SCIENCE, CURRICULUM,
AND
LIBERAL EDUCATION

JOSEPH J. SCHWAB

SCIENCE, CURRICULUM,
AND
LIBERAL EDUCATION
Selected Essays

Edited by

IAN WESTBURY

and

NEIL J. WILKOF

The University of Chicago Press
CHICAGO & LONDON

The University of Chicago Press, Chicago 60637
The University of Chicago Press, Ltd., London

JOSEPH J. SCHWAB is an associate at the Center for the
Study of Democratic Institutions. He is the author
of *College Curriculum and Student Protest*.
IAN WESTBURY is associate professor of secondary
education at the University of Illinois at Urbana-
Champaign. NEIL J. WILKOF is a law student at the
University of Chicago.

Library of Congress Cataloging in Publication Data

Schwab, Joseph.
  Science, curriculum, and liberal education.

  Bibliography: p.
  Includes index.
  1. Schwab, Joseph. 2. Education—Addresses,
essays, lectures. I. Westbury, Ian. II. Wilkof,
Neil J. III. Title.
LB885.S38S34   370   78–5848
ISBN 0–226–74186–9

Contents

IAN WESTBURY & NEIL J. WILKOF

Introduction

For nearly fifty years Joseph J. Schwab worked in the University of Chicago and lived in Hyde Park, the university's community. Entering the university at fifteen, he graduated in 1930 with a baccalaureate in English literature and in physics. In the fall of 1931 he began graduate work in biology, and he received his doctorate in genetics in 1939. He left Hyde Park for a year in 1937 to accept a fellowship in science education at Teachers College, Columbia University, where he explored the developing field of psychometrics and assisted in curriculum development while completing his doctoral research. In 1938 he returned to Chicago as an instructor and examiner in biology in the university's undergraduate college. He retired from the university in 1974 as professor of education and as William Rainey Harper Professor of Natural Sciences in the College. Subsequently he became a fellow at the Center for the Study of Democratic Institutions in Santa Barbara, California, an independent institute founded by Robert Maynard Hutchins, the president of the University of Chicago from 1929 to 1951.

Lengthy involvement in any institution with a strong sense of community profoundly colors the character of a man's work and actions. For Schwab, the University of Chicago was such a community. Arriving in Chicago as a youth from Columbus, Mississippi, he immediately made a commitment to the place and its people. Thirteen years later he became a faculty member in an institution which, because of the sweeping curriculum changes taking place within it, justified commitment. The reforming era in the College, which had begun in the thirties, had run its course by the early fifties, but for Schwab the collegiality, the forms of thought, and the practices of that period stayed with him, so much so that all of his subsequent writing and much of his later professional activity can be seen as successive efforts to explore the implications of his years in the College in broader and more varied contexts. Indeed, his book, *College Curriculum and Student Protest* (1969) can best be understood as the completion of an intellectual circle which had begun thirty years previously in a setting for what has been termed

1

"the most thorough-going experiment in general education in any college in the United States."[1]

Nevertheless, *College Curriculum and Student Protest*, as well as much of Schwab's other writing, has been uncertain in its impact. For some of those who knew him as a teacher, or for those who knew the College, his concerns and his approaches are accessible and enjoy a clear context. However, for many others the character of his thought has seemed unusual and puzzling. The medium of publication which Schwab used compounded the difficulty of understanding the totality of his concerns. Schwab is and always has been an engaged intellectual, writing for a particular occasion and purpose and using as his genre the essay, seeking by way of individual excursions into his problem area to create a tapestry which offers a single vision of one kind of education in one kind of college. There is in his writing a complex back-and-forth between the particular and the more general so that a grasp of any one essay requires appreciation by the reader of other essays, and of problems already discussed and closed. Yet, by the fifties and sixties, when Schwab was writing most prolifically, and for his largest audiences, the concern for the kind of general education, which is at the core of all of Schwab's work, had faded. Paradoxically, in a period of his career in which his writing and thought gained its widest recognition, as particular essays were anthologized again and again and as he gave many invited lectures, much of what he said often appeared puzzling even to those who half-remembered the idea of general education, and it was opaque to those who did not have any context in which to place Schwab's work.

In this introduction we will devote considerable attention to the task of sketching the field from which Schwab's work has sprung. We believe that an understanding of context is essential for a full appreciation of the character and scope of the essays presented here. But when context is known, something of the spirit with which Schwab wrote needs to be acknowledged. Thus, while the impulse of all his writing is a search for ways of giving new vitality to the ancient ideas of sociability, liberality, and civility, words that Sheldon Rothblatt suggests capture the most fundamental elements of the ideal of liberal education, his goal was never to provide a compendium, or a theory, of the practice of liberal education; it was rather to persuade readers to embark upon a practice.[2] As Schwab says about Dewey's style of philosophizing, he

1. Daniel Bell, *The Reforming of General Education: The Columbia College Experience in its National Setting* (New York: Columbia University Press, 1966), p. 26.
2. Sheldon Rothblatt, *Tradition and Change in English Liberal Education: An Essay in History and Culture* (London: Faber and Faber, 1976), p. 206.

renounced "any intention of 'proving,' in favor of moving men to reconstruct and test by practice. He points to weaknesses in men and society which exponents of the existing educational mode can agree are weaknesses, although he does not 'prove' that these weaknesses are failures of that education. . . . He then proposes a new and alternative scheme, though he does not, since he cannot, 'prove' that it is better" (p. 171 below).

Those remarks can serve as the epigraph for this volume. They define Schwab's intent, and his rhetorical problem, as a writer and teacher. Always he seeks ways in which he can achieve a mutuality with his readers so that each reader can find something of his own concerns being reflected in a particular essay. It is this mutuality which allows us as readers to overcome any puzzles and quibbles we might have about the particulars of an argument and to move along with it to the point at which we have to reflect on whether we accept or reject, agree or disagree, and why. In other words, these essays are invitations to enquiry[3] and reflection about the choices and alternatives that we must face as we think about the meaning of general education, the nature of science, and the character of educational thought. But, as we have suggested, we believe that there are difficulties in Schwab's work that derive from the ways in which he sees his problems, ways which are not as well known as they deserve to be. These problems interfere to some extent with the task of following the movement of the invitation to reflection which is extended here. We need, we believe, a sketch of the genesis of the essays reprinted here to ease entry to the thought represented in them.

I

In 1930, the year of Schwab's graduation from the University of Chicago, Robert Maynard Hutchins had just come from the Yale Law School to assume the university's presidency. Hutchins was young (thirty), immensely vigorous, and, most important for his impact on Schwab's career, was then developing an identification with a counterrevolution against the dominant forms of the American university of the interwar years. Indeed, given Hutchins' interest in education, his move to Chicago was in many ways paradoxical. By the late twenties

3. The spelling "enquiry" that is used in this volume is the one favored by Schwab. On his reason for adopting it, he remarks, in a letter to the editors of this volume: "In years centering on 1958, some educational psychologists became interested in the strategies children use to solve problems. The psychologists called this problem-solving 'inquiry'. To ensure that I would not be mistaken for one of these psychologists, I took to spelling 'inquiry' with an 'e'. Sometimes this could be forced on editors, sometimes not."

the University of Chicago had so deemphasized undergraduate teaching that it was seriously proposed that instruction in the first two years of the College be abandoned. On the other hand, however, because there was no strong commitment at Chicago to any particular form of undergraduate education, and so no strong tradition to terminate, it was a place in which a single-minded advocate of undergraduate education with a position such as Hutchins' could test the limits and possibilities of an educational ideal.

Beginning in the first decade of the twentieth century, the American university came to be seen by many of its faculty as an increasingly lost institution. There was a mood that demanded a discussion of what Lawrence Veysey has called "fundamentals." The focus of this dissatisfaction was, as Veysey describes it, the curriculum of the college, and particularly the elective system; but while there was a pervasive desire to reorganize the undergraduate curriculum in some way, there was little clarity about what the issues were and what was being proposed. Perhaps the only clear feature of the debate was a concern for what was seen as a lost ideal of liberal culture and for a reassertion of the honored place the humanities were seen as once having.[4]

By the twenties this widespread concern for curriculum change had become a reforming movement which, on the one hand, looked backward to the ideals of the traditional college and, on the other hand, generalized a despair over what was seen as the narrow scientific and vocational orientation of the university into a wholesale questioning of the value of American versus European culture and traditions. As Ronald Crane, one of the leading figures in the movement, which many saw initially as identified with Hutchins at Chicago, was to write: "the justifying faith of [the liberal arts college], the assumption upon which it is founded and continues to flourish, is that we can become educated men and women only by contemplating, in our youth, and learning the arts by which we may understand and emulate the best achievements of all kinds of which men have been capable, in sciences, institutions, and arts."[5] Crane, and others who shared his view, asked how an education based on student choice, which eschewed rigor, and in which contact with the humanities was too often only fragmentary could attain these ends. They believed it could not. Hutchins was to put this conclusion more forcefully: "The rising generation has been deprived of its birthright; the mess of pottage it has received in exchange has not been

4. Lawrence R. Veysey, *The Emergence of the American University* (Chicago: University of Chicago Press, 1965), Chap. 4.
5. "The Idea of the Humanities," in R. S. Crane, *The Idea of the Humanities and Other Essays Critical and Historical*, 2 vols. (Chicago: University of Chicago Press, 1967), 1:15.

nutritious; adults have come to lead lives rich in material comforts but very poor in moral, intellectual, and spiritual tone."[6] The need was for a new curriculum, one that would lead students to appreciate the western intellectual and spiritual tradition while, at the same time, capturing an understanding of the society that Americans shared in common.

The forces that lay behind the movement Hutchins was to identify with so firmly have never been adequately probed and are outside the scope of these introductory comments. Nevertheless, one can identify at the core of the campaign for renewal an attempt to recover ideals of liberal culture that were seen by many, particularly by those who were concerned with teaching rather than research, to have been lost with the development of the late nineteenth-century American university. As Schwab was to write many years later in a popular paper that sought to defend and explain the reforms that came at Chicago in the 1940s: "The early American college attempted to train men to be good men and able citizens. . . . These are the ends of the American college no longer. The American college has been engulfed by the backwash of factual, empirical, and specialized research."[7] Schwab's themes in this short article, virtue and citizenship, were the characteristic themes of the entire reforming movement, and the intellectual task of the movement was, as Veysey suggests, to find a way of blending the demands of a democratic education for the citizenry of a democratic polity with claims of liberal culture, vocationalism, and research.[8] The problem, in other words, was centered on finding a raison d'être for the conviction that the work of the undergraduate faculty was important and on giving teaching such a cast that it could stand alongside graduate study and the emerging scientifically based professional education.

The most characteristic expression of the impulse that moved many college faculty in these years emerged during the early twenties at Columbia College in New York City. Beginning in 1919, two courses were developed at Columbia to complement the major in a single discipline: one, Contemporary Civilization, sought to communicate an understanding of the problems confronting the West by way of a history of the intellectual tradition; the other, the Great Books course, sought to expose students to some classics of western thought by way of intensive, but not necessarily formal, reading of texts. The outcome of this reform was, however, one in which there was a fundamental tension: as Daniel Bell has written, "the yoking of these two produced tensions and paradoxes that were not always evident to the practitioners of general edu-

6. Robert M. Hutchins, Preface, *Great Books of the Western World*, 54 vols. (Chicago: Encyclopaedia Britannica, 1952), 1: xiii.

7. "The Fight for Education," *Atlantic Monthly*, 169 (1942): 727.

8. Veysey, *Emergence of the American University*, pp. 252–59.

cation. The Erskine [Great Books] program, with its emphasis on the classics of Western thought, constituted, as Lionel Trilling has put it, 'a fundamental criticism of American democratic education,' while the Contemporary Civilization course was an open and frank acknowledgement of the direct responsibility of the College to the stated democratic needs of society."[9] This antimony lay at the heart of the whole general education movement as it emerged in the interwar years, and it was one which the Columbia faculty that Hutchins was to recruit for Chicago were to seek to resolve.

While at Yale, Hutchins had met Mortimer Adler, then a member of Columbia's Great Books faculty. Through Adler, he met subsequently Richard McKeon, Columbia's first professor of renaissance and medieval philosophy, and Stringfellow Barr, a philosopher and the then-director of the School of Philosophy of the People's Institute of New York, an adult-oriented institution later associated with the New York Public Library. At this time Adler, McKeon, and Barr were working at the School of Philosophy trying to explore the implications of Columbia's Great Books course for the liberal education of adults. One issue in particular troubled them, the relationship between the ostensible aims of general education and the curricular and pedagogical means that were characteristic of the Columbia programs that they knew. What was the relationship between general education for all students in the college and the kind of honors programming that was being developed at Swarthmore and being widely imitated? Was the typical "belle-lettrist" approach to the Great Books an end or a means? Was the information communicated in surveys like Contemporary Civilization an end or a set of means? How could such information be in any way an educational end? If it was a means, how did it relate to an end?[10]

It was McKeon who provided a first solution to these puzzles for the group at the School. He was at this time working on the place and nature of the medieval liberal arts in the thought of such philosophers as Augustine, Abailard, and Erasmus, and, as he thought about this work, he concluded that perhaps it might be possible to resolve the paradoxes inhering in the common ideologies of general education by restoring the ancient notion of liberal arts to the center of the curriculum.

9. Bell, *Reforming of General Education*, p. 15. For a full discussion of the Columbia College developments, see Columbia University, *A History of Columbia College on Morningside* (New York: Columbia University Press, 1954).
10. This account of the collaboration of Hutchins, McKeon, Adler, and Barr is drawn from Amy Apfel Kass, "Radical Conservatives for Liberal Education" (Ph.D. diss., Johns Hopkins University, 1973).

Whether it is called the trivium or not, whether it is applied to old books or new books or even to oral presentations, whether or not principles are thought to determine the sequence, a student should emerge from such a general education with a knowledge of how problems, whether of life or of science or of art, have been treated, and with some insight therefore into how problems may be treated; and, joined to that knowledge, he should possess an ability to understand positions other than his own, to present his own convictions relevantly, lucidly, and cogently, and finally to apply informed critical standards to his own arguments and those advanced by others.[11]

McKeon's proposal was enthusiastically endorsed by his colleagues in New York—although its implications were far from fully developed and, as they were drawn, were to lead him, Adler, and Barr in different directions—and it was an emerging ideology of this kind that Hutchins heard when he first met Adler in 1928. It was a program originating in this kind of idea that Hutchins was to promote from the pulpit offered by his position at Chicago.

Hutchins moved on two fronts almost from the day of his arrival at Chicago.[12] In October of his second year he formally proposed the reorganization of the university and the creation of a separate undergraduate two-year college to explore the problem of a general curriculum. Included in the plans for the college he suggested were the conclusions of almost a decade's study by different faculty committees at Chicago about what an appropriate undergraduate curriculum should be like. Four one-year sequences in the biological sciences, the physical sciences, the humanities, and the social sciences were introduced as a foundation for the whole college experience; comprehensive examinations were substituted for credit accumulation, and mastery rather than time became the criterion for the attainment of a degree. At the same time, Hutchins suggested that Adler, Barr, and McKeon be appointed to the University of Chicago to continue the work they had begun in New York and, in so doing, to help create a new kind of basic intellec-

11. Richard McKeon, "Education and the Disciplines," *Ethics* 47 (1937): 377. For an example of the scholarship McKeon was undertaking in this period, see his "Renaissance and Method in Philosophy," in Columbia University, *Studies in the History of Ideas* (New York: Columbia University Press, 1935), 3: 37–114.

12. This account of Hutchins' activities at the University of Chicago is drawn from Reubin Frodin, "Very Simple, but Thoroughgoing," in *The Idea and Practice of General Education: An Account of the College of the University of Chicago*, by Present and Former Members of the Faculty (Chicago: University of Chicago Press, 1950), Chap. 2; and Kass, "Radical Conservatives," Chap. 3.

tual foundation for both the college and the university. While the plan for the curriculum was accepted by the faculty at large, Hutchins' attempts to bring the Columbia group to Chicago were bitterly resisted. Nevertheless he succeeded to the extent that Adler joined the University in 1930 and McKeon came in 1934. The first steps on the path that Hutchins had mapped in 1931 were taken:

> the College of the University of Chicago will contribute to the advancement of knowledge because it will be an experimental college. If this were not so I should recommend its abolition. . . . Few institutions in our area can do what we can do in collegiate education, and that is to experiment with it with the same intentness, the same kind of staff, and the same effectiveness with which we carry on our scientific work.[13]

In these first years of Hutchins' presidency of the University of Chicago Schwab was completing his baccalaureate and beginning his graduate work in genetics. He participated by invitation in one of the first of a series of Great Books seminars Hutchins and Adler were to offer during the 1930s and experienced there both the passionate convictions and the charisma of Hutchins. In addition, this seminar nourished the disposition to philosophical and ethical thought that Schwab had. This predisposition was to have only limited opportunities for concrete expression while Schwab was a graduate student in genetics; after his appointment as an instructor in 1937, however, the ideas which he first heard in the Great Books seminar and later encountered indirectly by way of friends who were working with McKeon and Crane in the graduate division of the humanities prepared him for his movement into the reforming camp that was centered on Hutchins and Adler. In fall, 1938, he became the first chairman of the newly developed Great Books extension program mounted by the university in its downtown evening college. He was to remain identified with this kind of public education for many more years and was ultimately to become a member of the editorial board of Hutchins' and Adler's *Great Books of the Western World*, a fifty-four volume collection published by Encyclopaedia Britannica of the western classics in all fields.[14]

13. Robert M. Hutchins, "The Chicago Plan and Graduate Study," in *The Idea of the University of Chicago: Selections from the Papers of the First Eight Chief Executives of the University of Chicago from 1891 to 1975*, ed. William Michael Murphy and D. J. R. Bruckner (Chicago: University of Chicago Press, 1976).

14. Robert M. Hutchins was editor-in-chief of *Great Books of the Western World* and Mortimer J. Adler was associate editor. The advisory board included Stringfellow Barr, Scott Buchanan, John Erskine, Clarence Faust, Alexander Meikeljohn, Joseph Schwab, and Mark Van Doren. Adler, Barr,

Yet, while Schwab's interest in the Great Books was an important determinant of the character of much of what he was to venture later, his other experiences in these years were equally important for his later contributions to both the development and implementation of the Chicago conception of general education and to educational thought more generally. As a graduate student of Sewall Wright, one of the preeminent biostatisticians of the time, Schwab was able to follow the work being done by Louis L. Thurstone, the first university examiner, with informed interest. During his year at Teachers College he spent considerable time with Irving Lorge, a major figure in the new field of educational measurement. As an examiner in biology he worked in the late thirties with Thurstone's successor, Ralph Tyler, and assimilated Tyler's concern for the articulation of courses and curriculum and testing procedures, with its implied self-consciousness about curriculum development, that was to become the hallmark of Tyler's contribution to the theory of curriculum development. At the same time, as a teacher, Schwab made an early mark in the College by introducing discussion methods into the undergraduate program, a development stimulated by a course he had taken as a beginning graduate student in which original papers were read and explored.

By 1940, when he was thirty-one, Schwab had become one of the key members of the group of faculty at Chicago committed to the reforming concerns of Hutchins. As a scientist with a sophisticated interest in general education he was prized by the group around Hutchins, Adler, and Clarence Faust, dean of the College from 1941; the integration of science into a scheme for general education had always been a fundamental goal of the general education movement but it had proved to be a quite elusive end because of the lack of interest of scientists in the issue. Yet, despite his interest in the idea of general education and his devotion to teaching in both the two-year program that had been created in 1931 and the parallel four-year college program that had been created in 1937 to offer terminal general education to students between grades eleven and fourteen, Schwab's conception of liberal education was essentially inchoate in 1940. He believed in discussion teaching, in the potential importance of the Great Books, and in the tractability of science for general education; he was passionately concerned with the relationships between science, values, and education—the theme of his first published paper on education.[15] He had not developed, however,

Buchanan, Erskine, and Van Doren had been associated with either the developments at Columbia College or the School of Philosophy. Faust was dean of the college at the University of Chicago.

15. "The Role of Biology in General Education: The Problem of Value," *Bios* 12 (1941): 87–97.

a coherent framework within which to place his ideas and concerns. It was not until he worked with Richard McKeon in 1942 in the course of the planning of the four-year college that was initiated in that year that he found the intellectual structures he needed to bring his ideas into focus.

The four-year college launched at Chicago in 1942 was the outcome of a heated debate among the faculty. In 1941, a group of younger faculty teaching in the College proposed to Hutchins that the time had come to institute the proposals he had made in 1936 in his book *The Higher Learning in America*[16] to create a four-year period of general education beginning in the conventional junior year of high school and continuing through the end of the sophomore year in college. They proposed that this be done at Chicago and that the College faculty should have the sole right to recommend students for a baccalaureate, which should be awarded after a four-year program of the kind Hutchins had sketched. Hutchins submitted this proposal to the faculty of the university, and after heated debate it was accepted. McKeon, then the dean of the university's Division of the Humanities, and Clarence Faust, the dean of the College, become the key personalities in the development of the new curricula that this structure required.

The boldness of the vision implicit in the proposal that became the 1942 College is manifest in the formal curriculum.[17] The four one-year introductory courses in physical and biological sciences, the social sciences, and the humanities of the old program were replaced by four three-year introductory sequences in the social sciences and the humanities and one- and two-year sequences in biological and physical sciences and mathematics. In addition, a one-year integrative capstone for the entire course of study, Observation, Integration, and Interpretation (OII), was introduced in order to explore the methods and interrelationships between the various field of knowledge studied previously. The curriculum was completely prescribed, at least initially, and examinations continued to be the sole measure of academic performance.

This structure for a program was accepted by the faculty. The curricular rationale that underlaid it did not capture the commitment of even a majority, but with the absences due to the war the curriculum and its particular rationale were able to control the development of a

16. Robert Maynard Hutchins, *The Higher Learning in America* (New Haven: Yale University Press, 1936).

17. The 1942 curriculum is described in *The Idea and Practice of General Education*. See also Neil J. Wilkof, "History and the Grand Design: The Impact of the History of Western Civilization Course on the Curriculum of the College of the University of Chicago" (M.S. diss., University of Chicago, 1972).

crucial set of new courses that did emerge between 1942 and 1946—
including a course in natural sciences that Schwab worked with as
chairman of the College natural science faculty.[18]

II

The underlying theoretical base for the boldly prescriptive curriculum
adopted in 1942 cannot be described as succinctly as can its structure.
After he came to Chicago in 1935 as dean of the Division of the Humanities, McKeon had withdrawn somewhat from the circle around
Hutchins and had carried forward the work he had begun in New York
by focusing his energies on the development of courses in the humanities
for general education and on the reorganization of graduate work in his
division. In collaboration with colleagues who shared his point of view
he pushed forward to the point that his colleague Ronald Crane, for
example, could observe that he had concluded that the "manner of
discussing the humanities [in education] which later generations inher-
ited from the Romans is by no means the only or inevitable mode of
approach." Crane suggested, for example, that instead of positing, as
most educational thought had done, that the *end* of education was
humanity and the task of educational theory was that of explicating
what that end consisted of and of finding the means by which the end
could be achieved, it might be possible to proceed in a different way:
to begin with the idea of humanities as human achievements and then
to explore that which contributes to *humanitas*. As Crane saw it, a
conception of education of this kind was quite different from traditional
conceptions: it required no end outside itself and the notions of humanity or *culture* became both ends and means. The curricular task was
one of ordering an approach to the significance of culture *seen in its
own terms* and of developing means and methods which might enable students to encounter the essence of this culture. As McKeon was
to write in an autobiographical essay published in 1953:

> We face [in our times] a *philosophic* problem of formulating
> the organization and interrelations of our knowledge and our
> values, the interplay of our ideas and our ideals, the influence
> of our new sciences in providing means for the solution of old
> problems and in laying the beginnings of new problems, and
> the distortions and misapplications of what is called scientific
> method and of what is claimed as democratic practice. That
> philosophical problem is inseparable from the *educational* prob-

18. For a discussion of this course see Chapter 1 and "The Science Programs in the College of the University of Chicago," in *Science and General
Education*, ed. Earl McGrath (Dubuque, Iowa: William C. Brown Co.,
1947), pp. 58–88.

lem of equiping men with abilities and insights to face the new problems of our times and to use the new instrumentalities with wisdom and freedom. The philosophic and educational problems are both implicated in the *political* problem of achieving common understanding among the peoples of the world who might, if ideas continue to become opaque in the oppositions of interests, be divided into parties determined by classes, the wealthy and the dispossessed, rather than by ideas and purposes.[19]

The central educational and, therefore, curricular tasks as they were seen by McKeon, Crane, and their colleagues were based on three key notions. One was the idea of culture and its elements while the second centered on the development of an understanding of what was problematic in the culture and on the nature of the changes that have taken place in the manner in which cultural elements are seen and experienced. Both of these concepts found their focus in the third idea—that of the person experiencing, and seeking to resolve, problems given him by his culture; as McKeon wrote in his autobiography, "the mind which is actively thinking is the objects which it thinks."[20]

It was an argument of this kind, with its foundations in the notions of *culture*, the *person*, and *community*, and its synthesis in the conception of *experience*, which justified, at the theoretical level, the 1942 curriculum; and it was Schwab more than anyone who was to articulate all of the elements of the rationale, although not for another decade. Initially the central place in the theoretical and practical development of the 1942 program was given to the task of ordering the array of "cultural elements as such and in their own terms."[21]

There was, of course, superficial classicism in both the emphasis on cultural elements and the approach to their exegesis by the reading of

19. In *Thirteen Americans: Their Spiritual Autobiographies*, ed. Louis Finkelstein (New York: Harper and Brothers, 1953), p. 113.

20. Ibid., p. 113. See also McKeon, "Education and the Disciplines"; idem, "The Nature and Teaching of the Humanities," *Journal of General Education* 3 (1949): 290–303; idem, "The Liberating Arts and the Humanizing Arts in Education," in *Humanistic Education and Western Civilization; Essays for Robert M. Hutchins*, ed. Arthur A. Cohen (New York: Holt, Rinehart and Winston, 1964), pp. 159–81; idem, "The Circumstances and Functions of Philosophy," in Fédération Internationale des Sociétés de Philosophie, *Philosophes critiques d'eux-mêmes*, ed. André Mercier and Maja Svilar (Bern: Herbert Lang, 1975), 1: 99–142.

21. These words are McKeon's as reported in the minutes of the History Review Committee, February 5, 1948, University of Chicago Archives, Papers of the Dean of the College. Cited in Wilkof, "History and the Grand Design," p. 114.

"great books," and this emphasis and approach posed many problems for faculty at Chicago and elsewhere. Part of the concern that was aroused derived from the complexity and novelty of the rationale being advocated, but part arose from confusions between the educational and curricular rationales being espoused by the group working on the 1942 program on the one hand and Hutchins' and Adler's differently conceived Great Books program. The confusions between these different positions were widespread, and they appear anew when the "Hutchins period" at Chicago is discussed. Adler, particularly, because of the attention he gave at this time to popular education was, and is, more widely read than McKeon, but it was McKeon's view that was to give Schwab the direction that he had been seeking until this point in his career. It is important for an understanding of the character of Schwab's later writing that McKeon's formulation of the philosophical underpinnings of this educational theory be acknowledged. We will suggest later that John Dewey, more than any other thinker, determined the character of the conception of liberal education that Schwab was to develop, but his encounters with McKeon's thought determined his approach to Dewey. McKeon had been a student and colleague of Dewey's at Columbia and offered Schwab direct access to his thought.

As both a historian of philosophy and as a philosopher, McKeon has been concerned most fundamentally with the problem of knowing how experienced thought about a problem can be understood. As he wrote in an early essay, "If the historian is something of a philosopher . . . he must be disturbed by the recognition that his history is the reflection of two independent systems of ideas, his own and that of the men whose careers he is recording."[22] The central task of the intellectual historian, he suggests, is that of understanding, in their own terms, what men have said, and this understanding is reached by the careful analysis of the texts they have left us. This commonplace conceals the question that in some ways has always most concerned McKeon—what is meant by the words that make up the pages of a text?

> History in its original sense is the study of concrete facts, but the concrete facts I was concerned with were the semantic structures, not the temporal succession of philosophies . . . the concrete facts I was concerned with were not the facts stated in true substantive propositions but the facts which marked the constitution and construction of a philosophically significant true proposition. . . . My studies of the structures of philosophy were in these circumstances more properly semantic studies of expression and what is expressed than historical studies of phi-

22. "Renaissance and Method in Philosophy," p. 41.

losophies, or philosophical studies of the resolution of problems, or scientific studies of the conditions of thought and action.[23]

The traditional discipline which has concerned itself with the task of the extraction of meaning from complex scriptural and philosophical texts is *hermeneutics* or *interpretation*, and this discipline more than any other has been a primary concern of McKeon's. The hermeneutic tradition offered him both techniques and methods that could be used for the interpretation of semantic structures of expression and, potentially, educational means. To read a text requires concern for both the text itself and the interpretative categories which the interpreter brings to that text. A curriculum which uses interpretation as its core method entails, then, a necessary focus on both the semantic problems inhering in the work being read and on the consciousness of students as readers.

In some senses, at least, the beginnings of a complete rationale for a liberal education can be found in the hermeneutic tradition. Such a rationale is inseparably linked with the concern for the liberal arts which had, ten or so years earlier, solved the difficulties that the Columbia program posed, yet it goes beyond this earlier formulation with its concern for the interpenetration of the structures of a text and the mind of the reader. When linked with an ordered array of fundamental cultural problems, for example, freedom in the state, there is in this tradition both a body of a curriculum content and a set of means. And, when the fruits of the semantic analysis of programs were seen, as they were by McKeon, as aspects of the liberal arts—inasmuch as a set of given interpretative schemata could be used inventively to comprehend new problems as well as old—there was a clear and direct linkage possible between the liberal eduction which the college might offer and informed and reflective participation in the commerce of ideas that is at the core of a participatory political and social community.

III

While the general outline of the educational theory implicit in the planning of the 1942 reforms of the College curriculum was well developed in the minds of the reformers, it was not particularly explicit nor had its implications been attended to outside the humanities. Nevertheless, Schwab's contact with McKeon in the course of his participation in the planning of the Observation, Interpretation, and Integration course seemed to give him a way of articulating in coherent terms his concerns as a teacher of biology and his interest in the potential of the Great Books as resources for liberal education. As he worked with the

23. "The Circumstances and Functions of Philosophy," pp. 107–8.

group planning this course, he was to assimilate a structure which was to determine what he was to do in the years that followed. While others were interested in the consequences of McKeon's thinking for their disciplines, Schwab almost alone was to seize upon the implications of McKeon's outline for teaching, as well as for the theory and practice of curriculum. It fell on him to search in these terms for a way of giving a complete expression to his emerging conception of what liberal education might be.

The first task that Schwab identified himself with in the 1942 College was that of developing a sequence of courses in the natural sciences, a problem that he would return to often during his career. The course and its development are described in Chapter 1 of this book, where the character of the task that he and his colleagues assumed is delineated succinctly. But there were also significant theoretical issues to be addressed prior to the work of curriculum development, and it was Schwab more than the others who taught in the natural sciences sequence who faced this problem. The first issue to be solved (and it was a pressing one, given the character of the curriculum of the College as Schwab saw it) was to define the place that the sciences should have in the program; it was this question that concerned him as much as the urgent problem of methods and means by which the form of the course might be executed. How could a program in science in a curriculum so self-consciously concerned with "culture" retain its character as science? This issue, the rock on which almost all attempts to assimilate science into the concerns of general education has fallen, is addressed in his essay on "The Three-Year Program in the Natural Sciences."

> By . . . distinguishing, but connecting, discipline and field, method and content, fact and idea, the science program attempts to determine its own duties, without neglecting the duties it shares with other programs of the curriculum. . . . It can leave artistic analysis to the humanities and doctrines of knowledge and being to philosophy, where these can be treated with wisdom and experience; it can concern itself with science; yet its treatment of science can be both sensitive and philosophical, without ceasing to be scientific. It is enabled to impart some knowledge of the world and yet construct a foundation for critical understanding of the limitations of human knowledge. . . . It can examine the contribution to science of both the eye and the human intellect without denigrating knowledge either to a catalogue or to a myth. Its attempt to do these things and its continuing effort to educate itself, to enlarge its competence for its task and to subject its principles to continuing re-examination are the bases for calling it a *liberal* program in the sciences (pp. 66–67 below).

Yet, while Schwab was concerning himself with the problem of the place of science in an overall scheme of general education, he was at the same time developing courses and teaching. The natural sciences sequence demanded an outline, topics, and reading. However, the development of any such course outlines presumed a conception of the course, and particularly the availability of interpretative structures which could serve to make the meaning of the texts that were to be used accessible semantically, and consequently available to the active consciousness of students. And, while the models that were available for the humanities courses indicated the general structure of such a framework, there was no explicit pattern at hand. Indeed, any search of the available literature of the philosophy of science would have contraindicated from the outset the very possibility of the kind of course Schwab sought.

Inevitably, the final development of the semantic mapping for science that Schwab's courses of the 1940s needed was long in the making. (Indeed, as is made clear in Chapter 1, the genesis of his thinking about the nature of an appropriate course for general education in science goes back to his teaching in the science courses of the 1930s.) But, already in the late forties, Schwab was formulating the basic outlines of both the philosophy of science he was to write about ten years later and, in the essay "The Nature of Scientific Knowledge as Related to Liberal Education" (Chapter 2), the preliminary taxonomy of the varieties of scientific enquiry that he offered as a "prefatory guide to the curriculum-planner in his choice of materials and subject matters and as an aid in the analyses of scientific researches which he and his students do" (p. 81 below). This paper complements "What Do Scientists Do?" (Chapter 7) both as a statement of the sources of this later work and as a discursive preamble on the purposes and the limitations of what was to come later.

As we have suggested, the work Schwab undertook in these years as chairman of the natural sciences sequences in the College, work in which he was developing a conception of the character of a science that was appropriate to general education, continued the line of thinking he had been engaged in since his appointment to the College in 1937. However, at the same time as he was focusing on the task of developing a curriculum for science, he was entering areas of enquiry which were to become decisive to his later intellectual development. He was teaching Observation, Interpretation, and Integration and beginning to explore Dewey's writings carefully. In 1948 he read the biological works of Aristotle to prepare the index of these works for the "Syntopicon" of the *Great Books of the Western World*, the last of Hutchins' and Adler's projects with the Great Books. In addition, he was beginning to explore psychology and psychiatry. And in 1949 he was appointed to the university's Department of Education, and there Ralph Tyler, the chairman of the department and Schwab's long-time colleague from the university examiner's office, encouraged him to turn his attention to the formal exploration of the rationale for liberal education. His gradually increasing involvement in teaching the philosophy of education in the Department of Education also pushed him in the same way, that is, to seek generalization of his experiences and concerns. All of this led him inexorably into the structures of thinking about the nature of education that were an integral part of the thought of McKeon, Crane, and their collaborators in the Division of the Humanities. The College of the University of Chicago in those years was a place in which conversation and the exploration of ideas was intense, and it was through dialogue as much as reading that the emerging modes of thought about education were apprehended and challenged. By the late 1940s, after seven years of actively developing and analyzing his ideas, Schwab was ready as perhaps no other of his colleagues were to turn his attention to the task of explicating in a more total and more formal way an educational rationale for the work he had been doing.

The first essay Schwab wrote that pointed the way to where he was to go intellectually was presented to the Educational Testing Service's Invitational Conference on Testing Problems (1950) and was, in some sense, a by-product of the work Schwab had done for over ten years as one of the College's examiners. His conference paper, "Criteria for the Evaluation of Achievement Tests: From the Point of View of the Subject-Matter Specialist" (Chapter 9 in this volume), is a statement which, while little known, can stand after twenty-five years as perhaps the clearest articulation that has been written of the potential relationships that might exist between the problematic notions of testing and the curriculum and the teacher.

In this paper, with its emphasis on process, communication, and the need to define problems through a search for ways of articulating and expressing *experience*, we see one of the first statements by Schwab that reflects the reading of Dewey that he had been doing in the late forties:

> a more valuable kind of test would be one whose items would serve to suggest to the teaching staff alternative or additional aims of education which deserve consideration. And still more valuable would be a test which would disclose the unknown and unanticipated consequences (in addition to those intended) which any effective curriculum inevitably must produce upon its students (p. 277 below).

Again and again in this paper he stresses the indeterminacy of what we think we know and the necessity of searching for ways of giving form to the "shadowy and incomplete condition" which is our world. Later he was to draw heavily on Dewey's particular construction of experience, but we see in this early paper one exceptionally powerful statement of themes which were to become fundamental to all of Schwab's thought.

> What is true of the concept of education's aim at Chicago is also true of . . . education's aim held elsewhere. The concept itself is incomplete and tentative. The terms which constitute it are only partly understood and are continuing subjects of investigation. The terms, in their shadowy and incomplete condition, are in turn represented by curricular intentions and programs whose appropriateness to the terms as ends is a matter of doubt and of continuing enquiry. Finally, the classroom practices which are supposed to realize curricular programs and intentions are valid only to the extent permitted by the competence, the experience, and the state of health possessed by the teacher at the moments when he teaches. A valid test in the ordinary sense is nothing more than an effort to measure the contours of a shifting and altering shadow (p. 278 below).

Yet while this paper offers a complex formal argument, it also reveals another aspect of Schwab's thought which runs constantly parallel to his philosophical concern. He insists upon exploring how a test can be used in a concrete situation. It was this practical trait of Schwab's personality, one that led him always to commit himself to action, that was the primary motivation of all that he was to attempt. If he was to teach in a way that satisfied him, he had to conceive of and develop means that satisfied his sense of ends. His problem was to develop an understanding of the ways in which the tools which those around him were exploring theoretically might be used as a basis for action and reflection on action.

The analytical and rhetorical force Schwab was to achieve as he addressed the problem of action was the result of a marriage of strong conviction with powerful methods. In an essay he wrote in 1951, "Dialectical Means vs. Dogmatic Extremes in Relation to Liberal Education," Schwab shows for the first time in a fully developed way (and in a manner which is more explicit than is seen in most of his later writing) his use of the forms of analysis and argument that McKeon (and, in a different way, Dewey) had drawn from the classical rhetorical tradition of *inventio*.[24] In its original context, this method consisted

24. "Dialectical Means vs. Dogmatic Extremes in Relation to Liberal Education," *Harvard Educational Review*, 21 (1951): 37–64.

of a comprehensive mapping of a territory of a given subject matter by means of a set of *topics* or *commonplaces* which ordered the possibilities that an orator might need to consider as he sought to develop his arguments. In the hands of McKeon this approach to invention was extended to encompass the possibility both of the development of semantic structures (it became a way of ordering an array of approaches to a text or tradition) and a way of exploring how a given problem, area, or subject matter might be brought within a comprehensive structure of address.

This topical style was to become the hallmark of Schwab's thought and writing, and when it was joined with the Aristotelian categories which he was beginning to use habitually as a source of commonplaces and with Dewey's construction of experience, it provided him with a distinctive way of approaching the problems which concerned him. Facility in inventive argument of this kind was, of course, one of the primary goals of the Chicago curriculum.

"Dialectical Means vs. Dogmatic Extremes" was much more formally structured than anything Schwab was to write later and in its own way represents a kind of byway in his thought similar to his Princeton paper. "Eros and Education" (Chapter 3), on the other hand, written four years later, is a first definitive statement of ideas and concerns which he was to explore again and again over the next twenty years. The paper is multifaceted, but perhaps its most revealing aspect is the shift in focus that it represents, away from the intellectual arts that concerned Hutchins and McKeon and towards the ideas of the person and liberal personhood and experience. Here, in Schwab's conception of education, we see perhaps the first marked influence of Dewey's emphasis on the place of continuity and growth in experience, although it was an influence filtered through both the psychoanalysis that Schwab was undergoing in these years and his reading of Aristotle's biology.

The "intellectual" arts and skills with which the liberal curriculum is concerned are not then intellectual as to subject matter, and thus exclusive of other subject matters, but intellectual as to quality. They are the arts and skills which confer cogency upon situations and actions whether these be scientific, social, or humanistic, general and abstract or particular and concrete. The liberal arts, however formulated, are to be understood as the best statement of our present knowledge of the human make, of the various means—some special in their application to specific subject matters, some general—by which the understanding frees us from submission to impressions, beliefs, and impulses, to give us critical and organizing power and deliberative command over choice and action. A liberal curriculum is one concerned that its students develop such powers.

With respect to ends as well as to means, then, the aim of a liberal education is not to "destroy the mammal within us." It is to harness Eros in the controlling reins of reasonableness in order that we may borrow energy from her for intellectual purposes and, conversely, enjoy to the fullest the capacities for feeling and action she confers upon us (p. 125 below).

This formulation is consistent with all that had been developed earlier at Chicago, but the debt to Dewey, and the consequent shifts in emphasis, are clear. The argument of "Eros and Education" achieves its linkages with its author's earlier work by using a set of topics which Schwab derived from Aristotle's *De Anima* and *Ethics*, Dewey's psychology, and Freud. Man has a rational faculty, that is, a capacity for reason, and an appetitive faculty, a source of emotion and sensation. Human behavior has its origins in both of these sources, but a developed, virtuous character is one in which the emotional faculties are formed so that they lead the person to take pleasure in those acts which make men good. Human behavior results from reason motivated by desire and desire formed by reason, and the developed personality is achieved by the training or habituation of the irrational faculties such that the person behaves in accord with reason.

Yet, now that Schwab had mastered the topical mode of reasoning that permitted him to bring his reading of Aristotle to bear on his concern for the ends of liberal education as seen from the vantage point of the individual, his sense of external structures that make up an educational institution both required and enabled him to address in this essay the particular question of the nature of the teacher's role in the process of education. This focus required him to treat the topic of method and means more explicitly than had either his colleagues or the works he had been reading. To address method, he draws on Freud and his own experience in analysis, but again he does this within the terms of a concern for a superordinate topical mapping of theories of personality and personhood.[25] With only the beginnings of such a structure (the search for a map of the domain of personality theories has been one of Schwab's continuing preoccupations) he was able to achieve in "Eros and Education" an exemplification of the kind of eclectic approach to educational problems that he had foreshadowed in "Dialectic

25. For an example of the kind of topical mapping Schwab was thinking about at this time, see Seymour Fox, *Freud and Education* (Springfield, Ill.: Charles C. Thomas, 1975). Professor Fox was one of Schwab's doctoral advisees and his book is based on a dissertation completed in 1966.

Means vs. Dogmatic Extremes" and was to spell out later in the series of papers on the "Practical" (Chapters 10–12 below).

As we have indicated, Schwab had been appointed to Chicago's Department of Education in 1949. As teachers of the philosophy of education in the graduate programs of this department, he and his colleagues had come to order discussions of the ends of education in terms of three commonplaces: conceptions of the individual, of society, and of knowledge. By implication, a complete rationale and prescription for *any* educational program had to address each of these ends if it was to hope for a polyfocal comprehensiveness, and this prescription was as true for liberal education as it was for the common school. Schwab's earlier writing had explored the commonplaces of knowledge and the individual. In 1955, he wrote "Science and Civil Discourse: The Uses of Diversity" (Chapter 4 below) to complete, as it were, the "coordinate" development of a conception of liberal education he was to urge later in his third "Practical" essay. As such, the paper represents a kind of termination of an exploration that had begun many years earlier, a purpose that is mirrored in the structure of the essay. It harks backward in its themes to offer, on the one hand, an informal history of the general education movement in the United States and, on the other hand, a commentary on the analyses of subject matter that had been undertaken in both the course Observation, Interpretation, and Integration and in Schwab's own work in science:

> A working knowledge of these principles [of scientific enquiry] is, in many important respects, the modern functional equivalent of the logic of the generalized liberal arts. The character of specialized problems and solutions, which makes them relatively inaccessible to generalized logic alone, accrues to them from such principles, that is, from varied and special conceptions of data, of possible connections among events and things to be sought for in enquiry, and of the units or entities in whose states or behaviors explanations are to be sought and from a conception of the states or behaviors which are relevant and important (p. 141 below).

But, although "Science and Civil Discourse" does review the idea of liberal education in the light of all three of the topics of ends, its primary focus is society and its implications for a liberal education. In developing this theme, the essay again follows the forms of Aristotle and Dewey with a discussion of the virtues that the citizenry of a state must possess for their society to cope with the problems that it might or must face.

"Current problems of the community, local as well as national, come to our attention embodied in the language of the specialist. And they come to us in this form not as a mere matter of vocabulary and formulation but in their origin and structure" (p. 138 below). Our elites are multiple in the specialties they do and must command. There can be no elite of elites with some set of general skills which can give them a mastery of the perspectives of specialists. What is necessary is communication within a community. All members of the society—specialists, officeholders, need "a working knowledge of each other's principles, enough to participate in the process of mutual education and, beyond that, in the process of modification of principle and remolding of formulation which is required for integration" (p. 143 below). The connection between the structure of the Chicago curriculum and this analysis of the needs of society is clear.

The last of the series of essays which Schwab wrote in the fifties when he was still teaching actively in the College is "Enquiry and the Reading Process" (Chapter 5 below). It is a less formally theoretical essay than "Eros and Education" or "Science and Civil Discourse" and reveals instead his concern for the practice of education. As such, "Enquiry and the Reading Process" is a primer of the hermeneutic rationale and methods characteristic of his teaching and serves to link the thinking he was doing about broader issues of liberal education and his return in the early sixties to the task of the analysis of the structure of science. In this regard, the most important characteristic of "Enquiry and the Reading Process" is its emphasis on the continuity which is a characteristic of reading—from this paper and this text to an understanding of context. Any paper is "such-and-such a treatment, in *these* terms but not *those*, of a certain part of a large subject disjoined from other parts, and providing a solution to this but not that problem involved in the subject" (p. 153 below). Such an analysis or interpretation is "participative," converting reading "from a view that symbols merely convey an author's meaning to a conception of discourse as the stimulus to a guided enquiry" (p. 157 below).

Such reading is a demanding process. It requires (and in this requirement lay the whole raison d'être of the efforts of Schwab's colleagues in the College) the reader to enter what Schwab called the "pragmatic space" of the investigator and his investigation. As he wrote in "The 'Impossible' Role of the Teacher in Progressive Education":

> Since scientific knowledge is couched in terms corresponding neither to "reality" nor to immediate human needs, we need to reflect on the relations of its conclusions to its forms and evidence in order to know what it is about. Its conclusions make sense only in the light of the way they were formed. And the *use* of the conclusions presupposes reflection which transforms

both the forms of scientific thought and the requirements of felt problems so that the two can be brought together (p. 178 below).

This is a description of what Schwab was later to call "fluid enquiry" and constitutes a key part of the end-in-view that lies behind "Enquiry and the Reading Process"—the introduction of students to the habits motivated in such enquiry. Yet, this focus highlights a recurrent ambivalence which is reflected in much of Schwab's thinking. Thus, with Dewey, he emphasizes again and again the discretionary aspects of individual and group behavior. He describes again and again *how* problems are to be encountered and resolved, but not *what* the solutions are or, in a specific sense, should be. In this sense, all of his writing searches for a characterization rather than a prescription of what teaching might be like, what a liberal education might be, how a curriculum might be developed. But there is, of course, a dilemma inherent in any emphasis of this kind on discretionary intelligence, a dilemma that Schwab acknowledged in "Science and Civil Discourse" and couched in terms of the needs of elites and the needs of the masses of the population. Schwab, there as elsewhere, rejected the need to make distinctions of this kind and sought always as both a consultant and a writer to communicate to as broad an audience as he could find. Yet, as we have suggested, by the late fifties, when the terms and forms of the general education movement had faded among those concerned with collegiate education, and as he sought to work with teachers and faculty of schools of education who had never known the general education movement, he increasingly began to encounter a problem of communication which he was never able adequately to resolve. Paradoxically, then, in a period in which Schwab was at his most productive intellectually and in which he received widespread recognition as a theoretician, his writing was seen as puzzling and enigmatic and more often than not was misunderstood.[26]

IV

By the second half of the fifties it was clear to all who had been involved in its development that the experiment in liberal education which Hutchins had initiated and nurtured in the College could not be sustained by the University of Chicago. The program was too different to win the support of other institutions; its premises went against the grain

26. Between 1960 and 1965 Schwab wrote three major theoretical papers, coauthored the teachers' handbook for the Biological Sciences Curriculum Study, and published twelve other papers. His papers were, in addition, widely reprinted during this period.

of too many of the faculty, even those who were committed to undergraduate education; and, most important perhaps, the very idea of general education was incompatible with the dominance of the conventional college which was, at this time, being increasingly seen by the population at large as the avenue to a good, or better, life. With the decline of the College that Schwab had been so closely identified with, he found himself in a situation of increasing personal tension. He had discovered in himself a need to find forms in which he could communicate his concern for and ideas about education, but at the same time his desire for efficacious action, for teaching and deliberation about teaching and curriculum, persisted. His role in the College permitted him to express both of these needs, but by the end of the fifties it was clear that his place in the College was increasingly marginal.

Schwab resolved this problem by accepting more and more responsibilities outside Hyde Park. In 1959 he became chairman of the academic board of the Melton Research Center of the Jewish Theological Seminary, where he worked on curriculum projects in Bible study and on programming for religiously oriented summer camps.[27] At the same time he became chairman of the committee on teacher preparation of the Biological Sciences Curriculum Study, one of a series of federally sponsored curriculum development projects designed to update what was seen as the obsolete content of the science programs of the high school.[28] This same year was spent away from Chicago on a sabbatical. All of this stimulated Schwab to begin the task of rethinking the work on science he had done ten years earlier and at the same time pushed his concerns in new directions, to thinking about community, tradition, and informal education.

During these years of the early sixties the curricular concerns of American schoolmen centered on the content of high school science. The slogan that became associated with this concern was "structure of the disciplines." Given his long-standing interest in the nature of an appropriate curriculum for liberal education in and through science, Schwab was seen as a spokesman for the importance of discipline-based teaching of science in the schools. His essay "The Concept of the Structure of a Discipline" and his contributions to two widely read symposia

27. Two of Schwab's published essays derive from the work he did with the Melton Research Center: "The Religiously Oriented School in the United States: A Memorandum on Policy," *Conservative Judaism* 18 (1964): 1–14; and, with Burton Cohen, "Practical Logic: Problems in Ethical Decision," *The American Behavioral Scientist* 8 (1965): 23–27.

28. As part of his work with BSCS he edited and coauthored *The Biology Teachers' Handbook*, American Institute of Biological Sciences, Biological Sciences Curriculum Study (New York: John Wiley and Sons, 1963).

on the theme of structures became basic texts for the structuralists in the schools and colleges of education; these, and other more popularly written pages, were often republished.[29]

Schwab did, of course, identify himself with the "structure of the disciplines" movement, although he well recognized that there was a fundamental difference between his conceptions and those of the more conventional disciplinary scholars who also figured prominently. But, despite this difference in viewpoint, it was his hope that something might be achieved that could be recognized as more "educative" than what had been done before. And while he did achieve some noticeable successes, including the publication of the BSCS *Teachers' Handbook* and the three different versions of BSCS biology, the evaluations that his own students were to conduct later suggested that much of the practice of even the teachers' institutes that were associated with the movement and the texts themselves were very different from what he would have wanted.[30]

Part of the problem that Schwab faced was, of course, the assimilation of his novel views of the structure of the disciplines into more conventional schemes. We can see the extent of this assimilation in the words of one recent commentator on his work. There is a theory, he writes,

> which has come to be known as the *structure-of-knowledge*, theory [which] has been described in the writings of Bruner, Schwab, [and others].
>
> All of these writers have argued that school subjects should serve as faithful and valid introductions to the academic disciplines whose names they bear. . . .
>
> The elements of the structure-of-knowledge theory can be economically expressed a few sentences. Knowledge is produced by a variety of *disciplines*. Each discipline operates upon a *domain*; practitioners of the discipline operate upon the domain by means of a *substantive structure* and a *syntactical structure*. The central thesis of this paper is that the substantive

29. "The Concept of the Structure of a Discipline," *Educational Record* 43 (1962): 197–205; "Problems, Topics, and Issues," in *Education and the Structure of Knowledge*, ed. Stanley Elam (Chicago: Rand McNally, 1964), pp. 4–47; "Structure of the Disciplines: Meanings and Significances" and "The Structure of the Natural Sciences," in *The Structure of Knowledge and the Curriculum*, ed. G. W. Ford and L. Pugno (Chicago: Rand McNally, 1964), pp. 1–49.

30. See, for example, Marshall D. Herron, "The Nature of Scientific Enquiry," *School Review* 79 (1971): 171–212, and Mary E. Diederich, "Physical Sciences and Processes of Inquiry: A Critique of CHEM, CBA and PSSC," *Journal of Research on Science Teaching* 6 (1970): 309–15.

structure of a science contains and generates different classes of *knowledge-statements*: definition statements, direct-observation statements, instrumental-observation statements. . . .[31]

While the terms used in these paragraphs were used by Schwab extensively in his writing on the structure of knowledge, the context and the intentionality of his formulation were very different from those suggested here. In the opening paragraphs of "Education and the Structure of the Disciplines" (Chapter 8 below) he writes:

> Before we ask about the structures peculiar to specific disciplines—before, indeed, we ask what "structure" is—there is a prior question: What relevance may the structure of disciplines have for the purposes of education? Why should the curriculum maker or the teacher be concerned with the structure of the discipline with which he or she works?
>
> There are two answers to this question. One answer is relevant when we conceive curriculum and instruction as concerned primarily with the imparting of knowledge. The other is relevant when we conceive curriculum and instruction as concerned primarily with the imparting of arts and skills. Since the reasonable curriculum maker is concerned with both of these, both answers are relevant here (p. 229 below).

Schwab was concerned, as he indicates here, with both science and the curriculum as knowledge and science and the curriculum as the representation of bodies of arts and skills, but his primary commitment was always with science seen as a certain kind of *habit of enquiry*. Thus, while he did not eschew the analysis of the ways in which a science might warrant its knowledge claims, the analysis of the nature of truth or knowledge claims per se was never his principal concern; rather he was interested in the description and analysis of why a particular science chooses at a particular time to emphasize one conception of verification over another.

Schwab's fundamental emphasis on the explication of the nature of the choices made by a particular science, or scientist, stems, of course, from the hermeneutic tradition which undergirded much of what had been attempted at Chicago in the 1942 curriculum. For Schwab, to "understand" a work or a body of work was to seek to enter the mind of the scientist or group of scientists with a consciousness of the theory that they held as lying itself in a tradition. Interpretation in this broad sense became coordinate with metaphysics, inasmuch as knowing any-

31. Paul Gardner, "Science and the Structure of Knowledge," in *The Structure of Science Education*, ed. P. L. Gardner (Hawthorn: Longman Australia, 1975), pp. 1–2.

thing implied a knowledge of a knower's knowledge and why he saw things in this way. It was this awareness that gave the Chicago group their most basic questions: Is this way of organizing the disciplines, the ways of knowing, the most appropriate one? Why? Is this way of rendering this subject matter an appropriate one? Why?[32] These questions were posed to students in manifold ways, and Schwab saw them, as he indicated in "Science and Civil Discourse," as the prerequisites for ready communication among the diverse disciplinary traditions of the modern university and polity.

A curriculum which emphasizes questions of these kinds needs a structure within the terms of which approaches to answers might be sought. In "Education and the Structure of the Disciplines" Schwab reviews many of the issues and approaches that he had used in the course Observation, Interpretation, and Integration, the College's capstone course that reviewed the problem of the organization of knowledge in the broadest sense.[33] In the parts of this essay we have used here, we see him exploring two themes from the broad set he had considered in his teaching of OII. First, he focuses on the question "How might subject matters be rendered?" and, as he explores this, he subordinates the problem of verification and the nature of truth to the prior task of examining what kind of claim it might be that we are asked to believe. The implication readily follows, and he immediately takes it up, that to appreciate the significance of a claim or observation in a text or a scientific report one must have a way of understanding its character, intent, and context.

Having made this point, Schwab goes on in "Education and the Structure of the Disciplines" to explore one way by means of which a reader can understand the twists and turns of the contexts and characters of scientific disciplines. In his extended discussion of the Comtean organization of the disciplines he explores the fundamental topics within the terms of which the characters of *all* scientific disciplines can be seen to be formed: fidelity to the complexity of a subject matter versus accuracy of statement about that subject matter; the understanding of patterns in a subject matter versus the identification of the elements of a subject matter; the understanding of the variety of ways in which patterns or orders of being might be seen. In developing this structure he draws again, as we have seen him doing throughout his work, on dis-

32. This view of the scope of the theory of interpretation is drawn from Arthur Child, *Interpretation: A General Theory* (Berkeley: University of California Press, 1965).

33. For a discussion of the scope of OII, see William O'Meara, "Integration: Observation, Interpretation, and Integration," in *Idea and Practice of General Education*, pp. 232–45.

tinctions which were first made by Aristotle, in this case the four causes.
Again Schwab insists that there is no single right way of approaching
the task of finding ways in which the significant aspects of natural and
human phenomena might be understood. Rather, there is a need for
both a "permissive eclecticism" as one thinks about the task of understanding the world and a need for some closure of the definition of the
set of ways that *might* be used so that the enquirer can order his approaches to his traditions and phenomena and the teacher can communicate skills which can be used to "penetrate language to arrive at the
purport which that language is intended to convey" (p. 241 below).

"Education and the Structure of the Disciplines" is a philosophical
essay that seeks to describe one way in which the character of the disciplines might be understood. It reflects the complexity of the task which
McKeon and Crane had set themselves, that of finding a way of understanding what man has achieved and ordering that understanding for
the purposes of instruction. The thrust of Schwab's other major essay
from this period, "What Do Scientists Do?" (Chapter 7 below), goes
in a different direction: it seeks to describe in explicit terms the semantic clusters associated with the process of scientific enquiry. Again, its
origins lie in the need to order the parameters of the interpretative task
that is at the heart of Schwab's conception of a liberal education. But
at the same time, it seeks to work through the influence of cultural
forms on the practice of enquiry. As such, this essay is close in spirit
to the thinking that is commonly associated with the work of Robert
Merton and Thomas Kuhn and should be seen as a prolegomenon to
the kinds of historical and sociological analysis which they have undertaken.[34] However, inasmuch as Schwab's approach to the problem of
understanding the nature of scientific enquiry is profoundly embedded
in the interpretative tradition, the underlying "paradigm" reflected by
"What Do Scientists Do?" is close in spirit to the hermeneutic sociolo-
gies of such scholars as Mannheim, Dilthey, and Habermas.[35] And,
because of the increasing influence of Dewey's thought on Schwab in
these years, we should also see this essay as an attempt to work out
Dewey's recognition "of the power exercised by cultural environment

34. See, for example, Robert K. Merton, *The Sociology of Science:
Theoretical and Empirical Investigations*, ed. Norman W. Storer (Chicago:
University of Chicago Press, 1973), and Thomas S. Kuhn, *The Structure
of Scientific Revolutions* (Chicago: University of Chicago Press, 1970).

35. For a discussion of Mannheim's theory of interpretation, see Child,
Interpretation, pp. 57–70; Wilhelm Dilthey, *Pattern and Meaning in His-
tory*, ed. Hans P. Rickman (London: Heinemann, 1962); Jurgen Habermas,
Theory and Practice (London: Heinemann, 1974).

in shaping the ideas, beliefs, and intellectual attitudes of individuals."[36] While the sociology and social psychology of science that Dewey foreshadowed is sketched only in the appendix to Schwab's essay, the thinking that is reflected in the main text is, of course, an inevitable first step to such a sociology of science.

"Education and the Structure of the Disciplines" and "What Do Scientists Do?" completed a cycle of thought that began with Schwab's first attempt to develop a sequence of courses in the natural sciences in the Chicago college. The whole cycle reflects a concern for the commonplace of knowledge. These essays illuminate this one topic from a number of points of view, but there is a sense in which the emphasis of the essays on the role of disciplines qua knowledge is atypical of Schwab's fundamental interests. Yet, while he had always been concerned with the intellectual ends of education (although from the perspective of intellectual arts and habits, not of knowledge), he had long appreciated that any exclusive focus on the intellectual denies the humanity which is integral to understanding man's search for understanding. As he had written many years before these essays were conceived:

> Not only the means, however, but also the ends of liberal education involve the Eros. For the end includes not only knowledge gained but knowledge desired and knowledge sought. The outcome of a successful liberal education is *actively* intelligent people. They *like* good pictures, good books, good music, good movies. They *find pleasure* in planning their active lives and carrying out the planned action. They hanker to make, to create, whether the object is knowledge mastered, art appreciated, or actions patterned and directed (p. 109 below). Education cannot, therefore, separate off the intellectual from feeling and action, whether in the interest of the one or of the other. Training of the intellect must take place ("must" in the sense of "unavoidably") in a milieu of feelings and must express itself in actions, either symbolic or actual. We may employ the emotional and active factors existent in student and teacher as means for intensifying and facilitating the process of intellectual education—or ignore them and suffer at the least a loss of them as effective aids, and possibly an alienation which places them in active opposition to our purposes (p. 108 below).

Paradoxically, in the sixties, as he attained visibility as a seeming exponent of the intellectual as a primary end of education, Schwab was

36. Jane M. Dewey, ed., "Biography of John Dewey," in *The Philosophy of John Dewey*, The Library of Living Philosophers, vol. 1, ed. Paul Arthur Schilpp (Evanston: Northwestern University Press, 1939), p. 17.

working in the context of the Jewish Theological Seminary's Melton Research Center seeking to understand not only the psychology of growth and development but also the place of tradition and community in the formation of character. He was not able to find a way of bringing this work into the clear focus that he needed to write effectively within the somewhat foreign context of confessional education, but the subsequent rise of the student protest movement and the clear alienation from the conventional university that it represented provided him with the occasion and the point of entry that he needed. The result was a reawakened concern for the exploration of the liberal education that had always preoccupied him, highlighted more than ever before by issues of community, of moral choice, and of deliberation and decision-making.

The question Schwab faced as he observed the protest movement was whether the conception of the ends and means of liberal education which he had so long pondered could be brought to bear on this new problem. The result of this thinking was *College Curriculum and Student Protest* (1969), an impassioned tract that takes as its occasion the protest movement but has as its most basic purpose the restatement of Schwab's conviction about the nature of liberal education. Ten or more years had passed, however, since his previous writing on this theme, and he had been giving serious attention to the problems of ethics and character. The outcome is a firm coordination of his concern for the intellectual arts and disciplines with the notion of *habit*, so that the primary focus of this book is the examination of the relationships between the curriculum in its manifold aspects and the education of a person of prudent and intelligent character. The search for a way of rendering his basic image of prudence into the terms of a curriculum took him in many directions; in this sense, *College Curriculum and Student Protest* is broader in scope than anything Schwab had done before. But, at the same time, the book is more narrowly focused in the concerns it reflects than is his earlier writing, inasmuch as it eschews further exploration of the nature of the liberal arts and liberal education in favor of a forceful articulation of the conclusions to his reflections about student protest. The outcome of this deliberation and analysis differs only in degree from what Schwab had written before, indeed it develops themes he had been exploring for twenty years. But the way he does this, and the manner in which he addresses a new problem, is a testament to the open-ended power of the intellectual forms which had controlled his thinking for so many years.

V

College Curriculum and Student Protest is, in some ways, Schwab's last direct statement about liberal education. Having outlined in this powerful book the continuing relevance of his conception of what a college might be, he was able finally to do what he had been unable to do earlier—address the study of education frontally. For many years he had been a member of a distinguished department of education, one that had a total commitment to research into educational problems, and while he had written occasional papers on educational problems formally conceived,[37] the theme of liberal education had been his overarching concern. The result of this shift of interest was a series of three essays on the "practical" as a language within the terms of which curriculum development and the "theoretical" discussion of curriculum development might be undertaken. The occasion was his perception of the failure of the educational research which he had seen to find a way of affecting the schools. His own career in education had been motivated always by a desire to act and (in his own words) "do good"— although experience had taught him that impulse needed to be tempered by both prudence and hard thinking. Neither of these traits were, it seemed, honored by educational research as he knew it.

This is not to say that Schwab's criticisms of conventional educational research reflected completely novel concerns on his part. In the discussion that followed his presentation of his essay on achievement testing to the Princeton conference in 1950 he vigorously asserted a complex view of the nature and place of testing in the college against what he saw as simplemindedness:

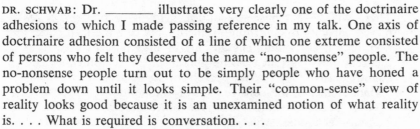

DR. SCHWAB: Dr. _____ illustrates very clearly one of the doctrinaire adhesions to which I made passing reference in my talk. One axis of doctrinaire adhesion consisted of a line of which one extreme consisted of persons who felt they deserved the name "no-nonsense" people. The no-nonsense people turn out to be simply people who have honed a problem down until it looks simple. Their "common-sense" view of reality looks good because it is an unexamined notion of what reality is. . . . What is required is conversation. . . .

DR. _____: I call this conversing you are talking about by teachers who don't know much about the facts of life a pooling of ignorance.

DR. SCHWAB: But that is precisely the way in which all research is done, isn't it?

DR. _____: That isn't the way I do it.

DR. SCHWAB: Then I really fear for your results, because it seems to me [that] the first condition of discovery is recognition of ignorance and

37. For example, "On the Corruption of Education by Psychology," *Ethics* 68 (1957): 39–44; "The Professorship of Administration: Theory, Art and Practice," in *The Professorship in Educational Administration* (Columbus, Ohio: University Council for Educational Administration, 1964), pp. 47–70.

[of] the delusion of knowledge; believing that one knows, for instance, what deduction or induction is, or that science is certain, firmly padlocks the door to any reinvestigation of the question of what science is.[38]

In his essay "On the Corruption of Education by Psychology" he had similarly (although less caustically) castigated his colleagues in education for a different kind of "doctrinaire adhesion," for their devotion to single-minded and simple views of what the subject matter of education might be.[39] The essays on the "practical," however, attempted a more formal and more systematic critique of educational research, one that drew on the thinking that he had done as he worked on the problems he had explored in "What Do Scientists Do?" and on his concern for the nature of deliberative and prudential action. In *College Curriculum and Student Protest* he had mocked political science for its attempts to reduce the complexities of political action to regression equations.[40] "This preoccupation with theory . . . is the self-imposed limitation of the academic. . . . The curriculum need not operate within this tyranny of the theoretic. It can function effectively (and cogently) with the crude facts, with 'life'. . . ."[41] In *College Curriculum and Student Protest* the terms within which Schwab explored the task of developing a curriculum that articulates intelligently and prudentially with "life" became those he used in the "practical" series of papers to address the problem of finding a more adequate conception of the character of educational theory.

> There will be a renascence of the field of curriculum, a renewed capacity to contribute to the quality of American education, only if curriculum energies are in large part diverted from theoretic pursuits (such as the pursuit of global principles and comprehensive patterns, the search for stable sequences and invariant elements, the construction of taxonomies of supposedly fixed or recurrent kinds) to three other modes of operation. These other modes, which differ radically from the theoretic, I shall call, following tradition, the *practical*, the *quasi-practical*, and the *eclectic* (p. 288 below).

He had urged his readers in *College Curriculum and Student Protest* to read Aristotle's *Nichomachean Ethics* and Dewey's *Human Nature and Conduct*; in the "practical" essays he attempts to present his understanding of the implications of his reading of these works for the nature

38. "Criteria for the Evaluation of Achievement Tests: Discussion," in *Invitational Conference on Testing Problems 1950* (Princeton, N.J.: Educational Testing Service, 1950), pp. 107–8.
39. See note 37.
40. *College Curriculum and Student Protest*, p. 75.
41. Ibid., p. 74.

of choice and action within education. In other words Schwab argues in these essays for a *reinterpretation* by education of its character and ends and its subject matter. Seen in this way, the forms in which Schwab states his "practical" thesis are, of course, those he had long used. His focus in his studies on the nature of science was the interpretation of a body of enquiries which had successfully interpreted their subject matters. In the "practical" essays he is exploring the task of the interpretation of a subject matter against the backdrop of a failure (in his judgment) of past interpretations.

While a number of scholars have offered commentaries of one kind or another on one or other of the three essays in the "practical" series, these commentaries have concentrated in the main on the particulars of the thesis he proposes and the argument he makes, without embedding their exegesis in the context of Schwab's earlier work.[42] This is appropriate, of course, for an examination of the significance of his analysis of and prescription for educational thought as such, but for complete understanding there is a sense in which it is important for these papers to be read in the context they have in this book. While they are different in theme from the earlier essays on liberal education and the structure of science, the connections they have with his other writing permits one to appreciate more fully the scope and character of the total body of thinking about education that he has offered.

Seen in this way, part of the linkage between the "practical" essays and Schwab's earlier writing is experiential. "The Practical: A Language for Curriculum" (Chapter 10 below) and "The Practical: Translation into Curriculum" (Chapter 12 below) seek to sketch the character of appropriate deliberation about a curriculum problem. The first essay in this book, "The Three-Year Program in the Natural Sciences," describes briefly the deliberations that yielded the courses in science that were Schwab's preoccupation for so many years. It is appropriate, we believe, to see these practical essays as an integrating attempt to formalize his recollection of this early work on science curriculum, his work as an examiner in the college, and his later discussions at the Melton Center and in the Biological Sciences Curriculum Study.

At the time, however, experience, if it is to become the basis for prescription, must be embedded in a context, and it was Schwab's read-

42. See, for example, Israel Scheffler, "The Practical as a Focus for Curriculum: Reflections on Schwab's View," in Israel Scheffler, *Reason and Teaching* (London: Routledge and Kegan Paul, 1973), Chap. 16; Max Van Manen, "Linking Ways of Knowing with Ways of Being Practical," *Curriculum Inquiry* 6 (1977): 205–28; Ian Westbury, "The Character of a Curriculum for a 'Practical' Curriculum," *Curriculum Theory Network*, no. 10 (Fall 1972): 37–44.

ing in other "practical" fields that provided him with the broader terms that he needed to generalize what he knew. We can see the basis for this generalization in *dicta* he offers but does not fully develop in "What Do Scientists Do?":

> A high ranking of interconnectivity over other criteria [for the evaluation of principles of enquiry] appears to stem from three (possibly four) sources. . . .
>
> . . . Arguments responsive to subjects come frequently from persons who give some of their time to the executive foci of the investigative disciplines: engineers, statesmen, and physicians. This is to be expected, for in these professions men encounter subject matters in a more nearly pristine state. The constituent matters of practical problems rarely conform to the boundary lines which insulate them from one another in the milieu of enquiry (p. 208 below).

Yet, experience, however wide-ranging in its scope, must be ordered. Consequently the most fundamental interconnection linking the "practical" essays to what had gone before is found in their forms of argument. The crisis that Schwab identifies in educational research lies in the ways it interprets its subject matter. This crisis in interpretation can itself be understood in terms of the language of principles. We can find ways of comprehending and *inventing* a formulation of this problem, and of its solution, within the categories that control our thought; for the purposes of topical ordering he invokes the Aristotelian distinction of "theoretical" and "practical." At a more detailed level there are further explicit linkages. In "The Practical: Arts of Eclectic" he restates in a different way his preoccupation with what he had called in "Education and the Structure of the Disciplines" *permissive eclecticism*, although in the latter paper, because of a different context, it becomes *polyfocal conspectus*. In "The Practical: A Language for Curriculum" he again deploys the Aristotelian causes to illuminate the intellectual territory under scrutiny in a manner similar to that used in "Education and the Structure of the Disciplines," albeit to order a different subject matter.

VI

More than anything else Schwab wrote, the "practical" essays capture the character and the style of his fundamental concerns:

> . . . curriculum is brought to bear, not on ideal or abstract representations, but on the real thing, on the concrete case, in all its completeness and with all its differences from other concrete cases, on a large body of fact concerning which the theoretic

abstraction is silent. The materials of a concrete curriculum will not consist merely of portions of "science," of "literature," of "process." On the contrary, their constituents will be particular assertions about selected matters couched in a particular vocabulary, syntax and rhetoric. They will be particular novels, short stories, or lyric poems, each, for better or for worse, with its own flavor. They will be particular acts upon particular matters in a given sequence. They will be perceptions conditioned by particular past conditionings of particular things and events. The curriculum constructed of these particulars will be brought to bear, not in some archetypical classroom, but in a particular locus in time and space with smells, shadows, seats, and conditions outside its walls which may have much to do with what is achieved inside. Above all, the supposed beneficiary is not the generic child, not even a class or kind of child out of the psychological or sociological literature pertaining to the child. The beneficiary will consist of very local kinds of children and, within the local kinds, individual children (pp. 309–10 below).

Instincts of this kind have through all of his career as a teacher and a scholar driven Schwab inward to *this* classroom, to a careful analysis of the characteristics of the students he had *this* semester, and always to a concern for the here-and-now of the next class, in *this* course, in *this* program. The origins of all of the essays presented here were of this kind: they were written usually for a particular occasion or to work out a particular preoccupation and only in the case of the "practical" series did he have an overt concern for the development of a theme that went beyond the essay at hand. In this sense Schwab's choice of the essay as his genre was a compatible one; it permitted him to bring the conclusions of his reflection to bear on something concrete and real, whether a theme or a problem.

Yet, as we hope these remarks have made clear, there are constants which run across all of the individual essays, creating a woof and a warp out of which the whole that we see here was constructed. We have emphasized the topical arts of invention which Schwab mastered, his explicit use of categories derived from his reading of Aristotle as topics, and his profound debt to the analysis of the proper nature of liberal education which he had heard McKeon and Crane discussing again and again. Emotionally he received from Hutchins a conception of means by which he could translate his zeal for improving the world into the context of education. From Ralph Tyler he learned the skills that were required to bring ideas to bear on concrete curricular problems and a sense of what it was to think about an educational problem systematically and from a distance. But while his intellectual debts are obvious and profound, Schwab integrated all of these influences in his own way and always made his own statement. He grew on and through his conversations with his colleagues at Chicago, but, as is clear from the discussion of his Princeton conference paper (see above, p. 31), he was from the beginning of his career his own man, argumentative, critical, dominating. He had his own sense of what was a problem and his own need to find a way of ordering his own concerns and insights into a satisfying whole. It was this need of Schwab's to articulate his concerns and conceptions into the terms of a whole and the particulars that he was able to derive from that whole that define the character of his contribution to educational theory.

Perhaps it was inevitable that as Schwab read the works of the philosophers who were influential in and on the Chicago milieu, that he was led ultimately to John Dewey. McKeon, in particular, had been Dewey's student and colleague at Columbia University and, as McKeon was to write later, he had learned from Dewey to seek the significance of philosophic positions in the contexts of the problems they were constructed to solve, to suspect distinctions and separations which remove the processes of thinking from the experience in which they originated, and to relate the formulation of problems and the discovery of solutions to the cultural influences which determine the manner of their occurrence.[43] And while this influence was always a constant at an overt level in McKeon's thought, being deeply embedded in his philosophizing, it was also penetrated by his understanding of what he saw as Aristotle's different kind of problematic method. The epistemological analysis of Aristotle offered an *organon*, a set of instruments for the appreciation and addressing of problems; but it was Dewey who gave the instruments of Aristotle a relevance and a life they did not have when seen as disembodied categories and methods, and he did this by embedding them in the commerce of individual perceptions that come from and make up these habitual modes of treating problems that are a culture.[44] As Schwab wrote in *College Curriculum and Student Protest*,

> Dewey and Aristotle are alike in their conception of the problem and subject-matter of morality. They are equally concerned that it be a morality of choice and action. Each sees choice and action becoming moral as they arise from good character brought to bear on the facts and existence and the desires of

43. McKeon, "Richard McKeon," in Finkelstein, ed., *Thirteen Americans*, p. 89.
44. McKeon draws, on a number of occasions, explicit connections between the methods of Aristotle and Dewey. See, for example, his "Philosophy and Action," *Ethics* 62 (1952): 79–100. For his interpretation of Aristotle, see Richard McKeon, ed., *Introduction to Aristotle*, 2d ed. (Chicago: University of Chicago Press, 1973), General Introduction.

men. Each conceives character as constituted of flexible, intelligent habits. Each recognizes a dual function of character-in-process—used on the one hand to reshape the facts of the environment which can alter the course of external events; used on the other hand to reshape the conditions of the environment and the behaviors which further modify and develop character itself. Yet, one of these men is, to put it briefly, Aristotelian; the other is pragmatic. Each, therefore, clarifies relations which the other does not; each makes distinctions which the other prefers to merge. The result is two perspectives on a nearly common object which, when taken together, are vastly more educative and informative than either taken alone.[45]

Schwab had read both of these philosophers carefully from the time of his first involvement in the 1942 College, and while it is clear that Aristotle's methods of philosophizing intrigued him, it was the influence of Dewey which was more profound. Dewey's corpus provided a framework which, more than Aristotle's, was compatible with Schwab's most basic concerns and convictions. The commerce of ideas that was so integral a part of Dewey's thought was the way of seeing and accounting for the importance of the community and the conversation which Schwab cherished; Dewey's descriptions of the process of enquiry captured what was happening in Schwab's world. As he wrote in 1950, discussing the need he saw for workshops which would be concerned with the tests and analyses representative of a variety of curriculums, such workshops

> would be concerned with the significance to each curriculum of the others it saw reflected in the variety of tests, and of the results exhibited by the measurement of achievement by its own students and those of other institutions, on the variety of matters tested. . . . Out of such workshops should grow a new and larger order of thought, experiment, and revision of curriculum than is remotely possible in the present insular state of most educationists and most educational institutions (p. 286 below).

And, as he wrote in 1976,

> First, community can be learned. It is not merely a matter of place, of village or small town, but a body of propensities toward action and feeling, propensities which can be expressed in many social circumstances.
> Second, human learning is a communal enterprise. The knowledge we learn has been garnered by a community of which we are only the most recent members and is conveyed

45. *College Curriculum and Student Protest*, p. 125.

by languages of work and gesture devised, preserved, and
passed on to us by that community. . . . Even experience as
a form of learning *becomes* experience only as it is shared and
given meaning by transactions with fellow human beings.[46]

Schwab began to read Dewey intensively as a part of his teaching
of OII and was to become one of his primary exponents in the College.
He wrote, for example, Dewey's obituary for the *Maroon*, the University's student newspaper, and in 1953 the *Journal of General Education*, a journal which was in the late forties edited in Chicago, published a lecture he had given in the college on Dewey's philosophic
method.[47] Increasingly Dewey was to become the thinker whose influence was fundamental to Schwab's thought—with the consequence that
his essay "The 'Impossible' Role of the Teacher in Progressive Education" should perhaps be read both first and last as one moves through
the pages in this book. Here, in paragraph after paragraph, the concerns which reappear again and again in individual essays are given
summary statement and embedded in the whole which provides their
context:

science, like practical knowledge, is fluid and dynamic. . . .
Since scientific knowledge is couched in terms corresponding
neither to "reality" nor to immediate human needs, we need
to reflect on the relations of its conclusions to its forms and
evidence in order even to know what it is about. Its conclusions
make sense only in the light of the way they were formed. And
the *use* of the conclusions presupposes reflection which transforms both the forms of scientific thought and the requirements
of felt problems so that the two can be brought together (p.
177–78 below).

. . . learning, for Dewey, is active participation in the pragmatic rhetoric—the recovery and test of meaning. Hence, the
effective "learning situation" is not the one which leads by the
quickest, most comfortable route to mastered habit and attitude, used precept and applied knowledge, but the one which
is provocative of reflection, experiment, and revision (p. 173
below).

Dewey sought, in education, the mutuality which joined society and separate persons. Development of the potentialities
special to each person, yes. But so that they be put in the ser-

46. "Education and the State: Learning Community," in *The Great Ideas
Today, 1976* (Chicago: Encyclopaedia Britannica, 1976), p. 235.
47. University of Chicago, *Maroon*, June 6, 1952, pp. 1, 3; "John Dewey:
The Creature as Creative," *Journal of General Education* 7 (1953): 109–21.

vice of society as well as in the service of the self. And development, too, of the common competences which serve society, but so that association may better serve the individual while individuals serve to improve the quality of association. Neither automatic conformity to socially accepted norms nor centrifugal scattering into privacies can be the useful rule. Where all conform, none question. There is no enquiry. Where belligerent individualism is the rule, we lose the fruits which require collaboration and, more important, lose the satisfaction of sharing, itself (p. 181 below).

In the text we used at the beginning of this introduction, from "The 'Impossible' Role of the Teacher in Progressive Education," Schwab emphasizes that Dewey does not offer a "theory" of knowing or of education in any accepted sense, but rather an invitation to enquiry, a polyprincipled *approach* to the task of persuasion of his readers to embark upon a practice. And, as we have suggested, the same is true of Schwab's writing and of his approaches to curriculum development. He sought, following an invitation which his reading of Dewey enabled him to articulate and order, a sense for ways in which a college might serve its students by providing them with the means that they might use to develop their capabilities and potentialities for dealing with the problems they might encounter as they traced their separate paths on graduation. He sought these ends in concrete ways, bringing to this task both sophistication about means and a clear sense of ends. He did not seek the solutions to the problems he saw with the clichés and platitudes that all too often pass for thinking about educational problems. His essays sought to communicate his discoveries and understandings so that others might follow the path he had trodden. They are instances of a style of thought which might be emulated but not followed as if it represented a prescription. But, as he offers such instances, he shows what thought about education might be, and how thought can bear on the work of the school and the college.

There are many reasons for pessimism about the salience of what Schwab was concerned with for the world in which most educators live and work. But the ideal of liberal education does linger. It might be that a conception of education that associates it with conceptions of sociability, civility, and self can be restored. And, if such restoration comes to pass, Schwab's essays and books will play an important part in the rediscovery of the meaning of these notions. He articulates a way of thinking which lets us see more clearly than does the way of any other contemporary thinker what thought about education *might* be and how it *might* be possible to give visions meaning. The burden of his work is an invitation to the reader to participate in the search that he ventured.

We wish to acknowledge the assistance given us as we prepared this essay by the following present and former faculty of the University of Chicago: Wayne Booth, Harold B. Dunkel, Richard McKeon, Kenneth J. Rehage, and Warner Wick. Ruth Murray of the Regenstein Library at the University of Chicago offered us unstinting bibliographical assistance. In addition we received invaluable help from Sylvia Ettenberg of the Jewish Theological Seminary, New York, and Rabbi Burton Cohen. Of course, our conversations with Joseph J. Schwab were a constant stimulus.

Part One

ON LIBERAL EDUCATION
AND SCIENCE

The Three-Year Program in the
Natural Sciences

The three-year science program exists [at the University of Chicago] in organic connection with other parts of the College curriculum.[1] Its structure and its function are therefore partly determined by the whole curriculum. In day-to-day practice, for instance, the discussion of materials in the science program takes cognizance of work which is going on serially or simultaneously upon related matters in the course in history, in the course in the interrelations of the fields of knowledge, and in the programs of the humanities and social sciences. Such day-to-day cognizance occurs in the sense that the work in science includes, on appropriate occasions, activities which are associated with the main responsibilities of other fields and also in the sense that treatment of materials ancillary to the main business of science is confidently left to other courses and programs. The practical connection of science to the remainder of the curriculum is an expression of common principles. These are, in the first instance, formulations of the ends of liberal education as a whole, but they achieve substance and the possibility of practical realization only as they divide the whole of liberal education into parts and assign to them different duties and responsibilities.

The science program, then, is part of a whole in three ways. First, its activities are connected with the activities in other programs and can be fully understood only in the light of these connections. Second, its main business is the consequence of a division of labor between specialized parts of the curriculum; hence, the character of the science

This chapter was previously published in a slightly different form in *The Idea and Practice of General Education: An Account of the College of the University of Chicago*, by Present and Former Members of the Faculty (Chicago: University of Chicago Press, 1950), pp. 149–98.

1. For students entering the University of Chicago at the first-year level (normally after two years of high school), the College offered a three-year program in science. For students who entered the College at the third-year level (normally after graduation from high school), a modified program which usually required two years for completion was offered. The three-year program consisted of a physical sciences component and a biological sciences component of approximately equal lengths.—EDS.

program is best understood in the light of the entire business being divided and in the light of the special aptitude of science (as against the special aptitude of the humanities, for instance) for certain parts of this business. Third, the science program expresses the principles of liberal education as a whole, but as mediated and modified by the qualities which distinguish science from the humanities and the social sciences; therefore, the science program is best understood in the light of what these principles become when expressed through the materials and procedures of science.

An adequate account of the science program will, in short, include a description of its matter and methods in relation to the matter and methods of other parts of the curriculum; it will state the specific aims and responsibilities of the science program in relation to the specific ends of other parts of the curriculum; and it will suggest the sense in which its specific materials, methods, and purposes realize the generic traits of the curriculum as a whole.

The subject matters treated in the science program reveal, at first glance, little effect of the operation of the principles of a liberal education. Taken separately, they show no notable departure from those which might be found in one or another conventional "survey" course or in one or another undergraduate pre-professional program, but in their number, their interconnection, and their degree of depth and detail they exhibit some of the significant features of the active plan of studies in the College.

As an introduction to the physical sciences the program begins with the simple Archimedean laws of equilibrium and of the lever. The first large unit, completed in about fifteen weeks, uses materials from the field of inorganic chemistry, with emphasis on phenomena of chemical and physical change as these lead to the development of molecular and atomic theories, which, in turn, give rise to the periodic table of the elements.

The second major unit of the physical science part of the program, by beginning with descriptive astronomy, makes a new start which appears, at first, to the student to be unrelated to the earlier unit. From the treatment of astronomy, however, the problems of motion develop, and, as solutions to them, the various conceptions and relations of classical mechanics and dynamics are expounded. The concept of energy is thereby introduced and, with it, the kinetic molecular theory. This is then seen as a solution to a number of unresolved problems deriving from the phenomena of chemical change examined in the first semester. In this way a relation between a problem in physics and one in chemistry is established as illustrative of the unifying function of scientific enquiry. The unit ends with a treatment of the special theory of relativity. The unity of this part of the program is derived from the study of motions as phenomena to be accounted for and as elements of theories which account for other phenomena.

The third unit deals with the rise of theories of atomic structure. The start is made not on the basis of materials already treated (such as phenomena of chemistry), which could have been employed to introduce theories of atomic structure, but by the exposition of a new body of phenomena, those of radiation. This provides a second illustration of the way in which scientific theory functions in the unification of apparently diverse bodies of phenomena. From the properties of visible light and the theories developed to explain them, the course moves to other forms of radiation and their connection with electric charge and with magnetic and electric fields. These phenomena and the problems which emerge from them are seen to be resolved in a progression of modern atomic theories, which includes Bohr's quantum theory of the hydrogen spectrum.

One and one-half academic years (i.e., four and one-half quarters, or three semesters) are assigned to the study of these phenomena, problems, and solutions.

The same amount of time is alloted to the biological part of the program. The first of its three units uses materials from physiology and anatomy, which treat two areas of problems and solutions: the transport and regulation of respiratory gases in the organism and the regulation and utilization of food material.

After a study of the gross anatomy and physiology of the heart and circulatory system, the unit turns to capillary anatomy and physiology as related to the transport of respiratory gases. It returns to a consideration of problems of the organism as a whole in relation to a changing environment involving the regulation of external and internal respiration and circulation.

To the previous exposition of the principles of structure and function, part and whole, and levels of organization, the second problem of the unit adds the factors of health and disease. These are treated both as problems for biological enquiry and as factors which contribute to the solution of its problems. The study of carbohydrate metabolism begins with an exposition of diabetic symptoms as a problem in the classification and description of disease. A characteristic contribution of pathology is exemplified by the identification of pancreatic lesions as a causal factor in diabetes, and clinical and pathological medicine are seen as contributing hypotheses to guide physiological investigations into structure and function. Exposition of the gross physiology of the pancreas, hypophysis, and liver as related to carbohydrate metabolism is followed by a view of the problem at the cellular and

chemical levels. Finally, in order to illustrate the existence of still further levels of the problem of the organism and its parts, and also the
tentative and incomplete character of scientific knowledge, the unit
ends with a treatment of psychosomatic factors in sugar utilization.

The second biological unit considers the developmental history of
the organism as an individual and as a member of a species. This unit
is, therefore, concerned with phylogeny, ontogeny, and genetics. An
exposition of Darwinian theory presents to the student a large body of
phenomena, terms, and concepts and poses problems of genetics and
embryonic development. These problems are pursued via experimental
data and theories concerning nucleus-cytoplasm relations, embryonic
regulation and induction, and the concept of organizers and gradients.
Genetics is pursued through exposition of primitive Mendelian instances, the phenomena of linkage and crossing-over, and quantitative characters. The unit ends with the modern, quantitative treatment of mutation, migration, natural selection, and chance as factors
of evolution.

The third unit of the biological part of the program draws its materials from psychology. The student examines problems and solutions
which are characteristic of the Gestalt, the behaviorist, the Freudian,
and the introspectionist conceptions of psychology.

In summary, the three years of the science program are divided approximately equally between biological sciences and physical sciences.
Taken singly, the topics chosen for treatment are representative of these
two major fields of scientific enquiry and exhibit no special features
stemming from the defining principles of a liberal education. Taken
together, on the other hand, the topics form a structure which departs
from that of ordinary "survey" courses and also from that of pre-
professional programs. From the point of view of pre-professional
programs, the topical structure is characterized by an unusual variety
of subject matters and of relation among the varieties. For instance,
in the case of the physical sciences, topics range over the recognized
areas of heat, light, mechanics and dynamics, inorganic chemistry, and
astronomy; and each conclusion drawn from these fields is expounded
not only in its own terms but also as relating to the problems, phenomena, and conclusions in other fields.

From one point of view, then, the science program is characterized
by an unusual variety of subject matters and an unusual emphasis on
the interrelations among this variety of specific and concrete matters
of fact and theory. On the other hand, viewed from the vantage point
of a conventional survey course in the biological or physical sciences,
the topical structure of the science program is characterized by considerable incompleteness and lack of variety. For instance, the con-

ventional topic of current electricity is missing. (To be sure, certain facts and theories concerning electrical phenomena are treated in connection with theories of atomic structure.) Similarly, in the case of the biological sciences, physiology is represented by only two topics rather than by a survey touching upon all the organ systems and most of the organs constituting the mammalian organism. The situation is similar in the case of embryology. This science is represented by a restricted series of experiments, with their data and conclusions, bearing upon a restricted but significant topic in the field rather than by a narrative of the development of the vertebrate or mammalian embryo.

In brief, by contrast with conventional survey courses, the science program treats a relatively small number of topics with an attention to detail and questions of evidence and interpretation reminiscent of a graduate seminar.

To combine what can be seen from these two points of view—that of the survey course and that of the pre-professional course—is to say that the unit elements of the program are not topics, strictly speaking, but problems. That is, the subdivisions of the physical and biological sciences drawn upon for materials are treated representatively, not exhaustively. The materials chosen to represent each field are, moreover, not only the conclusions of a representative part of that field but these conclusions together with the formulated problems, data, and the interpretations of data which yield the conclusions. Each field is taken, in short, not only as a body of knowledge but also as a field of enquiry, and one aim of this kind of material and treatment is to illuminate for the student the manner in which knowledge is obtained in each field, as well as the subject matters of the several fields (e.g., matter, motion, embryogeny). Further, the sequence and relation among the representative materials is made such that the problems, data, and conclusions of one field are often seen to have a bearing on similar factors in others. Problems in one field are viewed as stemming not only from previous solutions there but also from the knowledge and data of other, and sometimes remote, fields. Theories are presented as accounting for data in other fields, as well as for data in the field where they were developed; and theories arising more or less independently from diverse bodies of data are seen to pose problems of reconciliation and synthesis for the sake of unification of knowledge of nature.

A balance between depth and breadth is sought which is characteristic neither of the survey course nor of the pre-professional course but is somewhere in between. The excess of depth over breadth which appears by contrast with survey treatment of scientific material is constituted, in considerable part, of considerations bearing upon evidence and interpretation. For the rest, it consists of a concern for thorough treatment of conclusions as such and for avoidance of superficiality.

The excess of breadth over depth, on the other hand, which appears by contrast with pre-professional courses is constituted, in part, of a variety of problems and subject matters designed to exhibit the variety of ways in which the object of investigation of a science (e.g., the organism, in biology) can be examined in the light of varying principles, which pose different problems and suggest different kinds of evidence to be sought and conclusions to be formulated. For the remainder, the excess of breadth over depth which appears by contrast with pre-professional courses stems from the view that some aspects of the living and nonliving world are sufficiently important in themselves to be worth knowing about, even though the knowledge is gained only by some sacrifice of depth and of attention to questions of evidence and interpretation.

The present balance is the product of a long history of trials of differing proportions of these factors. The early efforts of the College science program were largely concerned with breadth, and with breadth of information about subject matter. Indeed, the earliest phase of development of the College science program was the prototype of the "survey" course. Its primary problem was choice of the subject matters appropriate to a "general education" and decision as to the amount of time and emphasis to be given to each. Its second problem was to choose a unifying theme which would bind together the diverse parts of its chosen subject matter so as to constitute a *narrative* whose structure would be an image or picture, which, though deficient in depth and detail, would be an informing and recognizable model of the world as then conceived by science. The name of the first University of Chicago science survey course, "The Nature of the World and of Man," is indicative of this goal.

This is not to say that science as a process of enquiry was ignored even in the earliest stages of development of the science program. Quite the contrary: a certain amount of time and considerable effort were devoted to an exposition of "scientific method." Nevertheless, the ratio of emphasis on conclusions to emphasis on scientific method was extremely high, and, moreover, method itself was primarily conceived as a subject matter. Its treatment was the same in kind as the treatment of other subject matters. It was the subject of a *narrative* account embodied in lectures and in chapters of a textbook. The student was expected to *know about* method in the same sense that he was expected to *know about* the structure of the atom or the age of the earth. Experience with a program characterized by relatively little emphasis on science as enquiry, by a tendency to understand enquiry in the narrow sense of "method," and by a reduction of "method" to the status of the subject matter of a narrative account led to dissatisfactions which promoted rethinking of all these matters. In 1943 a few members of the science staff were detached from duty in the parent-courses. They were expected to establish a new program in the sciences which, by practical operation, would provide a further and different body of experience wherewith to test our conceptions of the nature of scientific knowledge and the place of science in the liberal curriculum. The new program undertook neither to duplicate the method-content ratio of the parent-programs nor to invert it but, rather, to effect the union which is rather obviously suggested by the words "method" and "results." In other words, its responsibility was to avoid narrative discourse on either the conclusions of science or its method, by presenting "method" as the means by which conclusions are reached, verified, and related in science and "conclusions" as the consequences of the application of these means to an appropriate subject matter. By such a union, it was intended that the conclusions of science be given the cogency and meaning that is theirs when they are viewed in terms of the problems, the data, and the interpretations from which they stem. Furthermore, processes of enquiry which characterize science were to be exhibited only concretely and by example, that is, not as a doctrine about method but in the form of reports of problems formulated and data gathered and interpreted, which the student would need to grasp, point by point, as the necessary steps toward reaching a knowledge and understanding of conclusions.

The responsibility assigned to this new program was to effect a union of content and method in practice as well as in theory. A merely theoretical union would have admitted a continuation of narrative discourse as the principal means of instruction. The only change would have been that the units of the narrative would no longer have been aspects of the world or aspects of method, each taken separately, but units of analyzed and evaluated research. The mode of narrative discourse would have changed merely from the form, "The outer shell of the atom consists of . . . " or "There are N major divisions of the mammalian class," to the form, "On the heels of this discovery, Rutherford then investigated the magnitude of the charge . . . " or "The discovery of this particle forced a revision of the theory as follows. . . ." But a theoretical and practical union of "method" and "content" would assign to the student the task of understanding and following the stages of discovery and verification as the main route available to him for knowledge of the conclusions. By this means it was proposed to realize, in the area of the sciences, the notion:

> It is not the purpose of the College to instruct members of the rising generation what to think, but rather to teach them how to think. Its purpose is not indoctrination but the development

of power to form sound judgments. . . . This kind of competence, like skill in swimming, cannot be developed by learning
rules but only by exercise, and, since the methods by which
problems regarding the natural world are formulated and resolved differ from the formulation and resolution of problems
[in other fields], education in the formation of sound judgments
in these various areas requires practice in thinking about [these]
different subject matters.[2]

The practical union of "method" and "content" was effected by putting into the student's hands, as his primary materials, neither a textbook of the philosophy of science nor textbooks of science but, rather,
connected series of selected and edited papers and longer works drawn
from the research literature of each of the scientific fields. Instruction
consisted in careful reading and discussion of the papers, taken both
individually and in relation to one another. The means used was laboratory work for two hours a week and discussion periods utilizing three
hours per week. The aim of student and teacher was to take cognizance
of the phenomena about which a paper is concerned, to understand the
problem which is formulated in it, to see what aspects of the phenomena are embraced by the problem, and to follow the resolution of the
problem. In similar fashion, student and instructor worked together to
relate the researches and conclusions of the several papers of each
series.

The experience of the staff members engaged in the development and
teaching of this program produced both affirmative and critical judgments. The desirability and feasibility of using materials which enlisted
the students' participation in the processes of evaluation and synthesis,
which are ordinarily left to the instructor and lecturer, were confirmed.
The desirability of laboratory work was confirmed. The propriety of a
union of "method" and "content" was confirmed.

On the other hand, experience with the program in its earliest form
disclosed certain unexpected weaknesses and omissions; and continued
work with its later phases underlined the desirability of rectifying certain radical shifts in emphasis which at first were considered justified.
The undesirable features with which the 1943 program could reasonably
be charged were the following.

In the first place, the laboratory program and methods of discussion
which were developed in the course, though successful in guiding the

2. Clarence H. Faust, "The Problem of General Education," in *The Idea
and Practice of General Education: An Account of the College of the University of Chicago*, by Present and Former members of the Faculty (Chicago: University of Chicago Press, 1950), p. 17. (Clarence H. Faust was
dean of the College, 1941–47.—Eps.)

student to an adequate habit of interpreting and understanding individual papers, were not effective in teaching students the skills necessary for relating the conclusions of a variety of papers to one another. As a result, the scientific model of aspects of the world which was present in the documents was not vividly grasped by a large proportion of students.

In the second place, the models, even as presented in the papers, had more numerous and larger gaps than were noticeable before actual trial in the teaching situation. Adding further papers was not feasible: the amount of reading would have required an investment in time and energy not justified by the relatively small increase in reading and interpretive skill which might have resulted.

In the third place, the method of treating the materials in discussion had the undesirable effects of maximizing their role to the student as examples of scientific enquiry and of minimizing their role as sources of knowledge about the world.

Finally, the practice of treating "method" only by example and eschewing such formulas and formula words as "induction," "deduction," "hypothesis," "empirical generalization," etc., had the effect of leaving the student capable of understanding and even evaluating the process of enquiry disclosed by a given paper, yet unable to formulate a statement concerning the nature of one or another pattern of enquiry.

The faults and overemphases of the 1943 program were, with the possible exception of the last-named, at the locus of the strengths of the older program. Conversely, the experience gained in developing and teaching the 1943 program was useful at those points where the older program could be said to have its principal vices. As more and more members of the science staff participated in both programs and brought their combined experience to bear upon them, the aims, content, and method of the two converged. The present curriculum is the result of this exchange and pooling of insights and experience.[3] In so far as the previous programs converged toward a common point, the present sequence is that point. On the other hand, there is one sense in which it is neither the older program, that of the 1943 experiment, nor an eclectic composite of the two but, rather, a third plan, developing from principles of its own, whose tentative validity is warranted by the amount and diversity of experience employed in choosing and interpreting them.

The present program, for instance, leans heavily upon the reading and discussion of original works, but the gaps between papers, which were a vice of the 1943 program, are filled by materials which supply necessary and useful information about phenomena and conclusions

3. Under the administrative leadership of Benson Ginsburg, John W. Mayfield, Thornton L. Page, Aaron Sayvetz, and the author.

with the economy and in the manner of a good textbook. Moreover, the frequent appearance of these textbook materials and the manner in which they are treated in relation to the original papers appropriately bring to the student's attention questions both of the nature of scientific enquiry and of the nature of the world. The living organism, the nature of matter, and the nature of space and of motion are as much a concern of the student as are the patterns of enquiry which yield knowledge of matter, motion, and the organism.

Further emphasis upon the subject matter of science is achieved through the use of queries and problems which require, for solution, that knowledge of conclusions discovered in papers and textbook materials be brought to bear upon specific and concrete situations. Such queries and problems, together with textbook materials and a topical outline which contains the selected readings and textbook materials, also serve to achieve a connection between different conclusions. In the earlier years of the older program this connection was established by the instructor alone and communicated to the student by narrative; in the 1943 program it was not initially achieved to an adequate degree by any device.

These queries and problems are of different kinds. Some serve in a traditional way to illuminate the meaning and usefulness of scientific conclusions by applying them to practical or concrete situations. Some serve to interrelate different papers and textbook materials at the level of their conclusions. Others have the special function of bringing to students' attention the kinds of questions, which, by being asked of a given scientific paper, serve to connect its various logical parts (problem, evidence, interpretation, and conclusion). Queries of this last kind perform another function. They not only bring to the attention of the student the evidential relations of the parts of each individual paper to which they refer but, by an appropriate mode of repetition which introduces both specific variation and generic uniformity, teach students the kinds of questions and the various categories of answers which, together, constitute a knowledge of science as a process of enquiry. The chosen mode of repetition solves a problem which was not resolved satisfactorily either in the initial 1943 program or in the older one—the problem of a satisfactory and formulable notion of scientific method. If it could be charged that the older program, by expounding a narrative about method, reduced method to too simple a form, it could be charged with equal propriety that the initial 1943 program, by eschewing all reference to method as such, left its component parts so various and unconnected as hardly to permit an intelligent formulation by the student.

The materials, then, of the present program consist of series of research papers, monographs, and selections from textbooks representing the sciences by means of problems. Upon these papers and other materials a collection of queries and problems is directed in order to draw the papers together and to teach the student how to approach a statement in the field of science.

The use of primary or original source material in the program has elicited much comment and, apparently, much puzzlement also, for a variety of interpretations concerning the reason for their use has arisen, based on no more than the information that such materials were, somehow or other, employed in the course. It has been assumed, for instance, that the presence of original papers indicates that the science program has substituted the history of science for science proper. This would mean, supposedly, that the primary emphasis in the program is upon the shifts of research patterns or of principles or of scientific subject matter in succeeding epochs or in different places. This is not the case. It has been assumed that the presence of original papers indicates that the science program has substituted the sociology of science for science proper. This would mean, presumably, that the course conceives scientific investigation as largely or more significantly the creature of influences which lie outside science; for example, it might be thought that economic and technological factors are presented as determining problems chosen for research or that religious and philosophical factors are cited as determining the methods and canons employed for discovery and verification. This is not the case, either. Undoubtedly scientific enquiry is influenced by external factors, but such factors and their effects are not the concern of the science program, any more than the psychological determinants of a man's belief concern the scientist or detective who is trying to determine whether the belief is empirically warranted or not.

It has been assumed also that the presence of original papers means that the course has turned its back on science proper in order to treat scientific papers as humanistic objects, as creations of the human spirit. Nor is this the case. Undoubtedly, a few scientific works are works of art in the best sense. That is, they are complex wholes, woven of a multitude of parts whose relation to one another and to the whole are so complete and perfect as to constitute an aesthetic object. Darwin's *Origin of Species* is such a work. So also are Harvey's *Anatomical Disquisition* and Galileo's *Two New Sciences*. Parts or all of each of these works are used in the program. Nevertheless, the program is in no way concerned with these, or any other works, as works, i.e., humanistic objects.

An illuminating analogy for our use of primary source material is to be seen, rather, in a procedure found in the field of science itself—the practice of the graduate seminar. The "journal club," which meets to hear one or more of its members deliver an interpretation and analysis of a research paper or project, and the special-interest group, which meets to discuss current literature in its field of study, constitute practices familiar to most scientists, with aims and methods analogous to those of the three-year science program in its treatment of primary sources. The bibliographic graduate seminar, which systematizes the approach of journals clubs, is an even closer analogy. In such seminars the instructor presents a bibliography of papers and monographs from which each student selects his share of titles. Each student reads the articles chosen by him, writes abstracts of the papers for distribution among the members of the seminar, and delivers an extended interpretation and critical analysis of the work in question. Under the questioning of fellow students and with the guidance of the professor, students participating in such a program learn what is relevant and what is not to the understanding and judgment of both a scientific paper in the field and the kind of problem in question.

This practice is analogous to the use made of papers in the three-year program, but it is analogous only. It differs from that of a graduate seminar in ways which arise because the students are undergraduates and because the program is part of a liberal curriculum rather than a part of pre-professional training. The precise aim and practice in respect to the use of original papers are therefore best seen in terms of the educational principles which determine them.

The faculty of the College has chosen to divide its curriculum into three major parts, the humanities, the social sciences, and the natural sciences, because each of these areas of knowledge is large enough in itself and, further, because what is meant by knowledge in each of these areas differs sufficiently in origin and application. This division is made, however, without prejudice to the obvious (and sometimes subtle) relations which connect the fields of knowledge to one another. The problem of integration created by setting these boundaries is in part solved by integrative courses. Integration also takes place within the three principal programs as well as in the courses which are explicitly integrative, for this differentiation is a complex one whose basis is much broader than subject matter alone.

In fact, neither subject matter nor method nor purpose alone is an adequate criterion for discriminating and understanding the differences and similarities of the humanities, the social sciences, and the natural sciences. The end, method, and subject matter of each are found in some degree in each of the others. But it is also clear that any one of these criteria exhibits a predominant variant in each of the three fields. For example, in the area most relevant here, in respect to method and end, the process by which data are treated in ways which yield general truths, and primarily for the sake of these general truths, though to be found to a large degree in the social sciences and in the humanities, is nevertheless most prominent in the natural sciences. The same is true of subject matter. Nature, though treated by the humanities for its own purpose of finding models, means, and suggestions for its creations and though found in the social sciences in its specification to human nature, is pre-eminently the subject matter of the natural sciences.

The presence of all three components—humanistic, scientific, and social—in each of the three fields of activity is, therefore, one factor with which we must deal in understanding these fields. The predominance of each of these components in turn in the field which bears its name is another factor. These two factors, taken together in their bearing upon the differences and natures of the fields of the sciences, the social sciences, and the humanities, can be clarified by making explicit a distinction between a "field" and a "discipline." Let "field" stand for the combination of a plurality of subject matters, operations upon these subject matters, and the intentions of the operations, which are to be found in the clusters of organized studies that we call, respectively, the sciences, the humanities, and the social sciences. Let "discipline" stand for an organized activity brought to bear upon a subject matter, the activity achieving its organization in virtue of its purpose and in virtue of the way it takes (or views) its subject matter in order to make the activity, the purpose, and the subject matter appropriate to one another.

In these terms scientific discipline might be conceived as an activity of data-seeking and interpretation, brought to bear upon a subject matter viewed as a source of data capable of yielding general truths and pursued for the sake of such general truths. There would also be humanistic discipline, an activity of analysis and of recognition of relations, brought to bear upon a subject matter conceived as a human creation constructed of chosen parts and put together in chosen ways in order to constitute an envisaged whole, the end of the activity being a comprehension of the parts, their connections, and the whole; and that, in turn, is for the sake of appreciating the created object and for the sake of understanding the activity of choice and ordering of parts which produced it. There would be, finally, social-scientific discipline, an activity which orders knowledge of principles and grasp of particular situations and people to the determination of means-to-ends; this activity is brought to bear upon a dual subject matter, one conceived as giving rise to principles or general truths, the other conceived as setting a problem of choice of action; the activity is pursued for the sake of the choice of means-to-ends, or policy.

With these distinctions, we can then recognize the fields of the humanities, the social sciences, and the natural sciences as compounds of the same elements, but *chemical* compounds in which the characteristic differences of each field emerge as consequences of the differing proportions and connections *inter se* in which the three elements, the disciplines, appear in each field. For instance, the social sciences will have a humanistic and scientific component, but these will function primarily as they make it possible to know peoples, cultures, and societies for the sake of the ultimate determination of means-to-ends. In science, then, there will be a dole of humanistic and social-scientific disciplines, but only in so far as they serve the scientist in his elaboration of general truths from the particular facts of nature.

In terms of the three fields and their disciplines we may state the role to be played by each field in a liberal curriculum. First, each liberal program representative of a field will be concerned to convey to its students a knowledge of its subject matter. But it will be concerned to convey its knowledge to a degree and in a manner appropriate to its dominant disciplines: e.g., knowledge as an objective would loom largest in the field of science. Second, each program will accept responsibility for providing some practice in the liberal equivalent of those disciplines which are not primarily its own, though restricting this practice in kind and scope to the manner and extent that other disciplines function upon its own subject matter. Finally, each program will have a primary responsibility for providing the student with guidance and practice in the employment of the liberal equivalent of its own discipline.

The methods and materials of the natural science program of the College are determined by its share of these three aims. It is subordinately concerned with the disciplines of the other fields; but with these disciplines it is concerned only in so far as, and only on those occasions when, they are relevant to its major tasks. Its major concerns are to impart an understanding of the conclusions of science and to instill the abilities of thought and judgment by which the student may follow the application of scientific discipline in a particular instance to an understanding of the conclusions reached thereby: an understanding of conclusions both as warrantable interpretations of evidence and as instruments for the prediction and control of determinable aspects of nature.

The reason for the use of original research papers and the manner in which they are employed may now be clearer. The science program is not charged with responsibility for the humanistic disciplines, and its treatment of scientific papers does not take them as works of art, subject to the kind of analysis appropriate to a work of art. Therefore, the science program is not a reduction of science to the humanities. Similarly, because the responsibility for imparting knowledge of the social sciences is carried by the social science program and partly by the history course, the science program need not be, and is not, concerned with its material as evidence for conclusions about peoples, epochs, cultures, and trends. The science program is not a reduction of science to the history and sociology of knowledge, and its way of using scientific papers is not adapted to throw light upon such matters. The research papers are present as examples of enquiry, as containers of conclusions, and as centers for the kind of intellectual activity on the part of the student which will constitute practice of those abilities and powers of judgment which are appropriate to the discipline of science.

The student is concerned, in his reading of each reported investigation, with understanding its conclusions. He tries to determine and formulate the problem whose resolution is presented if that problem is not explicit. If the paper is a later one of a series, he tries to understand the problem in relation to the wider body of phenomena which the problems of other investigations have made clear to him. He then determines what kind of evidence is chosen for search by the scientist and why this kind of evidence is appropriate to the problem posed. The student then examines the data themselves and the degree to which they represent the phenomena for which they stand. He moves on to note the manner in which the data are interpreted so as to yield a conclusion, and he tries to determine the effects of the chosen method of interpretation upon the connection between the conclusions reached and the data. Now the student turns from conclusions as warrantable interpretations of data to conclusions as instruments of prediction and control. Through his knowledge of the sources and development of the conclusions, he attempts to understand to what phenomena they are applicable, under what limitations of circumstance and accuracy they may be applied, and with what power they may be expected to function.

The emphasis is also upon the paper as an exemplar of scientific enquiry. Although a single paper is but an instance of an isolated problem posed and solved, the variety of papers as a whole constitutes a cross-section of enquiry in their fields. As experience with one paper after another is established, there is a sifting of the numerous problems and solutions. Similarities and differences emerge. Questions to the students posed by query-sheets and discussions help him find, among the several varied papers, *patterns* of enquiry. He learns to recognize *types* of problems, *kinds* of data, and *modes* of formulation of knowledge.

He learns, for example, what causal enquiry aimed at biological subject matters is like: the kinds of data required, the difficulties of interpretation in such research. He will learn of the ways devised for resolving these difficulties or avoiding them. He will see differing conceptions of the constituent parts of an organism and of their relation to one another applied as tools for formulating problems and organizing research. He will note the advantages and disadvantages of differing principles by discovering what kind or degree of knowledge each yields and what each leaves unexamined. He will learn to distinguish such researches from those employing principles which lead to a different orientation of research, such as might be aimed at taxonomic schematisms or at comprehensive mathematical or mechanical theories. His study of the growth and development of the wave and the particle theories of radiation show him, for instance, what is involved in the development of such a model and what is done by science to combine breadth and flexibility of future application with precision of fit to existing data. He sees the differences in the sense of "verification" and what is experimentally and logically implied by "verification" when a taxonomic scheme is verified and how that differs from the verification of a mathematical model or the test of an assertion of causal relation.

The variety which is exhibited when each paper is treated as a singular solution to a singular problem is thus made intelligible by being seen as the expression of *types* of problem formulation and resolution. An inductive treatment of scientific enquiry replaces the more traditional narrative treatment, and enquiry itself is conceived as a process and an activity which is subject to indefinite variation and specification to particular problems, on the one hand, yet capable of intelligible formulations, on the other. This notion of enquiry is a far cry from its traditional treatment as a "method" to be formulated in a single set of general terms. The problems of enquiry, constituted of the special obstacles in the way of obtaining data and the special difficulties of interpretation which characterize different subject matters of science, as well as those which characterize particular problems, can emerge by an inductive treatment. An inductive treatment, moreover, provides a means by which the education of the student in respect to scientific enquiry can itself be an active scientific enquiry. The distinction of subject matter and student is made less rigid, and the student *does* what he is learning.

The textbook materials which accompany each set of original papers have their part to play as well. In respect to conclusions of science, the original papers cannot be expected to provide economically all that it is desirable to know about the phenomena treated in them. The textbook materials supply this lack: they occasionally provide the background of vocabulary or of unorganized knowledge of the situations with which the papers deal. More often they provide the background of previous theory and fact on which the papers depend or which they will reject, replace, or amend. The textbook materials are depended upon to enlarge and extend the conclusions reached in the papers read, and they supply links of knowledge between paper and paper and between the series of papers. In respect to enquiry, the textbook materials confirm and enlarge the students' understanding of various patterns of enquiry by tracing their effectiveness into areas not treated by the original papers.

The laboratory work of the program has special characteristics which parallel the use of original papers in the course; and, as a parallel to the presence of textbook materials among the readings, the laboratory work has its conventional side as well. The peculiar characteristic of the laboratory work is the marked paucity of explicit instructions for procedure and of predetermined "right" results, at which the student is supposed to aim.

Detailed procedural instruction and a mark to aim for are appropriate initiating devices for laboratory work, when the intention is to provide technique and to make vivid or meaningful the content of lecture and textbook. The laboratory of the science program accepts a measure of these responsibilities. It devotes much of its time to exhibiting the immediate phenomena with which papers or textbook materials will deal as problem situations. It must, for instance, exhibit the gross anatomy of the vertebrate animal; it must display such relatively commonplace phenomena as the solution and precipitation of solids, the behavior of gases during changes in temperature, and the behavior of solids in liquids relative to changes in density. At a more sophisticated level it must show the behavior of light, for example, in its passage through different media and the fact of the spectrum.

It is also through the laboratory that some features of the relation between fact and interpreted fact in science are conveyed. Here, for example, the student grasps by experience the difficulty, in experimentation, of realizing the conditions envisioned in a plan of experiment and the need and significance of the substitution of one procedure as the sign of another, as, for example, the chain of sign-signification relations which exist between the vertically falling body, the body on an inclined plane, and the pendulum. It is also through the laboratory that the difficulties in the way of attaining a required level of accuracy and precision of measurement can be appreciated and the importance of accuracy and precision be assayed.

A third familiar function of the laboratory work is that of making vivid and meaningful the conclusions of papers and text materials and the terms in which their problems are couched. The terms find their operational definition in the laboratory, and the conclusions find their extensional meaning and the limitations under which they have validity.

In a program aimed at comprehension of a discipline as well as at possession of information, however, the laboratory has a fourth function, and in this fourth function the initiating role ordinarily performed by detailed procedural instructions and a mark to aim at is more properly played only by a problem which is itself problematic, that is, a problem in the sense of a situation which invites investigation rather than a problem in the sense of a formulated query. The latter is, in fact, not a problem, strictly speaking, but a problem solved, the problem having been that of determining into what terms the problematic situation could be analyzed in a manner suitable for investigation. A formulated query, by indicating the terms in which the situation is to be analyzed, has also already solved the problem of determining what data are appropriate to solution and how such data are to be treated. A problematic situation, on the other hand, poses all these problems. And to be faced with all these problems is to be faced with the situation which confronts the scientist and which the discipline of science is intended to resolve.

It is for the sake of the light they can throw on the function and nature of the discipline of science that a very few (and these few only approximate) problematic situations confront the student in the three years of the program. Since the intentions of the program do not include the preparation of the student as a scientist, facility in the performance of the discipline of science is not an end, and therefore the number of such problematic situations is small. On the other hand, the responsibility of the program does include a comprehending and evaluating grasp of scientific discipline, and for this purpose a few confrontations with situations which are problematic to some degree have their use. This use has its analogy in the humanities, where some experience in the act of creating a poem or a painting has value not for the sake of making amateur painters or poets but for the sake of a more realistic and comprehending grasp of the artistic work.

Experience has taught us that multiplication of the number of confrontations with problematic situations beyond a few instances is unprofitable. They require much time and make demands upon qualities of originality and imagination which cannot be met by many otherwise highly competent students. It has been found more useful to inject a measured and appropriate degree of problematical quality into all laboratory functions rather than to employ dramatic instances of a wholly or largely problematical kind. This is achieved by reducing laboratory instructions to a minimum. Only a few instructions are written at all, and these in general terms. Rather, the laboratory work of a given week or period of weeks grows out of an initiating discussion of a selected facet of current work. This introduction serves to indicate the general problem area. Student teams then examine available equipment, formulate the problem to be solved, work out the details of experimentation, and proceed, on the basis of their own plans, to data-collecting and interpretation.

The same degree of independent work on the part of the student is achieved on the side of the discussions by a "reading period" which terminates the program. During this time the student pursues one topic through appropriate papers without the aid of class meetings and records the results of his independent investigation in an analytical and interpretive paper.

The distinction of discipline from field and the factors which this distinction emphasizes as aims of a liberal program in the sciences account for the presence and use of original papers and for some of the qualities of the laboratory work of the program. The specific mode of treatment of the papers, on the other hand—what is sought in them as relevant to their conclusions and to enquiry—is a consequence of the staff's conception of the nature of scientific discipline or enquiry.

Our conception of enquiry is an integration of two views which stem from a concern for subject matter, on the one hand, and a concern for skills and abilities, on the other, as the ends of education. Since the science program has both these aims and in relation to each other, its conception of enquiry must contain elements of both views, in proper relation to each other. If science in a curriculum is viewed solely or primarily as a body of conclusions to be narrated and learned, the appropriate view of scientific discipline is one which will assert the validity of scientific conclusions or state the component factors which constitute it. Validity is the only concern because, in respect to conclusions taken in relation to their objects, the principal question is only whether they are true or not. Moreover, where narration is the principal method of instruction, the validity of conclusions taken one by one is not a matter to be questioned or argued. That each separate conclusion is as valid as the method and subject matter permit is underwritten by the fact that they are chosen for narration by an able and informed authority, the teacher. What is required, therefore, is only that the *general* validity of the method employed in that given subject matter be conveyed. For this purpose, science may properly be conceived as a single, uniform procedure and the procedure be described within the limits of a single set of terms.

In point of fact, liberal programs in science concerned primarily or solely with conclusions hardly exist any longer. Yet the view of scientific enquiry appropriate to such a program persists as a vestige of the era in which the function of a general education was considered satisfied when a body of information was made available to the student. Views of this kind, which conceive science as a uniform procedure and describe it within the limits of a single set of terms, may be stated in a variety of ways. Science, for instance, is inductive, and what is not inductive is not science. Since induction implies a movement from particulars to more general statements, one can also say that science is a synthesis and interaction of facts and ideas. Or one can adopt procedural terms and describe science as a process with explicit steps (e.g., the observation of phenomena, the statement of a problem, the collection of relevant data, formulation of hypotheses, verification by prediction of consequences of hypotheses, and test for the presence or absence of predicted consequences).

Highly general formulations of this kind are true in their way, well adapted to a narrative method of instruction, and they serve well enough their purpose of conveying confidence to the student in the conclusions taught him. They have certain inherent limitations, however, and, practically, will not serve by themselves the purposes of a liberal program which is concerned with scientific discipline as well as information. Their limitation lies in the very generality and metonymy by which they are constructed.

Generality and its limiting effect can be seen in the stepwise formulation cited above. In order to reduce science to a conveniently narratable series of steps, the great variability which characterizes a given "step" when it is seen exemplified in different researches is lost. To refer to "formulation of hypotheses" as a step in scientific "method" is to give no hint of the great variety of *kinds* of hypotheses which are employed in different sciences and in different enquiries. Consequently, the fact that different kinds of hypotheses are so very different that each has its own definition of "relevance" in the notion of "relevant data" and confers upon verification its own operationally different meanings is hidden from view. The data and verification relevant to the hypothesis that *this* rather than *that* taxonomic schematism is best would involve an examination of the theories in which the schematism is grounded, a test to determine the value of the schematism in the solution of problems arising from these theories, as well as in a determination of the extent to which the schematism provides a place and only one place for each member of the universe to which the schematism is to be applied. A given taxonomic scheme is based upon a particular choice of qualities and properties of the objects to be classified, and the choice of qualities and properties is, in turn, determined by the use to which the scheme is to be put and the theories from which it arises. Therefore, a variety of taxonomic schemes applicable to a given universe and competent to provide each member of the universe with a place is possible. Verification of any one such scheme is therefore to be sought in a test of its usefulness upon problems and of its appropriateness to antecedent theories, as well as in a test by more immediate standards. A grasp of such ideas as these is not provided by the narration of a highly general, stepwise formulation of science, for, in their way, these ideas are themselves "steps" in scientific enquiry which are omitted from such a narrative.

The question of the data and tests relevant to the verification of a cause-and-effect hypothesis concerning a living organism and its parts presents its own complex features. Cause-and-effect researches in physiology involve notions of sufficient and necessary antecedent events and constituent parts. Hence one kind of relevant data and test of such a hypothesis will concern the consequence or lack of consequence of the presence or absence of designated parts or processes in the organism. "Part" and "particular process," however, are not objectively given pieces of the organism or of the life-process in time, and therefore the principles which determine the particular partitioning of the anatomy and activity of the organism are data relevant to a test of the hypothesis in question. Different researches employ different principles of partitioning which yield different parts (e.g., biochemical units as against organs, or organs as against organ aggregates), and therefore the test of a given hypothesis must include as relevant not only the data concerning ablation and replacement of parts characteristic of its own level of partitioning but also the facts concerning the consequences of the presence and absence of parts defined by other principles of anatomy.

Parts and particular processes in the living organism are also characterized by a peculiar fluidity. The structure and function of a given part, distinguished on whatever basis, vary with time and circumstance; its characteristics are a function of its environing neighbors and conditions, as well as of its own determination. Therefore, the changes in the organism as a whole under varied conditions and especially under the conditions of experimentation are valid data and part of the test of a causal hypothesis in the life-sciences.

Such matters as these escape a highly general presentation of the nature of science, in whatever terms it may be put. Large and important differences among various patterns of scientific enquiry are not raised for consideration. These differences need hardly be touched upon in a program concerned only with information, but a liberal program concerned also with scientific discipline requires a view of science which will permit a concrete and specific understanding of the individual examples of scientific enquiry examined by the student. A concrete understanding of particular researches requires a specification of general ideas to the matter in hand, and specification requires cognizance of sufficient diversity to make each paper intelligible in itself and capable of relation to other papers.

The need for simplicity and economy of narration which gives rise to highly general summaries of the nature of enquiry is also satisfied in many instances by metonymous procedures which achieve the same end by displaying a part of science as if it were the whole, that is, by describing a particular pattern of enquiry and omitting mention of others.

Metonymous formulations have the same limitation of usefulness to a liberal program as do highly general formulations: they do not suffice to make each enquiry intelligible in itself and capable of relation to other investigations. Metonymous constructions may, in fact, become more confusing than highly general constructions. The latter, though they fail to exhibit sufficient detail in a given example of research to permit its comprehension and evaluation, at least sketch a few broad lines which can be discerned in most papers. Metonymous constructions, on the other hand, may fail to fit (except by analogy) researches employing patterns of enquiry other than the one expounded.

At the other extreme from the general or metonymous narration of the nature of enquiry is the mode of presentation, with its attendant vices, which characterized the initial year of the 1943 science program. Then, as previously mentioned, formulation of the nature of enquiry in any terms whatever was eschewed. Enquiry was represented by individual researches examined in highly particular fashion; similarities and differences were sought, and thereby rough groupings of papers were noted; but the characteristics which bound one group of papers together as examples of enquiry and which separated that group from another were not distinguished and named, nor were the characteristics common to all the papers as examples of enquiry given adequate attention.

With such a procedure, the species of scientific enquiry become too numerous to function effectively as instruments of analysis; and the failure to establish them as species of a common genus by showing them as the varied application of common principles to a variety of problems leads to a failure to impart the notion of truth-seeking as such.

The failure to impart the notion of truth-seeking as such and a contrary failure in the case of general or metonymous narrations must be taken as representative of the inadequacies in practice of these ways of conceiving enquiry. General and metonymous narratives tend to lump all scientific conclusions together. Criteria of greater and lesser validity (as distinguished from true versus false) are not stated or applied. In consequence, all conclusions of science are understood as equally valid, and the level of validity is taken as absolute or very high. This view is likely to occur for psychological reasons, even if avoided in actual statement, for the lumping of all conclusions together at one level of validity requires that they all be accepted or rejected together. A total rejection is not likely. Total acceptance of conclusions requires acceptance of the allegedly common route by which they are reached. And the route itself has the same uniform validity conferred upon it that was attributed to the conclusions. Moreover, in the absence of a concrete study of varying scientific procedures and a consequent awareness of the complexity of the notion of validity, still a third mistaken factor colors the student's view of science: its conclusions are taken as all equally literal. The gram, the diameter of the earth, force in the Newtonian equation, the gene of Mendelian theory, the unseen x-tron of the latest mathematical exploration of atomic theory, and the automobile parked at the curb are assumed to have the same existential standing. That such a view leads to wild misunderstanding and confusion as to the meaning of conclusive statements in science goes without saying. The notion of science as a large body of equally true literal statements about nature, all arrived at by a common route, leads to a conception of problems and the difficulty of problem-solving equally wide of the mark. A problem appears to be something objectively given; the data seem to be waiting only to be recorded; and the solution seems to be something that supervenes automatically with the recording of the last datum gathered.

This simple and naïve empiricism finds its contrary error in the consequences of wholly individualistic treatment of enquiry. Many routes are seen to lead to as many conclusions, often mutually exclusive in their expression, yet, each in its own way, equally valid. The variety of procedures suggests the absence of canons of better and worse procedures. The variety of conclusions suggests the absence of canons of better and worse conclusions. Such a treatment often implants a conventionalistic view of scientific knowledge. Conclusions are conceived as mere plausible accounts stemming from the researcher's habitual choice of principles. Where the general narrative tends to implant naïve literalism, individualistic treatment tends to implant fictionalism—the notion that scientific conclusions are wholly metaphorical and to be judged only in terms of aesthetico-logical standards of unity, coherence, and economy. They come to be treated as useful myths among which choice is a matter only of custom and convenience. Problems appear to be merely invented, and data the product of an arbitrary choice.

Each of these approaches—the individualistic and the highly general —derives its prime weakness through ignoring the strength of the contrary view. The individualistic view tends to ignore the solid, factual basis of scientific knowledge. The general narrative ignores the constructive or inventive aspect of scientific theories and conclusions. A sounder view would incorporate and relate both. The science program attempts such an incorporation and relation of factual and ideational factors, both in its theory and in its practice. It does so by taking "problem" as a starting point rather than "data" or "conclusion." From "problem" it is possible to work in two directions. On the one hand, a problem can be seen in relation to nature as exhibited through other problems and thus be understood as an abstraction from the real and total situation with which nature confronts us. On the other hand, it can be seen as a statement which gives direction to enquiry and thus be understood as a meaningful question to which meaningful and valid answers can be given. From the first point of view, the incompleteness of scientific knowledge at any given moment and the significance of the variety of answers which it appears to give to a single question can be understood without recourse to conventionalism. They are seen as the consequence of the fact that problems are partial and abstract aspects of a larger complex of related matters. They are seen as consequences of a process by which more and more of the total situation called "nature" is encompassed and comprehended because the answers to partial problems lead to larger problems and their resolutions, which encompass more of the whole.

From the second point of view the validity of the knowledge of science at any given moment and the effectiveness of its answers as instruments for the control of nature can be understood without recourse to naïve literalism. They are seen as warranted answers to the questions-as-stated and also as milestones on the march of knowledge, since the amount of truth which they contain points to the knowledge which they do not contain and thereby they function as the germs of problems yet to come. By recognizing both the incompleteness of problems-as-formulated and the validity of solutions to such problems, a view of science is obtained in which its ongoing character, its continuing reconstruction of knowledge, and the practical truth of its views at a given moment in time are seen as faces of the same coin.

In practice, our treatment of instances of research follows this theoretical view. The student is concerned, first, with the problem stated, its relation to other problems, and, through these, its relations to nature. He then turns to the problem as relating to its resolution: he is concerned with matters of evidence, interpretation, and application. As experience with a variety of papers accumulates, he adds a concern for the modalities and the nature of enquiry itself: questions of types of problems and solutions and the canons of sound enquiry are raised and treated.

By thus distinguishing, but connecting, discipline and field, method and content, fact and idea, the science program attempts to determine its own duties, without neglecting the duties it shares with other programs of the curriculum, and to discharge these duties without doctrinaire adhesion to incomplete and warring dogmas. It can leave artistic analysis to the humanities and doctrines of knowledge and of being to philosophy, where these can be treated with wisdom and experience; it can concern itself with science; yet its treatment of science can be both sensitive and philosophical, without ceasing to be scientific. It is enabled to impart some knowledge of the world and yet construct a foundation for critical understanding of the limitations of human knowledge, without degrading the student to a parrot, on the one hand, or a snob, on the other. It can examine the contribution to science of both the eye and the human intellect without denigrating knowledge either to a catalogue or to a myth. Its attempt to do these things and its continuing effort to educate itself, to enlarge its competence for its task, and to subject its principles to continuing re-examination are the bases for calling it a *liberal* program in the sciences.

The Nature of Scientific Knowledge
as Related to Liberal Education

AGREEMENT AND DISAGREEMENT CONCERNING SCIENCE

What science is and, therefore, how to teach it are our problems. Yet, in one sense, there is no problem. We all know what science is. There is no difficulty in distinguishing its subject matter, as may be the case with the humanities. Its subject matter comprises all natural phenomena which can be made to yield general truths when subjected to the method of science. There is no controversy over the ends and methods of science, as is often the case in research within the field of the social studies. The end of science is the establishment of general laws or truths, and it achieves its end within the limits suggested by Dewey's descriptive phrase, "warranted assertibility." Its method is to establish the warranted assertibility of general propositions (which contain terms and relations not immediately derived from data) by referring them for verification to "stubborn and irreducible facts." This is a method which, though it may vary in detail from science to science or problem to problem, is called the "inductive method."

Described at this level of generality, not only is the nature of science well understood and agreed upon, it is also an adequate basis for many programs of study. Wherever a program is concerned only or mainly with the *conclusions* of science, and with them only for practical purposes, this general view suffices. This would hold for survey courses oriented to student "needs," where "need" is conceived only in terms of workaday applications to the technological devices of the modern home and office. It would hold also for engineering programs with a similarly restricted technological emphasis. Here the teacher may teach and the student learn the conclusions of science apart from the data and their interpretation which support conclusions, confident that the conclusions so taught and learned have all the validity which the method of science can impart. They can be sure that this validity is, on the whole, limited only by the incompleteness of data and the incomplete formulation of

This chapter was previously published in a slightly different form in the *Journal of General Education* 3 (1949): 245–66.

the problem to which the conclusions of science are always subject when withdrawn from the unending process of enquiry which produces useful conclusions but also continuously enlarges and modifies them.

When, however, the consideration of science goes beyond the general to a consideration of particular sciences as embodied in concrete examples of scientific enquiry (as it will when the objectives of a program of study go beyond the imparting of scientific conclusions for merely practical purposes), unanimity and simple certainty about the nature of science are displaced by differences of view. These differences arise when scientists and students of science are confronted by problems of method, end, and subject matter visible in concrete examples of scientific enquiry, though not noticeable from the distant and general view.

For instance, F. K. Richtmyer and E. H. Kennard, two highly respected physicists, have this to say of Newton's *Principia*—in the 1942 edition of their *Introduction to Modern Physics:*

> In this treatise the famous three laws of motion are assumed as axioms. Their greatest merit lay in the fact that they contain just enough to constitute a complete basis for the science of mechanics and no more. The laws can be expressed with a slightly greater clarity in modern terminology and we now realize that in part they express definitions rather than experimental facts, but it is commonly felt that no more *convenient* basis for mechanics has been proposed.[1]

On the other hand, R. B. Lindsay and H. Margenau, also highly respected physicists, have this to say in the 1944 printing of their *Foundations of Physics:*

> Granted our ignorance of force, . . . [Newton's first] law becomes a pious statement calling attention to a possible state of motion which may sometimes be realized in nature and sometimes not. . . . All this is very much tinged with anthropomorphism, and inasmuch as science tries to get as far away from anthropomorphic ideas as possible, is of doubtful value for mechanics. . . .[2]
>
> It is incumbent on us to provide some connected theoretical basis with which to replace the Newtonian laws and which will lead to the results which Newton and his successors have sought to draw from these laws.[3]

Clearly, these authors differ in their conception of what constitutes good science, and therefore they find in the record of Newton's research quite different characteristics to which they attach primary importance.

1. (New York: McGraw-Hill, 1942), p. 28.
2. (New York: John Wiley & Sons, 1944), p. 87.
3. Ibid., p. 91.

Richtmyer and Kennard's emphasis on "convenience" and Lindsay and Margenau's subsequent emphasis on an operationalist definition of an acceptable "connected theoretical basis" suggest the basis for their diversity of view concerning the proper criteria for judging the soundness of Newton's contribution to physics.

What is suggested by these quotations—that scientists differ widely in their views concerning the nature of science—is borne out if one looks to other fields and areas of science. One sees it in the contrast between the esteem in which the theory of relativity was held in Ernst Mach's later days by many physicists and this statement of his: "I can accept the theory of relativity as little as I can accept the existence of atoms and other such dogma." One sees it in situations where the criticism of a biological study as teleological is unanswerable, and the epithet "preformistic" is a sign of departure from orthodoxy. Sherrington testifies to this diversity of view by the fact that he finds it necessary to inveigh *against* the extremists on his own side in his plea for a physicochemical approach to problems in embryology:

> When we are told that the modern chemist and physicist cannot get on without the hypothesis that matter explains everything, a position is reached akin to that of initiation into a faith. A rigid attitude of mind is taken as an orientation necessary for progress in knowledge. Is there anything different between that and the efficacy of the spiritual exercises of St. Ignatius as introductory to mystic convictions expected to follow? What either expedient may possibly gain in intensity of insight is surely at disproportionately greater cost to breadth of judgment.[4]

As one moves closer and closer to concrete cases of scientific enquiry and further from sweeping and general views of the subject, the diversity of position among scientists becomes ever more real and significant in actually determining the direction of research and more necessary for understanding and relating researches to one another. The diversity becomes more significant because the positions involved deal specifically with questions of what kinds of data are to be preferred, what kinds of explanation or knowledge are to be sought, and what kinds of problems are to be considered most fruitful for attack in the subject matter in question. The opposition between physicochemical explanation and explanation in terms of function of parts relative to a whole (as seen in Sherrington's remarks), far from being the only conflict in biology, is only the container for more, and more specific, differences of approach. Even within the group which champions the physicochemical approach,

4. Charles Sherrington, *Man on His Nature* (New York: Macmillan, 1941), p. 136.

there is a division. In D'Arcy Thompson's *Growth and Form* we find, for example, this defense of the physical as against the chemical explanation as the preferred kind of scientific explanation:

> In short, it would seem evident that except in relation to a dynamical investigation, the mere study of cell structure has little value of its own. That a given cell, an ovum for instance, contains this or that visible substance or structure, germinal vesicle or germinal spot, . . . chromosomes or centrosomes, obviously gives no explanation of the activities of the cell. And in all such hypotheses . . . which attribute specific properties to micellae, chromosomes, idioplasts, ids, or other constituent particles of protoplasm or of the cell, we are apt to fall into the error of attributing to *matter* what is due to *energy* and is manifested in force: or, more strictly speaking, of attributing to material particles individually what is due to the energy of their collocation.
>
> If we speak . . . of . . . a substance . . . which hands on to the new generation the characteristics of the old, we can only justify our mode of speech by the assumption that that particular portion of matter is the essential vehicle of a particular charge or distribution of energy, in which is involved the capability of producing motion or of doing "work." . . . The *things* which we see in the cell are less important than the *actions* which we recognize in the cell.[5]

If we now turn from those scientists, who by the nature of their work give only occasional attention to the nature of science, to men with a special interest in methodology, the wide diversity of view becomes explosively clear. J. S. Mill and William Whewell are in direct conflict concerning the nature of induction itself.[6] Einstein and Henri Poincaré are polar in respect to one of the most critical aspects of method in the physical sciences—the relation of mathematical knowledge to the physical world.[7] Francis Bacon, Augustus DeMorgan, and Morris Cohen with Ernest Nagel represent three distinct positions concerning the propriety and place of hypothesis in scientific enquiry.[8] Descartes can

5. (New York: Macmillan, 1945), pp. 287–89.
6. J. S. Mill, *A System of Logic*, Book 3, chap. 2; William Whewell, *On the Philosophy of Discovery* (London: J.W. Parker & Sons, 1860), chap. 22.
7. Albert Einstein, *Sidelights on Relativity*, vol. 2, *Geometry and Experience* (London: Methuen, 1922); Henri Poincaré, *Science and Hypothesis* (New York: Science Press, 1905).
8. Francis Bacon, *Novum Organum*, Aphorisms, Book 1; Morris Cohen and Ernest Nagel, *An Introduction to Logic and Scientific Method* (New York: Harcourt, Brace, 1934); Augustus DeMorgan, *A Budget of Paradoxes* (London: Longmans, Green, 1872).

question the very use to which sense data are to be put.[9] Newton, in his aphoristic "hypotheses non fingo," inveighs against the use of *mechanical models* for explanation and asserts the superiority of conceptual *quantities* as the appropriate form of scientific knowledge.

Diversity of view concerning the nature of science is then an inescapable fact. And this inescapable fact implies one immediate caveat to architects of liberal programs in the natural sciences. The caveat is that no one doctrine concerning the nature of science can be exclusively employed as a principle of organization and interpretation or taught by the architect in the program he develops. To employ only one doctrine as a principle will give rise to a biased view of the nature of science, and to teach a single doctrine could be to the student only misleading or confusing or both, because no single doctrine is more than a partial statement—partial in the sense of incomplete and partial in the sense of being based upon a given set of epistemic or metaphysical presuppositions.

We shall discuss in a later paragraph a constructive proposal with which to replace the all too common doctrinaire treatment of scientific method. Our present problem, however, is to return to the inescapable fact of diversity of view concerning science and to note certain causes of this diversity which are themselves important considerations in planning and teaching a defensible liberal program of science.

Sources and Kinds of Diversity about and in Science

The causes of diversity significant to a liberal program in science are of three kinds. The first of these is found in philosophy. The second is found in science and concerns the reflexive effect of doctrines about science upon the practices of science. The third is also found in science and concerns the variety of problems and subject matters which science investigates.

Concerning the cause of diversity which is philosophical in origin, one must consider philosophy for a moment as a branch of scholarly enquiry. It has problems of its own which it investigates much as science does. The problems are various: they may be ethical or deal with aspects of the state and society; they may treat difficulties arising out of considerations concerning the nature of knowledge; or they may be involved in a theory concerning the nature of reality. For many of these problems, one aspect or another of scientific enquiry is relevant as a source of data. But, as the problem attacked by the philosopher varies, so does the aspect of science which is his source of relevant data, and the particular relevant aspect is incorporated into the solution to the philosopher's

9. René Descartes, *Meditations on First Philosophy*.

problem. It is appropriate there, and the conclusions embodying it, if valid when measured by the canons of philosophic method, are also valid if taken as applying only to the problem which the philosopher sought to solve. Difficulty arises when we interpret the philosopher's solution to his particular problem as being a solution to the general problem of the nature of scientific enquiry. So misinterpreted, the philosophic statement cannot appear otherwise than as incomplete and biased in favor of its own epistemic or metaphysical presuppositions; for it is then being mis-applied to a problem more extensive and more complex than the one it was intended to comprise. It *can* be made to throw light on some aspect of scientific enquiry and thus give us the benefits of scholarly study of the nature of science, but only if we are, first, careful to note the prob-lem to which it addresses itself and, second, willing to apply the disci-plines which enable us to see the particular aspect of science to which the problem is relevant and upon which the solution throws light.

David Hume offers a clear example. Misread as a treatise on the nature of science, he can be readily interpreted, and often has been, as showing the untenable character of causal relations as the object of scientific investigation. He is variously alleged to have sounded the death-knell of "cause," to have exhibited its viciously metaphysical nature, and to have shown that there can be no such thing as scientific evidence for asserting one class of thing or event to be the cause of another. If he is so misread, one is forced to wonder how biology, and especially physiology, could have been so stubborn as to have gone serenely on investigating causes, reporting them, and basing a reason-ably successful system of medical practice upon them. One answer is that Hume's document is not a treatise *on* science and does not condemn causation as an object of investigation. A glance at his title reveals that his work is a *Treatise of Human Nature*, in short, a treatise in psychol-ogy. In the light of that fact, a re-examination of his remarks on cause reveals that his principal terms are those of psychology: *idea, impres-sion, perception, association, habit, observation,* and *experience*. His problem, in so far as causes were concerned, was not whether the causal relation was a meaningful object of investigation but how it was to be investigated and how the results of investigation were to be interpreted. His conclusion, therefore, is not that knowledge of cause is untenable but only that it is probable rather than certain, that belief in a given causal relation is founded upon the repeated observation and experience of contiguity and antecedence-consequence between instances of the "cause" and instances of the "effect," and not upon detection of the act of *causing* itself. In short, he describes precisely how science investi-gates causal relations and the sense in which the products of such investigation are worthy of confidence. He condemns only a particular misunderstanding of the evidential and existential status of the relation we call "causation."[10]

Here, then, is an example of the way in which virtual or demi-philosophies of science tend to develop during the train of interpretations which usually intervenes between an original philosophical statement and classroom presentation. It points to the unsoundness or incompleteness which characterizes single doctrines of science and the teaching of a single, summary doctrine of science; it emphasizes the need for careful treatment of such doctrines. It suggests the need for presentation of several views of science in such a way that each doctrine will point to inadequacies or errors of others; for, although the example here given is one of overinterpretation of a doctrine, such doctrines, even thoroughly interpreted, are neither complete nor perfect theories concerning the nature of scientific knowledge. If, then, any given doctrine is either sweepingly general or, if specific, then also incomplete, to use one such doctrine is clearly to lay one's self open to the charge of falsehood or special pleading.

The second educationally significant cause of diversity is to be found not in philosophy but in science. It is, as suggested earlier, real variation in the pattern of scientific enquiry stemming from the reflexive effect of doctrines about science upon the practices of research scientists. From time to time certain "philosophies of science" or philosophic documents which can be read as treatises on science appeal to the practicing scientist, and his conduct of scientific investigation is modified to a greater or lesser degree by the doctrine that he has read and approved. This will often be true for significant segments of an entire field of science for a considerable time. Thus, despite the fact that, in one sense, methodological studies take scientific investigation as their data, it is also true that scientific investigation often stems from conclusions of methodology taken by the scientific investigator as guiding principles. Some of the same alternative epistemic and metaphysical presuppositions which initiate different doctrines about science, therefore, are also found initiating different researches in science itself. (It is of interest to note that this two-way relation between doctrines about science and scientific enquiry is the same two-way relation which holds between published discoveries about human behavior in general and the effects of knowing about these discoveries upon the behavior of the very organisms which they describe—the two-way relation which makes the problem of scientific knowledge in the social sciences so difficult.)

Examples of this influence of doctrine on practice in science are numerous and almost commonplace. The language and emphases of oper-

10. David Hume, *A Treatise of Human Nature*, Book 1, Part 3.

ationalism appear in the scientific literature of physics soon after the popularization of the doctrine as a philosophic point of view. The theological orientation of Newton's investigation of astronomy is no more obvious than the commitment of many twentieth-century physicists to the positivist doctrine of Ernst Mach. When we speak of the effects of new philosophic conceptions of knowledge and of investigation upon a Galileo, we are speaking of a kind of influence which continues to function. Espousal of a simple mechanistic position by zoölogists and psychologists in the years just before and after the First World War is no less a reflection of "usage . . . akin to initiation into a faith," than is Goldstein's contemporary insistence on a holistic approach in biology or than what is suggested by a recent meeting of biologists frankly entitled "Symposium on Teleological Mechanisms." Not only was Newton influenced by a doctrine; his work also became an influential doctrine. The years following the success of his *Principia* are characterized not only by the enormously successful effort to found other theories in physics and chemistry upon mechanics but also by a number of less significant biological researches which attempted to reduce a great deal of biology to fluid and solid statics and dynamics. In our own time the physiological and medical journals exhibit quite clearly a reaffirmation and new emphasis on a somewhat similar conception of physiological explanation following the successful extraction in useful quantity of heavy hydrogen and other isotopes. "Tracer" techniques quickened biological research along these lines; the increase in this kind of research was followed by emphasis upon the doctrine of physiochemical explanation as distinguished from organ physiology and explanation in terms of the relations of organs and organ systems to the organism as a whole. And the combination of these examples and precepts can be seen to have influenced biomedical research not only in the frequency of publication of this kind of research but also in the assignment of grants-in-aid by foundations and the policies of new institutes, subdepartments, and special projects in the biomedical divisions of universities and governmental research agencies.

A third kind of diversity significant for the planning of a liberal program in the sciences was earlier said to be that diversity which is concerned with the variety of subject matters and problems which science investigates. It would be tempting to say, for the sake of distinguishing sharply this and other diversities, that the third category *stems from* the subject matters and problems of the sciences. Such a characterization is plausible; even a casual contrast of representative researches in physics and biology, for example, exhibits a high degree of differentiation, if not a sharp demarcation, between the two in respect to the kind of investigation which is brought to bear upon their respective subject matters and the kind of knowledge of the subject matter which is sought. The attempt to determine covariant quantities and numerical constants is the commonplace of physics, for example, and rare in biology. On the other hand, the attempt to discover classes of events which are absolutely or usually invariant in their temporal sequence ("causes") is a commonplace of biology and rare in physics. The notion that this third category of diversity *stems from* consideration of the subject matter and problems is plausible, then. It is very difficult, how-ever, to establish by evidence. It is much more likely that, of the whole body of diversities of method which can be seen in science, some have undoubtedly been suggested to scientists in their struggle to comprehend their chosen subject matters, and others, whatever their origin, have come to be attached by scientists more to one subject matter than to another because of their peculiar appropriateness there. It would be best, therefore, to characterize this body of diversities as those which show definite correlations with one or another subject matter or with one or another kind of problem.

It should be emphasized that what is meant by "correlation" is not mere statistical frequency of association and disjunction, although this would be part of the story. What would distinguish this category of diversities from the others named is that here one finds associated with a given subject matter or kind of problem a kind of investigation, some properties of which have discernible relations to properties of the sub-ject matter. A high degree of variability is said to characterize a sample of any biological phenomenon, by contrast, for example, with the uni-formity of samples in chemistry. Such a high degree of variability in biology would constitute a special recalcitrance of such a subject matter to investigation aimed at formulating equations which express a fixed relation between quantitative variables. On the other hand, the concept of *organism*, with all that it implies concerning complexity and or-ganization, is far more meaningfully applied to living systems than to nonliving systems. Such a concept implies the notion of a battery of "functions" which analyze the whole activity of the organism into part-activities. These part-activities, in turn, suggest an analysis of the struc-ture of the organism into parts and extended research aimed at assigning structures to functions and also aimed at mutual correction and refine-ment of the original analyses. These steps describe a pattern of research, a "method" which is peculiarly suited to a particular kind of subject matter.

A further example of appropriateness of method to subject matter can be seen in the way that physical subject matters have been amenable in a high degree to a method for systematizing variability. The method consists in inventing and precisely defining certain "ideal" bodies, whose defined properties are such that variability in measurements of some property of real bodies can be referred to the "ideal" body and can be codified and measured with considerable precision as measured deviation from the "ideal."

One of the most obvious examples of codification in terms of an "ideal" is seen in the classical treatment of the impact and rebound of bodies. Data on comparative relative velocities of balls before and after impact suggested that equating momentum before impact to momentum after impact and relative velocity before impact to relative velocity after impact constituted central tendencies which expressed the behavior of bodies in impact, but with extreme variability from one kind of body to another. It was Newton who reduced this variability enormously by inventing the notion of "perfect elasticity" and so defining it that deviations from expected velocities could be expressed by a number which can be considered a measure of the deviation of real balls from "perfect elasticity" (the coefficient of restitution).

The "ideal gas" for the purposes of kinetic molecular theory is another case in point. So also was the "freely falling body" during the many years between Galileo's development of the conception and the production of vacuum pumps adequate to the task of creating nearly perfect vacuums.

Taken together, these cases exemplify the method of "idealization" which has been so fruitfully applied to the broad subject matter of the physical sciences and less so in the physiological aspects of biology. Taken separately, the same instances exemplify the diversity from problem to problem *within* a subject matter. Thus the coefficient of restitution is appropriate to one problem (or narrow subject matter) and the freely falling body to another.

Here, because we have moved away from diversities about science as a whole, through divisions of the sciences, almost to the level of particular researches, the diversity in pattern of research which can be seen is enormous. It is so large that one must legitimately raise the question whether any practicable account of it can be taken, even in specialized programs of education, much less in liberal programs which have broader responsibilities. The answer, it seems to me, is twofold. On the one hand, it is quite impossible to "cover" diversity at the level of particular problems, in the sense that survey courses try to "cover" a subject matter. On the other hand, the role of particular invented terms and conceptions in particular conclusions of science is both universal and decisive. Since liberal programs in science have as one aim to impart an understanding of the nature of conclusive formulations in science, illustration of the part that conceptions and terms play in these conclusions is desirable. Moreover, since liberal programs as well as others in science intend that conclusions learned for their own sake (rather than as examples of conclusive formulations) be understood as fully as possible, it follows that the conclusions which are taught should be taught with full cognizance of the meanings and roles of the particular terms involved in them. Thus two tasks can be performed at once. And the economy visible here is multiplied many times if, as will be suggested in detail later, the whole business of teaching the nature of scientific knowledge be performed inductively. For such a purpose the teaching materials would be sets of examples of scientific enquiry; each such example would serve simultaneously to impart subject-matter content and to illustrate aspects of the nature of scientific knowledge at many different levels—from the most specific level at which the paper falls (e.g., inferring causal connections in physiology from ablation and replacement experiments) through the level of the subscience (e.g., physiology) and the level of the broad special science (biology) to the level of science-as-a-whole.

One example will suffice to show the decisive role which terms and conceptions play in both the investigation of phenomena and the understanding of the conclusions so derived.

A few years ago, one interest of biologists in the behavior of lower animals took the form of testing their tropistic response to various stimuli. A tropism meant, among other things, a turning or moving in response to an environmental stimulus. The movement, if it occurred at all, could be either toward or away from the stimulus, such movements being called "positive" and "negative" tropisms, respectively. An investigation of tropistic response to light of a certain species was attempted by the usual method of so placing an aquarium containing the animals that light entered it from only one end, the other end being, in consequence, relatively dim. Other environmental factors were presumably equally distributed throughout the length of the aquarium.

One responsible investigator performed such an experiment and reported finding the population of the aquarium bunched very near its light end. He concluded, therefore, that the species in question was positively phototropic. Another responsible investigator reported a similar experiment upon the same species in which he found the animals clustered near the dim end of the aquarium. Hence he concluded that the species was negatively phototropic. Attempts to explain the apparent contradiction in terms of interfering environmental factors and in terms of differences between the two populations of experimental animals failed.

Eventually the difficulty was resolved by an examination and subsequent rejection of the term "tropism" for this particular purpose. Examination of the meaning of the term clarified its all-or-none characteristic.

That is, "tropism" could be answered to in only three ways: it could be positive or negative or not at all. Ignoring the zero state, since the experimental results did not require it, it became clear that the simple alternative of positive or negative *response* implied a similar pair of alternative *stimuli*, which in this case were lightness and darkness. The terms admitted any degree of undiscriminated *lightness* above some threshold, provided that a sufficient contrast of relative darkness were also available. The absolute intensity of light was not specified or suggested by the term "tropism." Discarding it, a third investigator examined the situation in the light of the notion that organisms moved not toward or away from a given stimulus but toward an "optimum intensity" of the stimulus. He was able, operating with this term, to demonstrate that the animals of the first and second investigations were at substantially the same absolute light intensity. Their movement toward the "optimum intensity" had been disguised as "contrary" movements by the interpretation which the term "tropism" had pressed upon the data. Results which appeared contradictory when viewed in terms of "tropism" became consistent and informative when viewed in terms of "optimal intensity."

Thus one's choice of terms is seen to emphasize certain facts in a situation at the price of obscuring others. One's choice of terms determines what appears relevant or irrelevant to a study; they indicate, literally *point to*, the area or aspect of phenomena from which data are to be drawn. It is this general function of terms which needs to be understood if the student is to have an informed understanding of the nature of scientific conclusions. It is identification of the particular terms involved in particular conclusions, and some appreciation of what phenomena are not indicated and which are emphasized by the chosen terms, that constitute an adequate understanding of the specific conclusions as valid statements applying to the physical world. To know the existence and effect of terms, moreover, is to grasp the fact that science grows not only by increased precision and discovery of new phenomena but also by redefinition and replacement of terms, so as to illuminate larger aspects of phenomena or to relate aspects of phenomena previously disjoined.

It should be noted that the "tropism" case cited as example is not to be taken as evidence for the universal superiority of "quantitative" over "nonquantitative" forms of knowledge. The tropism concept has been a fruitful source of knowledge and, indeed, has emphasized some aspects of animal behavior obscured by the notion of "optimum intensity." The point is not the superiority of one kind of term over another but the universal and decisive role which is played by terms in scientific knowledge.

A Prefatory Codification of Varieties of Scientific Knowledge

Presentation of a taxonomy of scientific enquiries would, under any circumstance, be an act of presumption. Where the taxonomy is for a special purpose, careful statement of limitations in validity are all the more demanded.

The tentative schematism to be suggested here does not pretend to be philosophically complete. It is intended only as a partial aid to the solution of a problem in the planning and teaching of a liberal program in the sciences. The problem is whether, in a liberal program, to treat scientific enquiry as consisting of one method or of many. The problem arises because liberal programs are committed to teaching students to understand the conclusions of science and to understand the nature of scientific knowledge. The problem, then, is whether the nature of scientific knowledge is understood as far as is useful or necessary for the purposes of liberal education if it is understood only as a single set of general terms. Such sets of terms do exist, and several of them can be defended as applicable to all scientific enquiry, as suggested earlier in this paper. Science, for instance, is inductive, and what is not inductive is not science. Since induction implies the movement from particulars to more general statements, one can also say that scientific knowledge is a synthesis and interaction of facts and ideas. In these, as in other general descriptions, however, the result is to make the term "science" highly ambiguous, since much humanistic study (e.g., history, philosophy, or art criticism) also moves from particular to general and involves synthesis of facts and ideas. Hence, even if liberal understanding means only the ability to distinguish science from other kinds of knowledge or enquiry, such uniform and general terms are hardly adequate.

Even if general descriptions of science permitted classification of an investigation as scientific rather than historical or other, they would still be inadequate for the purposes of liberal education. Liberal education aims at understanding. For the purposes of understanding something, to put it in a class has only a preliminary—though peculiarly important—function, and this important preliminary function is not served by classifying an investigation as simply scientific. To identify an enquiry as scientific rather than historical has only the same preliminary function as the identification of a pathological state as diabetes or of a book as a novel—namely, to guide one's further actions in respect to the thing classified. In the case of a literary genre we are guided in our reading and appreciation. In the case of a disease we are guided in the treatment aimed at cure or amelioration. In the case of an enquiry aimed at knowledge we are guided to comprehension and evaluation.

Comprehension and evaluation of a scientific investigation involves knowing the kind of data employed in an investigation. It means knowing the relation of the abstracted data to the whole body of phenomena from which they were drawn. It means knowing the kind of induction employed, that is, the kind of involvement of data with ideas which is used by the investigator to convert the particularity of his data into the general character of a scientific conclusion. Since there are several *kinds* of induction and since there are different kinds of ideas appropriate to different kinds of facts and related each to each in different ways, merely to identify the presence of induction or of interaction of facts and ideas is not a sufficient guide to comprehension and evaluation. One must know enough of the various kinds to grasp the particular interaction before one. One must know enough of the problems involved in the verification of each kind of induction or synthesis to estimate the adequacy of the case in question. In brief, operative understanding— knowledge capable of use—concerning enquiry must, like operative understanding anywhere, involve both the general and the less general, the concrete as well as the most abstract.

It is this need for generality *and* generic concreteness which points to the usefulness of a tentative taxonomy, for, if inoperative generality is one extreme, equally ineffective chaos is the other. In the one case, one merges all scientific enquiries into an indistinguishable mass. In the other, one equally oversimplifies the pedagogic problem by insisting on the individual difference of every enquiry from every other, on the unique standing of every investigation. Both are true. There is something common to all scientific enquiries. There is something unique to every one. These are obvious truths concerning any class and its members, and they are not the points at issue. The point is to find a pedagogically practicable mean between these two pedagogically inoperative extremes—one which will function in the student's mind as an aid to the analysis and evaluation of the particular scientific investigation before him.

It is to this practical purpose that our tentative taxonomy is addressed and not to the theoretical purpose of an exhaustive treatment of the problem. It is subject, therefore, to the restrictions and modifications applicable to any practical proposal. He who uses it must adapt it by contraction or expansion to the exigencies of his particular use— exigencies created by his faculty, students, and circumstances. Furthermore, it is not proposed as something to be presented to students to learn, for this could lead only to more detailed placement of things in categories. It is intended instead as a prefatory guide to the curriculum-planner in his choice of materials and subject matters and as an aid in the analyses of scientific researches which he and his students do.

So much for the restricted purpose of a prefatory taxonomy. It also has three serious limitations in subject matter of which the author is aware. Two of these stem from the fact that the scheme is not planned to distinguish the main subject-matter divisions of science from one another but treats science as a whole. One consequence of this is that the scheme must inevitably exhibit errors or omissions arising from the author's relative ignorance of those major subject matters in which his training is least. This can be remedied only by time and the criticisms and emendations of others. A second consequence is that, by being directed to science as a whole, matters special to one or another subject-matter division are lost. This should be remedied by supplementation. A third limitation is that the taxonomy presented here treats science only in terms of kind of conclusion, kind of data, and mode of verification. Epistemological and metaphysical considerations are minimized; that is, interpretations and evaluations of scientific as against other modes of knowing are not represented, nor is there any attempt at prescriptive statements about science based on epistemological or metaphysical doctrines. A compendium or schematism of interpretative and evaluative views of science is, then, another future agendum.

The prefatory taxonomy here presented has been constructed on the basis of three principles. The first principle defines the universe which the taxonomy comprises. The second defines what is meant by a pedagogically significant difference in method. The third principle orders the different methods so distinguished.

The universe treated by the taxonomy excludes methods which are only possible, hypothetical, or rare. It includes only such methods as correspond to a number of recognized and accepted researches in one or several fields of science.

The distinguishing definition is as follows: If a pattern of enquiry is characterized by aiming toward a kind of formulation of its conclusions which can be distinguished in form from other enquiries; and if that kind of conclusion requires a kind of data which can be distinguished from the data of other enquiries; and if for validation of the conclusion the data are related to the conclusion in a way distinguishable from the relations in other enquiries, then one has a pedagogically significant kind of scientific enquiry. In short, a "method" is deserving of separate consideration if the kind of knowledge that it aims at is linked to a kind of data and a mode of validation which differ from the kinds of knowledge, data, and mode of verification characteristic of other methods. The looseness of this definition would be inexcusable in a theoretical treatment. Its practical justification lies in whatever usefulness the results of its employment may have.

The third principle orders the distinguished methods according to their complexity and partly according to their incorporation into subsequent methods. Thus the first method is simplest in respect to the ordering among facts which it achieves, and its results are likely to be used as data or principles by methods subsequently described.

Taxonomic Science

The most ubiquitous of the kinds of scientific knowledge is taxonomic knowledge. Its ubiquity can be seen in the fact that some kind of classificatory schematism lies at the foundation of all the sciences and in the fact that the method is a conspicuous and active feature of modern zoölogy, botany, medical syndromy, and, to a lesser extent, geology and chemistry.

Taxonomy aims to establish a classificatory schematism as its form of scientific knowledge. Its first, raw data are all the members of the objectively delimited universe to which it addresses itself and all the properties of these members which can be discerned. Its method, in theoretical ideal, consists of determining (by "induction") the one or several "essential" properties from among the indefinite number presented by the members of the universe. These essential properties then define a set of classes among which each member of the universe will find a place and only one place. Verification, again in theoretic ideal, consists of demonstrating that the schematism in question does possess the properties of exclusive and exhaustive placement of the members of the universe.

Unfortunately, the conditions for this theoretical ideal either do not exist or are not now acceptable to scientists. The result is that, for each item characteristic of the method listed above, there is a "practical" substitute. Conspicuous among the absent or rejected conditions is the notion of "essential" property or properties. Some philosophers have warned against the notion, and many scientists have heeded them. The result is that the notion of "real" species with their "essential" features is practically never defended in practice. Instead, properties are chosen and classes established on the basis of these properties, in terms of an intended role or purpose of the schematism in some subsequent body of research aimed at other and more complex kinds of knowledge. Thus in zoölogy the primary taxonomy of animals is based on properties chosen for their capacity to relate their possessors according to evolutionary sequence and proximity of a common ancestral group. Thus "blood relationship" defines "real" groupings, and homologous structures (common embryogeny and presumptive common phylogeny) replace essential structures and properties. The result of this inextricable involvement of animal taxonomy with evolution is that researches with other interests require other taxonomies which cut across the primary, phylogenetic taxonomy. Ecological studies, for instance, require their own, based upon the environmental niches occupied by organisms or based upon the place of each organism in a web of predator-prey relationships.

A similar shift can be seen in the case of the physical sciences. Early physicists, concerned primarily with dynamics and statics, distinguished "primary" and "secondary" properties (e.g., size, shape, mass, and motion, as against taste, color, odor, texture, etc.) on metaphysical or epistemological grounds. Mechanics retained this same division of properties, but the primary properties are now seen as those appropriate to the problems which mechanics treats. As the chemical branch of physical science solved many of its problems and turned to others, more and more of the previously "secondary" properties were admitted to the "primary" rank and became involved in chemical taxonomy (e.g., color, taste, solubility, etc.).[11]

A second missing condition for an ideal taxonomy is that of an objectively delimited universe. The universes with which each taxonomist deals are bounded, but the boundaries are set by moving, rather than by fixed, criteria; for, in the last analysis, the universe within which a taxonomy is sought is itself a large class among a number of large classes. These large classes are the products of a taxonomy, usually historical rather than individual in origin, stemming from divisions of the sciences, specializations of techniques, and the existence of a number of separated theories and consequent groupings of unsolved problems. Thus even the taxonomy of animals differs in some marked respects from plant taxonomy.

In practice the universe within which a taxonomic solution is to be found is given to the researcher by the tradition which defines his field of specialization, by the theories which are current and effective, and by the problems which these theories pose. Then, as some of the problems are solved, the theories are revised to comprise the new solutions; the revised theories suggest new dimensions to the taxonomists and propose new problems; the new dimensions and the new problems loosen the boundaries of the universe treated by the taxonomist and admit new members to it. Often the new members of the universe find a place in a heterogeneous or "wastebasket" class developed for them; but eventually they are assimilated thoroughly into the

---

11. It is interesting to note, however, that mass (weight) and atomic number still play special roles in the periodic table of chemical elements.

taxonomic system by such revision of the whole system as will allow a place for them appropriate to the theories which introduced them and adequate to the new problems which these new theories pose. The major shifts in disease taxonomy (syndromy) illustrate the effective relationship between taxonomic and other activities in a science. Hippocratic disease taxonomy is centered around symptom-clusters, prognosis, and amenableness to certain treatments, with physical and personality typing and climatological factors taking a lesser place and material causative agents a role lesser still. With the growth of physiology and pathology and the advent of the germ theory of disease, the taxonomic schematism of disease underwent extensive revision, reflecting the new status given to causes and the consequent reduced emphasis on other properties of disease. At the present time psychosomatic theories are introducing another and similar alteration in medical taxonomy. Physical and personality typing is given greater emphasis; specific physiological and parasitic causes are subordinated to other kinds of causes, and the symptoms themselves are read differently and given new significances. The consequences to the taxonomy are the collapsing of some previously separated disease conditions into one, the separation of former single diseases into two or more, and the identification of new ones. This phase of medicine is, of course, only beginning, and its fate and the extent of the change that it may bring about in disease syndromy are not to be predicted. Nevertheless, it illustrates the process of change in taxonomic science and the relations of such change to established theories and currently given problems.

As a consequence of shifting boundaries and criteria, which move with the growth of knowledge, the third property of an "ideal" taxonomy is also lost—the property of exhaustive and exclusive classification of the membership of the universe. These properties are only approached, not reached. Borderline or ambiguous instances are commonplace, and a few unclassifiables are tolerated.

From the point of view of research, then, a practical taxonomic schematism is verified to the extent that its results are effective tools for the problems in which the classified universe is involved and the degree to which the properties of exhaustiveness and exclusiveness are reached within the system.

Analogically, for the purposes of liberal study, a given taxonomic system is understood when it is seen as one of several alternatives: when the properties on which it is based are seen in their relevance to representative examples of the theories and problems of the field which uses the taxonomy; when the lesser relevance of other properties to these theories and problems are noted; when the classes created by the chosen properties are seen effectively participating in other kinds of researches in the field; and, finally, when some of the doubtful areas of the taxonomy are seen and some of the reasons for their doubtful status understood.

Perhaps nowhere is there such violent contrast between common practice in general survey courses and what might be in a liberal program than in respect to taxonomy, especially animal taxonomy. A classification of the invertebrates and vertebrates is usually given with no sign of analysis or criticism, often followed by some single highly arbitrary phylogenic "tree," proffered with no more than a vague and general caveat, which then drops out of the student's sight and mind. The student is given access to the properties chosen for criteria and to the classes which they create, but the very existence of alternative properties is usually ignored and, along with them, the sound and good reasons for the use of the properties chosen.

Measurement Science

By "measurement science" I mean a simple, quickly describable pattern of enquiry at the roots of physics and chemistry and presently taking hold in biology. This pattern of enquiry has as its aim the measurement and consequent co-relating of changes in two or more varying, and presumably objective, quantities. The relation of degree of immersion of bodies to their specific gravity in hydrostatics is a familiar example. The relation of light intensity to distance from source is another. So also is the relation of vibration frequency to length in pendulums and stretched strings, and the behavior of freely falling bodies. This is the kind of science whose fruits are most commonly the referent of the term "scientific law."

Here the data required are obviously precise measurements; and verification is partly synonymous with precision and partly the problem of guaranteeing the absence of any effective variable except the ones measured. There are, however, two possible complicating features.

One of these complications is the notion of "ideal body" referred to above. Although in some cases what is reported as the fruit of measurement science is some statistical central tendency of actual measurements, such as mean or mode, it is often true that what is reported is some "ideal case" toward which actual measurements can be interpreted as tending. The inverse-square law of light intensity, for example, though based on measurements of light from real sources, is itself a report of the behavior of light from a "point" source, which is, by definition, an approachable but not attainable ideal. The notion of such ideal bodies and an understanding of the particular "ideals" involved in a given equation are necessary for a liberal understanding of the fruits of measurement science.

The second complication in measurement science arises from the abstractness or unreality of a statement of relations between two or three variables which are studied apart from the *N* other variables which may normally affect the measured ones. Such abstracted treatment is, of course, an entirely valid mode of enquiry. It is universally a part of science. But its existence and possible effect in each given instance should be a part of the liberal understanding of conclusions based upon it. The problem of abstraction will be treated more fully under causal science.

Causal Science

The term "cause" has become so generic that it is practically useless for a taxonomy of scientific enquiry. At one time or another it has been used as the name for the product of every kind of research. Currently it means about the same thing as explanation and description taken together and undistinguished. (Hence the commonplace textbook preface statement that "Science is the search for causes" is perfectly true because it merely says what the etymology of the word "science" says, namely, that "science" is the search for knowledge.) "Cause" is made to mean any knowledge whatever about a class of things or events which relates that class to some other class. Consider, for example, the discovery and report that all members of the class constituted of hydrochloric acid, sulphuric acid, nitric acid, etc., are made of some variable factor and a hydrogen ion. When it is interpreted primitively, one has simply identified the constituent material of each member of the class and noted that one such constituent, hydrogen, is common to all members. When interpreted in respect to the class, its material constituent is found to be hydrogen. This invariant constituent material can then be called the "cause" of acidity. Thus the "cause" of a class of things can mean simply the material substratum coexistent with a given bundle of other properties.

On the other hand, the properties which originally define the class are usually records of the interaction of members of the class with members of other classes. Thus acidity originally meant a sour taste, color changes in certain plant dyes, and combining with bases to form salts. These are events, motions, or changes over a temporal span, and one can ask the question, "What class of events invariably, in our experience, precedes *this* class of events, e.g., color change in the plant dye, etc.?" The answer to this question is then often called the "cause" of the color change, of the sensation of sourness, or of the formation of salts. Here "cause" means invariable antecedent event. Yet the color change of the dye, the sour sensation, and the salt formation are the defining properties of acids. Taken together they *are* acidity. Hence the discovery of the event or events antecedent to these defining events is as much the discovery of the "cause" of acidity as is discovery of the common material substratum of the things which possess the defining properties.

A third sense of "cause" is seen in researches aimed at determining a limiting stable state to a series of events arranged in their causal (in the sense described above) sequence. In such researches one first arranges the classes of events in their causal order as defined, then attempts to determine a stable limiting case in terms of which the preceding series of changes can be understood. The preceding changes or events are interpreted as tendencies, as steps or stages toward the limiting case, and in this sense the limiting case can be called the "cause" of the preceding events. In this sense "cause" means a concluding or climactic stage in a process. Active research along these lines is rare at the present time, but the products of past research of this kind are constantly in use. A descriptive embryology, for instance, which failed to relate the changes during embryogeny to the adult state of the organism would be enormously limited in its value to both practice (medicine) and theory (experimental embryology).

A fourth sense of cause arises when one attempts to combine all three of the kinds of causes into a single, unified scheme. When we see that a class of things made of a given material substrate participates only in certain classes of events (i.e., can have only certain effects) and fits only into a certain place in a series, many of us are constrained to act as if this concatenation, too, is not without significance, that there must be a reason (i.e., a "cause") why things made of this kind of matter behave in this way and have this place in a series. There thus arises the notion of a cause of causes, an essential cause. Sometimes the unity thus sought is found by identifying one of the three first-order causes as the essential one. The place of the class in its series and the effects that its members have on members of other classes are understood as derived from the material substrate; or its material substrate and its effects are understood as deriving from its place in its series; and so on. In other instances, however, a distinct *quartum quid* is sought as the unifying factor. The theory of atomic structure can be seen to play this role. The events in which a given chemical compound can participate, the elements which constitute it, and the place of these elements in the Periodic Table are all explainable in terms of the number and arrangement of particles which constitute the atoms of the elements comprised in compounds.

It is easy to see that the *quartum quid* in the case of atomic theory—and in many other cases, too—is not a distinct fourth. The particles of the atom are obviously a material sub-substrate of the original compounds. The absence in much research of a distinct fourth kind of cause can be interpreted as part of the rejection of the concept of "essence" mentioned under taxonomic science. Rather than seek a fourth kind of cause, most contemporary scientists prefer that its role of unifying other causes be realized by pressing one of the other three farther back: one seeks the material element of elements; attempts to place two or more series into a series of series; links antecedent-subsequent chains into larger and more complex webs.

What disposition are we to make of this congeries in a taxonomy of patterns of enquiry? In view of the confusion and ambiguity introduced by calling these several patterns of enquiry "causal," it would be helpful if we could distribute all of them into other parts of the scheme. To a great extent this can be done without violence to truth and with a net gain in pedagogic usefulness. Most researches aimed at discovery of material substrates are understandable for the purpose of liberal education as contributors to taxonomies, as one part of the problem of establishing useful categories and of placing members therein. Some part of antecedent-subsequent research can also be interpreted intelligibly in the same way. Another part of it is reducible to researches aimed at correlating quantitative variables. In similar fashion a large part of researches aimed at establishing limiting cases to steps and stages are interpretable in taxonomic terms, with the addition of the notion of hierarchical relation among the members of the class along with the notion of simple inclusion. Finally, almost all cases of research aimed at second-order causes (causes of causes) fall under the heading of analogical or *as-if* science, yet to be described.

However, when every defensible disposition of "causal" cases to other categories is made and every defensible translation into other terms of the notions involved in cause is achieved, there is a residuum. Some researches will fit into other categories only by Procrustean cutting and omitting. There is, in short, a kind of problem which requires a category other than taxonomy, quantitative correlation, and analogical relation. Moreover, this kind of problem shares sufficiently in the notions of cause outlined here to justify its being so named.

This causal science is found wherever some system of mutually interacting and mutually determined parts acts as a concerted whole. Such systems are seen in their most complicated and eminent degree in the subject matters of physiology and sociology. In the one science the organism is such a system; in the other, society.[12] The defining features

12. By linking the biological organism and society as two examples here, there is no intention of spinning a loose analogy whereby what is found true of biological organisms is also alleged of societies. Before such an analogy can be taken seriously, it would have to be shown that the relations of parts of the whole in each are substantially the same in three respects: (1)

(interaction, mutual determination, and concerted action) are clearly seen in both cases. In the case of society, interaction is seen in the extent to which the actions of each member of a community affect what others do. Mutual determination is seen in the extent to which it is true that the individual is a vicious abstraction—that is, the extent to which the traits and characteristics, the attitudes, abilities, and personality, of each "individual" are determined by his community and his part in it both as child and as adult. Concerted action is seen wherever communities act in relation to one another or in relation to a circumstantial problem.

In the case of the biological organism the same defining functions hold. The interaction of parts is the commonplace of physiological regulation, of maintenance of the internal environment. Mutual determination during development is the prime subject matter of embryology. Concerted action is, of course, the very sense of the term "organism."

Restricting ourselves, now, only to physiology, the problem of understanding such a subject matter as the organism is posed by the fact that the whole organism is far too complex to be understood in its unanalyzed unity. On the other hand, analysis for the sake of experimentation and understanding leaves us only with abstract knowledge of parts and pieces, radically altered by the very isolation which is required for experimentation. There is the further problem of somehow reconstructing knowledge of the whole from our merely compendious knowledge of the parts.

A start is made by the simple methods of ablation and addition. One simply removes a part or doubles a part of the organism and notes the differences between the nonnormal experimental organism and the normal. The variants of this primitive pattern are codified in J. S. Mill's "Four Methods of Experimental Inquiry."[13] These four methods—the Method of Difference, of Agreement, of Residues, and of Concomitant Variation—are the basis of a major part of the oversimplified and uninterpreted "scientific method" of elementary physiology textbook prefaces.

---

the extent to which each part's existence and activity are made possible by and subordinated to the whole; (2) in respect to the kinds of activities which are subordinated; (3) in respect to the nature of the relations which bind the parts to constitute the whole. These similarities have not been demonstrated and, as far as this author can see, do not exist. Society is a different kind of system, an "organism" in a sense as different from a biological organism as is, say, the "organism" of an organic molecule with its respective radicals occupying their place in its structure and playing their respective "roles" in the pharmacological effects of the molecule.

13. Mill, *A System of Logic*, Book 3, chaps. 7 and 8.

The prototype of this uninterpreted version of Mill is given by the question, "What organ or other part of the organism performs function X?" or by the converse, "What is the function of organ (or other part) X?" Says the Method of Difference: Consider the organs or parts A, B, C, D, F, among which previous knowledge gives us reason to think is the part which performs function X. By surgery, chemistry, or pathology remove or inhibit the action of organ A. Note whether function X has or has not disappeared. Repeat with each organ and each combination of organs. The results then tell us, says the oversimplified version of Mill, the sufficient and necessary cause or causes of function X. In the reverse experiment, the role of organ X in the intact organism is said to be given by the observed functional deficiencies in an organism lacking organ X.

Such an interpretation of the method of physiology would give us a catalogue of organs, each with its separate functions. This would be sound knowledge, were the animal or plant body assumed to be a compendium of objectively separable functions and anatomical parts. An organism, however, is a *system* whose parts and functions mutually determine one another and act in concert. Says Haldane:

> When we speak of the "function" of an organ and regard this function as what it does to restore the internal environment we are thinking in terms of a misleading conception of what an organ is and what an organism is: for we are thinking of only one side of its activities to the exclusion of others which are just as important. To put this into philosophical language we are thinking abstractly, or regarding only a part of the reality we are dealing with. We can speak more correctly of a function of a part of a machine: for this does nothing else than fulfill its function provided the machine is assumed to be perfect and stable. In a living organ however we are dealing with something of which the functions, if we speak of functions, are endless, since the activities are endless, constantly seeming to grow in number as we investigate further.[14]

Haldane could have said (and later does say) the same thing concerning anatomy as he here says of physiology: anatomizing (whether gross, microscopic, or chemical) yields parts which, if we can speak of parts, are abstractions. They are so far abstract rather than real "parts" that each "part" which is separated by anatomy and used for the purpose of research concerning functions can fruitfully be coupled with another "part" to constitute a larger and more complicated "part" or

14. John Scott Haldane, *Organisms and Environment* (New Haven: Yale University Press, 1917), pp. 84–85.

be further analyzed into smaller "parts," all of which, when employed in the Mill methods, yield more knowledge which must be built into the knowledge previously sought and found in terms of other degrees and ways of anatomizing.

These constitute two factors, then, which must be taken into account when interpreting the results of ablation and addition experimentation: the functions are abstractions, and knowledge framed in terms of them must be understood as restricted and qualified by the mode of abstraction. Parts or separated structures are also abstractions, and functions ascribed to them must be taken as meaningful only as related to researches which employ more minutely analyzed parts and more complexly related parts. These two factors are related to the notions of concerted action and interaction found in the definition of organism.

The third note of the definition—mutual determination—points to a third factor in terms of which isolated researches must be interpreted and related to other enquiries. There is sufficient evidence of "regulation" in even the most complex of organisms to make it highly improbable that an organism minus a part presents a functioning minus precisely the "normal" function of the part removed. There is too much known of "double insurance," compensation, and adjustment in the organism to assume that in any case of ablation some aspects of the normal role of the organ removed have not been compensated for— "taken over"—by what is left. Conversely, one cannot be sure but that some normal roles of organs anatomically intact have not been altered by the removal of another part. Thus the symptoms of diabetes following removal of the pancreas are far less acute if the pituitary gland is also removed.

The limitations here cited do not, of course, affect the validity of researches of this kind but only their oversimplified interpretation. In the progress of enquiry the anatomical identification of the adrenal glands is followed by their removal in physiological research. The complex of functions thereby discovered points toward further anatomical analysis of the adrenals and discovery of two anatomically separable parts, the cortex and the medulla. Separate querying of the functions of these parts leads to still finer analysis into more minute realms of histology and thence to chemical and physical "parts" and "functions." Thus more and more numerous, accurate, and detailed statements of functions are derived.

However, this progress opens the need for more enquiry in the contrary direction. As our knowledge of parts and functions becomes more numerous, detailed, and precise, the problem of *inter*actions and *inter*relations of these parts and functions becomes more pressing. The more parts we know more about, the more onerous and difficult is the problem of understanding their interconnections and thus constituting from our knowledge of the parts the knowledge of the whole which is our aim.

"Causal" research, then, upon a subject matter which is a complex of interacting and mutually determined parts constitutes a kind of science with its own problems of procedure and interpretation, differing widely from other patterns of enquiry. For a liberal understanding of the results of such researches, the student must be aware of the problems posed by the organism as a subject matter. He must be prepared to discover, in the records of such research, answers to the questions of what kinds of "parts" are being treated, what analysis of "functions" is being employed, how these "parts" and "functions" are related to the parts and functions of other related researches, and how, if at all, the researcher in question relates his discovered functions and parts to one another to constitute larger units more nearly approaching the unity of the organism as a whole.

Relational (Analogical) Science

By "relational science" I mean those patterns of enquiry which are most fully understood as aiming toward knowledge which attempts to "explain" or "account for" matters previously known by inventing co-related quantities which do not have one-to-one literal correlates among the phenomena to be accounted for, or by inventing mechanisms not directly accessible to observation but so conceived and applied to the phenomena to be explained that it can be said that certain things behave *as if* these mechanisms existed.

This pattern of enquiry may also be called "analogical," since it may be described as applying relations seen among one group of phenomena to another and thereby establishing a new relation among the two bodies of phenomena—the relation of analogy. The core of the method may be described in three steps. It consists, first, of the "borrowing" of sets or systems of relations dissociated from the relata among which they were found. The second step consists of finding those aspects of the phenomena under consideration which can be fitted as relata to the borrowed system of relations. The third step consists of elaborating the relations or adding or substituting others so as to assimilate more and more of the aspects of the phenomena under consideration into the system of relations.

Description in these terms throws an interesting light on a much-discussed point of scientific knowledge—the respective advantages of mathematical as against "model" explanations. Examined in the terms used here, this question reduces to a matter of two different sources from which relations may be "borrowed." In the case of "model" explanations, they are borrowed from other systems of physical things.

In the case of mathematical explanations, the borrowed relational system is a pure one, connecting no relata whatever until employed by the physicist or other relational scientist.

Certain advantages and disadvantages of each source are immediately obvious. Because mathematical systems of relations are free of physical relata, they are indefinitely flexible and various. They may take any form that the inventiveness of the mathematical genius can provide. As such, they constitute a source of novel and complicated systems of relations whose production is not limited by the progress of physical science.

On the other hand, to employ the knowledge of previous physical science (the term "physical" is here being used in contradistinction to the purely relational) is to tap still another source of relational systems of probably equal value. Systems borrowed from real relata have, however, one peculiarity in their use: the scientist who borrows them is usually never quite completely able to dissociate the relations themselves from the relata which they originally contained. The result is that he is both stimulated and restricted by the ghosts of these relata. He is stimulated in the sense that the ghost relata suggest ways of applying his borrowed relations to new phenomena. He is also stimulated or assisted by the ghost relata, in that they themselves function as connections or relations to still other phenomena with other relations on which the scientist may draw for needed additions or complications of his system. They act as restrictions in so far as they may blind the scientist to flexible uses of his relational system through restricting his examination of new phenomena to aspects suggested by the ghost relata but which are not necessary restrictions in the use of the relations. Thus many students of modern atomic theory have difficulty freeing themselves from the habit of trying to translate the mathematical relations which describe atomic structure into relations familiar in our experience of grosser bodies.

As representative of this kind of scientific knowledge, an interpretation of the Mendelian gene theory of heredity illustrates certain aspects of it which will be useful to our conclusions concerning science education. According to this interpretation, one emphasizes, first, the absence of one-to-one relations between the data and the terms of the theory. One notes that the immediate subjects of observation—the data —are simply the numbers of individuals in successive generations which resemble one parent, the other, or neither. These numbers are converted into ratios, and generalizations are then made concerning the ratio of offspring of given types to be expected from parents of specified types. So far, one has the kind of knowledge second in our list—the co-relating of variable and presumably objective quantities. It concerns hereditary *characters*, visible aspects of the organisms studied.

Mendel now turns to a discussion of quite another subject—hereditary *factors*, unobserved, unmeasured, taken as the causal precursors of the hereditary *characters* and assigned such frequencies and behaviors during germ-cell production and fertilization as would account for the ratios and combination series of *characters*.

At this point two different interpretations are possible. On the one hand, one can take the position that the "factors" of heredity and their postulated behavior constitute a physically stated model of the expansion of a binomial to the second power and of the combinations which are the products of two or more squared binomials. According to this interpretation, further research would consist largely of investigation of more varied and more complex breeding situations, with consequent complications of the algebra of particles which describes the results obtained. From such a point of view the hereditary factor has only a *conventional* status; it is a simple, clear, and economical way to talking and thinking about the relative numbers and combinations of hereditary characters.

On the other hand, Mendel's discussion of hereditary *factors* may be taken as a hypothesis concerning real, physical things—a hypothesis to be verified by an actual, visual search designed to reveal such particles, if they exist, and to make way for a direct investigation of their properties. According to this interpretation, the failure of such a search, after an appropriate interval, would require that the notion of such particles, however convenient for descriptive and predictive purposes, be dropped in favor of some other which would again be subject to direct, sensory discovery for validation. (In historical fact, both these interpretations were entertained and both kinds of research pursued successfully.)

Under the convenient, or conventional, conception, however, use of the notions, whether the particles were found to have physical existence or not, would continue to be proper as long as the notions were convenient and economical devices of description. Moreover, revision of the properties assigned to the particles could take place at each discovery of new aspects of breeding phenomena without reference to possible real properties of real particles. Conversely, if it should prove desirable to bring knowledge of breeding behavior into relation with knowledge of some other phenomena and if the new combination proved refractory to subsumption under the particle theory, the theory could be dropped forthwith in favor of some other which would serve the new and larger purpose.

From this contrast the nature of the data for such a mode of enquiry and what it requires for verification become clearer. The data appropriate for such an investigation are any data whatever which can be related to one another by being related to the borrowed model or system of mathematical relations. There is an important corollary to this conclusion, suggesting a balancing disadvantage to the breadth and freedom of investigation which characterizes this kind of scientific knowledge: Since any data which can be subsumed under the given model or system are appropriate, then any which cannot be so subsumed are inappropriate. This apparently empty negative assumes significance if one asks what might happen were a given model or system to prove extraordinarily successful. Should such a system or model be especially clear, precise, and economical in its subsumption of a given large body of data but be incapable of bringing that body of data into relation with some other, it is a question whether the previously successful model would willingly be dropped in favor of one which, though it subsumed both bodies of data, did so clumsily and uneconomically by contrast with the first. In such a situation previous success might tend to prevent the co-relation of phenomena which might profitably be related. Whether this extreme of conservatism occurred or not, it is clear that the data which would be sought by scientists in possession of a successful system or model would be those suggested by the model and its previously subsumed data. In short, one is forced to note that not only do data in part determine theory but that, conversely, theory tends to a similar degree to determine what data are sought and co-related to each other. Theory certifies the relevance of data as much as data certify the validity of theory.

What constitutes verification of this mode of knowledge also becomes clear. It consists, in the first place, of the precision and completeness with which the system in question subsumes the data for which it was chosen. In the second place, the curiously aesthetic criteria of simplicity, economy, austerity, and elegance apply. And, in the third place, the capacity of the system to assimilate new data—that is, to exhibit relevance and connection among phenomena previously unrelated in our knowledge—takes a high place.

Here, then, are four modes of scientific investigation, four species of enquiry, distinguished in terms of the form of knowledge which they seek, the data that they require, and the canons of validity that they employ. The differences among them are such that the conclusions arrived at by each can be well understood and evaluated only if one has operative, effective knowledge of their mode of validation and of the difficulties of interpretation, limitations, and qualifications which stem from the data sought, the formulations aimed at, and the relation of these data to the formulated conclusions. Without this knowledge, the conclusions so achieved by science are only half-appreciated or more than half-misunderstood. With this knowledge, on the other hand, the student is prepared to evaluate and comprehend the fruits of science. And by coming to such knowledge through informed discussion of the records of such enquiries, by an inductively aimed analysis of scientific works, the student comes to knowledge both of nature and of scientific enquiry; he learns to appreciate both the subject matters of science and science as a subject matter. The study of "method" and the study of "content" rather than being divorced, to the impoverishment of each, are thoroughly wedded, to the enrichment of both. Scientific knowledge thus gained is least likely to be parrot-knowledge, for the student knows each conclusion in terms of the evidence which established it, the competitions with alternative formulations through which it has won its way, and the revisions which it has undergone in the continuing process of enquiry. Knowledge *about* science thus gained could not be parrot-knowledge, for there will have been no speeches or prefaces about science to copy. Instead, the knowledge will be operational—gained, practiced, and perfected by operations of analysis, comparison, contrast, and criticism practiced upon varied examples of scientific enquiry.

Before we go on to a summary discussion of the educational implications of this diversity of science, one generic feature of the four species here described should be pointed out. This feature is related to the notion of the cumulative character of scientific enquiry, the idea of an ongoing process of enquiry which always assimilates the past into the present and prepares present knowledge for assimilation into knowledge of the future. This cumulative character of science is often pointed out in general terms. Here in the four species described we see its origin and nature. In taxonomic science the need for a taxonomic system arises from the pressure of unsolved problems of many kinds. The schematism constructed successfully in the light of these needs solves many of the problems which gave rise to it. In this sense the taxonomy is seen to assimilate the past knowledge which generated the problems which, in turn, gave rise to the taxonomic system. But, in turn, the knowledge realized in the solutions stemming from the taxonomic scheme give rise to new problems, usually involving new data. A solution of these new problems requires a new taxonomy, and the cycle repeats itself again and again.

The same tentative character is seen in the other species of enquiry; each conclusion of science not only solves one problem but creates another; each kernel of scientific knowledge contains the germ of its own revision by pointing toward matters hitherto unknown and unrelated to one another. In causal knowledge of organisms each bit of anatomical knowledge gained through hypotheses stemming from physiology or pathology points back to needed revisions in the parent-physiology or pathology. Conversely, physiological knowledge gained through an enquiry which began with a given anatomical analysis points to revision or enlargement of its anatomical parent. In analogical science the understanding of a body of phenomena gained by setting them in a chosen system of relations points to new phenomena not previously subsumed. The assimilation of new phenomena into the old requires revision, emendation, or even substitution of new systems of relations, and so on. It is this ongoing, unclosed character of science which creates the crucial problem of liberal understanding of scientific conclusions. And it is grasp of the specific origins of each kind of ongoing tentativeness which is the starting place for a solution to this problem of liberal understanding.

SOME EDUCATIONAL IMPLICATIONS

We have tried to describe three kinds of diversity in and about science: (1) diversity of doctrines concerning the nature of science; (2) broad diversities in science, stemming from espousal by scientists of different doctrines of method; (3) specific diversities in patterns of enquiry related to differences of subject matters and problems in the several sciences.

From all or parts of each of these come problems to face the architect of a liberal program in the sciences. We shall first state the problems, then proffer a systematic solution to the group of them.

The fact of diversity itself poses the problem; for to ignore it in an educational program creates in our graduates evils and inadequacies, some of which are of deep seriousness and are obvious and visible in our students' behavior. One brute fact is that the *natural world* is a complicated affair, and no scientist worthy of the name pretends that the world in all its complications is successfully ensnared in even today's successful science. A second brute fact is that *science* is complicated; scientists who have engaged in research can view only with impatience the claim of any single system in logic, any one theory of history, any broad, sweeping philosophic view, that it describes and explains the problems which the scientist faces in his effort to wrest knowledge from the world. He may find the effort to explain his activities an interesting and fruitful one; he can no more accept one of several competitive views of his activities as definitive than he can accept one of two competing theories in science as definitive.

If, in the face of this, we teach the conclusions of science as simple and definitive solutions to its problems and, similarly, teach our personal choice of conclusions about science, we set in motion a train of evils. In the first place, we block progress toward one of the most widely held, if impossible, goals of liberal science training: to provide the student with an adequate picture of the world. To give a simple picture of a complicated world is not to give the scientist's picture of that world. By so doing we make the picture not only inadequate (which it will always be) but false. In the second place, by giving a simple picture of science we give the students a conception of the nature and magnitude of an intellectual problem shockingly different from a sound conception. What can we expect from this falsification, repeated *ad nauseam* throughout their training, except men who will find only frustration when they meet problems in all their magnitude and complication, or who will blindly simplify and vulgarize them until they fit the measure that we have taught?

The three kinds of diversity sharpen and specify these problems. Ignorance of diverse doctrines about science not only will be a contribution to the generic evil of oversimplification but, specifically, will generate academic chauvinism and intellectual intolerance. We have all seen these in two forms, not only in our students but in ourselves. One form which they take is the elevation of science above other scholarly disciplines, largely by elevating science to a level of definitive truth that it cannot rightfully claim and by denigrating the social studies and humanities to the level of sophistical refutations and defenses of opinions or to preoccupation with the unimportant. The effective and positive contrary to this state of mind is not respectful but uninformed ignorance. It is rather an informed understanding of the several disciplines by which man solves his problems and creates his worlds. It is to this understanding that an examination of diverse views about science makes one of its most direct contributions; for it is here that the similarities *and* the differences among man's several paths to truth emerge most clearly. It is only here that one can see the complex pattern of relations which bind the questions that men ask to the faculties that they have for answering them and to the world in which the raw stuff of answers lies. It is only here in the same sense that it is only in physics that one learns about falling bodies. Knowledge of both falling bodies and the processes of human enquiry can be acquired otherwise. But they cannot otherwise be acquired systematically and with economy.

The second form of intellectual intolerance is the corruption of discussion into debate: the transformation of a process of mutual aiming toward better approximation to truth into polemical defense and attack. Discussion starts with the clear admission by all participants that one's own conclusions are based only on an incomplete view of the problem in hand. Discussion assumes that other participants may have seen more, or at least have seen other, facets of the problem. Discussion assumes, moreover, that differences in view (quite literally differences in view) can be understood and related to one another in such a manner that inferences from the larger and more encompassing whole can be made and understood and can replace the narrower and less complete views with which discussion began. Such discussion is a habit as well as a body of skills. It must begin with such experience as makes emphatic the complexity of problems and the incompleteness of answers. It must continue with such experiences repeated again and again. And it must go on to mastery of the skills by which the different facets of different kinds of problems are recognized, fittted to one another, and employed as basis for better, but still tentative, conclusions. This means, first, that where diversities exist within the subject matters of liberal education that fact itself should not be obscured. Second, the mere fact of diversity must be supplemented by substantial samples of it. Finally, the diversities themselves must be treated, not merely exhibited. Naïve relativism which replaces a dogma with diversity of dogma is no net gain. One must go on to instruction and exercise in the disciplines of comparison, contrast, choice, and synthesis appropriate to the field in which the diversity occurs. These statements are applicable to the fields of science itself, as well as to the field which treats science as its subject matter. In the latter case examples of interpretations of science—including the historical, philosophical, and methodological—would be read, discussed, and analyzed. They would be so analyzed in terms of the criteria appropriate to historical, philosophical, or methodological problems and treatments.

In the former case instruction and exercise would treat examples of scientific investigation. It would educate, encourage, and exercise the student in applying appropriate canons of comprehension and evaluation to such examples of scientific enquiry. It is here that the varieties of scientific enquiry again become relevant; for from these come the notions of data and evidence and relation of conclusion to evidence which determine what comprehending and critical queries are appropriate to the scientific investigation in question. However, the act of critical analysis must begin with a decision as to the particular pattern of enquiry with which one is dealing; for this will determine what questions to put to the scientific paper and what kinds of answers one can expect. Since this is so, it follows that categories and kinds of investigation—scientific or otherwise—must be learned as operative judgments, not as mere schema named and described but not employed.

The existence of varieties of scientific investigation also sharpens the need for sound knowledge of science itself. Even where the conclusions of science are to be understood only in relation to the physical world which they order and describe, and not as examples of the fruits of enquiry, they cannot be understood alone. Their meaning resides in the data that they subsume and the manner of subsumption. To say that a dog is a mammal; that A causes B; that $F = MA$; that atoms have such-and-such arrangements of particles or fields are enormously ambiguous statements taken alone. They are ambiguous not only because of the uncertain meaning of such technical nouns as "mammal," "force," "field," and "electron" but also because of a similar ambiguity in the meaning of such apparently common words as "is" in the sense of classificatory inclusion, "cause," the notion of transitive relation in the sign for "equals," and the notion of "is" in the sense of having a nature or structure. Thus the varieties of scientific investigation pose the problem of adequate instruction in science, even when and if the aim of instruction is limited to the conclusions of science themselves.

The pedagogic problems can be summarized as follows: how diversity in science and diversity about science can be treated in a fraction of a college career, especially in view of the hierarchies of diversity which exist—that is, in view of the fact that scientific researches exhibit not only a few broad differences based on doctrinal grounds but also, within these broad differences, more specific differences related to species of problems and subject matters; and, within the species, still more particular but important differences involving particular terms and conceptions employed upon particular problems.

To this summary problem a summary solution can be proposed. The broad doctrinal differences in science, the specific differences, and the particular differences do not require independent exemplifications. Moreover, the exemplification of all need not be done independently of subject-matter mastery; for any good scientific paper is all of these at once. It is the bearer of a portion of the knowledge in its field. It "illustrates itself" as an example of scientific investigation. It illustrates the species of which it is a member and the genus to which its species belongs. (Moreover, it is a datum to the historian, philosopher, and methodologist, a point we will consider next.) Since it is all these, a knowledge of the paper can become a contribution to the student's knowledge of each of these not only in turn but to some extent simultaneously. All that is required is that instruction teach the student to ask the question of a given paper which directs his attention to each of these aspects of the paper. There will be questions directed to the comprehension of the conclusions of the paper:

What was the problem that the author set out to solve?
What are the terms in which he seeks his conclusions?
What, for him, were the data appropriate to such a problem?
What difficulties did he encounter in gathering such data?
How did he overcome them?
In what ways did he treat the data in order to move from them
    to conclusions?
What larger aspects of the phenomena treated were excluded
    by the formulation of the problem?
What, then, is the area or sense in which the conclusions are
    valid?

These questions and the seeking for answers to them in a scientific
paper would be aimed primarily at mastery of the paper's conclusions,
at understanding the subject matter of science. The paper would not be
treated naïvely as a perfectly transparent and plane-parallel window
looking out onto an immediately knowable world. But neither, on the
other hand, would such questions treat it as a datum of history or
philosophy.

Now, however, on subsequent papers, couple each such question as
those above with questions calling for comparison and contrast:

How does A's notion of the problem differ from B's?
What shifts in terms or their meanings can be noted?
What difference in treatment of the data can be noted as stem-
    ming from differences in formulation of the problem or of
    terms?

By seeking the answers to such questions as these, the student will add
to his informed and qualified understanding of conclusions a growing
understanding of the magnitude of problems in science, the strengths
and weaknesses of scientific ways of solving them, and the varieties of
ways of solving them. He will, moreover, be teaching himself to ask
such questions of papers that he will later read and even, perhaps to
prefer, for reading, materials worth such questioning. Finally, he will
be teaching himself *to* read and understand. He will be liberating himself to some extent from the need for a living teacher. And this last
is the sign and sense of a liberal education.

The first part, then, of a systematic solution to the problems posed
here is that liberal programs in science consist of (or contain) original
records of scientific research, series of papers containing the knowledge
of whatever subject matters seem appropriate and treated analytically
and critically in the ways and for the ends suggested above. One will
certainly sacrifice thereby the alleged "coverage" claimed by survey

courses, but it can be questioned whether the loss is real, since it is questionable whether the "coverage" seen in arrays of lecture topics and syllabus tables of contents is ever "coverage" by the student; he may "cover" but he rarely "contains." What one gains by this sacrifice can be minds aware of what a problem is and what a solution is; men and women committed and habituated to thoughtfulness and flexibility of mind within the limits of their powers.

The second and last part of the systematic solution here proposed is that doctrines about science be avoided in the science program proper and appear in a separate and later course devoted to them. This is for two reasons with a common base. The common base is that we do not want merely to substitute a conspectus of dogmas for a single dogma but to make the treatment of diverse doctrines about science serve not only the purpose of informing the student of the complexities of science, philosophy, and history but also as the occasion again for the learning and exercise of analytic and critical skills. This base supports two reasons for placing doctrines and interpretations of science in a separate and later course. The first of these is that philosophical and historical doctrines concerning science are, by analogy *to* science, theories concerning the significances of scientific activities. As such, their data are the records of scientific activities, the journals and monographs of science. It would be unscientific indeed to treat any theory apart from its data, and no less so for historical and philosophical theories. Thus the later and separate course in the nature of scientific (and perhaps other) knowledge would fall back upon the earlier substantive courses as data and, at the same time, would serve to integrate and relate the earlier courses to one another.

The second reason for placing doctrines about science in a separate and later course is a practical one. The doctrines, as has been said, are the products of historical or philosophical disciplines. Their criticism and analysis depend, then, on methods and criteria appropriate to these disciplines and differing from those appropriate to scientific works. Such materials require men trained to teach them. Ideally, the faculty of a liberal program can be expected to possess disciplines beyond the ones learned in their profession, but practically they will come to possess them only by participation in courses which require and evoke them and which are manned in the first instance by teachers who have them already. This suggests a program established by philosophers and historians from whom the scientists can learn, just as it would be wise for the science part of the program to be established by scientists from whom the historians and philosophers would learn. Such an administrative procedure has an advantage beyond adequate staffing. It would create a situation in which—in respect to one subject, at least—each staff member would be undergoing the same liberal training intended for the students. And liberal training is infectious.

· 3 ·

Eros and Education: A Discussion of
One Aspect of Discussion

Discussion, by itself, does not constitute an education. There are many
things it cannot do or cannot do well. It cannot teach the whole art of
reading well. It cannot do much toward teaching a student to write with
clarity and to the point. It cannot efficiently give one the statements of
fact or the experience with concrete things which knowledge and wisdom must sooner or later include. It cannot substitute for the solitary
labor of organization and memory which underlies knowledge. Nor is
it the place for the work of lonely creation which crowns knowledge
if one is lucky.

Yet discussion in one form or another—with others or with one's
self—is indispensable to a good liberal education. For in the last analysis, discussion is not merely a device, one of several possible means by
which a mind may be brought to understanding of a worthy object. It is
also the *experience* of moving toward and possessing understanding,
and a liberal education is concerned with the arts and skills of understanding.

This is not to say that a liberal curriculum in which discussion has
an indispensable place is *not* concerned with specific understandings of
specific objects, knowledge which is useful and desirable in itself or
for the sake of its application. It is. But it is also concerned with such
objects as termini of processes of intellectual activity, desirable because
they mark the successful traverse, originally by a scholar or a researcher
and now by a student, of a pathway toward understanding. In a curriculum concerned primarily with specific understandings of specific
objects, discussion as a device of instruction may be defended as a
peculiarly powerful teaching instrument, in view of the depth of understanding and the greater degree of retention which characterizes the
knowledge it imparts, but it cannot be maintained that for a curriculum
so oriented discussion is indispensable. It is merely one of several usable
techniques; the question is one of better-or-worse which must be settled
in terms of greater and lesser costliness.

This chapter was previously published in the *Journal of General Education* 8 (1954): 54–71.

In a curriculum, however, which aims to impart intellectual arts and skills and habits and attitudes, as well as bodies of information, discussion is not simply efficient or powerful but indispensable, for the same reason that the act of swimming is indispensable to teaching that art and practice on the piano indispensable to learning that. Discussion is an engagement in and a practice of the activities of thought and communication.

The idea of the "intellectual skills" and the notion of the "liberal arts" are peculiarly liable to misinterpretation. "Intellectual" is likely to evoke an image of large eyes behind horn-rimmed glasses, of arms too thin and voice too rich. Or, again, the eyes behind the lenses may be alertly malicious rather than innocent, and the mouth shaped to smile at the coarse antics of the human monkeys on the other side of the pale. There is truth in these fantasies. No greater injury has been done the intellectual than by some of his proponents. In the upper reaches of American education, some teachers have misconceived the intellectual as standing in contrariety to the physical and material and upon this misconception have built courses and coteries which encouraged in students already partially isolated from reality contempt for the concrete, the impulsive, and the earthy. In the face of these and similar consequences, it is no wonder that some of us have grown uncompromisingly suspicious, if not of the intellect, at least of people who talk about it apart from other aspects of human kind.

Our suspicions are well founded. There are neither biological, psychological, nor philosophic grounds for isolation of the intellectual as a principle of education. It is indissolubly a *part* of the learning organism.

In this view the "intellectual" is conceived as excluding the material and physical. Another view sets the intellectual apart by treating it as excluding the aesthetic and practical, and, in this form, isolation of the intellectual is frequent enough in our literature and our schools to have produced a general and regrettably mistaken notion of the intellectual. Relative to the practical, the intellectual is often taken as a flight to a world of "pure" ideas and to speculation unresponsive to physical things and events. To be intellectual seems to mean in this context to know all about "Constitutional Government," for instance, but nothing about log-rolling and compromise as inevitable parts of the democratic process; to be able to discuss "Justice" and "The Judiciary" at length, but not to know about bailiffs and their relationship to judges. There is talk about ideas and about classes of ideas, without cognizance of the particulars for which they stand.

Relative to the aesthetic, intellectualization is often taken as displacement of artistic works and of their appreciation by substituting abstract constructions which become the subjects of conversation. A reading of

Lear seems to become only an occasion for discussion of "Tragedy" or "The Tragic," on the one hand, and for the construction of an "analysis," a kind of detailed but abstract blueprint, on the other. The concrete, particular drama and its unique artistic effect seem to be tossed aside.

These are, however, not the consequences of employment of the intellect, but a corruption of it by education which arises when reason is conceived as opposed to other constituent functions of the human psyche. Differentiation of the intellective, active, and aesthetic has its place in philosophical analysis and as a heuristic ground for psychological research, but it is a dangerous doctrine for the liberal educator. It leads to an incomplete curriculum whose shortcomings can be defended only by the hopeful assertion that "life" (as opposed to "school") will supply enough and to spare of the active and the moving.

The doctrine arises from a misunderstanding of what it means to be human. But it is no mere empirical error, stemming from poor observation of human behavior. It is a large-scale error of conception, arising in biology and carrying over into logic, concerning the meaning and relation of genus and species and applied to the notion of man as generically animal and specifically rational. The error assumes that the generic and specific exist as separate, insulated, determining agencies in the organism, each having its appropriate effect on the finished product, but none upon each other. The specific is conceived as merely superimposed upon the generic. It is as if sodium chloride were conceived as an inclosing stuff within which a sodium atom has acted to produce some of the properties of the stuff, and a chlorine atom the remainder, rather than as an entity in itself arising from the interaction and coexistence of its constitutive elements. At the least, genus is to species as matter is to form: the specific is a modifier and modulator of the generic. An isosceles triangle is not triangle *and* isosceles, but a figure whose triangularity is of a particular kind. Indeed, the relationship may go farther, to become one of mutual determination. In an adolescent gang not only does the adolescence of its members confer a special quality upon the "ganginess" of the organization, but, conversely, the gang organization modifies and specializes the attributes of adolescence in the persons so involved.

As an educational doctrine, the isolationist error is exemplified by the dictum (sponsored by at least two educators of note) that "the aim of man should be to destroy the mammal within us." It is assumed that the mammal dead can leave the man alive—and better. The suggestion is that man's specific rationality has simply been stacked upon his generic mammalarity and that, so situated, each competes with the other for man's time and energy. That either of these constitutive elements may dispossess the other is assumed. That the existence of each is contingent upon and coextensive with the other is not dreamed of. Yet this is the case. Man is no more rational *and* mammal than a snub nose is snub and nose. Snub is a modifier and modulator of nose. Reason is a modifier and modulator of mammalarity. A snub nose is a special kind of nose. A man is a special kind of mammal. Snub noses do not provide passage for air in quite the same way as do other kinds of noses, and human females suckle their young with concomitants and consequences not found in all other mammals. Man's actions and emotions are rife with reasonings (some good, some bad), just as his reasonings teem with consequences of his actions and emotions.

Education cannot, therefore, separate off the intellectual from feeling and action, whether in the interest of the one or of the other. Training of the intellect must take place ("must" in the sense of "unavoidably") in a milieu of feelings and must express itself in actions, either symbolic or actual. We may employ the emotional and active factors existent in student and teacher as means for intensifying and facilitating the process of intellectual education—or ignore them and suffer at the least a loss of them as effective aids, and possibly an alienation which places them in active opposition to our purposes.

One sees precisely the latter consequence in many institutions. Because the emotional and active are considered as apart from the intellectual and of no concern to the teacher, practically all feeling and propensities toward action on the part of the student are attached to the extracurricular. The curriculum becomes a bore, an unpleasant duty, a necessary evil, and, consequently, the recipient only of energies left over from the more compelling activities of campus life. Thereupon, we the teachers develop the legend of wayward youth wherein only the exceptional or the sick young person has intellectual interest. By this myth we protect ourselves from a view of our failure as teachers.

The legend is a legend. *Sub specie aeternitatis*, the young are potentially capable of a vast and omnivorous appetite for learning, for deliberate as opposed to capricious action, and for aesthetic and creative experience. It is the legend, reflected to each generation of students by upperclassmen, by campus tradition, by the weary skepticism of some professors, and by cynical indulgences by clowns among the faculty, which the young, respectful of their elders, hear, accept as true, and try to realize, thus conferring upon the legend a semblance of reality.

This is a reversible trend. The findings of modern psychiatry and psychology amply evidence the merely local and cultural determination of normal campus youth toward indifference or distaste for the intellectual. The same sciences join hands with older findings stemming from ethics and religious practice to give us a sense of the nature of the youthful person and of his potential proclivity for pursuit of solutions to problems, of consequential activity, and of aesthetic enjoyment. And with this sense, the educator of ordinary sensitivity, reasonable maturity, and a certain energy can reverse the trend, create the kind of social and emotional climate in which the intellectual, the deliberative, and the artistic potentialities of the young will receive a fair share of energy, interest, and affection.

Appetite, emotion, and reason, then, can be abstracted from one another for purposes of thought but not in action. If we are to act upon and with another human person, as in his education, these factors must be understood and employed in their interaction and interpenetration. The fact of their interpenetration is one of the starting points, one of the principles, for consideration of education whether in respect to ends or means.

Eros, the energy of wanting, is as much the energy source in the pursuit of truth as it is in the motion toward pleasure, friendship, fame, or power. Any means or method of education taps this energy source to the extent that the method is at all effective, and the best means of education will be one which taps it most effectively. (Though the best educational means must be measured against other criteria as well.)

Not only the means, however, but also the ends of liberal education involve the Eros. For the end includes not only knowledge gained but knowledge desired and knowledge sought. The outcome of a successful liberal curriculum is *actively* intelligent people. They *like* good pictures, good books, good music, good movies. They *find pleasure* in planning their active lives and carrying out the planned action. They hanker to make, to create, whether the object is knowledge mastered, art appreciated, or actions patterned and directed. In short, a curriculum is not complete which does not move the Eros, as well as the mind of the young, from where it is to where it might better be.

Enquiry into the means of liberal education must then seek answers to two questions concerning the affective factor in education. To what objects does the youthful Eros readily attach? Which of these can be sufficiently ambiguous to serve not only in satisfaction of present needs but also to generate or bring to consciousness more enduring satisfactions?

To locate something in practice which fulfils these two conditions is to initiate the only practical means by which the Eros may be moved to more enduring objects. It is also to initiate and energize a highly efficient process by which the student may learn to discriminate these enduring objects from others, to master the arts or skills or methods necessary to their pursuit, and to digest the knowledge which bases these arts and skills. It is, in short, to initiate the climate in which liberal education can take place effectively.

The usable object of the youthful Eros as so defined can be described concretely. It is a nexus of four factors, constituting a situation. The situation so constituted is the initial phase of discussion as it functions in the liberal curriculum. The first and central factor of the situation is a certain face-to-face relation between teacher and student. The other three are enabling factors involving the administrative organization of the institution, the physical conditions of instruction, and certain characteristics of the curricular materials. These subsidiary factors are important in order to establish the face-to-face relation and in order that its effects may be channeled toward the envisaged outcomes of the curriculum.

The central factor is establishment of a distinctly interpersonal relation between the teacher and the members of a group of students, the effect of which, in the student, will be to evoke those propensities toward action which are conventionally known as liking and respect. It may be that for teachers who are consummate actors an interpersonal relation is not required. For such persons, it may be possible to determine the appearance and manner appropriate to evocation of liking and respect and to play the determined role so effectively that the student is moved to the desired response. It is my impression, however, that the best teachers, and the majority of teachers, cannot rely on a merely conscious and deliberate determination of manner and appearance. Rather, the manner and appearance which will evoke liking and respect in the student will arise only as the teacher does, in fact, respond to the persons before him. (It is the reciprocity of evocation and response which constitutes a genuine interpersonal relationship.)

If, in the first moments of the first meeting of a new class, the teacher's gaze wanders first to one, then to another and another of the anonymous faces before him, those faces which are not readable yet as to promise and performance, and if, in this wandering inspection, two or three students answer his regard in a way which signals to him their curious awareness of him as a person, a start has been made. The person who is thus aware of me is a person of whom I become aware. The wandering movement of my eyes is stopped. They return to him or her. (From an anonymous sea of faces, from the mere collective, individuation has begun; "the class" is beginning to be "persons.") The teacher thus answers the awareness he feels in the student; he examines more closely the person who has signaled interest in him. In reciprocity, this new inspection is no longer felt by the student as mere curious awareness, but as awareness of himself as a person. More, the student feels his own movement from item to individuality, from anonymity to personality. And he is grateful.

For the Eros which appears in its most obvious guise as a hankering after externals is, in a deeper analysis, a regard for self, a desire for selfhood. To experience another's recognition of one's self is to receive reassurance of that self's existence. Such assurance initiates further growth of self. Gratitude follows.

But there is one more phase to the cycle which establishes our interpersonal relationship. The grateful warmth in the student is felt by the teacher. And for this, he in turn is grateful. At that instant, liking is born. His gratitude is not for the self's assurance which comes from recognition, for he has not suffered from anonymity in these moments. (There is only one of him, whereas the students are many.) Rather, he is grateful for that reassurance which arises from notice of usefulness, of neededness. In a sense, he is grateful for the student's gratitude, for the sign that he has been useful. It is a parallel of Descartes's *Cogito, ergo sum*. I have affected, therefore I am.

It may be objected that, if liking is contingent on this last phase of the cycle, liking and respect are incompatibles, that respect will be founded on the teacher's maturity and competence, and that maturity in the teacher disallows grateful response to an adolescent. One answer, I think, is that no man's self, however full his life, is ever so complete that this species of assurance is no longer welcome. It is true that maturity is partly measured by decreasing *need* for this kind of assurance and increased emphasis on the maturity of him who gives it, but not by decrease of its welcome. (That is why, with increasing maturity, self-love can emerge more and more serviceably as love for others. The teacher for whom the average-to-good student is too pejoratively adolescent to be regarded in this light is not so much mature as ill perhaps, or immature, or in a hurry.)

Another and complementary answer is that the teacher is not being asked to like what is infantile in the student but what is adolescent in its accurate and least pejorative sense—what is *growing up*. It is the germinal maturity in the young—germinal maturity of Eros, germinal maturity of intelligence—which he evokes and to which he ought to respond. And this should not be shameful to any man.

This complex but nearly instantaneous transaction need not take place with every student, nor necessarily in the first moments of the class. In fact, were it attempted with most students and all at once, it would fail, by virtue of the fact that the young are as much aware as adults that not everybody is as much a person as everybody else. The automatic assumption of pea-in-pod equality leads to the false-hearty, or to broody-hen behavior, which the student will reject. Three or four genuine transactions are enough at the start. In successive meetings, as successive students respond by revealing one or another quality of individuality, it is to be honored in its own right, as the teacher feels it. Thus a further level of individuation is reached; not only are persons individuated from the amorphous "class," but, of different individual qualities, each is honored in its own way and degree.

Respect arises out of liking when the teacher successfully traverses the straight road between the extremes suggested above. On one extreme he may be overanxious and overstate a wish to respond or like; in this case, respect will be lost. On the other extreme, he may be too cold, or perhaps too impatient or preoccupied, to note signals of invitation and response; in this case, some liking may be lost, for, once rejected, good students are cautious about trying again.

After the earliest establishment of interpersonal relations, almost every student will engage in an active, personal test of the teacher's judgment. This can occur in a tremendous variety of ways, but the essence remains the same; it consists of presenting for possible approval behavior which is false (i.e., manufactured), qualities which are irrelevant to the real business of the moment, or behavior designed to disrupt or impede the felt intention of the instructor. These are to be understood by the teacher as *provocative*. They are designed to seduce him. Pretended eagerness, fake interest, manufactured questions, test the teacher's capacity to distinguish the real from the false. Disclosure of irrelevant or inappropriate virtues tests his maturity. If he has immature needs for warmth, for the disparate friendship (or admiration) of the young, for instance, he will respond despite the irrelevance of the virtues shown. The teacher who responds to the sexual attractiveness of a pretty girl earns a lively interest which is not liking or respect but a measure of contempt. Or imagine a student who learns of a chemist's interest in music, is himself an able musician, and in a discussion of a chemical problem manages to intrude the fact of his musical competence (e.g., by using a far-fetched analogy). The teacher who responds to this provocation has also earned contempt—and, in fact, to a greater degree than has a male teacher who responds to a girl. For sex is recognized as a powerful drive, difficult to control; love of music is not.

For the normal student engaged in provocative testing of a normal teacher, the range of behavior is likely to extend from the exhibition of irrelevant bits of knowledge and irrelevant capacities, no further than to insistence upon intruding into the discussion expressions of belief, opinion, and preference, and questions of meaning or application of the materials under discussion, which are tangential to the detectable main line of discussion, or beyond or beside the range of interest and comprehension of the group as a whole. The proper response to these "normal" provocations is a clear communication to the student of the teacher's awareness of the questionable usefulness of the proffered contribution. This response is not always easy, for it must take a form which does not reject the student along with his offer. It should not reject him, in common justice, since he is not wholly aware of the meaning of his action, and its origin is not malice but need. It must not reject him, if the "erotic" aims of this phase of discussion are to be achieved, for a rebuff at this early stage will be interpreted as evidence of a specific weakness in the teacher, a self-doubt concerning his status as authority.

The simplest and most literal way of treating the offering without attacking the student is often the most effective. To a student's query concerning an esoteric application or source, "Ask that after class; it's a bit special"; to the expression of irrelevant opinion or fact, a patient waiting out of its statement and simple return to the business in hand without communication by facial expression or bodily poise of contempt, of impatience, or of patronizing patience. Or one can repeat what the student has said and indicate its connection with an aspect of the problem other than the aspect under discussion, in a way which does not blame him for its present irrelevance. (This must be done briefly, however, since to spend much time upon it will be to succumb to the student's seduction.) Too, one can simply ask the student's permission to postpone consideration of his point on grounds of the prevailing interest of the group or as a matter of personal privilege.

The evidence of thorough success in meeting these small crises lies in the student's subsequent behavior: in the first place, he continues to participate, but his contributions are fitting, and, in the second place, he "forgets" the invitation to reopen his tangential point or question. Only partial success, as indicated by continuing and fitting contributions accompanied by prompt presentation of the teacher's promissory note, or no success at all, as indicated by continuing provocative behavior, may characterize one's efforts with particular students. There is no general remedy for this situation. In some cases the student will be satisfied by two or three further provocative tests met as the first one was. In a few cases he will never be satisfied, and his provocative behavior will become a regular feature of the class meetings which will not be changed even by expressed cognizance and dislike on the part of the remainder of the class.

Such cases are not necessarily failures on the part of the teacher—in the sense that had he done otherwise, the outcome would have been cure. In any student body there are some individuals for whom establishment of a working relation with what is to him an authority-figure is a task which rouses great anxiety. Such a young person cannot respond to *this* teacher, *this* class, *this* moment, for all these are bound up with past adults, past moments, and past relations, and his responses are to the unhappy mixture. Two possibilities exist for the improvement of such a young person. One is psychotherapy in the strictest and most exclusive sense. For this task, the teacher is both incompetent and irresponsible. The other lies simply in the student's discovery and repeated rediscovery of profit, of pleasure, and of the absence of injury in relationship with an adult. For this "therapy," the good teacher is preeminently qualified and responsible. His role and responsibility relative to it is to be a good teacher and a just and responsible person, and these he is, or should be. By so being, he constitutes himself a curative experience.

In addition to provocative behavior, the characteristic quality of which is inappropriateness, there is another kind of testing action which takes the form of an expressed eagerness to talk, to contribute to the discussions of the earliest class meetings, or in some other way to attract the attention of the teacher by means which are at least superficially appropriate to the classroom situation. These are testing actions in a sense different from those which are provocative. "Appropriate" testing actions are designed to estimate primarily the psychological space, the degree and kind of tolerance which the student may expect from the teacher, rather than the teacher's capacity for appropriate judgment. To be recognized as awkward, to be caught in error, to be seen to misapply his intelligence or judgment is far more painful for the young person than for the mature adult. The young person's self is far from complete; his confidence in his individual existence is not great. He doubts not only his competence to cope with the real world but even whether he, as independent of controlling parents and copied manners and mores, does in fact exist. To the extent that successful and accepted actions give him the kind of reassurance that permits to him a new unit of self-growth, to the same extent failure and nonacceptance incite regression or postponement of new growth. These conditions of his self appear to the young person in the guise of a need to be assured that attempts at doing and thinking will be accepted as attempts, as trial runs and practices, and not as definitive measures of his powers or limitations.

The young student has not often had that reassurance in the teaching situation. The common run of instructors at the college level are unaware of this condition of the young, or indifferent to its magnitude, and consequently hold the student to the kind of responsibility toward words, toward choices and decisions, which is appropriate to adults. A surprising number of teachers go even further and employ instances of this nonresponsible condition of the young student as occasions and excuse for a destructiveness toward the student's efforts which is wholly gratuitous in its intensity. Occasionally, an instructor will, through this destructiveness, reduce an entire class to silence in a matter of a few weeks, and thereafter, of course, resent even more the students who now sit as silent witness to his aggression. Still other teachers, at the opposite extreme, frustrate the young student's attempts at intelligent activity by accepting any contribution whatever without estimate or critical comment, thus reducing the teaching relationship to a species of saccharine wet-nursing. In view of these altogether too common unsatisfactory experiences, many students feel compelled to discover the worst as soon as possible.

It is at this point in the initiation of relations within the group that one of the greatest losses of potential future participation may occur. The uncertain student who receives at this early moment a response to his testing which is "wrong" for him may not again open his mouth except under strong provocation of interest or welfare. The "right" response depends on a sensitive and charitable awareness of the peculiar helplessness, the vulnerability, which is conferred by the combined status of adolescent and student. The teacher must feel, or at the least be aware of, the conflict of impulses, part bravado, part appeal, part reckless plunge, part deeply insecure hesitancy, engendered by this vulnerable condition and must comprehend the gaucherie which will inform behavior arising from such a conflict of impulses. With this kind of empathy, the teacher's response is less likely to be "wrong," and a higher potential of teaching effectiveness for the group will be preserved.

This empathy and the sensitively measured response to student stimuli which is likely to flow from it cannot be replaced by a generalized receptivity, an uncalculated and wholesale acceptance of student offerings with a uniform kind and degree of "permissiveness." The student wants to be taught, not merely and unqualifiedly "accepted." He wants to be accepted as a learner, which means that the teacher must teach. He no more enjoys the transparently false pretense that he is complete than he enjoys attack because he is not complete. He wants neither syrupy friendship nor awful judgment but correction and assistance. These he can accept without anxiety from a person he likes and respects. He likes what is measuredly and discriminatingly kind; he respects what is unpretentiously able and competent.

"Testing" behavior, then, is designed to estimate the teacher's Eros for the student, his charity. Impeding and provocative behavior test the teacher's strength. If any person is to put himself in some way into the hands of another, he must have assurance both of his gentleness and of his strength and competence. This is no less true of student to teacher than of woman to man or friend to friend. Hence the testing and the seducing, provocative acts. The former are done in the hope that they will succeed. The latter are done in the hope that they will *not* succeed. If the first hope is betrayed, the student retires into passivity. If the second hope is betrayed, if the provocative acts succeed instead of fail, the person betrayed will take his revenge. This revenge is the origin of practically all teacher-student relations involving "disciplinary problems." Quite simply, the students find the teacher undeserving of respect, guilty of not being a man, and punish him for failing them.

There are then two pairs of pitfalls to be avoided by the teacher. One pair bounds the pathway which leads to recognition by individual students and by the teacher of each other as proper objects of Eros, their likable and respect-deserving individuality. The pitfalls for the teacher are coldness, on the one hand, and overanxiety to be liked, on the other. The second pair of pitfalls bounds the pathway which leads to that relationship between the student and teacher which takes account of the Eros of the student for himself—his wavering uncertainty which arises from his incompleteness. The pitfalls are peremptory judgment, on the one hand, and indiscriminate permissiveness, on the other. Provocative behavior helps to guide the teacher past the first set of pitfalls. "Testing" behavior helps guide him past the second. If these pitfalls are avoided, liking and respect will arise. These feelings come to be not serially, but concurrently, with a phase-lag of respect upon liking. Liking increases as more numerous interpersonal relations are established and as those made earlier ripen through recognition, acknowledgment, and tolerance of more and more of the individual traits in the persons involved. Respect ripens as the provocative testing process ensues upon liking and is satisfied. At the rate of three meetings per week, a normally heterogeneous group of approximately twenty-five in a well-planned curriculum and in the absence of spectacular external diversions (e.g., a climactic football game) will have completed this initial phase in the establishment of discussion at the sixth to the tenth meeting.

At this point, the teacher has in his hands a potent instrument for good influence or bad. As the next stage in the Eros aspect of discussion, he is now to use it to evoke in students a drive to emulate his professional activity and interest and a desire for his approbation. He is to convert liking and respect for his person into pleasure in practicing what he is and does as a liberally educated person. This is to say that, ultimately, the student's Eros is disengaged from the person of the teacher and fastened upon those qualities and capacities which make any man complete. The Eros, in this last state, is attached to the qualities and the capacities in their own right, and not as qualities and capacities of the teacher. The student learns to like them (through being brought, originally, to like their possessor) because they are good, to enjoy their exercise, and to desire them for himself. The student who remains attached to the teacher for long after their relation as student and teacher has ended has not been taught so much as he has been enslaved or used.

It is quite clear that the relationship involved in liking and respect can be misused. It can be corrupted by an ignorant, a weak, or a neurotic teacher in many ways. The ignorant teacher may employ it as a powerful device of propaganda and indoctrination. The weak teacher may direct the Eros, not through himself to the objects of the curriculum, but upon himself. The seriously neurotic teacher may move in any one of many directions. He may engage in deliberate manipulation of a captive audience for the sake of a sense of power. Very often, he will be exhibitionistically preoccupied with evoking applause and admiration. He may use his students as objects of destructive aggression. He may even try to corrupt accessible members of the group to a state which fits his own neurotic symptoms.

But these possibilities do not constitute an argument against the use of affective interpersonal relations in education. The neurotic teacher will use them in any case. As for others, any device or means is capable of misuse, and a powerful means toward a good end is likely to be almost as potent in misuse as in a defensible function. The physician-patient relation is susceptible of a similar corruption. So is that of father and son. In the last analysis we must depend upon the integrity of the men *selected* for the task. The teacher-student relation, at any rate, is accessible to a control which cannot reach parent and physician: the rule of *Caveat administrator.*

Let us turn now to the conditions under which the interpersonal relation can best be established and employed—the administrative organization, the physical circumstances, and the curricular materials in and through which affectively energized discussion can take place. The administrative organization of the school becomes important because it may impose upon student and teacher relations which are inimical to the liking, respecting "friendship" which is to be developed. Physical circumstances intrude in so far as they impede or facilitate the sometimes subtle, and often wordless, communications by which the relation is established and maintained. The curricular materials are obviously important, since they embody the purposes for which the relationship is established.

The father-child relation offers us an analogy to that of student and teacher which, in certain respects, can guide our examination of administration, physical conditions, and curriculum. By ordinary custom and institutional structure, the teacher, like the father, is taskmaster and inquisitor. He establishes the course or program, assigns and receives, probes and examines. At best, therefore, he is obeyed when it is convenient, evaded with all the ingenuity of which the intelligent adolescent is capable, is the recipient of masterly instances of dissembling and pretense. At worst, he is disliked or even hated. The teacher is also a source of material and emotional welfare. He is the giver or withholder of approval in the form of pass or fail, high grade or low. He must be cajoled. For on the passing grade the undergraduate is dependent for continuation of his student status—either through the institution's rules or parental willingness. And on the better grade many an adolescent is dependent in the same way, though not in the same degree, as the child is dependent for emotional well-being on the approval of father and mother.

But the friendship relation of parent and child sets the model for the affection relationships of teacher and student. This rare relation comes into being when a series of transactions between child and adult have their origin and direction given by a task in which they are jointly engaged. If the task is "real," that is, if it embodies creation of something admirable or useful to others, the experience involved becomes the most complete of which the young is capable. The feeling experienced can be atomized into a sense of the smooth flow of muscle and movement, a sense of increased stature (the child literally feels himself taller) and of increased clarity and scope of vision, hearing, and touch. These sensations are felt as if they were a translation or representation of something occurring in deeper and more intrinsic levels of the child's personality. That "something" is growth of the person; the body translates this to consciousness.

The experience comes as a smooth flow of creative volition in which the makers, the object being made, and the materials and actions of its construction become one organic and unfolding whole. It is the experience for the child of the growth of its ego, of its capacity for Eros. It is felt with intensity when the several constituents of this growth of self are present unalloyed: the young ego with nascent potentialities; another ego, more complete, more capable; an object, something admirable to be made or done.

The elder ego functions as a catalyst and a bridge. As catalyst, it marshals the capabilities of the young ego. This catalytic power arises from union in the elder ego of factual and emotional accessibility as a model. It is factually a model if it owns powers possessable but not yet possessed by the child. It is emotionally accessible as a model if it has invited the child to be like itself. Because the invitation arises from an ego of superior capability, it has validity: the possibility of being "like" is guaranteed as possible. Because the invitation is to be like a superior person, the child's ego is recognized and complimented; it is assured, not merely of its existence, but of its capacity for increase. A second condition is required for emotional accessibility. There must be no demand upon the child other than participation, no insistence on right methods or standards which would change the child's view of its incompleteness from capacity for growth to mere incompetence.

Thus the elder ego can function as bridge, taking the child by one hand and the task of creation by the other. Since it is an emotionally accessible model, its competence is not a threat to the child but a promise of aid; and the task, which is really beyond the immediate capabilities of the child alone, seems possible of achievement. Meanwhile, the competence of the elder ego guarantees to the child the worth of the selected task. Thus the child is persuaded to stretch, to extend itself, and so to assimilate to its actual capabilities its nascent potentialities.

These same elements are required in the relation of teacher and student (thought their fusion is different). There is the young student with certain potentialities to be developed; there must be a teacher who can appear to the student as competent in the first place and as an ally— an emotionally accessible model—in the second; there must be a task whose end is admirable and whose difficulty is such as to challenge the capacity of the student and employ the competence of the teacher to such a degree that his participation with the student in the work to be done will not be mistaken for patronizing or contemptuous bending of giant to pygmy, of adult to child.

The systematic difference between the "friend" relation of parent to child and the analogous relation of teacher to student lies in the phrase "adult and child." In the case of parent and child, the parent is an adult, the child a child. The adult status of the parent can be recognized by the self-avowed child and received, not as an intimidation, but as a solace. The young student does not admit, however, to an inevitable and necessary childishness; consequently, he cannot accept mere adulthood on the part of the teacher as the equivalent of superiority. On the contrary, if he is to participate fully with an adult, it is at a price: he demands and must receive the right to judge the teacher and admit him, or not, to the role of adult, of teacher. (Otherwise, he will merely submit grudgingly to the pressure of institutionally conferred authority and behave accordingly—at his whim, with evasion and pretense, with some profit but much friction, and with little pleasure in the tasks which accrue to him in the role of enforced recipient. Under such circumstances, the school will neither employ the Eros of the young student to further the ordinary purposes of education nor be able successfully to include among those purposes a development and organization of the Eros.)

Because of this new condition for emotional accessibility, the roles which are mere handicaps to the parent become much greater obstacles to the teacher. The roles of taskmaster and inquisitor, of giver and withholder of marks of progress and success, not only adulterate the quality of the experience of conjoint action to a desirable end but make it virtually impossible. If bread-and-butter love is called into being, the affection which will marshal capabilities and lead to intellectual and emotional growth is likely to find no support at all.

In the usual school organization, these undesirable roles are vested primarily in three transactions: the police work of "calling the roll," the examining function, and the vestiture of course-planning exclusively in the person of the individual teacher.

The first of these may appear trivial, and in some sense it is. But nowhere else in the teaching situation is the entire tone of proceedings set so definitely at the start, and so regularly, by an action which asserts to the student that he is a subject, subordinate to discipline and obedient to rules in whose formation he had no hand. It is questionable whether entirely voluntary attendance at all ages or years in the college program is the solution to this difficulty. Students come to different colleges at different mean ages and at even more variable levels of maturity and capacity for voluntary administration of their time. It would be desirable to move in this direction, nevertheless, as experimentation with particular student bodies indicates what degree of freedom is optimal. Several schemes are possible. Attendance may be required in the freshman year, or the first two years, and made voluntary thereafter. It may be required in the first year, made contingent on performance in the second, and voluntary thereafter. It might be required in the first few weeks of each semester or quarter and made voluntary after that. In any event, it is desirable that the police function be divorced from the teaching function and from its place as initiator of class work. To this end, the device of placing responsibility for check and enforcement of attendance upon the students themselves might be tried. Through student government or class organization, this alien and inimical duty might be removed from the teacher.

The handicap created by investing course-planning functions exclusively in the individual teacher is not obvious. (Neither is it as pervasive as the effect of the police function or as serious in effect as the examining function.) It arises because it puts the teacher in the position of inviting the student to participate in tasks which he and only he has set for them. The only reason the student has for accepting the invitation to participate in the work of the course is the reason of force, the power and status conferred on the teacher by his official position. It is an impressive sign of students' tolerance and charity toward teachers that they perform as well as they do on tasks they must take blindly and without reason.

This condition is most simply ameliorated institutionally by the device of a corporate staff or committee which is responsible (and known by the students to be responsible) for course-planning. Knowledge on the part of the student that such a committee is responsible for the planning of his work has two desirable effects. In the first place (and most important), it guarantees to the student that what he is asked to do has been devised and decided by a meeting of minds, by discussion, by oppositions and compromises among different opinions of what is proper, and thus removes the structure of the course from his consciousness as a series of tasks imposed through the whim of a single individual. Second, it insures a divorce between the giver of tasks and the helper in the doing of tasks sufficiently to permit the teacher to exercise the latter function without handicap from the former.

It need not be argued, I suppose, that the common examination system of the American school is, in general, a vicious one, if the willing and independent quality of a student's work is of any concern to the teacher. The work cannot, by the farthest stretch of the word, be called willing when it is done perforce under the whip of an imminent inquisition. It cannot be called independent when it must meet a test arbitrarily set by the same man who sets the work. The custom of frequent examination will not be altered in our generation: the system is too firmly fixed in our school and social tradition. But the second of these conditions, the identity of teacher and examiner, has been removed in many institutions and can be removed in more if the teaching staff so desires. It is fair to say that ingenuity could not combine the inimical effects of bread-and-butter love and submission to the taskmaster and inquisitor more effectively than does the institution of the teacher-set examination. Without its removal, the possibility of establishing a sound teaching relation with the vast majority of students is well-nigh nil.

Experience has shown that the solution to this difficulty is as simple as the difficulty is great. It does not consist in the establishment of a wholly independent examining body. (Indeed, a wholly independent examining body is not desirable for many reasons.) It consists rather of the same device which can provide effective divorce of the planning and teaching functions—the device of a corporate staff or committee. As in the case of course-planning, the student is satisfied by the existence of such an examining body that his examination is the product, not of whim but of community judgment. His own instructor can appear before him, not as inquisitor but as the source of aid which is required for conjoint action toward the aims of the program. The quality of this change is further enhanced if the examining function is exercised through the corporate staff or committee by a technical assistant, the Examiner, whose primary duty it is, but whose work is constantly checked as well as planned in conjunction with the staff.

Through these administrative shifts—the removal of the police function and divorce of the teaching function from planning and examining —the teacher is freed from the roles which handicap his function as a teacher. It remains to discuss briefly the physical conditions of discussion, and the materials of the curriculum through which the initial relation of liking and respect can be translated into that conjoint attack by teacher and student on a problem challenging to both, which is the epitome of the teaching relationship.

As trivial as the roll-call function, but also as important, is the fact that the worn tradition of teaching as dictation is embodied in a classroom structure and arrangement which virtually forbids students to see one another and requires them to look as steadfastly at the teacher as a subject is required to eye a hypnotist. Chairs are arranged in serried ranks. The students gaze at teacher or at the backs of one another's heads. To sneak a turn of the eye to right or left is to catch a glimpse of an evasive profile and to feel guilt at inattention to the authority at the front of the room. These are not the conditions under which casual conversation, much less serious discussion, can take place. "Face-to-face" communication is more than a metaphor. It is a description of the conditions under which words and sentences whose purport is of the subject in hand, whether science or politics or literary criticism, is made to carry a second meaning, the emotionally laden communication by which a person signals to another his interest in and attitude toward that other person. It is the condition under which as empty a salutation as "Hello" can carry to a communicant the full sense of the speaker's good will, indifference, dislike, or resentment. Discussion, then, even to be discussion, much more to be affectively energized discussion, must take place face to face.

The most obvious means of achieving this condition is the arrangement of chairs in a rough oval. This results in a curious identification of bodily protection and ego-security. The seated person exposed to the gaze of others feels a peculiar sense of vulnerability, of nakedness, which inhibits free exchange of thoughts and feeling. If, however, the members of our potential group are placed around a table, the sense of vulnerability and its consequent hesitancy disappear. The cause seems to lie in the secrecy the table affords for movements of the hands, of the body, and of the legs as means by which each person is able to express for and to himself responsive feelings he is not prepared to communicate to his neighbors. Later, when the group has come to know one another, and when a number of relationships bind members of the group to one another, this cautionary device is no longer necessary, and discussion will occur freely under any circumstances in which the communicants can see one another's faces. An oval table, capable of seating twenty-five in comfort, seems to be the optimal equipment. Larger and smaller tables have been tried. The larger tends to create a sense of great distance and of psychological remoteness between those at the farthest points of the oval. Smaller tables are appropriate where the number in the class is smaller.

When classes are larger than twenty-five, the table which seats twenty-five is still appropriate. Chairs placed back of those at the table are then occupied by students who choose them. They are not improperly excluded from a sense of membership in the group by their second-row position. On the contrary, this second row provides a kind of psychological bay, a second line of defense, behind which those more timid than their fellows can test out the situation and participate in the way they find most comfortable with the least sense of compulsion and exposure. If interpersonal relations are successfully established, the event will be marked by the drift of some of the second-row occupants to the table, a drift for which room is often automatically made by the spontaneously friendly gesture on the part of other students of drawing their chairs away from the table so as to make room for the person who has now signaled his or her readiness to join fully in the group. It is a moving and important action.

If an affective situation which can serve the ends of a liberal education is to be established, the materials of the curriculum must be at least as fit for the purpose as the administrative and physical conditions of instruction. The earliest relationship established in the group is that of liking and respect for the teacher on the part of the student. This relationship is to go through many stages as part of the development and organization of the Eros. In its first condition, the Eros, thus organized, engenders a wish for the teacher's approbation. This approbation, the student is to discover, arises from his effective use of what powers he possesses upon the work in hand. Call this, if you will, Eros for the teacher. In the second stage, he is to discover, through the work which earns him his approbation, the greater pleasure in the experience of conjoint work with others. And the earliest phase of this is pleasure in conjoint work with the instructor. Call this, if you will, Eros for the remembered experience of "friendship" with the parent. The pleasure so earned and the organization of the Eros which results prepare him to surmount the competitive feeling toward peers he originally experiences in the presence of the liked and respected elder ego and to try the experience of conjoint work with his peers. Ideally, the Eros is then shared with the objects of conjoint, creative action and, ultimately, in very rare instances, with the work of creation itself.

We are concerned here only with the first and second stages. If the movement from first to second stage is to take place, the possibility of real conjoint work with the instructor toward an admirable goal must be actual. For this purpose, it is necessary that some parts of the content of the curriculum be materials which offer as much challenge to the instructor as they do to the instructed, for otherwise there will be nothing in which the teacher may genuinely participate; there will only be opportunity for condescension and consequent increase rather than decrease of the psychological distance between student and teacher. In the case of music appreciation, for example, some of the works employed can be short, trivial, or vulgar, but attention to these materials must lead, at the last, to analysis of some works of sufficient stature and complexity to make clear to the student that the teacher and he are one in their recognition of the challenge and inexhaustible magnitude of the work. In the case of science teaching, some of the problems set for laboratory and discussion may be simple "exercises" invented and set by the teaching staff, or selected, simplified summaries of experimental work ("junior monographs"), but these must at last culminate in problems or reports of researches which bear the stamp of authenticity and which are clearly seen by the student to pose to the teacher as well as to him challenging problems of comprehension and understanding.

It is precisely these conditions which discussion in its liberally educative function is designed to fulfil. Discussion is, therefore, in one sense only a systematization, a conscious and controlled development, of what every good teacher tends to do and what he would want to do, had he only the appropriate climate in which to function and a curriculum which provided the necessary raw material of discussion—problems to be solved, dignified occasions for deliberation on policy and action, and unsentimental occasions for apprehension of works of art. He wants something more for his students than the capacity to give back to him a report of what he himself has said. He wants them to possess a knowledge or a skill in the same way that he possesses it, as a part of his best-beloved self. He does not want his teaching to be mere phonography, although the administrative structure of education often prevents his being more. He wants to convey not merely what he knows but how he knows it and how he values it. He wants to communicate some of the fire he feels, some of the Eros he possesses, for a valued object. Discussion in its liberally educative function has in it, then, a great deal of Mark Hopkins on one end of a log, but it is a Mark Hopkins with something *in his hand*, a Mark Hopkins with something to impart other than his mere self. His controlled and conscious purpose is to liberate, not to captivate, the student. The log is not his home.

Education can no more afford to separate the intellectual from the active and affective as objectives of the curriculum than it can to separate them as means. The effect of a curriculum whose end was training of the intellect, pure and simple, would be a crippled intellect. It would be crippled intellect in the simplest possible sense—one largely incapable of intelligent direction of actions and emotions, an engine without a load. The educated man is not one whose "life of the mind" is ordered while his emotions run hog-wild and his actions are aimless. Rather, the educated man is one who, while he enjoys a "life of the mind," also leads an active life in which zest and impulse restore, instead of exhaust themselves by having aims given them by thought. Similarly, the educated man's response to music and works of other arts is not limited to evanescent nostalgias and maudlin feelings of power, self-pity, and Oceanic escape. Thanks to his mind, he appreciates the art work instead of depreciating it. Rather than reduce it to a mere springboard or occasion, he gives it, through his knowledgeable eye and ear, the power to affect him by all the ordered structure and meaningfulness which the artist put in it in the first place.

The "intellectual" arts and skills with which the liberal curriculum is concerned are not then intellectual as to subject matter, and thus exclusive of other subject matters, but intellectual as to quality. They are the arts and skills which confer cogency upon situations and actions whether these be scientific, social, or humanistic, general and abstract or particular and concrete. The liberal arts, however formulated, are to be understood as the best statement of our present knowledge of the human make, of the various means—some special in their application to specific subject matters, some general—by which the understanding frees us from submission to impressions, beliefs, and impulses, to give us critical and organizing power and deliberative command over choice and action. A liberal curriculum is one concerned that its students develop such powers.

With respect to ends as well as to means, then, the aim of a liberal education is not to "destroy the mammal within us." It is to harness Eros in the controlling reins of reasonableness in order that we may borrow energy from her for intellectual purposes and, conversely, enjoy to the fullest the capacities for feeling and action she confers upon us. The liking and respect, the Eros, which the instructor moves to attach to himself as the initiation of discussion, has a function beyond the energizing of discussion and its attendant labors. This latter it must do, at the start and throughout the weeks of work. But Eros functions in the curriculum, not only as a means, but in its own right as well. An education becomes liberal only if the Eros is moved from one successive object to another until it comes at last to the objects of the curriculum.

If discussion is to achieve this purpose, it must do more than impart specific learnings. It must take cognizance of its "erotic" purpose *and* its intellectual aims, and it must take action in respect to them together. The movement of Eros and the movement of the mind cannot take place separately, converging only at the end. In the person, the student, they interact and interpenetrate. They must be treated so in transactions with a person. They must be moved together. Consequently, the quality of effective discussion will reflect this conjoint purpose.

The quality of discussion appropriate to this conjoint purpose can be stated as three functions which, ideally, every discussion, and every segment of discussion, will serve. (It is not practically possible, of course, that every query and every hour of discussion will serve equally well all three functions. It is enough if the three show a proper balance in the long run.) First, each query or discussion must serve as an efficient means of arriving at a specific, intended understanding of some specified object of knowledge. This is the function of discussion which is most commonly understood. Second, each query or discussion must function as an instance of movement toward understanding. It must represent that kind of attack upon the problem at hand which would be found appropriate and proper, defensible as a part of the discipline of the field in question, by a master of that field. We are trying to impart, not only knowledge, but a species of activity ("method," if you will) as well. We are concerned that the knowledge we impart be sound. We must be equally concerned that the activity be sound; and the activity which matters in the teaching of it is not the "method" we talk about but the method we actually employ in the sight of our students and persuade our students to employ. Third, each query or discussion must function as a stimulus to the student to try the activity in question, the activity which can eventuate in the immediate understanding sought. It is this function which most obviously involves the Eros.

The three functions of discussion may be restated as three criteria by which the instructor may judge the efficacy of a proposed plan or query. He asks: (*a*) whether it is an efficient means of arriving at a specific, planned goal; (*b*) whether it is a defensible instance of movement toward that kind of understanding; (*c*) whether, in view of the bent and interests of his students, it is likely to rouse two or three of them so to move. We may call these, for convenience, the substantive, the exemplary, and the stimulative functions of discussion. Taken together, they represent the three conjoint categories of the aims of liberal education: knowledge, power, and affection.

It is important not only that these three functions be served by the long run of discussion but also that they be served in a proper balance. Yet the balanced functioning cannot be described, for it is a dynamic mean. It varies from group to group, from instructor to instructor, and from time to time in the course of discussion. The group of low energy or of scattered interests needs more of the stimulative, for example, than of the exemplary and the substantive. A tense and anxious group, hounded by competition, by social or economic pressures, requires little of the stimulative. But it may need much of the substantive to assuage anxiety through concrete signals of achievement; and certainly it needs much of the exemplary, in order to mediate the headlong and uncritical rush toward the substantive which its anxiety motivates.

The teacher with a flair for insights and inspirations, whether about his subject matter or about the course of discussion, is one who must attend much more to the criterion of exemplariness than to the substantive and the stimulative. Conversely, the teacher in whom circumstance has created remoteness from the young needs to be most attentive to the problems of the stimulative.

With respect to the time factor also, the balance point is variable. For an average student group with a well-balanced teacher, for example, the stimulative will exceed the other functions, and the substantive will exceed the exemplary, early in the course of discussion. But soon thereafter the exemplary must be introduced more and more until it exceeds, first, the substantive and, later, the stimulative aspect of the situation. The mean or balance cannot, then, be given both a general and a precise formulation. The extremes, however, can; and in terms of these, the teacher may locate the mean for himself.

The tendency to plan a discussion as a dramatic dialogue with beginning, middle, and triumphant end epitomizes the tendency to bury the exemplary and stimulative functions of discussion under its role as means to a specified understanding. The end is reached in the allotted time, as a rule, and the student *seems* to move to and grasp the conception, theory, or view which the instructor had in mind. It will be found, however, that at best the student moves from one carefully fashioned query to the next one in much the same way a woman in high heels uses stepping-stones across a brook; the far shore is arrived at with a sigh of relief. The goal is reached, but no cognitive map of the route persists in the mind of the student. In fact, the goal can be said to be reached only if it be taken as a decidedly illiberal one; that is, if it is a theory, a conception, view, or what-not which is to be accepted as authoritatively given rather than understood in terms of the argument, evidence, or usefulness which warrants it. For even if the elements of the dramatic dialogue are in fact exemplary of steps in the argument, deliberation, or treatment of evidence which warrants the end-point of the discussion, they will not be understood as such nor, in fact, understood at all. They will function simply as the stones which, having got one across the creek, are forgotten.

The exclusively exemplary discussion is as seductive under some circumstances as the dramatic tendency is in others, but it is not a temptation to which one is likely to succumb unawares. The consequences are too obviously an abandonment of discussion to pass unnoticed. The teacher assigns a reading. When the class reassembles, a brief period is given over to student questions. Then the teacher takes over. If the work is a scientific paper, he formulates the background of the problem, exhibits the principles of attack, analyzes the evidence presented, and shows the cogency of the conclusions drawn. In dealing with tragedy or the novel, the teacher sets forth the details of character, plot, and scene, exposes their beautiful appropriateness to one another, and exhibits in his own person the aesthetic pleasure evoked by the artistry his sensitivity and analytic powers have detected and disclosed.

Overemphasis on the exemplary function can occur in a different way. It may arise from the teacher's mistaking himself for the curriculum. He may treat himself as the object to be taught. In the social sciences, for example, the teacher may make each class period a time for exhibition of himself as the Objective Social Scientist, superbly nonethnocentric, indeed with no center at all, sticking to The Facts, eschewing all mere Value-Judgments. Or he may prefer the role of Emancipated Soul, owing nothing to Class and Caste, or be the antithesis of the Assertive, Aggressive, and Competitive member of a Vertically Mobile Society.

The teacher who teaches himself is more than a joke. He points up the danger of pure Mark Hopkinsism, the educational theory which makes the "good" (i.e., "fascinating") teacher so much of an educational principle that nothing else matters much. The danger of this view rests, not in the occasional exaggerated spectacle of the one-eyed leading the blind, but in the fact that none of us is entirely two-eyed. No teacher constitutes in himself a liberal education. That is why it is desirable that we function as the agents of education, not as its subject matter. That is why, too, it is desirable that the content of the curriculum be the product of staffwork, arising out of debate and discussion, not of individual choice. That is also why it is desirable that the curriculum comprise, in part, materials not of our own making. What we produce, or what is produced by our equivalents in other institutions, can reflect only what we are and what our times make prominent. A liberal curriculum needs more than that. More is needed for our own continued education, for a check against presumption, and as additional sources for our students. The recent textbook and the homegrown syllabus are important, are practically indispensable, but are not sufficient. What is wanted, in addition, is materials outside of and, if possible, beyond ourselves. Such materials act to check the tendency in us, the teachers, to mistake our own incomplete learning for eternal wisdom. They enable the student to be not quite so blind to our one-eyedness.

In the case of overemphasis of the stimulative, there is a threefold mistaking of part for whole. The activity of Eros is mistaken for its organization and development. Powers of communication are confused with the larger set of powers involved in the objectives of liberal education. And that amount of knowledge which can be drawn from limited experience is mistaken for enlightenment. By omission of the substantive function, only the students' experience remains as a subject matter and as a ground of discussion. By omission of the exemplary, what little is available for subject matter is treated only by means of the limited terms and methods already familiar to the participants. The combined omission of both has as its consequence increase of a drug-addictive taste for talk itself. Discussion is corrupted into bull session.

The largely stimulative discussion becomes druglike in its fascination, but it reveals its hollowness after the fact. When one leaves a traditional bull session, reaction sets in. The sense of comradeship fades; disgust displaces one's former sense of special competence and strength; able thought and apt expression are seen as self-display. The similar hollowness of the overstimulative discussion does not reveal itself as readily because of the disparate status of student and instructor. The instructor may know that he has not taught, for nothing new has been constructed by him with and for the students. But he can believe that the students stand looking with new eyes at experiences they had formerly taken with only a portion of their signification. He assures himself that his possessing no new thing is because he was the midwife only. The students had the baby. In part, of course, he is right. The organization or reorganization of experience already possessed is an essential part of a liberal education. It is the way one weaves the web which binds past experience and new capacities for experience, by which new terms, new "frames of reference" are moved from the status of a mere equation to that of a formula (a flexible one) with which real ingredients may be compounded into meaningful experience. It is the means by which, quite literally, theoretical knowledge may be realized. But its enlightenment is limited to the little knowledge and experience which the student already possesses. It is a gross corruption of Dewey's "growth is growing."

Omission of the exemplary and substantive components of discussion necessarily restrict discussion to the resources immediately accessible in the student group. Omission of a substantive component means restriction of the content of discussion to what the student already knows. Omission of an exemplary component means that what will be done to and with the subject matter by way of understanding and evaluation is confined within the means already at the disposition of the student. With regard to the Eros the exclusively stimulative discussion centers each student's attention on himself: *his* knowledge, powers, and opinions. Consequently, the effect is to confirm complacent self-love as the proper condition of the Eros.

The merely stimulative discussion is not only a privation of possible and desirable ends but becomes positively miseducative. Its very virtues —reintegration of opinion and of experience—are distorted in character and consequence by its isolation from substantive and exemplary components. It tends to reinforce in the student the view that his particular store of knowledge and his particular habits of thought are to be defended in their status quo rather than enlarged and reordered. Since the prevailing climate of the stimulative discussion is one of debate and polemic, each participant finds sanction and encouragement for defense of what is his own and for attack upon the opinions, organizations, and treatments of others. In such a climate, errors of fact, of logic, or of principle discovered in one's own position take on the character of weaknesses to be hidden from an enemy. Admission of them is equated to defeat. On the other side, devices of *ad hominem* appeal, ambiguity, and confusion which succeed in obscuring a cogent fact or treatment in an "opponent's" position take on the character of victory. They are things of which to be proud.

In two respects, then, the merely stimulative discussion becomes positively miseducative. First, intellectual growth is discouraged. The drive and energy which is constituted in any situation by the prevailing activity and the prevailing sanctions of a group is put squarely in opposition to intellectual growth. Such growth, consisting of the assimilation of new knowledge and new principles and their reintegration into the body of opinion previously held is made to appear, in the polemical contest, loss of face. Second, organization and direction of the Eros is diverted. Such increase in rhetorical and expressive skill as accrues from the polemical exercise is corrupted from its potential character as a means for the clarification of opinion and knowledge, and therefore as means for initiating intellectual growth, into weapons in a battle for domination of one individual by another. What might have been a conjoint inquiry, engendering the satisfaction which comes from collaboration with others toward an admirable objective, is converted into an experience in the art of verbal warfare and into a taste of (and for) successful aggression.

Neglect of the substantive component is effectively built into the polemical situation. Even though opinions are challenged, they are challenged only in terms of their dissidence from other opinions held by other members of the group, and judgment among the several opinions is rendered sophistically on the basis of the prevailing opinion of the closed group as a whole. The essential feature is closure. The group is taught to take itself as the measure of true and false, better and worse; by extension, each member of the group is taught by the experience of the polemic to take himself as a similar measure in other situations. An unrealistic valuation of common sense and common knowledge, which is already a prevailing attitude in our society, is reinforced and confirmed. Realization that common knowledge and common sense are the result, through education, of what was once special knowledge and special sense is obscured. That common knowledge and common sense can increase by assimilation of what is currently special knowledge and special sense is tacitly denied. Rather, they are placed in opposition, and "common sense" is given that peculiarly normative meaning in which it is set over against special knowledge as "good" sense opposed to the vagaries of some bizarre point of view.

The desirable alternative to this habit of self-measured judgment of self-held opinion is constituted of two factors. The first is the habitual recognition that common knowledge and common sense are to be supplemented and corrected by special knowledge and special sense when problems arise which are new and important. The second is the habit (coupled with the appropriate abilities) of searching out and evaluating sources of special knowledge and special sense concerning the problem in hand. By these means, we avoid disdain of the specialist tacit in the merely stimulative and polemical discussion, disdain which, in a polity and economy as complex as ours, is as fatal as passive submission to his dicta.

Inclusion of the exemplary in its critical function means the deliberate introduction into the curriculum of the "confusion" of *differing* solutions to important problems, solutions differing in the terms and methods by which they interpret their data and differing in the data they conceive to be relevant and important to the problem. On such materials, the union of stimulative and exemplary components would be directed first to the *felt* recognition by the student that men of good will can arrive at different answers to problems because differences in terms, "frames of reference," and methods yield differing formulations of the problem, differing delimitations of the data relevant to the problem, and differing ways of extracting conclusions from the data. Discussion would then be directed toward identification of the prevailing "frames" and methods which characterize each field of knowledge and toward grasp of the emphases and omissions which characterize each set of "frames" and methods. Finally, discussion would be brought to bear upon practice of the arts by which the terms, "frames," and methods employed in a given work are identified and their effect upon the scope and quality of solution is estimated and understood.

This is a difficult undertaking. It involves on the part of us who are teachers assimilation of modes of analysis appropriate to materials in our subject fields which are not often a part of specialized, graduate training. It involves development of patient and effective techniques of discussion which are not the rule in most institutions. The rewards, however, are great. Neither disdain of the specialist and glorification of common sense, on the one hand, nor enslavement of the layman by the unexamined authority of the specialist, on the other, would come to characterize our students, but rather intelligent communication between layman and specialist, in which each recognized his need for the other and was confidently aware of his own role and value to the society in which he participates. Between laymen, where common problems but differing views enforce transaction, the relation would tend to be one of a common enterprise, a pooling of conceptions of the problem and partnership in a search for solutions, with an eye to the quality of the ensuing action rather than to the possibilities for personal domination inherent in the situation.

When all three factors are present in discussion and the goal for the Eros is firmly set on attachment to conjoint work with others toward an admirable objective, there is a little-used classic term which describes the temper of this union. It is the contrary of "polemic": the word "irenic." Etymologically, the word is derived from Irene, the goddess of peace, who was the daughter of Zeus and Themis and half-sister to Prometheus. This ancestry tells us much more than does a definition. Irene's peace is not the peace implied by "conciliatory," the peace of sleep, of quietude, of the suppression of self, of the absence of strife because of the absence of life. Her peace is the peace of work, of activity, of doing and making made orderly and rewarding by its aim. Her father, Zeus, is the god of moral law and order. Her mother, Themis, is the goddess of the law and harmony of the physical universe. Irene's half-brother, Prometheus, is the giver to man of fire and of the arts. Irene, then, is the goddess of those activities of men which employ her brother's gifts in the search for knowledge and mastery of the laws of the universe; those activities with knowledge and creation as their goal which bring into being the Eros which embodies moral law; the activities which take place in and through the Eros and have its increase as their goal.

· 4 ·

Science and Civil Discourse

The Uses of Diversity

I propose to examine here certain consequences which accrue to the liberal curriculum when one takes account of the vastly enhanced practical role which scientific enquiry and its fruits have come to play in recent years. I shall first describe what I understand to be the character of enquiry. I shall then examine its current practical role. From both character and role I shall draw certain conclusions concerning the liberal curriculum.

Enquiry is partly constructive, in the sense that conceptions—principles—must be invented or adapted by the investigator in order to determine his subject matter and his data. Before a scientific investigation can properly begin, there must be a restriction of subject matter, a choice of some part of the complex of things and events. A part is to be torn from context and studied as if it were, for the purposes of study, a complete and self-supporting whole. In fact, of course, it is in determinative connection with a vastly greater body of events and things. Consequently, to remove it from context is to disconnect it from part of itself. It is distorted by this tearing from context, and it is made incomplete. A given conclusion in science is therefore about a taken something, not an objectively given something; the conclusion is true only of that something as it is, and it seems, in its incompleteness and distortion, out of connection with much that would normally alter and affect it. When Heisenberg points out that the position or velocity of a fundamental particle can be investigated only by altering one or the other, he is pointing only to a special case of what is true of all enquiry. Every subject matter, precisely because it has been made a fit subject for investigation, is to some extent artificial.

Not only the *what* but the *what-about* are determined by enquiry. When our matter is made a subject by tearing it from context and forcing on it some conception of self-supporting unity and completeness, there is also a restriction of what to investigate about it. The effect of

This chapter was previously published in a different form in the *Journal of General Education* 9 (1956): 132–43.

principles which make a material investigatable at all by impressing on it an appearance of unity and completeness is complemented by further effects which determine the form our knowledge will take. In biology, for instance, whether we shall seek knowledge of the organism in terms of separate structures and their unique functions or in terms of the contributions which all organs make to the maintenance of certain life-equilibria is determined by such principles. In history, to take another example, shall we encompass our subject by seeking out the presiding genius and spirit of each age or by relating successive events one to another as causes and effects? The principles which determine such matters restrict and name the particular similarities, differences, elements, interactions, or other relations, among the many available, to be noted and measured as the raw material from which to mold our finished knowledge. They determine what we will take as our data.

This constructive character of scientific knowledge suggests expansion of the liberal curriculum beyond the rhetoric of conclusions which is its usual content. If a theory is to be known as a showing-forth of some aspect of the world, we must also teach what the theory is a theory of and what about that subject is and is not incorporated in the theory. We must add to Lord Kelvin's dictum, that we do not know until we measure, the further dictum that we do not know until we know what was measured. If we are to do what the dictum suggests, we must have something more in the materials of our curriculum than theories themselves, for the restrictions which define what the theory is about are not readily found in the theory itself. The theory is only the terminal part of an enquiry. We need what comes before the end, the early and middle parts of enquiry, in which its guiding principles can be found, in order to discover what the theory is a theory of and what aspects of its chosen subject matter are embraced.

Another effect of principles is to make scientific knowledge fluid. The knowledge produced in one enquiry is changed in the light of the results of subsequent enquiries. The change, moreover, is not mere increase. It is revision. The meanings of the terms of the theory are altered; their relations to one another are revised; some of the terms, as time goes on, may be discarded and new ones introduced.

This revisionary character of scientific knowledge also suggests expansion of the materials of the curriculum beyond a rhetoric of conclusions. For a rhetoric only of conclusions in no way prepares the student for the fact of change; and, when it occurs, he is stripped by the event of a part of his capacity for rational judgment, forced into generalized mistrust of professional competence and knowledge. If, on the other hand, the curriculum illustrates with care and clarity the participation of principles in the construction of knowledge and exhibits the growth of knowledge which occurs via the increasing adequacy of successive principles imposed in enquiry, the student can see the ground for change and revision. He sees that authority consists not in possession of information but in possession of competence in enquiry; change in what authority says no longer appears as a sign of confusion or mere change in fashion but as a sign of the progress of enquiry. The student can understand that to be true does not necessarily mean to be fixed and eternal; that what is said in one set of terms may give way to something else, not because the first was false or has become unfashionable but because it was limited; that a new formulation may arise and be more desirable because it encompasses more in more intimate interconnection than did its predecessor. Consequently, the event of change will no longer be ground for generalized mistrust of the soundness of all knowledge.

The curriculum can profitably go a step further. Such generic knowledge of the origin and process of change prepares us in a general way to receive and understand change, but it does not help us to understand the changed thing. For this, we need cognizance of specific principles and their action. We need to have possessed our first organized knowledge of a subject matter in the light of its principles, and we need to be able to trace, in reports of new formulations, the changes in principle which have brought the revision about. This means an analytic and constructive grasp of knowledge, in the first place, and skill in analysis and reconstruction, in the second. The student needs to know, for instance, that, when he speaks of a person as involved in an Oedipal situation and explains some facet of conduct by reference to an internal conflict, he is seeing personality in terms of a certain psychological anatomy and embryogeny. He needs to know that these conceptions of psychological organs and maturation are the principles of a particular way of studying personality and behavior; he needs to understand how these principles guided Freud's choice of data and his interpretation of them. He needs also to see what other potentialities inhere in this scheme of principles (for instance, a different anatomy of the psyche, an evolving, instead of a fixed, maturation process; sources other than parental personality for its modulation) and what changes in form of knowledge would be consequent on their use. He needs, in addition, at least a little insight into other possible schemes of principles (personality expressed through various functions or various needs rather than a various anatomy, for instance). Finally, he needs to have acquired this knowledge of the specific connections of a body of knowledge to its principles through such guided practice in the art of disclosing them that he acquires not only the knowledge but also the skill of tracing such connections. He needs that skill if he is to achieve understanding of materials which arise after formal schooling is over and if he is to relate new formulations to what he was originally taught.

When multiple enquiries on a similar subject matter take place, a third characteristic of knowledge arises. Often the richness and variety of a subject matter make possible the simultaneous application of several sets of principles. Each such set gives rise to a form and kind of knowledge distinct from that produced by the operation of other sets. Each such body of knowledge often turns out to have its own peculiar value and usefulness. On the practical side, one form of knowledge will be more easily or more effectively applied to one body of problems, and another form to other problems. On the theoretical side, one set of principles and the knowledge it yields will open lines of investigation which another does not, and, conversely, this other will prove the key to doors which the first will not open. To realize the value of such plural bodies of knowledge calls again for grasp of each formulation in terms of the principles which define its subject matter and its data. For it is these principles, the subject matter they delineate, and the data they determine which can guide us to a wise choice of the formulation to apply to each problem we may face.

We need, finally, to note that enquiry affects problems themselves, as well as knowledge. The very fact that we possess knowledge couched in a given set of terms, treating an aspect of the world by recognizing in it certain parts and certain interrelations of these parts, means that problems which can be treated in terms of these partitionings and these connections are not only successfully treatable but successfully treated. From the moment the knowledge is acquired, the problems appropriate to it begin to be settled problems. And, as fast as they are settled, new kinds of problems arise, generated by the solutions of the old ones, involving a different partitioning and other connections. For, when we have effectively solved a problem, we have diverted, in some respect, the flow of events. Some things and circumstances being made different now from what they were, new connections become probable, and new ways of interacting can arise. This means the emergence of problems which have a touch of novelty. It means also that the knowledge with which we achieved this alteration of the world has been made a little obsolescent by its effective use; the world reflected in its purport is not quite the same world as that which now exists. The subject matter has undergone a change.

This continuing shift in the practical validity of knowledge and the character of problems, brought about by solving problems, poses its own curricular responsibility. If knowledge is to be possessed in a maximally useful way, it must be characterized by plasticity. The knower must be prepared to recognize the small but crucial change of the shape of his knowledge required by the element of novelty in a problem, and he must be able to mold his knowledge to fit the need. This readiness involves three factors. The knower needs to recognize in specific, posed problems their deviation from the typical; he needs a sensitive awareness of the terms in which his knowledge is couched; and he must be ready to adapt the latter to the former.

This is to say that even the use and application of knowledge involve something of the art of enquiry. Knowledge is not made on one hand and used on another. "Laws of Nature" are as constantly remade in the using as are laws of nations. Just as the decisions of courts and judges remake and reinterpret civil laws to achieve a maximum of justice, so also does the intelligent use of scientific law achieve a maximum of goods. Both of them, viewed from the practical side, are flexible rules of conduct.

Let us turn now to a brief examination of the liberal curriculum in terms of its traditional function—the preparation of a leadership.

The liberal arts were thought to suffice as the formal school contribution to the needs and conditions of leadership. The task of the school was to provide the verbal arts, some taste and experience of the fine arts and literature, a modicum of mathematics, a great deal of history, and a larger and more heterogeneous society than that afforded by the home environment—this last to provide experience of men and of the manners and morals of leadership. Of these, only history was treated primarily for the sake of its content, as a subject matter. The rest were taught largely as tools, arts, skills: the skills of reading, writing, thinking, conversing. Grammar, rhetoric, and logic were practiced through the media of languages, classic and modern. Mathematics were present by name. Music, the appreciation of order, proportion, and elegance, were represented by history, by architecture, and by literature.

The common accent and common body of tastes and experience of the fine arts so provided sufficed to complete the unity of leadership which was thought desirable. History provided the models and precedents which defined leadership. Mathematics and the trivium supplied the tools by which information needed in the execution of duties of office could be garnered. The trivium in another function sufficed for the tasks of persuasion, which constituted the public moments of leadership.

The leadership for which such an education was thought to suffice no longer exists, at least in the United States, for three great changes have taken place. First, diversity among leaders rather than unity is now honored. If once in our history the law, the land, and the church were the principal sources of leadership, then, later, industry and business, such identifications are no longer made. Our leadership is drawn from the leisured, from business and industry, from labor, from the academic, from professional and military administration—indeed, from all enterprises (with the possible exception of the plastic arts) in which excellence, in one form or another, can be identified. In the second place, the process of leadership has changed. It is no longer a matter of drawing information from specialized sources, then applying this knowledge to the formation of policy without further recourse to experts, and finally engaging in the forensics which forge a party. Rather, the expert participates in leadership; policies are impossible of formation without him. And adoption of a policy requires not only the forensics which yield agreement but the more intimate communication which enlists cooperation. The third change is the major source of the other two and the one which will concern us most. It is the rise from theoretic to practical importance of specialism and the specialist.

Current problems of the community, local as well as national, come to our attention embodied in the language of the specialist. And they come to us in this form not as a mere matter of vocabulary and formulation but in their origin and structure. Problems arise from existing practices and policies, and for many decades our practices and policies have been determined as much by specialists as by traditional policymakers. Economists, sociologists and psychiatrists, physicists and chemists, mathematicians, pathologists, physiologists, entomologists, bacteriologists, and botanists constitute a large bulk of our civil service. They contribute also to the lower echelons of corporation executive bodies—a group which functions in America as an auxiliary civil service. These specialists, with all their special knowledge, are firmly imbedded in our culture, for better or for worse. The problems facing our community leadership come to us, consequently, as special and technical problems; we are advised upon them by specialists; and the policies we formulate on the basis of specialists' advice we turn back to specialists for execution. The phenomena of subatomic particles, of supragalactic space, of the unconscious reaches of the human psyche, of cellular physics and chemistry, have their consequences and concomitants in the world we consider ordinary. Diplomatic decisions, labor policies, road-building programs, the court-martial of a returned prisoner of war, armaments—all the problems of peace and of war involve one or more of them and must take account of them. They constitute part of the matter with which a community leadership currently must deal.

To cope with problems such as these, a body of generalized liberal arts is not enough. The grammar and rhetoric of the generalized liberal arts were designed to effect communication among men who spoke a common language, not a variety of special languages. The logic of the generalized liberal arts was designed for analysis of arguments and evidence adduced in debate about principles which arose from practices that had a relatively uniform and common body of principles. One mathematics was applicable; it was not yet conceived that the geometry of common space might have to exist side by side with other and apparently contradictory geometries. Even the arts spoke the common language. Lyric poetry, for instance, dealt with common experience and drew its language and imagery from sources available to all educated men.

The generalized liberal arts are still, of course, useful constituents of a liberal curriculum, for there is still a common language and a body of practices rooted in the common principles of the nineteenth century. In addition, the languages of specialities, in so far as they have not become mathematical, are still species of a common language, using a large part of its vocabulary and, on the whole, the common grammer, syntax, and logic. The need, therefore, is not for discard of the generalized liberal arts but for additional means which will supplement them and enable us to specify them to meet the new requirements involved in judgment and decisions about specialized problems.

What is needed is a body of knowledge which can enable a leadership to comprehend and to exercise its judgment upon the specialized component which will be present in almost all its problems. Since the specialized components will be numerous, various, and recondite, the task of supplying such a body of knowledge appears to be insuperable. It seems to imply imparting familiarity with the phenomena and the conclusions of all special sciences, which would be, of course, a task of impossible magnitude.

The earliest American effort to supply this need was to draw together in one undergraduate program the several elementary courses already existing in the various departments of the university. This effort failed because elementary courses were planned as only preliminary to a course of training in which the particularized and relatively primitive facts of the elementary course were to be supplemented by more complex data and submitted to organization in later courses. The elementary facts without the comprehensive theories which organized and related them to one another proved inadequate to the needs of a community leadership. The leadership possessing only this training found that, although it had some idea of what specialists were talking about, it could not deal with what the specialists were saying about that subject matter. The leader's training prepared him to do little more than know what specialist to call upon to deal with a given material. For a time it appeared as if a democratic leadership would have to abdicate much of its function in favor of a technocracy.

The second American response to the need for a specialized component in liberal education arose in reaction to the first. If the elementary facts were not adequate to the demands made upon a general, liberal education, perhaps the most firmly established and widely accepted general conclusions of each field might suffice. This conception of the proper complement to the generalized liberal arts launched the survey courses of the 1920s.

These survey courses were collections of "principles," conclusions, and theories selected from the total body of finished material in each science.[1] They were chosen on the basis of two criteria: first, the materials were to be those most relevant to the practical problems of family and political life; second, they were to be the most firmly established and most widely accepted theories and conclusions. These theories and conclusions, once selected, were then simplified; made brief and compact enough to fit within the time available for instruction; and molded into some unifying scheme which served to give at least a superficial connection from one topic to the next.

The survey course, though still in use, has shown serious weaknesses of two kinds: superficiality and dogmatism in its graduates and obsolescence in its content. The simplification which the structure of the survey course imposes on its materials produces a superficial knowledge almost as inadequate to the needs of leadership as acquaintance with unorganized, elementary facts. Cut off from the data which justify and give meaning to theories and conclusions, the knowledge gained of them becomes so merely verbal that its possessor frequently fails to recognize in problems the very situations to which the theories apply. He makes inferences but fails to identify the physical things and events to which the terms of his conclusions apply.

When, in addition, the materials learned in survey courses are cut off from their qualifications and alternatives, they take on an easy, dogmatic character in the minds of graduates which becomes a formidable barrier to communication with persons familiar with the material and leads to the habit of drawing fluent, plausible, but often unjustified inferences and implications from them. The dogmatic habit is further enhanced by the very neatness of organization in which the materials of survey courses are often presented. With loose ends and unanswered

---

1. The application of the word "principles" to conclusions and established theories in science by the architects of the early survey courses has a curious philosophical significance. The word in this usage has not lost its basic sense of "that which is first," leading, guiding, ruling. Obviously, however, conclusions in science are not its leading, guiding principles but that which literally comes last. In what sense, then, could conclusions and theories have been thought of as playing the role of principles? The answer lies in the fact that the conclusions of scientific enquiry were taken as fixed and literal truths about their subject matter. Consequently, they could be conceived as principles for thought and action on that subject matter.

questions infrequent, submerged, or absent, the theories and conclusions of the usual survey course present a misleadingly finished and conclusive appearance.

This conclusive appearance becomes even more misleading in the light of the fact that theories of long standing and wide acceptance include most of those which prove to have been on the verge of obsolescence. Thus, by the time graduates of the traditional survey courses reached the point in their careers when they most needed their scientific knowledge, much of that knowledge was out of date.

It is here that enquiry, with an emphasis on the organizing, conceptual principles of investigation, finds its place in the liberal curriculum. Such principles have the desired properties which the isolated facts of the elementary course and the simplified, curt conclusions of the survey course do not possess. Because they are organizing principles, such concepts have the wide applicability and instrumental character required for leadership and lacking in the elementary facts of a science. Because they are *working* principles, serving to direct and control the enquiries which give rise to a succession of conclusions and theories, they have a much longer life-expectancy than does any one group of the theories and conclusions which are the products of their use.

A working knowledge of these principles is, in many important respects, the modern functional equivalent of the logic of the generalized liberal arts. The character of specialized problems and solutions, which makes them relatively inaccessible to generalized logic alone, accrues to them from such principles, that is, from varied and special conceptions of data, of possible connections among events and things to be sought for in enquiry, and of the units or entities in whose states or behaviors explanations are to be sought and from a conception of the states or behaviors which are relevant and important.

One or a very few sets of such conceptions characterize a science in a given epoch, and they persist far longer than any one theory investigated and formulated in terms of them. Their life is longer, mainly because they become established in a science by far more varied and extensive tests than is any single theory developed by means of them. Just as every inductive generalization, whatever its specific subject matter, is a test of the general notion of the uniformity of nature, so every theory successfully invented, developed, and tested in terms of a given conception of the units and behaviors appropriate to a special subject matter is a test of that conception. One particular theory concerning the particular particles, masses, charges, and motions which constitute the atom may, for instance, have a very limited life and a limited applicability; but the technique of seeking explanations of physical and chemical phenomena in terms of particles of some mass, charge, and motion will persist as long as theories of this kind have their usefulness and continue to be capable of revision and enlargement to encompass new phenomena. Of course, these conceptions, too, come to the end of their usefulness; theories developed in terms of them become clumsy, and phenomena arise which they cannot easily be made to encompass. But where the life of a given theory may be measured in years or a few decades, the concrete guiding principles in terms of which the outworn is to be revised or replaced will characterize a larger epoch of a science. They are durable enough to serve the purposes of a general, liberal curriculum where theories in particular are not.

If, however, knowledge of guiding principles such as these is to serve the needs of a leadership, the principles must be dealt with in the liberal curriculum in the contexts of proof and discovery in which they have their origin and function. They are not amenable to being abstracted, codified, and presented merely as linguistic principles. In the first place, they are not merely a convenient new language but concrete principles referring to phenomena. In the second place, they are usually much more than merely new combinations of accepted notions already in our common language and derived from common experience. They are virtually inventions, new conceptions arising from a specialist's experience with phenomena which are not yet encountered or not yet perceived in the course of ordinary existence; they contain the very essence of the speciality of the specialized sciences. Consequently, they are not amenable to the ordinary techniques of exposition in which what is unfamiliar to an audience is defined and described by reference to familiar things and ideas. They take their origin from the needs posed by the study of phenomena in the special sciences, and their meaning can be found only in reference to these phenomena.

Moreover, these guiding principles are developed in order to formulate problems which are involved in these phenomena and in order to account for the phenomena, to relate them to one another and to phenomena already known. They cannot, therefore, be treated merely as new nouns pointing to new facts. Their meaning must be sought not only in the unfamiliar phenomena to which they are applied but also in the use which is made of them in formulating problems and theories concerning those phenomena. They need to be examined at work, in connection with the phenomena which first demanded their invention and in connection with some of the theories and conclusions which they make possible.

It is not only the nature of principles which calls for a working knowledge of them rather than a formal grasp of them in isolation from the products and raw materials. The use to be made of them by a leadership also requires such a working hold. The change which the nature of leadership has undergone includes a change from a rhetoric of persuasion to a catalysis of cooperation. It was once sufficient if a leadership, in the person of a lay, non-specialist officer, mastered the facts necessary for solution of a problem by employing the general liberal arts on written or living sources of information, formulated a policy involving them by means of related arts, and then, through mastery of rhetoric, persuaded colleagues and constituency to accept his policy. Today no such isolation of the layman and specialist is possible. The specialist is no longer merely the source of information, and the lay officer the maker of policy. The specialist, of necessity, participates in policy-making, and the lay officer can no longer, by himself, determine and correlate the relevant facts.

The lay chairman, administrator, or executive, even if he still played the old special role of policy-maker, has a much more strenuous task to perform. Even to get facts into relevant connection with one another, he must be able to combine the resources of many specialists. This he can no longer do by privily consulting first one and then another. For each specialist must relate his relevant knowledge not only to the problem in hand but to the relevant knowledge of other specialists. For the lay officer to function as sole intermediary in such an enterprise would require a depth and breadth of cognizance concerning the principles of many fields which no liberal curriculum so far devised can confer. Rather, the specialist concerned and the lay officer involved must engage in continuous, joint communication. They must instruct each other concerning meanings and scope and validity. They must recognize in each other's principles the points of contact through which their several bodies of information can be joined. They must participate in a joint process of each altering his own principles to fit the other's to the extent necessary to permit integration of their specialized contributions.

In such a pooling of knowledge, the role of the lay officer is a new one. First, he is the mediator not of bodies of information but of communication. Second, there is a sense in which he is a specialist, too, for he represents and presents the terms of the problem which is the occasion for the pooling of information. He plays vis-à-vis the terms of the administrative, social, or political problem the same role which each specialist plays vis-à-vis the terms of his body of knowledge. Thus all of them—specialist and lay officer alike—need a working knowledge of each other's principles, enough to participate in the process of mutual education and, beyond that, in the process of modification of principle and remolding of formulation which is required for integration.

A further function of a working knowledge of principles appears as one takes cognizance of the change which makes it no longer possible for the lay officer alone to play the role of policy-maker. The time was when the problems of a nation or smaller community arose, or seemed to arise at any rate, from the society, the polity, or the commonwealth. They were conceived to be and were called "social," "political," or "economic" problems because they seemed to arise from one or another of these sources. And they did arise from one of these sources in the sense that it was the lay officer, the social or political executive, or the administrator of the commonwealth who recognized them and estimated their urgency or importance. It was in the hand of the lay officer that responsibility for the recognition and solution of problems lay. The specialities of the natural and social sciences were invoked only after the problem appeared and was recognized.

Today, the situation is very nearly reversed. We see the problems from farther off. They no longer seem to arise from the mysterious workings of society or the economy, for these workings are no longer quite so mysterious as they once were. On the one hand, the problems are seen to arise from the operation of factors and forces in the society and economy which are now the province of specialists. On the other hand, they are seen to arise from the impact upon society and the economy of factors and forces which the special sciences and technologies have themselves unleashed. It is the physicist, the ecologist, the medical expert, the economist, and the social psychologist who see many of our problems first and estimate their importance and urgency. It is their task to bring these problems to the attention of the executive and participate with him in determining their relation to other factors and their relative importance to other problems arising from other factors and in other areas. Thus the specialist participates with the lay executive not merely in the solution of problems but in their recognition and estimation, and, since this is so to the extent that it is only through and with him that the magnitude of problems can be estimated, he, too, participates in the formation of policy, as does the executive, and not merely as a source of special knowledge.

Thus specialist and lay member of a leadership must alike engage in a process which involves reconciliation of a plurality of opinions and advices, the integration of a variety of bodies of special knowledge, and the estimation of the scope, adequacy, and relevance of the principles behind given formulations of advices and problems.

(I take special exception to the notion that a liberal training can produce lay generalists capable of sitting in judgment on the expertness of an expert. This relegation of the possessor of special knowledge to the role of talking book is no more valid that the technocratic view that experts can divide the problems of government and leadership among themselves and relegate laymen to the role of grateful subjects prospering at the hands of expert shepherds. The same point indicates the invalidity of both views. To the extent that experts are engrossed in the problems of their own field and habituated to the use of their own principles and points of view, they are rendered alien to the felt wants and needs of others and tend to apply the canons and principles of their own field to the problems of other fields. It is here that the lay executive exercises judgment. He judges not the expertness of the expert, but the relevance and adequacy to the *common* problems of those principles of the expert's field which the expert chooses to employ in making his contribution to the common problem. And even here, it is not the layman by himself who can make this judgment. He must be assisted by the exchange among different representatives of the same field, by their debates among themselves, and by their critical estimates of one another.)

This *instrumental* knowledge of guiding principles, which their origin and projected use demands, can arise when the liberal curriculum provides a view of principles, in a context of phenomena and of the operations of enquiry which are the locale of their meaning, and provides ample opportunity for the student to analyze and understand the relations among principles, data, interpretations, and conclusions which illuminate their function. This means, in effect, that the liberal curriculum will be heavy with content, but it will be a content which is neither largely of fact isolated from comprehensive theories which give them meaning, as in the common elementary course, nor of theories and conclusions isolated from the data and operative principles of enquiry which give them validity, as in the common survey course. It will be a content of theory and conclusions, together with their data and with the interpretations which derived them from their data.

In effect, I am suggesting that popular education has two quite different responsibilities. There is not only the responsibility for bringing all our population into the fold of literacy and of making accessible to all the common school and the common skills. This responsibility is recognized and generally accepted. Alone, however, the meeting of this responsibility can move the half of our population which is least well educated toward the modal education of the population as a whole. If education is to continue to do for us what it has done in the past by way of improving the quality and quantity of self-determination, the modal level of education must itself be raised along the scale.

Our present modal level of knowledgeableness and reasonableness in the solution of our problems is not very high by comparison with the levels which are possible and which the complexity of our problems demands. Columnists and commentators who array reasons and arguments for their readers do not usually speak as peer to peers. Rather they speak as popular educators. They give neither all the reasons they have considered nor all the interrelations among those they do present. They oversimplify and sugarcoat. They select the kinds of reasons which experience has taught them are presently accessible to readers and suppress the rest. Many of our schoolbooks, be it added, do much the same. And to the very great extent to which this is done, the degree of our self-determination is not being raised at all. Rather, the degree already attained through education is merely utilized and maintained.

There is a considerable danger involved in this limitation of education to mere maintenance and further spread through the population of our present level of reasonableness. It produces and extends the sense of capacity for self-determination while effectively hiding those complexities of problems with which our present capacity for reasonableness is not prepared to deal. Thus there arises a Hobson's choice. On the one hand, being unapprised of many of the facets involved in problems and unaware that we are unapprised, we may proceed to take the whole task of decision-making to ourselves and come to choices and actions based on only a fraction of what is involved. When this occurs, the frequency of poor decisions can only rise and the magnitude of undesired consequences increase. Much more common will be the other alternative: fullest consideration of problems will take place on high. Decisions will be made there, and the rest of us will then be manipulated into agreement. We will be flattered by being asked our opinion. We will be presented with carefully selected fragments of facts and arguments for our consideration. We will be encouraged to debate, to come together in block organizations, community meetings, town halls, and panels but will be left unsupplied with the facts and skills necessary for full self-determination. And as long as we are kept in the dark about the complexity of problems and the full scope of the process of decision-making, we will have the illusion of full self-determination. We will be willing victims of our own subjugation. This second alternative is no projected fantasy. Techniques of "consensus engineering" are already in use by self-selected elites and taught by them to chosen disciples. The mastery of these techniques constitutes the new demaguery. These are its new methods.

If we are to create the necessary defense against the new demagogue and increase the soundness of those decisions which we ourselves do make, it is necessary that an education be accessible which will disclose much more of the complexity of problems, of meaning, and of knowledge and a fuller scope of what is involved in the making of defensible decisions. To do otherwise, to maintain as the curriculum of most of our institutions of "higher" education one which disposes the elements of problems in their simplest form, inculcates a simple rhetoric of conclusions, and provides synthetic conclusions, is to play into the hands of the new demagogues and to halt the progress which the democratic system of public education initiated.

Unfortunately, this responsibility, unlike that for universal literacy, has by no means been well recognized or widely accepted. Many of the community colleges now being developed in our larger states are openly committed to supplying no more of an education than is required by a local labor force serving the needs of local industry and business. Average reasonableness, average knowledgeableness, average propriety of speech and manner, are the typical aims. In states which use the very large central university instead of local colleges, some spokesmen for the "general education movement" openly, even belligerently, assert a dedication to the current average to be the first principle of general education. Its generality is defined as general accessibility. They propose to teach, not for an increase in what can be understood and used, but only such materials as the existing educational milieu has already prepared students to comprehend.

I do not, for one moment, suggest that, were a curriculum generally introduced which attempted to disclose much of the structure of knowledge and the complexity of enquiry, it would be immediately successful with most students. We do not know how much of such complexity can be mastered by how many. The most seemingly self-evident facts about the educability of large numbers of people seem to say that such a program would be a failure. "Common sense" of the most rudimentary sort seems to tell us that students have all they can do to master the content of merely inculcative curriculums. But the same apparently obvious facts and rudimentary common sense spoke to the impossibility of widespread literacy when it was first suggested. And the first efforts at invoking literacy in those disinherited from any expectation of it were stumbling and of scant success. Then two spreading changes occurred, one on the side of educability, one on the side of competence to educate. The increase in literacy, as initial efforts were successful with the more educable, spread the *atmosphere* of literacy. As the number of literate persons increased, the number which expected literacy as a birthright increased. This expectation itself did away with many of the barriers to learning to read and write—the infrequency of need for it, its remoteness, its association with a distinct other group and class. Babies were born, not with an increased educability in this respect, of course, but into a milieu which prepared them for it with such ease and automaticity as to be equivalent to a genetic increase. Their parents read. So did many of their parents' friends. Books were read to them, and they became aware of the pleasure to be had from the printed page. The capacity to read to themselves became, conventionally, one of the first symbolic steps toward growing up, toward independence of adults. Then the usefulness of a round hand and a capacity to read when it came to getting jobs came into sight, and so on. Meanwhile, on the teacher's side of the desk came the discovery of better and more efficient ways of teaching. They, too, were affected by first success with the more educable. They were encouraged to find new means, new methods of instruction, which could reach those inaccessible to the first means tried. One does not need to remark on the present outcome of these two processes.

It is by similarly making no limiting, a priori assumptions as to who are the educable in respect of sounder views of knowledge and more complete modes of enquiry that we can find out how many can and how many cannot master them.

If a student is to acquire such instrumental knowledge, it is clear that the traditional curriculum must undergo radical revision in both the form of its materials and its way of treating them. The materials must reflect enquiry, and treatment of them must constitute a second enquiry, engaged in by student and teacher alike, aimed at practicing the arts of enquiry and at grasp of that full meaning of a body of knowledge which only the enquiry which produced it can supply.

· 5 ·

Enquiry and the Reading Process

> The impossibility of separating the nomenclature of a science
> from the science itself is owing to this, that every branch of
> physical science must consist of three things; the series of facts
> which are the objects of the science, the ideas which represent
> these facts, and the words by which these ideas are expressed.
>
> A. LAVOISIER, *Elements of Chemistry*

This document invites the humanist to make a contribution to general
education which no one else—least of all, the scientist—is as competent to make. I am not, however, sanguine about positive responses
to the invitation, for him on whom I would prevail is too prone to sulk
in his humanistic tent.

For a good many humanists, this tent is made of eighteenth-century
sensibility. These gentlemen—who resemble Achilles in few other respects—will have nothing to do with the teaching of expository work
in any mode, unless the exposition be of the variety known as the
"familiar" essay, written at the level of a Gilbert Highet, designed to
amuse, to "delight," and to flatter the reader but hardly to inform him.
I can expect no help from them.

For other humanists, the tent is spun from "semantics," a doctrine
bearing about the same resemblance to the discipline of semiotic as
does a newspaper account of satellites to a good physicist's statement
of a scientific theory. This doctrine closes the humanist in a safe world
of words supposed to constitute a system of such rigor and potency that
knowledge of its laws and usage will function as a key to knowledge
of everything else. Language is treated as if it were a battery of flaw-
less and focused lenses through which one can simply look and thereby
apprehend everything thought and experienced which anyone sufficiently
master of language has seen fit to report.

This chapter was previously published in the *Journal of General Education* 11 (1958): 72–82.

Those who hold this doctrine will not be pleased at what I have to say, for I suggest that language is not transparent and, though capable of leading a reader to water, *not* capable of making him think. Nevertheless, it is to these humanists that my faint hopes are pinned and to whom this document is addressed. They and I share an interest in valid meaning, and it is of the *construction* of valid meanings that I speak. I shall describe (and exemplify in some detail) two additions to the ordinary "semantic" reading process which embody the factors necessary for construction of meaning which are neglected in the "semantic" view.

When a speaker or writer asks of his discourse, "Am I communicating?" the question is usually addressed to three levels of his system of symbols: Are the separate words of the discourse within the reach of the audience and sufficiently unambiguous in their reference? Are sentences constructed to serve their several purposes? Is the organization of sentences and paragraphs into a whole sufficiently clear and simple?

At first glance, these three levels of questioning appear to include all that one need include—whether to check the adequacy of one's own discourse or to comprehend the discourse of another. To understand the meaning of each word, to understand the structure of the sentences in which they appear, and to understand the significance of the order of sentences and paragraphs would seem to constitute understanding of the discourse. These three levels—the commonplaces of grammar, syntax, and rhetoric—comprehend, indeed, the matter of the popular doctrine which I here call "semantics." This doctrine further asserts that the answers to these questions can be found entirely within the discourse, if the reader has a proper store of language knowledge and skill in certain language arts.

According to the semantical view, the grammatical question, addressed to the single word elements of the discourse, is answerable because a word—any word—is supposed to have one or a very small number of meanings conferred on it by proper usage. Consequently, a memory store of words and their meanings, plus a glance at context, is supposed to suffice for discovering the meanings of these elements.

The syntactical question, addressed to the structure of sentences and to words as *parts* of the speech therein, is supposed to be answerable because the structure of a sentence is itself constituted of a fixed, small number of substructures, and each substructure, in turn, is such that the words in it play one or another of a few, universally applicable roles: qualifier, subject, predicate, object, and so on. Thus the meanings imparted by syntax are supposed to be accessible to anyone who understands, in general, the parts of speech and the structure of sentences in his language. So equipped, the reader *receives* the meaning of a sentence. He need contribute nothing himself.

When the rhetorical question is addressed to the structure of the discourse as a whole, it seeks for the meanings which lie in the *ordering* of sentences, paragraphs, and larger divisions of the whole. One detects, first, those "joints" of the discourse which conventions of punctuation, indentation, subtitling, and so on do not indicate automatically, such as the "business" which partitions the flow of a dramatic scene, the cadential rhythm of a sentence which marks the end of a narrative episode, or the conclusive construction which marks the termination of an argument. Once the parts are noted, one goes on to discover the meaning they confer through their identity and serial order.

There are supposed to be three groups of meanings to be found through rhetorical analysis. First, one discovers the subject of the discourse. Second, one discovers what is being done to it *by* the discourse, how it is being treated. Third, one discovers what the parts of the subject are. Although these three groups of meanings alone constitute the fruit of rhetorical analysis, one makes the analysis, not once but several times, at different levels of organization—for the discourse as a whole, for its largest parts, for smaller parts, for paragraphs. One makes similar discoveries even for sentences. For syntax treats each sentence as a unity. Its syntactical subject is seen in isolation, whereas the rhetorical analysis which puts a sentence in relation to its neighbors discloses the subject of each sentence as a part of the larger subject treated by the larger units of the discourse.

As in the cases of grammar and syntax, access to the meanings disclosed by rhetorical questions is allegedly given—in the case of rhetoric, by a highly abstract and universally applicable "logical" apparatus. The alleged potency of this apparatus rests on the assumption that there are only a few ways of treating a subject and only a few kinds of subjects, each with its own fixed kinds of parts. As far as treatments go, one can only describe, narrate, infer, or induce, and each of these treatments is supposed to have its own proper structure which will characterize the discourse which embodies it. As far as subjects are concerned, there is a similar finitude. *Change* as a subject admits only of sequential, temporal parts. *Process* calls for temporal parts and a relating of each part to the end (or beginning) of the process as a whole. *Whole things* have a material constitution, a form, and a union of the two, which constitute "meaning." A *partial thing*, such as an organ of the body, has its material constitution and a courtesy form and meaning understood in terms of the function that the part has in the whole thing. An *idea* as the subject of discourse has meaning and instances. Every *meaning* has a general essence and a differentiating one. An *action* has an agent, a subject or "patient," purpose and consequences.

Thus each of a not very great number of matters to talk about is supposed to have its own inalienable parts and therefore to be subject to fixed ways of treatment, because of the fixed nature of the world and corresponding fixed capacities of the human mind. Hence, just as syntactical meaning is supposed to be accessible to a reader through his knowledge of the parts of speech, so rhetorical meaning is supposed to be discoverable through equally general and abstract knowledge of the parts of thought. Grammar, syntax, and rhetoric are supposed to constitute the whole logic of discourse.

The details of this semantical doctrine of discourse, in which symbols are supposed to have the power, by themselves, to yield all meaning, have much to commend them. In the first place, the differentiation of grammar, syntax, and rhetoric, as stages in the discovery of meaning, is applicable to practically all discourse and is fruitful in application. If one admits that change may occur in the meanings assigned to words and in the usages of sentence structure, thus avoiding the notion of a fixed, prescriptive grammar and syntax, use of the doctrine imparts a good fraction of the meanings involved in ordinary discourse. Moreover, even the fixed metaphysics, by which rhetoric prescribes the wholes and parts of the world, has its usefulness. The metaphysics which talks of things and species, essence and accident, cause and effect, process and end, and so on continues to be used, and used effectively, as the basis for solving a good many of the problems of the everyday world.

The doctrine, however, is not so adequate a doctrine as it is a guide. Its assumption of a fixed and universal metaphysics is one difficulty. But more important to our purposes are the limitations set by the doctrine to the locus of meaning and to the ways in which meaning is found. It speaks as if the meaning of a discourse could be found entire in the given statement. And the search for meaning is treated as largely an uncovering, a learning, of what the speech or essay has to tell us. Neither of these limitations fits the facts. A given discourse has a context of other discourses in the same way that one of its paragraphs has a context of other paragraphs. And a reader brings meanings to symbols, just as symbols bring meaning to him.

The character of enquiry indicates clearly enough the sense in which a context of discourses is required to illuminate the meaning of a single expository discourse. First, the subject of a given discourse is usually only a part of a larger subject. Second, the terms in which a discourse treats its subject may be only one set of terms among several which can be brought to bear on that subject, or only a few members of a set of terms, others of the set being omitted. Third, the problem to which a discourse speaks arises in a constellation of other problems connected with the same or related subject matters.

These contexts give added meaning to a contained single discourse in much the same way that the organization of sections and paragraphs adds meaning to the subjects and predicates of separate sentences. The subject which seems complete in the separate sentence takes on a fuller meaning in the light of the related subjects of other sentences. And when several sentences are disclosed and combined by the act of interpretation, they give us not only knowledge of a larger whole but fuller knowledge of any one part of that whole. In the same way, knowledge of a context of discourses gives us, for any single discourse of that context, a fuller knowledge of the scope and meaning of its conclusions.

We need, therefore, to add to grammar, syntax, and rhetoric a fourth level of interpretation in which a whole discourse is "placed" as providing such-and-such a treatment, in *these* terms but not *those*, of a certain part of a large subject disjoined from other parts, and providing a solution to this but not that problem involved in the subject.

We may, if we like, provide a name for this level of interpretation which will assimilate it to the notions of grammar, syntax, and rhetoric. When the question of communication is addressed to a context of enquiries, the question speaks to the problem of dialectic—whether those meanings are grasped which accrue to an inquiry by seeing its subject, principles, and conclusions in relation to subjects, principles, and conclusions of other, related inquiries.

To the question how big a context constitutes the proper context for a reported enquiry there is no answer. But the principle which should govern a practical context is clear enough: any apparently definitive or highly persuasive solution to a clearly defined problem ought to appear in a context which will indicate that there is yet more to know or more to know about. Take, for example, an essay on the aims of education which treats the problem in terms of a conception of human nature. Its conception of human nature may be precise and sound. Its logic, as it proceeds from its premises about human nature to its conclusions about the aims of education, may be impeccable. But there will be other terms in which sound and precise views of human nature can be conceived. And certainly there are other principles which speak to the question of the aims of education: the nature and content of our extant knowledge, for example; the character of a good society; or the political and economic problems which face the polity and its members. And there are other essays on the aims of education which treat the problem in one or more of these other terms. Often the practically desirable dialectical context can be provided by one such *other* essay. Two, however, are usually preferable because the total of three—three parts to a problem or subject or three sets of terms—avoids the peculiar proclivity we all have for treating a *pair* of alternatives as if they constituted an exhaustive whole.

The second inadequacy of the semantical doctrine, its merely passive conception of interpretation, can be repaired by turning to still another context which it overlooks. This is the context of alternatives which an author conceives in the auctorial process and from which he draws the words, constructions, and organizations which constitute the discourse before us.

The author with a precise meaning to convey and the intention of conveying it precisely conjures up such alternatives for a number of purposes. He chooses one of several synonyms in order to convey an idea as accurately as possible. A sentence structure is selected, not merely to convey ideas with accuracy and completeness but also to distribute appropriate emphases among its several ideas. An organization is chosen in order to set before the reader subordinations and co-ordinations which are themselves parts of the author's intended meaning and to illustrate, by the parts of subject matter it distinguishes and the divisions of treatment it uses, what the author considers to be the principles appropriate to his problem.

If a reader could have access to the alternatives from which an author thus chose his key words, the structure of his key sentences, and his organization, he would have at hand a remarkable aid to interpretation. The reader could contrast a word chosen by an author with those he had discarded and thus arrive at a much more precise understanding of the meaning that the word was intended to convey. He could proceed in the same way to discover a fuller or more precise meaning for chosen sentence structures and organizing principles. In general, by bringing to bear on symbols and meanings the same process of comparison which enables us to identify the otherwise undistinguished character of one of a collection of similar physical things, the reader could participate in a part of the act of authorship.

We cannot, of course, gain access to the set of alternatives from which an author made his choices. Indeed, in most cases they pass even from the author's memory in a few moments after his choice is made. But we do have access to approximate resources which much enhance the process of interpretation. These are the alternatives, drawn from the common resources of language, which the context of a discourse makes plausible. A sentence of F. H. Bradley's affords an example at the level of syntax.

The relevant part of the sentence reads, "A man is moral when his actions are conformed to and embody a good will. . . ."[1] Assuming the sense of the separate words, the meaning derivable from passive notice can be paraphrased thus: "A man is moral when his actions are consistent with a good will and when those actions include that good will as a constituent." This paraphrase takes account of the two predicates which Bradley refers to actions—"are conformed to" and "embody." It ignores, however, the peculiar fact that, in the latter predication, actions are active; they "embody," whereas, in the former, actions are passive: they do not "conform"; they "are conformed to." The immediate context of this second predication makes it plausible that it too might have been in the active voice but is not, that its passivity is the result of a significant choice by the author. To note that the author has chosen to say that actions are conformed to, and not that actions conform, adds a meaning wholly missing from our first paraphrase. This meaning involves the point that actions (of a moral man, at any rate) are malleable, are subjects of the actions of some agent which molds them, rather than automatically arising in conformity to the will, even in the man of good will. Further, this meaning alerts the reader to a problem which he ought to expect the author to solve, the problem of what it may be that molds or conforms actions, whether, for Bradley, it is the will or something else. In short, the paraphrase which would result from a participative interpretation of this kind would read, "A man is moral when his actions are *made* to be consistent with a good will (by some as yet unspecified agent) and when those actions include that good will as a constituent."

At the level of grammar, participative interpretation proceeds in much the same way as it does at the level of syntax. A discourse uses, for example, the three words, "individual," "particular," and "specific." We may therefore take it as plausible that these three words constitute alternatives from which meaningful choice has been made in most instances. We note the shades of meaning which, through usage, distinguish the three words: the connotation of membership with others of "specific," the connotation of unity and wholeness of "individual," and the connotation of idiosyncrasy attached to "particular." We read its own connotation into sentences which use one of these words, and we explicitly exclude the others. And we do this for all the sentences which use these three words. Proceeding thus, we shall discover one of three things: a more precise and more complete meaning of the discourse than we otherwise would have had; a wholly unexpected meaning de-

1. F. H. Bradley, *Ethical Studies* (New York: Liberal Arts Press, 1951, p. 82.

riving from novel use of one of the words; or the fact that inconsistency rules out any such subtlety of sense in this author. We gain from the process, whichever of the possible outcomes we find.

At the level of the discourse as a whole, participative interpretation proceeds in a somewhat different way. Since we are here dealing with the organization of that whole, it cannot supply us with the context from which to derive our plausible alternatives: only one set of organizing principles can constitute it, and we must look elsewhere for the alternatives which other parts of a discourse supply in the case of grammar and syntax. The elsewhere, of course, is the context of enquiry. It is here, as we have seen, that we can locate the larger subject which makes the subject of any one discourse only a part and its terms only one of several sets of terms. Hence, in participative rhetoric, we read outward, from part to whole, instead of inward, from larger to smaller part of discourse. We note the terms in which a treatment proceeds, what subject, and what division of it are treated. Then, if the terms and subject are aspects of a body of enquiry which is already familiar, we use this knowledge to determine what selection from what alternatives the discourse represents and what significance the choice itself may have. (We shall later on illustrate in some detail.) The participative dialectical analysis can also take place reflexively. When the document under consideration belongs to an enquiry with which we are unfamiliar, we can note the terms and subjects but not what selection they represent. We save them in memory, and only when we add to that memory notice of later treatments in which different terms are used and the subject has different boundaries and divisions, can we come to understand in retrospect what our first discourse had selected and from what.

At the level of a body of enquiries, there can be no participative interpretation, in the strictest sense, for here we are dealing, by definition, with the largest whole of all (or, in the practical program, with the largest whole normally accessible to its students). There is nothing beyond it, in the way of discourse, to supply a context from which we can derive plausible alternatives. What does lie beyond it, however, is the possibility of new enquiries which will treat a new version of the subject by new principles. Should our reader invent such a new pathway of enquiry (or one new to him), he can use it to supply him with a perspective. But if he does so, he is no longer conducting an enquiry into enquiries but has come face to face with the subject and problem. He will have taken a further step to enquiry itself, a step which is to participative interpretation what participative interpretation is to its passive form.

The fact that it is but another step from participative interpretation to enquiry proper emphasizes what is already clear—that a shift from passive to participative interpretation is no mere addendum to the semantical theory of meaning. It is a conversion of it from a view that symbols merely convey an author's meaning to a conception of discourse as the stimulus to a guided enquiry.

This revised view of the character of interpretation can be put negatively by noting that one can never know whether an author did carefully choose one of several alternatives and, if he did, whether his alternatives were those which the participative interpreter considered. In the first place, the author may have been slovenly. He may have had no precise meaning to convey or have failed to give energy to the task of conveying it with precision. If this were indeed the case, our participative process of interpretation would usually include its own corrective for the assumption of reasoned choice. The meanings we assign to certain symbols at one place will make hash of the meaning derived from the same symbols at another place, and we would thus soon see that the author is not precise—itself a valuable discovery if we are concerned with enquiry. But there is always a remote chance that his accidental choices will support a coherent meaning. In that case, we will have been led to construct an enquiry with outcomes of worthwhile meaning which were never in the author's intention.

Where an author used reasoned choices to convey a precise meaning, we too may arrive at a precise meaning but one which is not necessarily the author's. Participative interpretation begins to construct its alternatives by recourse to common usage—usages, that is, which are common in our time and place. That they were also the commonplaces of the author, we cannot be certain. Even were we to correct our first choices by reference to historical studies of usage at the author's time and place, we could not be sure. For usage depends not only on time and place but also on the locus in enquiry of the author. A specialist in a field will assign meaning to a word which is not the same as the meaning given it by a non-specialist or by a specialist in another field. And a specialist working at the frontier of a field of enquiry may assign meanings to words which differ from those assigned by tillers of its central acres.

Again, we have correctives which tend to resist our pushing meanings very far from the alternatives used by an author. If he is a specialist and uses his words in a special way, then, as we become more and more familiar with the body of enquiry in which the author worked and which he knew, the more closely will our sets of alternatives probably conform to his. And the more we push our meanings into the context of his own enquiry, the more will we tend to correct in ourselves those usages of his field which he has abandoned in favor of his own frontier meanings. Nevertheless, there still remains a chance that we can go "wrong"—arrive, that is, at something more or something less than the author intended us to find. In the last analysis, there is no certainty that one has received an author's intended meaning. One can only construct a meaning coherent in itself and consistent with the text.

Participative rhetoric and participative dialectical analysis present serious problems of instruction. Not only are the processes themselves new to the student, but the meanings they aim to uncover are meanings of which many students are unaware. They have usually been taught to conceive the structure of a whole work as a mere "outline," a convenience by which a large subject is broken into parts for presentation in theme or essay. It is not only that they fail to identify the structure of a document with the terms its author used for investigating or thinking about his subject; they do not possess the notion of terms chosen and subject defined as steps in enquiry. They have been exposed to knowledge as if it were information, objectively given facts, passively noted by an investigator and passed on through discourse to a reader. Consequently, the process of initiating the student into participative rhetorical and dialectical interpretation must also be a process of initiating him into the existence of enquiry, of exhibiting to him the extent to which organized knowledge depends on terms chosen and subjects defined, and of showing him how he can identify these terms and definitions and trace their effects upon the knowledge which embodies them.

The work of such initiatory discussion would be done best with a text which presents few problems other than those of participative rhetoric and dialectic—problems of discovering its terms and subject limitation and of apprehending the function of such terms as instruments of enquiry. An unfamiliar subject or an analysis in unfamiliar terms may defeat the intended purpose, since they impose on the work of discovering the factors and effects of enquiry the further work of comprehending a combination of materials remote from possessed experience.

The starting point for such initiatory work consists in a form of question which suggests the novel operation and challenges the student to find, not the answer to it, but its meaning. In effect, one puts the student on notice that an operation is possible (both abstractly and to him), in a familiar area (reading), which is new to him but which is not unrelated to familiar operations. He is invited to conceive procedures apparently appropriate to the process and to test them for their appropriateness.

I have chosen for illustration a philosophic text which is brief and has the desirable familiarity of content and language. The text, from Book II of Aristotle's *Physics,*[2] is as follows:

2. Richard McKeon, ed., *Introduction to Aristotle*, 2d ed. (Chicago: University of Chicago Press, 1973), pp. 122–23.

Of things that exist, some exist by nature, some from other causes.

"By nature" the animals and their parts exist, and the plants and the simple bodies (earth, fire, air, water)—for we say that these and the like exist "by nature."

All the things mentioned present a feature in which they differ from things which are *not* constituted by nature. Each of them has *within itself* a principle of motion and of stationariness (in respect of place, or of growth and decrease, or by way of alteration). On the other hand, a bed and a coat and anything else of that sort, *qua* receiving these designations—i.e. in so far as they are products of art—have no innate impulse to change. But in so far as they happen to be composed of stone or of earth or of a mixture of the two, they *do* have such an impulse, and just to that extent—which seems to indicate that *nature is a source or cause of being moved and of being at rest in that to which it belongs primarily*, in virtue of itself and not in virtue of a concomitant attribute.

Let us assume that this brief text appears as the first of a series of enquiries into the problem of what sciences there are and what their fundamental differences and characters are and that an introduction has apprised the group that this is the problem. Assume, further, that the grammatical difficulty of the title "Physics" has been disposed of: the students understand it as an equivalent for "natural sciences" and understand that the work before them is to be taken as dealing with the character and differentiation of the natural sciences.

The key question which is to suggest a novel procedure to the students and invite them to discover it is asked: "What is the author *doing* in the first, short paragraph?" The instructor's voice does not underline "doing" and the question is asked soberly and simply—without calling attention to its novelty. The point is to invest the work of analysis with no element of special importance or reconditeness but, rather, to indicate that, though novel, it is not difficult and, though important, is not an end in itself.

The particular student addressed will usually be mentally deaf to the "doing" of the question and respond with a paraphrase of the text, e.g., "He says that some things exist by nature and some from other causes." With great frequency, the student seems almost to memorialize his rejection of the puzzling word "doing" by prefacing his paraphrase with "He *says*. . . ."

The teacher then restates the question, remarking that the first response speaks to the question of what the author is *saying*, not to what the author is *doing* or has done and is reporting through his words. This contrasting of the actual query with another (itself instancing use by a speaker of participative interpretation of his own statement) serves as a first step toward the sense of the question: that it is concerned, not with the surface of the words of the text, but with something behind them which they represent and which cannot be stated by a paraphrase.

That the thing wanted, back of the speaker's words, is an operation of enquiry is not, of course, at all clear. Consequently, the second response to the question usually takes one of three unsatisfactory forms. If the student is extremely puzzled or has not yet overcome self-consciousness, he may again reject "doing" and give another paraphrase. If he accepts the puzzling word, he will usually move in one of two directions. He will give the word the highly general meaning which permits him to fall back on stereotyped "parts" of essays and themes, answering that what the author is doing is to give his introduction or to introduce his subject. Or the student will translate "What is the author doing?" to mean "What is the author's private and hidden motivation?" The latter is hard to sustain with the present text, as it would be with texts from the natural sciences, but, with works of criticism or materials from the social sciences, it is an appealing and plausible hypothesis concerning the useful sense of the teacher's question.

If the second response again rejects "doing," the instructor again points to it, turning, if he notes signs of too much frustration in his vis-à-vis, to another student or to the group in general. When a response accepts "doing" and supplies it with a meaning, the process of clarification goes another step. Whatever the student's hypothesis concerning the intention of the question, whether one of the probable two suggested or a third, it is used to point more clearly to the desired analysis. Thus if, for instance, the response takes the question as referring to the stereotypes of introduction-argument-summary-conclusion, the instructor remarks that, though helpful in general, such an analysis is only preliminary; it is too general to tell us what this particular investigator in this particular enquiry is doing here and now; that what is needed is attention to how *this* worker introduces—how he takes hold of—*his* problem.

The aim of this kind of response by the instructor is threefold. It aims to give the student's hypothesis its due, not to reject it as ridiculous or wrong but to table it as inappropriate to the present problem—this for the sake of communication as transaction. His second aim is to indicate that the analysis presently desired is not a one right way of doing the work of interpretation but is only the one now needed. His third and central aim is to use the weaknesses of the tentative hypothesis to narrow and direct the search for another. Thus, in the present example, the generality of "introductions" permits two important points to be made: first, that there is a plurality of ways of "introducing" and that some one way is used in *this* introduction and, second, that an introduction is not merely a transaction between author and reader but also one between them and problem-materials, that it is the author's way of introducing not himself to us but *himself and us to a problem*. The second of these points constitutes the crucial narrowing of the issue; it transforms it from an issue of the meaning of mere words to an issue concerning an operation of problem-solving, a question not of language but of enquiry—the essence of participative analysis.

Two or three such essays toward probing the meaning of the question are usually sufficient. The group emerges to cognizance that the author's first paragraph constitutes a classification (analysis) of the collection, "things," on the basis of their "cause"; that what it says emerges from and represents the act of classification of a particular, chosen collection on the basis of a chosen principle of classification.

One inadequacy of the present selection for its intended purpose lies in the fact that the classificatory process is so familiar—because of the pervasive influence of Aristotle on common habits of thought—that the student is permitted to distract himself, silently or aloud, by the protest that he saw *that* all along but considered it too obvious to mention. If this objection is raised aloud, it can be turned to the same account that was made of unsatisfactory hypotheses concerning the sense of the original question. The instructor agrees that the point is obvious, once it is noted, but that the usefulness of noting such processes, this obvious one or some other, is not obvious and, indeed, has yet to be proved. He may then usefully digress to a brief interlude of participative interpretation by inviting the group to suggest other ways by which other investigators might initiate work on a similar problem. Identification of two or three by the group serves to show that, since there is more than one way to initiate the process, there was something to be sought and distinguished by asking what the present author is doing.

The classification by causes having been identified, one moves on to note that the second paragraph of the selection focuses down from the collection of things to the established subclass *natural things* and defines it by "extension," i.e., by instances. One may, by way of giving the student a sense of participating in a professionally close analysis, ask whether the array provided by the author (animals, their parts, plants, simple bodies) comprises mere instances or constitutes an exhaustive reference to the members of the subclass. Students will often, having looked again to the list, note with satisfaction that it is, in fact, a principled listing, proceeding from what can be taken as most complex to simplest. He will often also identify "simple bodies" as elements in the sense of the irreducible and uncompounded.

Then the third and last paragraph is identified as defining the sub-class, natural things, by "intension," by locating its differentiating qual-ity as possession of an inherent tendency toward certain changes or stabilities.

The contrast of the inherent tendency toward change of natural things to the external source of the changes which affect artificial things may be noted as identifying one of the cryptic "other causes" of the first paragraph. One may or may not, as the temper of the group dic-tates, then assay another brief participative digression into what other "causes" there may be besides art and nature. And one similarly deter-mines how far finer details of the discourse (e.g., the parenthetical list of "motions" and stabilities; the fact that "nature," as against the sub-class "natural things," is defined only tentatively; the notion that arti-ficial things must be made of natural materials, etc.) can be made to yield still more meaning.

This phase of interpretation is then concluded by a synoptic summary which identifies the enquiry as one for which things and causes are prin-ciples and for which classification and definition are principled methods. One may wish to close as one began, making this synopsis a second occasion for probing a novel concept, by posing the question "What then, may we say are the principles of this enquiry?" and using a series of answers to provide an implicit definition of a principle.

Now one moves into an emphatically participative phase by recalling the context in which this particular enquiry is being investigated. The group is concerned with enquiries into classification of the sciences. This is only one such enquiry. It is possibly only one kind of approach to the problem and may offer only one of a plurality of solutions. Doubtless, its place in a larger body of enquiries will be most clearly disclosed by contrasts with enquiries yet to be examined; but, mean-while, what tentative part of possible approaches to the problem can be assigned to this one? Concretely, this text of Aristotle's attempts to deal with the problem of the *sciences* by starting with *things*, specifically with natural science by way of natural things. What are natural things to the natural sciences? And, by extension, what are things in general to sciences in general? And, most important, what other components of a science are implied by the role we shall find things to play?

A tentative structure usually flows simply and quickly from such queries. Natural things are the *subject matter* of the natural sciences; they are what the science seeks knowledge of. And things in general are the subjects of sciences in general. A subject of a science implies a sci-entist and an emerging knowledge as two other necessary terms or parts of this notion of "a science." Moreover, if there are different sciences, each concerned with an essentially different kind of thing, there may be quite different methods and capacities of the investigator which are brought to bear in each case. Further, if the subject material, methods, and capacities are different, the outcomes may differ also.

Thus a schematism of enquiries into the problem of classification of sciences emerges. One may classify sciences according to the "essentially" different kinds of subject matter on which they are brought to bear. One may also classify sciences by differences of method, of outcome, or by differences in the abilities required of the investigator.

Then, since each of these principles of classification implies the other three, an adequate enquiry of the kind initiated by the report being examined ought to include and correlate all four.

Thus, as in the case of the sentence from F. H. Bradley, participative interpretation moves from mere reading of a given discourse to anticipation of a larger whole of which the given discourse is a part. And in the present example, where the interpretation is rhetorical and not of the lesser elements of syntax, as in the case of the Bradley sentence, participative interpretation moves from construction of a meaning for a text to a measure of participation in the enquiry itself.

Part Two

ON THE FOUNDATIONS
OF THE CURRICULUM

· 6 ·

The "Impossible" Role of the Teacher
in Progressive Education

Since the earliest entrepreneurial efforts to institutionalize "progressive" education, most of what has been said by and for educators in the name of Dewey has consisted of distorted shadows and blurred images of the original doctrine—epitomes, diverse in content and tending to oppose or exclude one another.

Many of the epitomes, despite their diversity of content, exhibit two significant similarities. In Dewey's original statement, the members of a numerous set of terms were placed in new and fruitful relations to one another: time, fact-idea, change, freedom, organism-environment, experience, individual and society. In each epitome, on the other hand, only one or two of these terms appear, and conclusions about the character of education are drawn from them alone. Thus each epitome inflates what was a part of the original into an alleged whole.

The second uniform feature of the epitomes follows from the first. Since the one or two terms used in each epitome are now merely isolated terms rather than members of their original related set, they must be rendered with a specious simplicity and ambiguity to make the oversimplified statements of doctrine plausible. The result is to confuse or suppress reflection on the matters represented by the terms.

These uniformities point to a single degenerative process as the source of the various misinterpretations which Dewey has suffered. This process is one of selection which seeks a single evident principle on which to found a policy for education. The effect of this process, despite the variety of epitomes it produced, was to leave out of account three crucial aspects of Dewey's pragmatic method and content—precisely those three which treat of the function of numerous terms and how to cope with them. It is my intention to outline these facets of Dewey's view and suggest how they may be used to correct and organize the various epitomes which still represent Dewey's thought to substantial segments of our world.

This chapter was previously published in the *School Review* 67 (1959): 139–59.

In the past few years, something has taken place in education which renders this intention very much to the point. One sees emerging in recent school practices and in the utterances of creative teachers increasingly adequate reflections of Dewey's original views. The blurred images are beginning to come into focus; the shadows are taking on a third dimension. This change, itself, arises, as we shall presently see, from one of the facets of Dewey's doctrine and procedure. Teachers are discovering, from looking at their own practices and the consequences of them, some of the inadequacies of the epitomes they have used. They are beginning to see the omitted factors which, if added, would help constitute a defensible and effective scheme of education. The lack of reflection which the epitomes induced in the midst of the overt activity they evoked is being overcome as a result of that very activity. It is my hope to contribute a little to this process.

The three facets to be dealt with are simultaneously parts of Dewey's content and parts of the process by which that content is constructed or communicated. We may call them: (1) Pragmatic Rhetoric; (2) Intelligence; (3) Polyprincipality.

In its most general sense, rhetoric is the process by which what is "true," "right," or "better" is convincingly communicated by one man to others. Every philosophy has its own version of this process, appropriate to what it means by truth and its discovery.

For certain rationalistic views, for example, rhetoric consists of finding the true first principles from which one's scattered items of knowledge can be inferred. This discovery yields an effective rhetoric since true first principles, in such a view, are self-evident, seen immediately and without argument as true. Hence, if one can find and voice such a principle and show the bits of knowledge which can be inferred therefrom, these bits of knowledge will be accepted by the hearer as true and meaningful.

For an empiricist view, the true rhetoric consists of rubbing the learner's nose in the "facts." This conception rests on a premise very like that of rationalism, that "facts" carry their own self-evident guarantee and convey the same conclusion to all men.

On the other hand, for philosophies dominated by political views and a notion of a natural aristocracy, rhetoric becomes the process of finding the words, the attitudes, and the arguments which will rouse and marshal passions on the side one wishes to have affirmed. This is the rhetoric appropriate to such a philosophy because the ability to appreciate evidence and argument is the property of the few. The many must be moved by their passions.

Dewey's conception of rhetoric differs from all of these. It is grounded in the notion of warrantable statement (as against "truth" in the traditional views) and concerns reconstruction of solutions to problems rather than the implanting of conviction. Dewey's concept of rhetoric is crucial to an understanding of Dewey in two ways. It is a part of his conception of education. It is also the means by which he attempted to convey that conception. Without an understanding of it in this second function, the remainder of the doctrine is liable to crippling misinterpretation. It is this rhetoric which it is our present business to describe.

One aspect of the confusion which came to characterize the "new" education has its origin in the fact that Dewey set forth a doctrine whose radical novelty lay in an unfamiliar way of constructing a doctrine. This way of building produces a structure of meanings which will not yield to the kind of reading and interpretation which the educated man (including the educators) of the first to fourth decades of this century was commonly taught in the schools and conditioned by habit to use. It is as if Dewey had been grossly ignorant of, or indifferent to, his audience.

Yet the fault is not Dewey's. He had no choice in the matter. This is a hard saying. Let us see what leads to it.

The new education proposed by Dewey differed fundamentally from common theory and practice. Its aims and methods took their meaning from a new view of intelligence or enquiry: a new conception of knowledge, of knowing, and of that which is known. Thus his doctrine was, in two ways, something more than a theory of education. In the first place, it was not about education taken as something apart. It was about knowing, knowledge, and the known. Because of the view it took of these matters, it was also about human action and communication and human goods. In the second place, it was not a theory in the received meaning of the term. Its aim was not to explain and provide settled "understanding" but to persuade its readers to embark upon a practice.

This aim was inherent to the very view of knowledge which it proposed. For Dewey, any theory of practice, including his, finds its full meaning only as it is put into practice and gains its "verification" only as it is tested there. A theory includes a body of "logical forms," conceptions designed to embrace and relate to one another all the facts in a problematic situation which are seen as relevant to its resolution. These logical forms take part of their meaning from the facts they are designed to hold, and another part from what they do to the facts by way of making them signify actions to be taken. Hence, the theory cannot be understood until the facts are experienced in the form given them by the organizing conceptions of the theory; and "experienced" means that they must be seen and felt and that the actions they signify must be undertaken.

Further, the theory is "verified" only by such an undertaking, for a theory is good to the extent that it does take account of all the pregnant facts and leads to actions which resolve the problem to the satisfaction of those who are caught up in it. Hence, the problem of pragmatic rhetoric is to move men to an informed and reflective practice.

Now, it must be remembered that this view of knowledge plays two roles. In part it is the conception of education which Dewey hopes to convey. At the same time, it represents to him the way it must be conveyed. Remember too, that it is a wholly novel view of meaning and of truth. To this day, it remains far from being generally understood. If these three points now be joined, something very like a paradox emerges.

Dewey seeks to persuade men to teach a mode of learning and knowing which they themselves do not know and which they cannot grasp by their habitual ways of learning. It is the same problem of breaking the apparently unbreakable circle which Plato faces in *Meno* and Augustine in his treatise, *On the Teacher*.

To appreciate this seeming paradox more fully, let us turn to an analogous but simpler situation. Suppose a man wishes to show that the classic logic can lead to error. The one thing he cannot do is to give a classic argument which leads to this conclusion. For, if the classic argument does so lead, the conclusion, for that very reason, is suspect. Nor can he hope to succeed by arguing for his new logic by means of the new. For then he follows rules which his hearers do not know, much less agree to. This is a true dilemma—the live equivalent of a paradox.

We can begin to see Dewey's solution to this problem by continuing the analogy. Suppose that the man with the new logic changes his intention. He proposes, not to "prove" the fallibility of the old logic but to persuade men to try the new system which he conceives to be sounder. By this change of intention, he opens for himself a new route. He points out many assertions which his hearers will agree to be erroneous. He then points out that these errors were conclusions arrived at by the old logic. He does not (for he cannot) show that the fault lay in the old logic itself rather than in its faulty application. Hence, by these "pointings" he *proves* nothing. But he has, perhaps, raised a reasonable doubt in the minds of reasonable men. He has created a situation in which some men of good will may be moved to try the new logic and thereby submit it to the test of practice—provided they can understand it.

This last is the remaining great stumbling block. If the enterprise is to be successful, it is the new logic and not some radically mistaken version of it which must be tried. Yet this is the unlikeliest outcome of all. For, if the new logic be described in its own new terms, its hearers must struggle hard for understanding by whatever means they have. These means, however, are the old modes of understanding, stemming from the old logic. Inevitably, the new will be altered and distorted in this process of communication, converted into some semblance of the old.

As we shall see, this is not a fatal objection, but it might appear so when first discerned. Hence, an alternative way of conveying the new logic might be sought, and there is a seeming alternative. The exponent of the new may prefer, for the sake of communication, to distort his own doctrine, converting his new conception into something thinner and less complete for the sake of transmitting it in the old, familiar terms. Thus he might get immediate comprehension. And what was comprehended would deviate from the original no more than (if as much as) the notions conveyed by the first technique.

This analogy pretty well describes the situation as Dewey's view of knowing and communication required him to see it. He too renounces any intention of "proving," in favor of moving men to reconstruct and test by practice. He points to weaknesses in men and society which exponents of the existing educational mode can agree are weaknesses, although he does not "prove" that these weaknesses are failures of that education. He points to omissions in current educational doctrine which are omissions even by that doctrine's standards. He then proposes a new and alternative scheme, though he does not, since he cannot, "prove" that it is better. And he, too, by so doing, runs the calculated risk of serious misunderstanding.

In one respect, however, the analogy does not hold. For Dewey, the two alternative routes to misunderstanding are not real alternatives. Only the first is feasible. The reason is simple. If the new doctrine is entirely converted into the terms of the old, a static and unrecognized misunderstanding is likely to result. The poisoning occurs at the source. The hearers experience no struggle to comprehend. Hence, they do not know that they do not fully know. A new practice may ensue, but it is unlikely to be the testing practice which discloses that the policy it rested on was an imperfect shadow of what it seemed to be.

This follows from the fact that complex problems and what would be solutions to them are not "given" and "objective," and thus seen as the same by all men—any more than are the means for solution. Such a community of problem and desired solution characterizes only those situations which are the same for all of us by virtue of our common biology or a common culture, thoroughly shared. Neither of these conditions holds for problems of education. We play different roles in our society and occupy varied parts of it. We have different personal histories which confer on us widely varying wants and capacities for satisfaction. Hence, an imperfect and partial understanding of a theory, leading to an incomplete practice, may yet seem to us satisfactory. It may have outcomes which fulfil some of our needs. Some of the needs it does not fulfil may not be our needs here and now. We may not be so placed as to see that their privation in others will later hit us where it hurts. In the same way, some of the outcomes of that practice may be deleterious to others, and eventually to us, but as long as they are not damaging to us here and now, we may, again, easily overlook them. Still other needs the practice fails to fill may be ours here and now, but we guess that they are needs whose satisfaction should be sought elsewhere or at another time.

Thus many a man-in-the-street has no use for the Humanities. "What good is it?" meaning, "How will it fill my belly?" is his present looming problem. He does not know that, when his belly and the needs it figuratively stands for are satisfied, he will discover new wants which art and the novel would fulfil had he learned access to them. Many a teacher "has no use for theories of education," meaning, "How will they help me keep order in the classroom and help my students get good grades?" She is not so placed that she can see that new subjects and new disciplines proposed by the theory are intended to solve problems on the part of government or science or industry of which she and her students will eventually feel the pinch though she is not aware of them now. Many an editor urges that this or that aim of the school be "returned to the home where it belongs"—not knowing, or perhaps not wanting to know, that the homes of many of our children are no longer capable of serving the aim.

In brief, a pragmatic theory does more than merely suggest means for solving problems. It also points both to the problems themselves and to what a solution might be like—seen by the pragmatic theory-maker because his special stance affords him a view of problems which are visible to others only part by part.

Since pragmatic theory does contain a "pointing" to possible problems and possible aims, as well as to means to these ends, it must, in its own right, be in good part understood. It is not enough that a pale shadow of it be comfortably taken for the real thing, on the supposition that practice will soon disclose its weaknesses and lead to their correction. Hence, for Dewey, the alternative rhetoric which consists of thinning out and "dumbing down" at source is not a real alternative. It will not lead to test and understanding.

Only the first and thornier route is feasible. If the new is presented mainly in its own new terms, a quite different situation is created, uncomfortable but productive. From the first, hearers must struggle to understand. As they translate their tentative understanding into action, a powerful stimulus to thought and reflection is created. This stimulus acts in two ways. On the one hand, it creates new food for thought. The actions undertaken lead to unexpected consequences, effects on teachers and students, which cry for explanation. There is reflection on the disparities between ends envisaged and the consequences which actually ensue. There is reflection on the means used and the reasons why their outcomes were as they were. At the same time, new competences for taking thought are roused. The new actions change old habits of thought and observation. Facts formerly ignored or deemed irrelevant take on significance. Energies are mobilized; new empathies are roused.

There thus arises a new and fuller understanding of the situation and a better grasp of the ideas which led to it. A revised practice is undertaken. The cycle renews itself. As long as the struggle is—and is felt as —indecisive, there will be such a continuing re-examination and reassessment of what is thought and done.

The significance to education of pragmatic rhetoric is twofold—corresponding to the two roles which the rhetoric plays for Dewey. As part of a conception of education, it becomes part of the meaning of "learning by doing." What one learns is considerably more than habits, attitudes, precepts and doctrines presently true and useful. These, yes. But they are only the first order of learning. Each such instance of first-order mastery is, in addition, the occasion for a learning of a second order, a learning of what it is to learn. And learning, for Dewey, is active participation in the pragmatic rhetoric—the recovery and test of meaning. Hence, the effective "learning situation" is not the one which leads by the quickest, most comfortable route to mastered habit and attitude, used precept and applied knowledge, but the one which is provocative of reflection, experiment, and revision.

As the means by which Dewey hoped to convey his view of education, pragmatic rhetoric points to the fact that Dewey's evangelists rendered him a poor service when they interposed between him and the teacher a series of deceiving simplicities which purported to contain the "new" view of education. This point applies to the present as well as the past. If teachers are effectively to guide their students through and to the exercise of intelligence, they cannot, themselves, be unreflective. The teachers college and the administrative structure of the school cannot afford, therefore, to repeat the error of the epitomists, to provide their teachers with fixed techniques, content to be learned by rote, and imposed curriculums. Teacher training ought, in some measure, to become teacher education despite the pressure of an expanding population. It ought to exhibit the material which their students will teach as matter for reflection rather than as matter for docile mastery. It ought to exhibit proposed ends and methods of instruction in some of their difficult, tangled, and doubtful connection with the imperfect and incomplete researches on society, the learning process, human personality, and similar topics, from which they stem. The schools, in turn, ought to be so organized that at least some of their capable and energetic teachers find in the classroom and in each other the opportunity to reflect on ends and methods and try alternatives which experience and reflection suggest.

Luckily, Dewey's influence penetrated areas other than education. He laid the ground for dynamic theories of personality. His criticism of the rigid Pavlovian notions of conditioning modified research into learning and thereby affected our views of human intelligence and its operation. His conception of human association influenced many sociologists and, through the results of their researches, modified the very social structure in which we live. By these means, Dewey created a learning situation much broader than the classroom. Out of that situation, many American scholars, including some educators, have moved into the region of pragmatic intelligence. Let us look now at the scope and character of that space.

Dewey's problem in constructing that space was to rejoin what decadent memories of ancient philosophies had struck apart, to reestablish circuits through which divisions of human thought and interest could find each other. There were the urgencies of human needs, the "practical," left, in their isolation from science and scholarship, to seek each its own means to satisfaction with indifference to the farther future and with frightened inattention to the consequences of taken actions on areas of other needs. There were the fields of science and scholarship, enjoying an integral character which the practical lacked but preoccupied each with the intricate relations among its own conceptions and growing sterile from lack of contact with the arena of human needs and with each other. There was the area of value—of duty and enjoyment —treated as something opposing or beyond the condition of man and the circumstances of existence. There was the area of fact treated as ultimately unresponsive to man's wishes and irrelevant to his highest aspirations.

Pragmatic Intellectual Space is Dewey's solution to these problems. The solution is remarkable in that these divided factors are placed in communication with one another without sacrificing the special character of each one. Science and scholarship retain their integrations; the practical, its competence to cope with urgency. Art and aspiration continue to look beyond the present and the presently possible. The anchoring recalcitrance of fact is not denied. But while each retains its special advantage, each can repair its lack by connection with the others. Science finds refreshment and new impetus in problems posed it by the practical. The practical finds organization of means and consequences and refinement of its aims in science. Art and aspiration find test, support, and material for realization in the world of fact and of the practical. Facts are made more pliable by science and placed in the service of art and the practical.

These connections are achieved by discerning new guiding patterns and outcomes for the exercise of intelligence, replacing the older ones. In older guiding views, for example, science consisted in the pursuit of one or another eternal stability: irreducible elements of which the world was supposed to be composed; or the ultimate formal patterns which organized each subject matter; or the system of natural classes to which each natural thing belonged. The very universality and ultimacy of these directive notions was what cut science off from the practical. Similar directives walled off art from "life" and ethics from ordinary affairs.

We can catch a glimpse of Dewey's revised channels of intelligence by examining briefly the topography of pragmatic intellectual space with special reference to theory and practice, science and daily problems.

The (literally) fundamental differentiation of pragmatic space from other views of intelligence lies in the discard of the notion of brute and given fact observed. The doubtful notion that facts are seen "objectively," without reference to the seeing thing, is replaced by the notion of "situation." The primitive intelligent act is apprehension of need, requirement, imbalance, in one's relation to surrounding circumstance. From apprehension of imbalance we move to specification of it—what there is about us and circumstance which is teetering, open, needful: we locate the problem which the situation poses. The process moves to its climax when we find a way of acting which promises to restore balance in the situation—a way to solve our problem. The process is completed when we master the pattern of action which does, in fact, resolve the problem by creating a satisfactory state of affairs.

If we look closely at this idea we can see what replaces "brute" fact and plants the germ of an integration of theory and practice. There is a primitive knowing here—a forecast of science. There is a primitive practicality—the resolution of an imbalance involving us. And the two are closely joined. What we know is not facts *sub specie aeternitatis*, but facts as parts of a practical problem and as means to its solution. In the opposite direction, what we achieve is not merely satisfaction of a need but a new condition in the world around us, an experiment, if you please, which will evoke new situations posing new problems which will present new facts for us to know.

The first level of pragmatic space is, then, a mastered pattern of action to an end. But, says Dewey, this is an artifact, an abstraction. No single pattern of action to an end exists alone—even in animals "lower" than man. No two situations are precisely alike; single, rigid patterns of action will not continue to master situations. So a second level must intervene before we can reach the level of reflection. At this level, we achieve, for each kind of problem and situation, flexible ways of acting, modified steps and alternative sequences designed to meet the flux of materials and events.

This state of affairs is a marked improvement; it is intelligent. But it is not yet reflective; we have not reflexed, looked back. On the side of means, we have not yet noted why certain actions were effective, others not. On the side of aims, we have not yet compared them with one another. We are *too* responsive to the flux of materials and events; too little its master.

The third level of pragmatic space—the first level in which reflection appears—fills this gap. At this level, we take note of connections between different things done and different resulting consequences. Thus we compile a catalogue of means to ends, a body of practical knowledge. Then we look to connections among differing consequences and the differing satisfactions which ensue, yielding knowledge of wants and their objects—what there is that satisfies and in what degree. Thus reflection provides us with tested means by which to meet similar situations in the future and with alternative aims by which to guide the use we make of these situations. We become good, practical animals.

This sort of practical knowledge suffices for some parts of some lives, but it is too much chained to the past to anticipate adequately the changing future. It is reflection on past means and ends. It can serve to anticipate only such futures as are notable in the past; but there is reason to be sure that the future will pose problems markedly different. We have ourselves set in train events which will change them. Each resolution of a past situation has been successful because it changed something. Very often, the change is small, and what follows from it is equally small. But some solutions to problems are far-reaching in their effects. Agriculture, for example, has changed the face and climate of vast areas. Urbanization has altered the waters we drink and the air we breathe. And while these changes take place on the circumstantial side of situations, the other side—ourselves—changes too. By the act of solving problems and by living with their solutions, we alter ourselves. Our competence is enhanced, and our wants are changed. When problems of mere survival are overcome, we look for comfort. When this is found, we uncover higher aspirations. From being satisfied with outcomes of our acts, we turn to pleasure in the act well done; from being satisfied with other men as henchmen, we look for men as friends. So, in respect of both ends and means, the future poses problems which may differ radically from those of the past.

If this condition is to be met, the pursuit of knowledge must race ahead of practical problems posed and do without their aid. It must be unchained from past experience, even from the present. It must go on "for its own sake," for the future. This process is the birth of the sciences—those which concern ourselves as well as those concerned with the surrounding world. We now arrive at the fourth level.

We already have the makings of a modest science in the form of known means to ends. But the linkage of each bit of knowledge as a means to an end is the chain to the past. It makes a catalogue of our knowledge which can be enhanced only as new problems permit us to discover new means. What we need is a way in which knowledge of means alone will point to sources for new knowledge. This is achieved when we disconnect each means from its end and invent a new form of organization which binds our bits together as coherent knowledge of some extensive part or aspect of the world. Where we knew before, for example, that heat hardens clay and eggs but softens meat, we are now to forget about dishes and stews and concern ourselves with heat and with the structure and states of matter. Thus we transform knowledge from knowledge of means to tentative knowledge of the world.

This reorganization, remember, is not invented to give more practically useful structure to what we already know but to point to new things to know and new ways of disclosing knowledge. There is a dual significance to this function of scientific structure. In the first place, it means that the organization is still instrumental (not "real" or ultimate or "true") as was knowledge when organized as means. Only, the end has changed, and the instrument is a new instrument. The end is knowledge, the instrument is an instrument of enquiry. It is designed to show us how to create problems deliberately instead of waiting on them and how to create just those problems which will create new experiences to enlarge our body of knowledge. This is the activity of experiment and research.

To say that scientific knowledge is organized instrumentally is also to suggest the second significant point: that its organizing forms (atoms, electrons, wave-motion, reflex arcs, cultures, civilizations) are not the forms of things, an ultimate or "true" picture of a static world, but the forms which serve us well, in the present state of our knowledge, as means for pursuing more knowledge. In consequence, the forms will change. As they succeed, they change the state of our knowledge. New forms become necessary as the potential of the old ones is exhausted. So science, like practical knowledge, is fluid and dynamic.

This last fact has explosive meaning for the conduct of the school. It points to the pervasive place of reflection in all educative experience. The pervasive dynamism of things and knowledge, practical and theoretical, means that at no level of pragmatic space can education rest on inculcation only. There are no dependable patterns of reaction, no permanent catalogue of means and ends, not even a permanent body of scientific knowledge, which, once known, can be the unreflective basis of all other action and reflection. We need to reflect on our acts in the light of knowledge of means and ends and to reflect on this knowledge in the light of what science has to offer.

But this reflective motion downward from above is only half the story. Since scientific knowledge is couched in terms corresponding neither to "reality" nor to immediate human needs, we need to reflect on the relations of its conclusions to its forms and evidence in order even to know what it is about. Its conclusions make sense only in the light of the way they were formed. And the *use* of the conclusions presupposes reflection which transforms both the forms of scientific thought and the requirements of felt problems so that the two can be brought together.

Mirroring these needs, pragmatic intellectual space supposes two sets of reflective motions. There are, first, the motions which make each level: the trying-out which yields patterns of effective action; the cataloguing which yields knowledge of means and ends; the enquiring which yields science. But these cannot go on (or, if pursued, be completed) without reflection that oscillates between each level and the others. Seeing problems in the practical freshens the forms of enquiry; seeing practical possibilities in the structure of scientific knowledge enhances the life of everyday. These are the dynamics which link the levels to one another and enable them to serve their function in the system.

With the fifth and sixth levels of pragmatic space we shall deal very briefly. The pursuit of new scientific knowledge is guided by the organization with which we structured the old. This structure, embodied in such "theoretic" concepts as atom and electron, organ and organism, culture and civilization, cause and kind, creates and constrains the methods of science. The effectiveness of each science is thus determined or limited by the adequacy of its forming concepts. These may be more or less effective for the purposes of enquiry. But effective as they may be at any given time, they may reach the end of their usefulness, require refreshment or replacement. Hence, there must be reflection on the means and ends involved in the discovery of knowledge, a reflection that judges and measures. This is the level called Logic.

Finally, there must be an activity of supremely creative reflection, a process dedicated to the invention of new concepts, new logical forms by which to restructure knowledge and guide its increase. This is the level of Mathematics.

THE DYNAMICS	THE ACTIVITY	THE OUTCOME	THE NAME
5th →Reflection on knowledge of discovery	Invention of means and ends of discovery	Mathematics*
4th,→ Reflection on the conduct of discovery	Critical knowledge of scientific method	Logic
→ Reflection on ends and means; deliberate pursuit of experience	Knowledge organized for pursuit of further knowledge	Science, including the Social
→ Reflection on actions and consequences	Knowledge organized as tested ends and means	Technics; Practical Ethics
3d		
→ 2d Sensitive mastery of variable problematic situations	Flexible ways of acting in each such situation	Flexible habit; Artfulness
1st → → → Mastery of problematic situations	A way of acting in each such situation	Mere habit

* "Mathematics," as used here, covers more than the number system, algebra, and geometry taught in the schools. It includes all invention of formal devices and relations.

FIG. 1.—The levels and dynamics of pragmatic intellectual space

Let us summarize the scope of pragmatic intellectual space in the diagram in Figure 1. This diagram omits two extremely important matters. One is the place of art. The other is the dimension of human association and communication. Perhaps also there is a seventh discipline, "Critic," combining logic and mathematics and applying to the entire space. This would be the discipline used by Dewey himself.

We turn now from knowledge and knowing to what is known—to the subject matter of reflection. Of the three factors we shall have discussed, this one is the simplest. It may be put bluntly thus: no dependable, anticipatory judgment can tell us that *one* of the terms into which a problem can be analyzed is its first, most proper, or only principle. *All* the terms that men severally have recognized should be considered as relevant, interacting factors. Reflection is the better as it puts together what other men have put asunder. Where one man may judge a wrong-doer by his motive, a second by the effect of his act on others, a third by looking to upbringing as an extenuation, and so on, Dewey insists that all such factors must be considered. He puts it thus: "It is the business of an intelligent theory to ascertain the causes for the conflicts that exist and then, instead of taking one side or the other, to indicate a plan of operations proceeding from a level *deeper and more inclusive* than is represented by the practices and ideas of the contending parties."[1]

A glance at some of the epitomes spoken in Dewey's name will clarify the point. Let us begin with the following pair:

1. The school must educate for present living. Our tradition is a great one but its organization and content grew out of conditions and circumstances which are mostly over and done with. It must give way to what is live and real: to the conditions, the situations, the problems and instruments of the present.
2. A good education must be education for change. We live in a dynamic world. The present, by its very nature, is senescent. It is the blossoming future, with all its unknowns, that the child must be prepared to face.

Each of these, taken alone and without reflection, is plausible. But taken together they exhibit the "either-or," the signal that each is contributing a *part* of the story of education while ignoring the part contributed by the other. The first celebrates the present while ignoring the future and condemning the past. The second condemns both past and present in the interest of the future.

For Dewey, on the other hand, these parts of time were to be brought together. Reflection and enquiry take from the past and project toward the future. The learning experiences of the child, taking place in a childish present, are nevertheless to acquire a structure and organization as they extend over the weeks and months, embracing the formulated knowledge which we take as the gift of the past. Meanwhile the vivid presentness of experience serves the future by vivifying knowledge gained, insuring that it will be accessible as means to ends and as means for judging ends.

Let us take another pair:

3. We cannot impose a single norm on all individuals. Each differs from the other. A good education aims to develop whatever potentials each individual may possess. It identifies and then nurtures to maximum growth the uniqueness in each child.

1. John Dewey, *Experience and Education* (New York: Macmillan, 1939). Italics mine.

4. Man's sociality is an inescapable fact. Each of us finds our effectiveness and our satisfactions in concert with others. Education must, therefore, develop each child into an effective, co-operative member of a group, competent and happy in his social life.

Here, the obvious opposition lies between the members of that time-worn pair, the individual "versus" society. Number 3 harps on uniqueness without noting that even the "nurturing" it recommends is a social act in which the nurturer and the nurtured must have much in common if nurture is to succeed. The nurturer will sacrifice some of his uniqueness in order to serve the child, while the fact that the child will learn much from the teacher as a model will make them much alike. Meanwhile, Number 4, by the unexamined ambiguity of "sociality" leaves unvoiced the extent to which a group requires differentness, uniqueness, among its members, and the similar extent to which individuals are rendered a service severally as well as collectively by being a member of a group.

Dewey sought, in education, the mutuality which joined society and separate persons. Development of the potentialities special to each person, yes. But so that they be put in the service of society as well as in the service of the self. And development, too, of the common competences which serve society, but so that association may better serve the individual while individuals serve to improve the quality of association. Neither automatic conformity to socially accepted norms nor centrifugal scattering into privacies can be the useful rule. Where all conform, none question. There is no enquiry. Where belligerent individualism is the rule, we lose the fruits which require collaboration and, more important, lose the satisfaction of sharing, itself.

Let us end with two further specimens:

5. Ultimately, the goal of education can only be to provide means for adjustment to the environment. Man's means for meeting the conditions of life may be far richer than those of other species and his needs more complex. But in the last analysis, whether we seek merely to live or to live well, we share with all organisms our dependence on the environment.

6. To live is to do. It is a concrete shaping of events and things to serve our needs. Education too, unless it be for an ivory tower divorced from doing and undertaking, must occur through and for concrete doing and making. There is no place in it for the inactive, the abstract, the verbal; for academic "thought" and "logic" not focused on a concrete problem to be solved, an existent need to be fulfilled.

Between these two we see, first, the same kind of opposition visible in the others. Number 5 can speak of adjustment to the environment while giving hardly a hint of the fact that we may often (and perhaps much more satisfactorily) adjust the environment to ourselves. Number 6 is opposed to Number 5, but its emphasis raises another pair of factors. It attacks thought and logic, words and abstraction, with just the touch of ambiguity which leaves the unwary reader supposing that somehow these are alternative to action, to doing and making, rather than their aids and correctives. It leaves unvoiced the point that the active doing which Dewey commended to the schools was not for its own sake but as the occasion and condition for learning and reflection. To "learn by doing" was neither to learn only by doing nor to learn only how to do. Doing was to go hand in hand with reading, reflecting, and remembering. And these intelligent activities were to eventuate in something more than efficient coping with the bread-and-butter problems of existence. They were to yield the capacity for rewarding experience, a doing and undergoing not merely for the sake of the material outcome; often, not for that outcome at all, but for the satisfaction of the work itself. Here lies the region which involves enjoyment—of problems and of work, of art, and of our relations with our friends and neighbors.

In brief, Dewey's effort in his work on education was to join together many factors, not to substitute one for another. He was concerned to find the "deeper and more inclusive ideas" which would *relate* past and present, doing and thinking, individual and society. So also for terms we have not illustrated: work and play; art and life; ends and means; impulse, discipline, order, and spontaneity.

What, then, is the "impossible" role of the teacher in a progressive school and curriculum?

It consists, first, in the fact that the teacher must be a learner—even unto the fourth level of Dewey's intellectual space. It is not enough for the teacher to master certain ways of acting as a teacher. This is only a capable apprentice. It is not enough to be master of flexible ways of acting. This is only to be a competent "hand" who can function well when told what to do but who cannot himself administer. It is not even enough to possess organized knowledge of ways and means. This is to interpret a policy and tend to its efficient execution but not to be able to improve a policy or change it as problems change.

Only as the teacher uses the classroom as the occasion and the means to reflect upon education as a whole (ends as well as means), as the laboratory in which to translate reflections into actions and thus to test reflections, actions, and outcomes against many criteria, is he a good "progressive" teacher.

Meanwhile, he must be a teacher too. As a teacher, he must aim to carry all his students to the third dynamic of intellectual space, some to the fourth, and be alert to find those few who may go still farther. To aim for less than the third is to fail to test the possibility of a democratic society, to capitulate to the notion of Mass and Class—the latter managerial and manipulative; the former, managed servants, unaware.

· 7 ·

What Do Scientists Do?

Man is by nature metaphysical and proud.

Claude Bernard

AIMS AND PROBLEMS

Certain debates among scientists perennially reflower in their literature and their symposia and perennially fail of resolution. These debates concern the way in which enquiry should be conducted. Patterns of actual enquiries exhibit the same variety and persistence. Different scientists do different things. A mode of enquiry discredited by one scientist, dismissed at one time, discarded in one science, reappears and is fruitful in other hands, at other times, or in other sciences.

Three further points suffice to bound our problem. In the course of their professional lives, a few scientists change their habit of enquiry or the position they defend but many do not so change. Second, the practices and positions encountered (and the arguments in their defense) are remarkably constant from science to science and from epoch to epoch. Third, the order in which different modes of enquiry appear is *not* constant across different fields, different subject matters, different problems. What in one science is a starting point, in another is a middle or a climax.

To take account of these matters, we make four suppositions: (1) the alternative patterns of enquiry accessible to the man of science are few in number and capable of formulation; (2) a relatively stable personal preference contributes mightily to the view of a scientist about what ought to constitute his science; (3) these personal preferences represent a configuration of personality types among scientists which is relatively stable over time and sciences; (4) this personal factor and ephemerals of circumstance rather than inexorables of logic or of history often determine what is better or best for a given science or scientist at a given time.

This chapter was previously published in a slightly different form in *Behavioral Science* 5 (1960): 1–27.

What follows is the fruit of an effort to realize the first of these suppositions. It is also a framework through which to investigate the others. It consists of a scheme of the decision points in the process of enquiry and of the choices available at each such point.

The decision points and choices summarize what I have seen in some 4,000 scientific papers written by European and American scientists over the past five centuries in the biological sciences, the physical sciences, and three "behavioral" sciences. Most of the papers are from the last two centuries, from the biological sciences (including clinical medicine and psychiatry) and psychology.

THE DECISION POINTS

The six decision points, briefly sketched below, obviously do not include all the points which exist in and around enquiry. I have not considered decisions involved in larger operations for which enquiry is only a ploy; e.g., careers toward administrative and political functions; careers of popular authority and entertainment; the keeping of academic posts and the advancement of salary. I have also omitted such obvious and preliminary choices as that of science as a career and of a subject field in science.

Of the six decision points, three occur seriatim in the course of enquiry. Two others are labor-divisional choices in which some one phase of enquiry is chosen for repetition, eschewing the remainder of the process. The sixth represents a *0* choice which will replace our initial pretense that all scientific enquiries originate in efforts to make a contribution to knowledge of a subject matter.

The brief descriptions here are intended to serve only as a preliminary guide. Their full sense will be expanded later.

Point 1. Invention or selection of a form of principle for enquiry. Five forms of principle are available, three with subdivisions.

Point 2. Judgment of proposed principles relative to enquiry *in medias res.* Four criteria are used. None is wholly ignored, as a rule. Choice consists of the relative weighting given each of the criteria.

Point 3. Selection among alternative sets of specific terms for detailed enquiries. Two criteria are used. Unlike the criteria of Point 2, these two criteria are often weighted in ratios approaching 1:0.

Point 4. Selection of "stable" or of "fluid" enquiry; that is, the pursuit of conclusions with terms hypostasized or pursuit of conclusions as tests of the terms of the enquiry.

Point 5. Selection of one phase of enquiry for repeated endeavor. Although enquiry can be divided into at least five tasks capable of being executed independently of executing others, only three are commonly discriminated for choice by the working scientist.

Point 0. Displacement of "knowledge of the subject matter" by other desiderata determining researches pursued. Two alternatives are conspicuous.

THE FORMS OF PRINCIPLE FOR ENQUIRY (DECISION POINT 1)

We shall use "principle" to stand for the ideas which initiate and guide any planned activity. "Principle of enquiry" thus stands for the notions which initiate and guide the course of a line of research. The biologist who wonders "which of the virus strains causes distemper?" uses *cause* as one part of his principle and notions about the taxonomy of microorganisms, the relation of invaders to the body's economy, and of disease "entities" as other parts.

A principle of enquiry in this sense may arise from a doctrine consciously known and espoused by the scientist or it may be simply his habit, his unexamined way of recognizing his subject matter and his problems. Whatever its status in this respect, it remains, for our purposes, a principle of enquiry.

We are similarly indifferent to the original reference among philosophical commonplaces of a principle of enquiry. It may originally specify the nature of things, of method, of "mind" or knowledge without affecting its status for us as a principle of enquiry.

A group of notions achieve the status of principle of enquiry when they succeed in *bounding* and *analyzing* a subject matter so as to make it fit for enquiry. Bounding is exemplified when, say, a primitive psychology conceives "learning" as the retention of nonsense materials under conditions which minimize or exclude motivational factors and interpersonal relations. It is seen when economists discriminate a "free market"; when factors of shape and medium are excluded from kinematics; when the distinction of chemical and physical change restricts the subject matter of chemical enquiry. It is seen again when a primitive physiology conceives its "organism" as that which (a) stops at the skin, (b) during maturity, (3) under "normal" conditions.

The analytic function of principles consists in identifying the meaning-units or meaning-elements which are to be treated in enquiry into the subject matter. Thus a primitive physiology treats its organism as constituted of organs and their functions. The principles of another physiology identify homeostases and their supporting mechanisms as the elements of research. A third (within a different bounding) conceives the organism as a chemical-energetic system indefinitely interpenetrating an environment.

More disparate forms of principle are seen in the Freudian personality with its psychic organs and functions, by contrast to the Sullivan-ian in which "I" am the intersect of my friends and enemies and they, in turn, are the intersects of me and others.

The first specific service of principles to the course of enquiry is to provide it with terms in which to couch its problems. Thus, for our primitive physiology, the problem of enquiry is of the form, "What is the function of Organ X?" or, "What organ performs function Y?"

By way of the terms of the problem, the principle then determines what shall constitute the data required by the enquiry and outlines the procedure which will elicit the required data. Thus our physiologist must know what alterations in the behavior of the organism ensue upon suppression of a part, and he is instructed to remove an organ and contrast the deprived animal with a normal one.

Finally, the principles of an enquiry restrict the form which knowledge of the subject will take by indicating how the data are to be interpreted. Thus, an organ-function physiology leads to a catalog of assertions of the form, "The function of X is Y."

Of principles in this sense, we find five kinds: reductive, rational, holistic, anti-principled and primitive. Reductive, holistic, and anti-principled principles are each represented by subspecies. (The historian of philosophy will find none of these unfamiliar. Plato, Aristotle, Augustine, Plotinus, Comte, Mill, Mach, Whitehead, *et al.*, appear to have influenced a certain number of scientists—or to have read a certain amount of modern scientific literature.)

Reductive Principles

Reductive principles are the grey flannels of enquiry; serviceable and wearable almost anywhere by anybody. They rest on the notion that things are as they are because of what they are made of. A subject of enquiry is treated, not as a thing which is, but as a something constituted. The scientific account is sought in the constituents.

Atomic Reduction

If one insists on recognizing *orders* of phenomena, the stage is set for atomic reductive principles. The world is seen as literally *compounded*, in the style of a nest of Chinese boxes. Thus physical particles constitute the organizations called chemical. Chemicals constitute each physiological. Society is the structure of physiologicals.

Comte, of course, is the familiar spokesman for such a view. It is in deference to him that I have made the hierarchy read as it does. We would currently need to state it thus: physicals, chemicals, biologicals, psychologicals, socials.

Says Comte, "to study social phenomena one must start from a thorough knowledge of the laws pertaining to the individual."[1] This states the paradigm which atomic reductions copy or outdo. Atomic reduction would embark upon an enquiry by more or less abandoning the subject of interest in favor of a study of the behavior and properties of its immediate constituents. Thus the behavior of human groups is treated as a function of their physiology; physiological knowledge is sought in terms of chemistry; and chemical phenomena are explained in terms of the masses, charges, positions, and motions of physical units. Pavlov's *physiological* reflexes as the determining constituents of behavior and the multi-enzyme system as the determining constituent of the organism are modern cases in point. In general, constituents are treated as determinative of the constituted and never the reverse.

Two varieties of this doctrine can be distinguished, though they do not deserve the privilege of a nomenclature. On the one hand, there is the variety which departs from Comte's paradigm. In this belligerently held version, the subject of interest is abandoned as the subject of enquiry. It is enough to know the constituents in their virgin state—not as constituents but as solitary items. From their properties seen in that condition, says this extreme view of reduction, we can infer, and predict, the organizations into which they might enter and the character that would result.

In the more temperate version, the subject of interest is not abandoned. It is treated as serving two necessary functions. Through it, one finds the properties and behaviors which are to be accounted for by a study of constituents. Second, it is only by way of behaviors exhibited in the constituted order of phenomena that one can detect some of the most important properties of the constituent elements, since some of these properties will be potencies exhibited only in unions and combinations. Thus, it is in a study of the properties of chemical compounds that the chemist locates many of the problems he proposes to solve by study of their elements; and it is in the processes of combination and separation that important properties (e.g., valence) of the elements are seen.

Modern reductions depart from the Comtean pattern in still another way. The reduction may leap several steps at once down the Comtean hierarchy to rest on some constitutive factor held to be determinative of the behavior of all or several "orders" of phenomena. (And the determining constituents may be immaterial.) We have, for example:

1. A. Comte, "A Course of Positive Philosophy," trans. A. C. Benjamin, in University of Chicago, The College, *History of the Organization of the Sciences* (Chicago: University of Chicago Press, 1943).

The problem of the physical sciences is thus finally determined; to reduce the natural phenomena to unalterable, attractive and repulsive forces whose intensity depends upon the distance.

. . . Its task will be complete when the reduction of phenomena to simple forces is complete, and when at the same time, it can be proved that the given reduction is the only possible one which the phenomena admit. Then this reduction would have been proved to be the necessary conceptual form of the theory of nature; so there would then be justified as well the ascription to it of the objective truth.[2]

In these several versions of reduction, the constant mark consists in the fact that causal efficacy is wholly located in the chosen constitutive elements. The constant mark of atomic reduction consists in the fact that the efficacious elements are treated as of a different order from the constituted subject.

An atomic reductive bias in the scientist (especially its belligerent version) is often used to relegate ultimate responsibility for the soundness of knowledge to the scientist of the lower order of phenomena while the investigator of the higher order maintains an amateur status which yet permits him to flaunt before his non-reductive colleagues a prestigious knowledge they do not possess. A great deal of this was visible in physiology before biochemistry and physics were common requirements in the field. Mathematics is currently used in a number of fields in the same way.

(Piety requires me to remark that Comte was not himself a heavily biased reductionist. What appears to be that in the *Positive Philosophy* is only an installment of a story which is completed in the *Positive Polity*. In the story as a whole, there are three related "methods": "objective," "subjective," and "synthetical." The first is atomic reductive; the second is what we shall describe as "rational"; the third is partly rational and partly a union of enquiry, morals, and social action into a single process.)

Molecular Reduction

As in other cases, brothers in science are likely to quarrel more bitterly than cousins: those who espouse molecular reductive principles bitterly dislike atomic reduction. B. F. Skinner exemplifies the point, and in such wise that he provides an apt statement of the distinction between the two subspecies while nicely illustrating the affect which

2. H. Von Helmholtz, "Uber Die Erhaltung der Kraft" (1847), trans. H. Stein, in University of Chicago, The College, *Relation of Physical and Biological Sciences* (Chicago: University of Chicago Press, 1955).

marks such choices. The object of Mr. Skinner's first aversion is a holistic principle.

> Behavior has that kind of complexity or intricacy which discourages simple description and in which magical explanatory concepts flourish abundantly. Primitive systems of behavior first set the pattern by placing the behavior of man under the direction of entities beyond man himself. . . . In more advanced systems . . . , the ultimate direction and control have been assigned to entities placed within the organism and called psychic or mental. Nothing is gained by this strategem. . . . Some conceptions of the "mind" and its faculties, and more recently the "ego," "super-ego," and "id" are examples of inner agents or organisms, designed to account for behavior. . . .[3]

He now moves in on atomic reduction:

> The important advance from this level of explanation that is made by turning to the nervous system as a controlling entity has unfortunately had a similar effect in discouraging a direct descriptive attack on behavior. The change is an advance because the new entity beyond behavior . . . has a definite physical status of its own. . . . Its chief function with regard to a science of behavior, however, is again to divert attention away from behavior as a subject matter. . . . The more sophisticated neurological views generally agree with the popular view in contending that behavior is itself incomprehensible but may be reduced to law if it can be shown to be controlled by an internal system. . . . Facts about behavior are not treated in their own right, but are regarded as something to be explained or even explained away by the prior facts of the nervous system. . . . Worst of all, it [physiological behaviorism] carried on the practice of seeking a solution for the problems of behavior elsewhere than in behavior itself. . . . The altogether too obvious alternative to a mental science was a neural science. The possibility of a directly descriptive science of behavior and its peculiar advantages has received little attention.[4]

3. Mr. Skinner has the distinction of being one of the first American scientists to use "magical" instead of "metaphysical" as a major epithet. However, the fact that epithets of this kind are not the exclusive property of the "hard fact" men is seen in the following: "During the 1920's and 1930's psychologists were, on the whole, rather averse to theory. Governed by a naive metaphysical belief, they were apt to consider 'fact finding' the only task of 'scientific' psychology . . ." (Kurt Lewin, *Field Theory in Social Science* [New York: Harper, 1951]).

4. B. F. Skinner, *The Behavior of Organisms* (New York: Appleton-Century-Crofts, 1938). The attack on a holistic principle in this paragraph is obscured by a simultaneous attack on anything without a "physical status."

First, then, the demolition of holistic principles and nonphysical terms: "magical concepts," "strategems," "mind," "ego, super-ego, and id." This is followed by attack on atomic reductions (neurology and physiological behaviorism) and praise of treatment of the phenomena of behavior "in their own right." The latter phrase is the common presenting symptom of preference for molecular reductive principles.[5] Skinner then proceeds to bound his preferred subject matter ("Behavior is what an organism is doing—having commerce with the outside world") with a further exhibition of his presenting symptom: "the peculiar properties which make behavior a unitary and unique subject matter."

He now thrusts at one form of anti-principled principle:

> We may proceed to a kind of description of behavior by giving a running account of a sample of behavior as it unfolds itself in some frame of reference. This is a typical method in natural history and is employed extensively in current work. . . . It may be described as narration. . . . From data obtained in this way it is possible to classify different kinds of behavior, it is not a science in the accepted sense. We need to go beyond mere observation of a study of functional relationships. We need to establish laws. . . .[6]

Skinner is now ready to describe and praise his own reductive molecule:

> It is presumably not possible to show that behavior as a whole is a function of the stimulating environment as a whole. A relation between terms as complex as these does not easily submit to analysis and may perhaps never be demonstrated. The environment enters into a description of behavior when it can be shown that a given part of behavior may be induced at will by a modification in part of the forces affecting the organism. Such a part of the environment . . . is traditionally called a *stimulus* and the correlated part of the behavior a *response*. Neither term may be defined as to its essential properties without the other. For the observed relation between them, I shall use the term *reflex*.
> The difference between the demonstration of a reflex and mere narration is . . . that no lawful relation . . . is asserted. . . .

5. For a further example of this presenting symptom, see Emile Durkheim, *The Rules of Sociological Method* (Glencoe, Il.: The Free Press, 1950), chap. 1. It is interesting and touching that whereas most psychologists can now take physiology or leave it alone, a great many sociologists are still extremely tetchy about psychology. Thrice in a week I have heard young sociologists respond to a remark by the phrase, "Well, if you *must* psychologize. . . ."

6. Skinner, *Behavior of Organisms*. "Mere" rivals "metaphysical" as a favored epithet in defenses of form of principle.

The story is told simply of something that has once happened. The isolation of a reflex, on the other hand, is the demonstration of a predictable uniformity of behavior. In some form or other, it is an inevitable part of any science of behavior. . . . Current objections to the reflex on the ground that in the analysis we destroy the very thing we are trying to understand, scarcely calls for an answer. We always analyze. It is only good sense to make the act explicit. . . .

So defined a reflex is not, of course, a theory. It is a fact. It is an analytical unit, which makes an investigation of behavior possible. . . .[7]

Molecular reduction is, then, the effort to find the irreducible minimum of the subject matter under investigation. Among such paradigmatic molecules we have "the family" of one political sociology, the "cell" of nineteenth-century general physiology and the "two-person group" of some recent sociology.[8] In the case of B. F. Skinner, the telling sentence is: "Neither term [stimulus, response] may be defined as to its essential properties without the other."[9] That is, the reflex, constituted of stimulus and response, is asserted as the ultimate reduction *of behavior*. If what "stimulus" names is discussed apart from "response" (as it can be), the conversation is no longer about behavior but about something else—physical or meteorological or chemical phenomena. Similarly, "response" without "stimulus" would be physiology or biochemistry, not behavior, and, for that reason, unacceptable.

From the point of view of enquiry as against enquirers, molecular reduction tends to shade off toward the atomic by invoking numerous *different* elements as determinative constituents. Pre-Mendelevian chemistry is a case in point; so also the general physiology which moved from "the" cell to three, five, or ten kinds of cells (e.g., secretory, epithelial, nervous, muscular, germ). A similar psychology would arise from an attempt to discriminate classes of reflexes and to account for complex behaviors as combinations. Even in such cases, however, the personal loyalty of the enquirer appears to attach to the molecular character of the simple: that it is a simple which is peculiarly chemical and not physical; or social and not psychological; or behavioral and not neural.

7. Ibid. Scattered through these quotations are indications of a choice at Decision Point 3. We shall deal with this later.

8. The phrase "dyadic group" frequently replaces my "two-person group," not only because it sounds impressive but because it better asserts the "right" unit; i.e., a dyadic group is *a* something with two parts, not two somethings interacting. It is a social molecule, not psychological atoms—as Skinner's "reflex" is a psychological molecule whose wholeness is not to be divided.

9. Ibid.

The fact that molecular reductions are incomplete principles of enquiry lends credence to this hypothesis. Unlike atomic reduction to a field of enquiry which has terms already laid down, the molecular reduction requires further invention. Given the stimulus-response reflex, for example, the enquirer must still decide what to observe or measure about that molecule and how to interpret his data. For this purpose he must append additional factors and these may be taken from one of the other forms of principle: holistic, rational, anti-principles—even atomic reductive. In brief, molecular reduction often serves only to dignify the science by asserting the existence of a unique subject matter requiring its service.

> Practically all sociologists now demand a separate existence for their science; but . . . the common-sense view still holds that sociology is a superstructure built upon the substratum of the individual consciousness. . . .
>
> What is so readily judged inadmissible in the matter of social facts is freely admitted in the other realms of nature. Whenever certain elements combine and thereby produce, by the fact of their combination, new phenomena, it is plain that these new phenomena reside not in the original elements but in the totality formed by their union. The living cell contains nothing but mineral particles, as society contains nothing but individuals. Yet it is patently impossible for the phenomena characteristic of life to reside in the atoms of hydrogen, oxygen, carbon, and nitrogen. . . .[10]

And from the psychiatrist Maslow:

> This conclusion exposes the essentially theoretical nature of the entire reductive effort. . . . It is simply a reflection or implication in science of an atomistic, mechanical world view that we now have good reason to doubt.[11]

Holistic Principles

Holistic principles are most conspicuous in the frankly taxonomic sciences—zoology, botany, mineralogy—and in physiology from William Harvey to recent times. Holistic principles require an account of the subject matter of interest in terms of the combination of qualities or constituents which, as organized, sets that subject matter apart from all others. Parts or constituents are used, as in atomic reductive principles, but the properties of the constituent factors do not provide an

10. Durkheim, *Rules of Sociological Method*, p. xlvii.
11. Abraham H. Maslow, *Motivation and Personality* (New York: Harper and Row, 1951).

adequate or complete account of the whole. *That* is sought in the whole itself, as well as in the parts. Indeed, some properties of the constituents are sometimes treated as conferred by their place in the organization of which they are parts. For this reason, such principles are sometimes called "organic." The original Aristotelian prescription of such principles is still viable:

> the organizing principle is the starting point in natural things as it is in those things which are made by man. Consider how the physician or the builder sets about his work. He starts by setting for himself a definite picture, the physician, of health, the builder, of a house. This picture he uses as the guide and explanation of each subsequent step that he takes. . . . In the works of nature, the organizing principle is even more dominant than in works of art such as these. . . .
>
> . . . there is also a factor manifested which may be called contingent necessity. For if a house or other such object is to be realized, it is necessary that such and such material shall exist; and it is necessary that first this and then that shall be produced—and so on. . . . So also is it with the production of nature. The starting point for living things is that which is to be. But this, being of such-and-such characters, necessitates the previous existence or production of this and that antecedent. . . .
>
> The fittest mode, then, of treatment is to say, a man has such and such parts because the organization of man includes their presence and because they are necessary conditions of his existence.[12]

And from Maslow:

> One essential characteristic of holistic analysis of the personality . . . is that there be a preliminary study or understanding of the total organism, and that we then proceed to study the role that our part of the whole plays in the organization and dynamics of the total organism.[13]

Formal-material holistic principles

Formal-material holistic principles follow the Aristotelian prescription in assigning roles to both the material constituents and to the organized whole. For example,

> The atom, we now find, is . . . a mechanism or organism in which the properties of the whole depend not *solely* on the nature of its parts but *also* on the peculiar relatedness of its parts;

12. Paraphrased from *Parts of Animals*, 1.1.
13. Maslow, *Motivation and Personality*.

while an organic molecule . . . is, again, a mechanism or organism in which the properties of the whole depend upon the relatedness of its parts as well as upon their nature. Now for *descriptive* purposes, and for visualization, the parts of the atom or molecule must be in our minds; and we cannot therefore dispense with the results of analysis. Yet in spite of such knowledge of the parts certain fundamental properties of the *whole* will elude us in each case unless we study it while intact. We can only properly define the whole in terms of its activities. . . . In all cases structure, internal events, and functions must be thought of as inseparable if we are to grasp the essential nature of such systems. . . .[14]

In a less dramatic form, such a principle is seen in a physiology which first assigns certain necessary activities to the organism (e.g., ingestion, digestion, excretion, reproduction, etc.) and then describes each organ, tissue, and enzyme-system by reference to what it contributes to one or another of these defining activities and how it does so.

Formal holistic principles

When the distinguishing character of the subject of interest is treated as capable of embodiment in any one of a variety of materials or sets of parts, the holistic principle becomes formal. Enquiry guided by such a view may use material parts as evidence of the character of the whole since they are taken as effects or requisites of it, but the stable object of enquiry is the pattern, organization, or form exhibited *via* the material. For example:

Democracy—like forms of group living—cannot be defined adequately by isolated elements of conduct, rules or institutions; it is the larger *pattern* of group life and the group atmosphere which determines how society is to be classified.[15]

and from Maslow again,

Since these specificities have the same source or function or aim, they are interchangeable and may actually be thought to be psychological synonyms of one another. . . .[16]

Such enquiries entail a search for a variety of embodiments. One set of material parts, being only one means of expression, may, as stub-

14. J. Needham and E. Baldwin, eds., *Hopkins and Biochemistry, 1861–1947* (Cambridge: W. Heffer and Sons, 1949), pp. 179–90.
15. Kurt Lewin, "Group Living: Autocratic, Democratic, and Laissez-faire," in *Modern Political Thought*, ed. W. Ebenstein (New York: Rinehart, 1954).
16. Maslow, *Motivation and Personality*.

born matter, either fail to express the full pattern or mix its own properties with it. Hence, the nature of culture is sought in cross-cultural
study. The nature of the organism is sought through numerous experiments in which parts are altered and the coordinate changes in all other
parts are scrutinized in order to determine the stable pattern which is
reconstituted by all such sets of changes.[17]

Needless to say, the exponents of such principles, dubbed mystics, do
as they are done by, especially to atomic reductionists; e.g.,

> . . . the orthodox credulity with which so many writers continue
> to refer to the "mechanisms" of various living activities is to
> my mind pathetic in its blind clinging to what has come to be
> regarded as a sacred scientific authority.[18]

It is worth noting that holistic principles share with molecular reductions an emphasis on the apartness of the subject of interest. It must be
studied "in its own terms." I suspect, however, that a factor analytic
study would show that scientists' adhesion to holistic principles is heavily loaded with a passion for wholeness or something of which wholeness is symbolic rather than with a need to create an independent domain of investigation.

Rational Principles

If atomic reduction seeks its likely story in "downward" terms, while
moleculars and holists try for a statement of the subject in its own
terms, there is a remaining malapropic possibility: reduction upward.
Principles of this kind require that the subject of interest be seen as
given its character by its place in some larger determinative whole or
by some *ratio* imposed from without.[19] Such a principle is seen in one
of its simplest guises in socially dominated theories of personality in
which the human organism is treated as a nearly blank slate on which
the society writ small is what is mistaken for a person.

Most such principles have a distinct Platonic, Cartesian, or Deistic
cast. That is, the process of determination is rarely referred to a *vera
causa* or to specified processes, as introjection and identification are

17. See, for example, J. S. Haldane, "The Universe in Its Biological Aspect," in his *Materialism* (London: Hodder and Stoughton, 1932).

18. Ibid.

19. A word about the word "rational." In this context it does not mean
—honorifically—logical, reasonable, or sane, thus suggesting that other principles are unreasonable, "merely empirical," or insane. Nor does it mean, as
does the pejorative "rational*istic*," the elaboration of "self-evident" premises
into conclusions to be accepted without recourse to empirical data. What it
does mean, the text will try to show. My apology for the misleading word
is that I can find no better one.

used by some of the conservative social personologies. Rather, the determiner is seen as some sort of rational structure of relations with no particular *relata* (a "configuration"), either subsisting in its own right or as the defining part of the material, determinative surround. The Keplerian conic sections, the relativity field (insofar as it is not the product of objects in the field), and Lewin's psychological field (in part), are cases in point.

Einstein succinctly describes this rationality as follows:

> When I speak here of "comprehensibility" the expression is used at first only in its minimal signification. It signifies that by the creation of universal concepts and relations among these concepts, and also by stable relations established somehow or other between concepts and sense-experience, the latter are brought into some sort of order. . . .
>
> All that is essential is that attempt to present the manifold of concepts and propositions which are close to experience as propositions logically derivable from a basis—as narrow as possible—of fundamental relations which can in themselves be freely chosen [axioms]. . . .[20]

By "a Platonic, Cartesian, or Deistic cast," I mean to suggest a common quality of the enquiring principles but not to suggest that idealist metaphysical views are necessarily espoused. What justification will be used in defense of such principles is hardly predictable beyond the fact that very frequently they will be asserted to be "best" or "true" or "most widely accepted" science. Clark Hull's book, *Principles of Behavior* is a case in point.[21] Here, amid echoes of J. S. Mill, William Whewell and more recent logicians, deductive systems (involving primary terms which are hardly Keplerian or Einsteinian) are defended partly on the ground that if empirical generalizations can be incorporated into a deductive system, *post facto*, their credibility is somehow enhanced.

It should be noted that rationally instituted theories are not to be taken as identical with bodies of theory presented as deductive systems. The mark of a rational system is not in its form but in its content. It consists of assignment of causal efficacy "upward," whether to the configuration of a material "whole" of which the subject of interest is a "part" or to a Platonic-Cartesian *ratio*. Though some deductive systems

20. Albert Einstein,"Physik und realität," in University of Chicago, The College, *Methods of the Sciences*, 6th ed. (Chicago: University of Chicago Press, 1955).

21. Clark L. Hull, *Principles of Behavior* (New York: D. Appleton-Century, 1943), chaps. 1 and 20.

are fruits of enquiry pursued in this way, some are not. The deductive structure may be merely imposed on the results of enquiries instituted by other principles, e.g., the Clark Hull material cited above. (See also the section on Imposition of Deductive Structures.) On the other hand, a theory developed in terms of a rational principle may be presented apart from a formal, deductive system.

A further difficulty exists in the distinction of rational from formal-holistic principles since the latter appeal to a *ratio* as do some of the former. The distinction rests on the fact that the *ratio* of formal-holistic principles is something peculiar to the whole investigated while the *ratio* of rational schemes is a form whose variants or subspecies reign over greater reaches of investigable phenomena. Thus the normal curve, other probability functions, exponentials and other algebraic functions are characteristic *ratios* of rational schemes since they may be applied indifferently to the investigation of any subject matter or all subject matters.

The fact that ratios are characteristic of formal-holistic schemes as well as of rationals also complicates somewhat the question of who prefers what among principles. Two pairs of factors intersect one another in this case. On the one hand, there is the choice between universal and local subject matters. On the other hand, there may also be a tendency to prefer *ratios* as such or to reject them as such. Thus four classes are generated, only three of which are readily identifiable. A preference for *ratios* and for a local subject matter is satisfied by formal-holistic operation. Preference for *ratios* and for a universal subject matter yields rational schemes. Rejection of *ratios* and preference for local subject matter can be satisfied with formal-material holistics. But rejection of *ratios* and preference for a universalized subject matter constitute an extremely obscure class. These may be the men who practice holistic enquiries but persistently preach vague or arbitrary sermons about the need for synthesis, integration, or unity of the sciences.

By contrast to such ordered structures as those of Einstein, von Neumann, and others, an entirely *ad hoc* example is seen in the following:

> Thus in general, the spatio-temporal pattern of activity would be determined . . . by three factors: (i) the microstructure of the neural net and its functional properties; (ii) the afferent input; (iii) the postulated "field of extraneous influence". . . .
>
> It can be claimed that no physical instrument would bear comparison with the postulated performance of the active cerebral cortex as a detector of minute "fields of influence" spread over a microscopic pattern and with temporal sequences of milliseconds. The integration, within a few milliseconds, of "influence" picked up at hundreds of thousands of nodes would be

unique, particularly when it is remembered that the integration is no mere addition, but is exerted to modify in some specific way "a shifting harmony of sub-patterns" of neuronal activity, achieving expression through the modifications so produced.

Thus the neurophysiological hypothesis, is that the "will" modifies the spatio-temporal activity of the neuronal network by exerting spatio-temporal "fields of influence" that become effective through this unique detector function of the active cerebral cortex. . . .[22]

Anti-principles

The most conspicuous of anti-principles arise from and embody the familiar view that science ought to avoid principles all together (or may avoid them without loss) and be content to report the facts. What properly constitutes "the" facts then becomes the covert issue of principle. The schism on this score creates two large departments.

A third department arises from modern vestiges of the view that some things of this world are not lawful—or are otherwise insusceptible of scientific enquiring.

"Laws of Nature"

On the one hand, "the facts" take the form of "laws"—algebraic or verbal equations whose terms are alleged to be in one-to-one correspondence with sense-experienced and "objectively" discrete aspects of the subject matter. Thus, "the facts" are the sensible covariances of measurable parameters. It should be emphasized that the mathematics involved in such enquiries is treated as a system of notation or measurement. There is abhorrence of the rationalist notion that mathematical functions express rational structures to which the world might be expected to conform. Indeed, anti-principle equations might well run to seven or eight powers were it not for the relative ease with which one parameter can usually be split into two or three when the number of inflection points grows too big for comfort. Mach's familiar strictures on Galileo constitute a case in point:

> In Galileo's conception of the universe, the *formal, mathematical*, and *esthetical* point of view predominates. . . . The planetary system had not yet taken the shape of a *genuine physical problem* for him.[23]

22. John C. Eccles, *The Neurophysiological Basis of Mind* (Oxford: Clarendon Press, 1953), p. 277.
23. E. Mach, *The Science of Mechanics* (Chicago, Il.: Open Court, 1902). Italics mine.

This theme is addressed to Newton with even greater violence by Karl Pearson:

> I have accordingly expressed my own views on the subject; these may be concisely described as a strong desire to see the terms matter and force, together with the ideas associated with them, entirely removed from scientific terminology, to reduce, in fact, all dynamics to kinematics.[24]

"Causes"

Elsewhere one finds "the facts" defined as antecedent-consequent "causation." This way of enquiring differs in no important wise from the J. S. Millsian formula. The world is seen as a web of partial uniformities whose separate strands—of invariant antecedent-consequent relations —are the only proper objects of enquiry. The webbing, itself, the frequent or invariant recurrence of N antecedent-consequent strands to constitute, e.g., a man or a swan, is treated as a locus of problems but not *as* a problem for enquiry.

For the purposes of an etho-psychological study of the scientist, it is useful to note that the causal anti-principle is Millsian also in the fact that it invites the "method of differences" in all its compact neatness as the basic experimental design. Indeed, both forms of anti-principles correspond to the textbook ideal of "the controlled experiment."

Adherence to this anti-principle in opposition to concern for the webbing or whole as constituting the central problem of enquiry lies at the base of much of the perennial strife over "teleology" in the biological sciences. It is rarely the case that "teleology" is, in fact, espousal of a notion of a conscious "wisdom of the body" or a similar conscious wisdom on the part of birds or earthworms. Partisan attack will often so describe it, but the researches attacked usually disclose only that the researcher has embraced a material-formal holism. He treats the distinguishable parts and processes of the organism as matters fully understood only when interrelated, as constituting a whole, the organism. In Aristotelian terms, formal and final causes are identified: that which is the final cause and that which is the formal cause are taken as the same —the mature organism; and an account of efficient and material causes is given in terms of the role or function of, the service performed by, each efficient cause relative to the whole going concern. It is this account which is deemed "unscientific" by adherents to causal antiprinciples. (In animal behavior studies [e.g., E. S. Russell] the opposition is made more poignant by translation of the "going" concern into one or several massive *hormes*, as food, nesting, mating, etc.)

24. Quoted in W. K. Clifford, *The Common Sense of the Exact Sciences* (New York: Knopf, 1946), p. xiv.

In attempting to identify studies guided by the causal anti-principle, it is important that it be not confused with concern for described or narrated facts in general. Publications consisting of "pure" description or narration are often preludes to studies whose controlling notion is quite otherwise. The most "teleological" of embryological investigations may involve numerous publications of plates, drawings, and verbal descriptions devoid of coherent interpretation in those particular papers. The same holds for accounts of animal behavior, individual and group human behavior, physiological and biochemical studies, which may be holistic, atomic reductive, or even rational in their completed form.

Finally, it should be noted that biologists and psychologists adherent to these anti-principles have an extremely hard time being faithful. The word and the notion of function creep in time and again; so does "teleology" in the guise of "drive," "anticipation," "adaptive value," "operant behaviors." I suspect that the anti-principled scientist's losing struggle to defend his virtue is due to the exigent demands of the organism as a subject-in-fact.

Particularities

One or another plausible distinction between what is matter for enquiry and what is insusceptible to scientific investigation have been commonplaces of "philosophies of science" since Aristotle. The line was early drawn between non-living material on the one hand, and life, human life, art, and morals on the other, all the latter being distinguished as "free" in some sense where matter was "fated" or obedient to law.

This location of the dividing line persisted through almost the end of the nineteenth century. Physicians spoke up from the floor of Medical Society meetings to reject general statements about organisms and about disease as, *qua* general, contrary to fact. (Even Claude Bernard, apostle of positive science, was constrained at one point to describe the organism as held in lawful bounds only by the constraints of the physical environment.) And, of course, the free will of man was interpreted by many as placing human behavior, and especially the behavior of valuing, far beyond the limits of the investigable.

It is often said that modern scientists make no such distinction, on the ground that the only persuasive demonstration that some class of matters is incapable of scientific investigation is the durable failure of efforts to investigate them. This is not the universal view, however. The line has been moved up but not off. Sporadic but not rare expressions of scientists now place it so as to mark off particular events, and especially the particular human event (whether social or individual) as beyond the scope of scientific enquiry, however effective enquiry may be in dealing with *classes* of events.

Some truth lies back of this, of course. The scope of an enquiry rarely includes the full richness of its subject matter and what is omitted from its formulations is most vividly seen in the individual case which acts "contrary to the scientific law" because what is acting is something more complex than the subject-of-enquiry subsumed in the "law" in question. It is also the case, however, that, quickly or slowly, enquiries expand their purview to include more and more of the details which constitute their subjects, and there is no substantial reason to suppose that this expansion has limits (sub-atomic particles excepted) prior to the limits of the subject matter itself. We shall further discuss this aspect of enquiry later, under the heading of "Validity." Meanwhile, we must leave a place among the ranks of the "anti-principled" for the view that science should not spend its substance on certain problems because they are incapable of solution. A case in point is Franz Boas:

> it seems justifiable to question whether any generalized conclusions may be expected that will be applicable everywhere and that will reduce the data of anthropology to a formula which may be applied to every case, explaining its past and predicting its future.
>
> I believe that it would be idle to entertain such hopes. The phenomena of our science are so individualized, so exposed to outer accident that no set of laws could explain them. It is as in any other science dealing with the actual world surrounding us. For each individual case we can arrive at an understanding of its determination by inner and outer forces, but we cannot explain its individuality in the form of laws. . . .
>
> In short, the material of anthropology is such that it needs must be a historical science, one of the sciences the interest of which centers in the attempt to understand the individual phenomena rather than in the establishment of general laws which, on account of the complexity of the materials, will be necessarily vague and, we might also say, so self-evident that they are of little help to a real understanding.[25]

Primitive Principles

John Dewey pointed out that one of the origins of knowledge of subject matters (scientific knowledge) is in the effort to codify and extend knowledge of ways and means (commonsense knowledge). This partial dependence of science on common sense is usually conceived as expressed in only two contexts: historically, in the sense that the origin

25. Franz Boas, *Race, Language, and Culture* (New York: Macmillan, 1955), pp. 257–58.

of science as an enterprise is thus explained; and sociologically, in the sense that social approval and disapproval of scientific enquiries via the status accorded, financial support afforded or withheld and so on, go far toward determining what enquiries proceed and which are retarded or stopped.

In point of fact, however, there is a third expression—an ontogenetic repetition of phylogeny. Immature sciences and sciences in moments of frustration and regression often refresh their enquiries by renewed contact with the earth of common sense. Conceptual frames which never were or which seem to be exhausted are replaced by numerous *ad hoc* investigations framed in the terms of the queries which would normally speak to practical problems.

For example, one current investigation of cancer discards all conceptions of the micro-chemistry and biology of the cell in favor of *ad hoc* tests of the effects of an array of chemicals chosen almost at random. Political scientists ask such questions as, "What filiations and adhesions are correlated with the voting behavior of such-and-such group?" "How did Smith reach his present position of power?" "Who actually controls such-and-such?" Thus scientists ape the questions men ask in order to plan a political campaign, a personal career, or other efforts to get one's way. Studies of small groups in terms of what will increase the efficiency of workers and their loyalty to management is another case in point. So also some studies of learning in terms of the enhancement of scholastic achievement.

On "Models" and "Model-Building"

"Model" and "model-building" are currently words with which to conjure, though not yet, like God and Game Theory, spelled with uppercase initials. Their referents add little to the scheme of principles so far described but require comment nonetheless since they represent emphases which bestow some advantages on enquiries under certain circumstances.

A heterogeneity of four activities and devices are found labeled as models by enquirers. Two of them instance or approximate the use of rational principles; one represents the attempt to incorporate the fruits of an enquiry into deductive structures; the fourth is simply the self-conscious use of plausible analogies.

Rational models

Full and explicit use of rational structures as "models" is exemplified by the attempt to relate any large-scale mathematical structure, such as Game Theory or a probabilistic calculus, to a body of phenomena.

Thus, the activity is pretty much the same as Einstein's application of Riemannian geometry to space, including the premises underlying that application, the operations required, and the fruits which accrue.

The premise concerns the mathematically ordered or orderable structure of the phenomena in question. Either the world is ordered in this way or it is heuristically valuable to constrain those portions of it which will so submit to the structure of a logical scheme.

The operations involved are simply describable but extremely difficult in practice. Factors are sought in the subject matter which can be assigned as the referents of some of the terms of the mathematical structure. By this means, the theorems (and corollaries thereof) of the mathematical structure are transformed into existential assertions. The truth or falsehood of these existential assertions are then tested. If the tests reveal that the effort is entirely successful, we now have a demonstrated theory of the rational kind. If the effort is partially successful, either of two alternative procedures may ensue. On the one hand, there can be an effort to discriminate that aspect of the subject matter which conforms to the rational structure, to distinguish it by definition from that which does not conform, and to retain the fitted and its fitting structure while relegating the remainder of the subject matter to an agenda of future enquiry. On the other hand, there may be an effort to modify the rational structure itself so as to adjust it to the subject of interest. (The choice between these two procedures is involved in decision points 4 and 5 to be described later.) If the effort is a failure, the investigator may try some other rational structure.

A successful effort of this kind has precisely the value which an investigator may assign to rational structures. If he prefers them above all others, the effort constitutes a great new synthesis. If he does not approve, he will demand that the rationalist investigator ocularly demonstrate the existence in fact of measurable entities corresponding to all the terms of the rational scheme. In either case, however, it is desirable to note that the use of a ready-made mathematical structure has the advantage, if it works, of presenting by a single *coup* a great number of inferred consequences of the implied hypothesis.

Miniature use of rational models is seen in efforts to fit some part or aspect of known data to a standard form of algebraic or differential equation, or other small-scale scheme of related symbols. This activity is usually undertaken (e.g., bio-mathematics) with the same valuation in mind as in the full-scale case. If the effort is successful it is usually followed by the second alternative described above. That is, the investigator, having achieved a mathematical first approximation to known data, now attempts a more adequate approximation.

Imposition of deductive structures

Modeling of a different kind can be invoked near the termination of a course of enquiry. A subject matter having been defined and a few general terms discriminated, numbers of pairs, triplets, or slightly larger sets of more specific terms will be devised independently of one another and the entailed enquiries of each set pursued independently.

The aggregate of these several researches may then be brought together and the services of a logician or analyst requested. His task is to determine whether the compendium of terms, "laws," conclusions, etc., is capable of rearrangement in the form of a deductive system and to develop such a system if it is possible (e.g., Clark Hull).

The advantages which may accrue to such an undertaking are three. First, a specialized training is invoked which may be better able to detect ambiguity or vagueness in the terms of the enquiry than was the original investigator. Second, incoherence among the terms or contradictions among their containing propositions are likely to be identified. Third, inferences may be derived whose purports imply new experiments which might not otherwise have been envisaged. Needless to say, these outcomes are valuable. Whether a logician is likely to be inclined to undertake such a task after the fact of conception and ensuing enquiry is another matter. His position is almost as bad as that of the statistician whose help is sought only after the experiments are done and the data collected.

Self-conscious trials of analogies

When new principles are required in a field of enquiry, they are usually sought from two sources. They may be borrowed from another field (preferably a "neighboring" one). They may be devised by a variant specification of a general and common idea, such as that of "particle." Both sources are common. Both are entirely legitimate.

In the past few years, use of the first of these sources has been dignified by calling it model-making or -seeking. Thus a physiologist proposes that a society or culture be treated as if it were an organism. A social scientist may try to examine an area in which two peoples have come into extensive contact by asking whether the biological phenomenon of hybrid vigor, "heterosis," has a social analogue. Neuropsychological investigations are instigated in terms of computing machines and their functions, and so on.

The advantages of such a procedure are the advantages which accrue from seeking and finding any new terms of enquiry—when they are needed—whatever we may call the search. There is even an advantage in pursuing the search self-consciously: we look systematically for new and likely terms. There is also a disadvantage: a pretentious new name for the process may cast such an aura of prestige that the search for new terms is pursued when new terms are neither necessary nor desirable.

CRITERIA FOR THE JUDGMENT OF PRINCIPLE (DECISION POINT 2)

Principles for enquiry are not, of course, accepted out of hand by the scientific community. Nor are they usually private inventions privately used. On the contrary, they are required to be presented to the community where they are scrutinized, debated, and then accepted or rejected for the more searching and expensive test which consists of their use in enquiry.

The arraignment of principles for debate is commonly instigated from one of two sources. On the one hand, no principle may have proved of extensive and durable worth in the field thus far. In such a case, numerous principles and numerous proponents of principles will compete for the attention and approval of the participating community. This situation is, so far, continual in the *methodenstreit* disciplines: psychiatry, psychology, sociology, political science. One hesitates to assign a number to the variety of conceptions of the person, of learning, of society, and of political action now in use.

In other fields, such crises are recurrent rather than continual. New phenomena are discovered; the effectiveness of an old set of principles has been exhausted; a current set has been effective enough to reveal complexities in the subject matter which the revealing principle cannot encompass. In such crises, new principles are proposed or, more often, revisions and emendations of existing principles.

Thus, in 1919, E. M. East meets an alleged inadequacy of the Mendelian conception of the apparatus of heredity. Biologists assert that the Mendelian scheme must be discarded since it cannot take account of characteristics of a species which exhibit continuous variability. East responds by exhibiting the genic apparatus as a mechanical model of the expansion of the binomial, and the normal curve as the limit of such an expansion. In two beautifully designed papers, he then shows that these notions, together with a few corollaries, enlarge the then-current view of the gene mechanism so that it can encompass "blending" characters as well as those which fall into a few discontinuous classes. More recently, inadequacies of the notion of dominance-recessiveness in genetics are remedied by the added notion of penetrance. The Lorentz note on the Michelson-Morley experiments is a more drastic case in point.

The documents which propose principles or their revision and the critical statements which the proposals generate show the existence of four major criteria by which judgments are made.

The four criteria are: interconnectivity, adequacy, feasibility, and continuity. Interconnectivity concerns the extensive domain of subject matters subsumed by the proposed principle. Adequacy concerns its intensive domain, the degree of complexity or "completeness" with which the principle subsumes the details of the subject matter. Feasibility concerns the ease, economy, precision, and consistency with which the data required by the principle can be collected. Continuity concerns the ease or difficulty with which the new principle can be made to contain the bodies of knowledge previously formulated in other sets of terms (i.e., by translations or by subsumption as a special case).

The referent qualities named by these criteria are not exclusive of one another nor are they often treated as if they were. Hence, at this decision point, unlike the first, preference is not for one as *against* the others nor is preference usually shown by attack on other criteria. Instead, choice is exhibited as a rank-ordering or weighting of the four. In proposing statements, weighting is seen in what the author presents as the advantages to future enquiry of his proposed principle and in those possible effects on the ensuing enquiry on which he is silent or brief. Among critical statements, the weighting is seen in the character of the shortcomings which are selected for attack and in the advantages which are alleged as reasons for acceptance.

Interconnectivity

Emphasis on interconnectivity is seen clearly and briefly in the following:

> Not infrequently it has been stated that theories which merely explain known facts are of no particular value. I cannot agree with this view. Particularly if the theory combines into one logical system known facts which previously had to be treated by separate theories, it would have a definite advantage as an organizational device. . . .[26]

A major emphasis on interconnectivity is seen in Einstein's argument for field theory as against classical mechanics and suffices to exhibit the character of this criterion:

> In spite of the fact that today we know for certain that classical mechanics breaks down as a ruling basis for the whole of physics, it still stands in the center of physical thought. The reason for this lies in the fact that . . . we have not yet arrived at a new basis for physics *from which we can be certain that the entire manifold of investigated phenomena and successful special theoretical systems can be logically deduced.* . . .

26. Kurt Lewin, *Field Theory in Social Science* (New York: Harper, 1951).

To the attempt to make mechanics fundamental to the whole of physics, light and electricity present insurmountable obstacles. This leads to a field theory of electricity and beyond this to the attempt to base the *whole of physics* on the concept of field. . . .[27]

A high ranking of interconnectivity over other criteria appears to stem from three (possibly four) sources which may be psychologically independent. These sources are, respectively, a sensitivity to subject matters, a sensitivity to processes of enquiry, and what appears to be a generalized Oceanic state.

The first is seen in pleas for interconnectivity ("interdisciplinary approaches") which argue, for example, for a psycho-social economics because of the influence of status structure, wants, etc., on the market; or for certain dynamic theories of personality as against others because of the need adequately to recognize the roles of culture and society on personality formation; or for a psychological political science for similar reasons. Arguments responsive to subjects come frequently from persons who give some of their time to the executive foci of the investigative disciplines: engineers, statesmen, and physicians. This is to be expected, for in these professions men encounter subject matters in a more nearly pristine state. The constituent matters of practical problems rarely conform to the boundary lines which insulate them from one another in the milieu of enquiry.

Similar arguments which are not quite the same are seen in pleadings which carry the Durkheimian need for a self-sufficient science with a peculiar subject matter one step further; they speak for principles which will unite the subject matters of several sciences under the aegis of one of them as queen of the sciences. Claude Bernard's notion of the proper dominance of physiology over anatomy, pathology, and medicine is a case in point. (*An Introduction to the Study of Experimental Medicine.*)

The argument from commitments about the character of enquiry is exemplified by Ludwig von Bertalanffy:

> Modern science is characterized by the trend toward continually increasing specialization. This development is unavoidable in view of the ever-increasing amount of facts. . . . It is generally acknowledged, however, that this specialization entails grave dangers for the development of science. . . .
>
> On the other hand, the modern development in the various sciences shows a remarkable parallelism in basic viewpoints and constructs. This parallelism . . . indicates a hitherto unsus-

27. Einstein, "Physik und realität." Italics mine.

pected unity of the modern world-picture, and a uniformity or isomorphy of constructs and laws in different fields.

In view of these facts, the present author has proposed a new basic [sic] discipline, called General System Theory, which aims at establishing those principles which are common to, and thus applicable in various fields of science from physics to biology to psychology or the social sciences.[28]

In recent years, such arguments are commoner among philosophers, especially logicalists, than among working scientists.

The Oceanic plea for interconnectivity seems to depend for evocation on no specific occasion in either the relations of subject matters or of enquiries. The argument is of the form: The World is One; therefore, Science should be One. And unity is sought as much for literary criticism and biology as for, say, psychology and neurology. The argument is indigenous to history but occasionally seen in other disciplines.

A class intermediate between the Oceanic and the subject-matter sensitive is represented by such items as a plea by a psychologist to base literary criticism on psychological principles; by a physiologist to base ethics and politics on the behavior of cells and tissues; by sociologists to assimilate history to sociology. I have tended to treat these as vulgarities irrelevant to enquiry.

This may be an error. The poignancy or pointlessness to *us* of a given plea for interconnection depends on the extent to which *we* see the subjects involved as related or irrelevant. This, in turn, depends, not on the facts objectively given by the subject matters, but upon the state of enquiry at the time. That is, related or "neighboring" fields are those which, literally, *have been related by enquiry*. They are the fields between which the terms of enquiry (or the terms for solving practical problems) have already managed to establish a few connections. And "irrelevant" subject matters are those for which connective terms have yet to be devised. Hence, the Oceanic pleader or the pleader for connection between such "remote" areas as ethics and physiology may well be a man who sees farther into a possible future than we do.

This point also bears on the problem of estimating the ranking of interconnectivity relative to other criteria in a given science at a given time. For, where some connective principles between the field in question and another do not exist, the scientists in that field who put a high value on interconnection lack channels for exhibiting their preference.

28. Ludwig von Bertalanffy, "A Program of Systems Research and Inter-disciplinary Synthesis" (Palo Alto, California: Center for Advanced Study in the Behavioral Sciences, n.d.) (mimeographed). Similar comments may be found in papers by von Bertalanffy in: *The British Journal for the Philosophy of Science* (1950); *Human Biology* (December 1951).

Thus, a good judgment of the ranking of interconnectivity as a criterion must be made by reference to the actual interconnections which exist at the time the enquirer is exhibiting his argued preferences among principles.

The Criterion of Adequacy

Where the interconnective potency of a principle bears on the relations established among subject matters the adequacy of a principle refers to the connections it makes *within* the immediate subject matter, to the "completeness" or complexity with which it identifies components, factors, variables, and promises to establish satisfactorily complex connections among them. Thus Clark Hull praises the "goal-gradient hypothesis":

> It is hardly accidental that a single principle should be able to . . . integrate such diverse phenomena as the choice of the shorter path, Weber's Law, the elimination of blind alleys, the order of their elimination, the rate of locomotion through the different portions of a maze, the short-circuiting of symbolic-act sequences, and the origin of ideomotor action.[29]

So similarly, does Koffka argue for the notion of "figure";

> Very good, you may say, but what is the advantage of this new way of describing simple experience? It seems on the face of it so much more complicated, so much less systematic, than the old way. This, indeed, is a fundamental question. But it cannot be answered by argument—only by facts. It must be shown that in all fields as well as in the field of choice-training (*Wahldressuren*) this new description explains the facts of experience more easily and better than they can be explained by the traditional view.[30]

Enquirers see a need for more "adequate" principles in three sources. First, it is seen in the subject matter as currently known through existing principles: e.g., that the notion of independent "traits" is inadequate to the interactive character of problem-solving competence; that mass and charge are inadequate to represent the differences among fundamental particles, and so on.

Second, it is seen in what is *not* known about the subject matter, i.e., in problems formulable in the currently orthodox terms but not solvable

29. Clark L. Hull, "The Goal-gradient Hypothesis and Maze Learning," *Psychological Review* 39 (1932): 43.

30. Kurt Koffka, "Perception: An Introduction to Gestalt-Theorie," *Psychological Bulletin* 19 (1922): 544.

therein, as when, for example, "contradictory" or incoherent results are obtained. Such an inadequacy occurs in a physiology pursued in terms of single-function organs which discovers an organ with two functions, or in the "paradox" of an a judged equal to b and a b judged equal to c when a is judged greater than c (e.g., Stumpf's paradox).

Third, and much more radically, it may be seen in the possibility of posing new problems and addressing novel questions to a subject matter: the Lorentz suggestion of dependency between velocity and length; studies of emotional determinants of susceptibility to infection; the Haldaneian effort to ask what changes in a supposedly stable anatomy and biochemistry can be brought about as adjustments to radical and persistent environmental changes; efforts to investigate alteration of a supposedly stable intelligence quotient.

Among these three sources there is a suggestion of a conservatism-freedom scale, the first being most conservative of existing principles. This property may be relevant in an investigating scientist's prejudices.

It should be remarked that discrimination of adequacy and interconnectivity is relative to the state of enquiry in much the same way as is the notion of "relevant" or "neighboring" fields. Whether the failure of an existing principle is a failure in interconnectivity or in adequacy is a question of whether elements left unrelated by that principle are understood as parts of "one" subject matter or of "two," and this is a function of the principle or principles operative at that time. Thus, at one point in the psychological literature, "individual behavior" and "social behavior" are spoken of as independent fields requiring some measure of interconnection. Later, similar matters are named as aspects of a single "subject" whose mutual dependencies require more thoroughgoing investigation. Adequacy and interconnection require discrimination, nevertheless, for debate concerning competitive principles does, in fact, occasionally turn on the relative weighting of these two criteria.

The Criterion of Feasibility

Little need be added to the remark that feasibility concerns the ease, cost, precision, and reliability with which the data required by a principle can be collected. In many cases, this is only a matter of pointing to ways in which familiar techniques and instruments can be adapted to the new purpose. In other cases, unfamiliar forms of data, new experimental patterns, or new devices are required. It is in the second kind of case that differences in weighting of feasibility as against other criteria become most visible. On the one hand, high cost in time or money, the unproved accuracy of new devices, and so on are given as reasons for rejection of the principle. On the other hand, the defending or proposing document may consist in large part of efforts to disclaim such handicaps or, better, to remove them by reporting success in overcoming them.

The papers of E. M. East, mentioned earlier, constitute a case in point. It is a curious commentary on the biologists of the time that what East proposes is not new. The conceptions themselves and the greater adequacy they would confer on enquiry into genetics are visible even in Mendel's original paper. Still other papers have already reasserted the same points. The major contribution of East is to exhibit the feasibility of the conceptions, or, rather, to make them feasible by explaining precisely where and how to use them. He explains the significance of certain parameters of a frequency distribution as data of inheritance. He explains what new kinds of crosses and breeding patterns are required, why they are significant and how the resulting data are to be interpreted. This is done, not by a pure exploration of the conception, its corollaries and their consequences, but in the context of two fullscale researches which are nothing more nor less than exhibitions of the fact that the data required by the conceptions can be collected and interpreted. In effect, these papers exhibit the weight put by East's audience on feasibility, or, conversely, the weight which East puts on adequacy. (Here, as in the case of the sources of inadequacy, a conservative-free factor is suggested. East is ready to abandon or change current notions of the meaning of breeding data, and curent experimental patterns and learn a little statistics; his audience is reluctant.)

The Criterion of Continuity

This criterion brings into even sharper relief the role of a conservative-free factor operative in the weighting of criteria. The notion of continuity concerns the extent to which new principles arise from or can be connected with extant principles; and, consequently, how readily the knowledge accumulated in terms of older principles can be assimilated to the knowledge which may arise in terms of the new. Insofar as the new principle departs radically from the old, there is scope for the play of a conservative-free factor. For the advantages of a new principle lie in future enquiry and new knowledge, and these advantages, in the case of principles which are radical departures, are costly as far as existent knowledge is concerned. The old knowledge may require extensive reformulation. Extensive re-education and sweeping rewriting of textbooks and monographs may need to be done. And some failure of communication between two generations of investigators may have to be accepted.

Among the weightings and oppositions of these four criteria, two are conspicuous as foci of conflict among enquirers. One consists of continuity and feasibility taken together and opposed to adequacy and interconnection. The other consists of interconnectivity alone as object of exceedingly passionate loyalty and equally passionate attack.

There is also noticeable connection between interconnectivity and certain choices at the first decision point. High ranking of interconnectivity and preference for atomic reductions or rationals are often seen together; there is negative correlation with choice of formal-material wholes. These relations are to be expected since scope for interconnection is provided by the first two and excluded by the latter. It is interesting, however, that interconnectivity is more frequently linked to rationals than to reductives, since it would appear as if either would serve the purpose.

RELIABILITY—VALIDITY (DECISION POINT 3)

An effectively instrumental principle of enquiry must almost always include a series of terms of decreasing comprehensiveness and increasing specificity of connection with the data-yielding components of the subject matter. The invention and debate we have so far discussed concern themselves mainly with the higher terms of the series.

We are now concerned with what happens in the choice of the lower terms of the series. The more general terms of a series limit but do not wholly determine the "lesser" terms. For example, a conception of organism and of structure and function may be developed and accepted with no specified scheme within which to discriminate one structure from another—or there may be two or more alternative schemes. Hence, different executors of specific research programs must usually develop or choose different sets of lower terms with which to work, even though they are operating within the same general scheme. Each of these choices will usually be defended as most efficacious of the available alternatives for guiding successful enquiries, the issue turning on different weightings of two criteria of "success": reliability and validity.

Reliability stands for the following cluster: the extent to which the terms of a research program are free of vagueness and ambiguity; the extent to which the referents of the terms are given distinct and unequivocal location and limit; the extent to which the manipulations and measurements indicated by the terms can be undertaken with precision and repeated with uniform consequences. This is one ideal of enquiry.

Validity stands for a less easily specifiable property: the extent to which the terms of a research program approximate to the presumptive richness and complexity of the subject matter; the extent to which abstraction, in its sense of simplification by removal from context, is eschewed as a species of cheat. This is a second ideal of enquiry. (It includes *adequacy* and *interconnectivity* but in opposition to *reliability*.)

Reliability and validity thus name two obligations which scientists, collectively, recognize as co-ordinate and complemental. One concerns the knowledge produced. The other concerns the subject of that knowledge. On the one hand, the scientist is responsible for making conclusions which are as clear, dependable and precise as the state of his art permits. On the other hand, he is responsible for seeing to it that the subjects and predicates of these conclusions—the central emphases of his enquiry—be as "telling" as possible, that they represent as much of the extent and complexity of the subject as the state of the art permits.

The contrast of the two is seen throughout the fields of enquiry. One biologist restricts the meaning of "sexual act" (in the human male) to an ejaculation and proceeds to count their frequency and to characterize their circumstances by reference only to the age, sex, and species of the partner, if any. Another includes fantasies as well as overt movements, searchings as well as satisfactions, symbols as well as actual objects; and characterizes the circumstances of the act in terms of interpersonal components such as possessiveness; guilt, anxiety, and shame; dominance-submission; fusion and confusion of identities. One ethnologist examines friendship by reference to the number of hours per week which each member of a group spends with one other, two others, etc. A second proposes a study in terms of the needs which are satisfied by association, the activities used as the occasion for association, the frequency and intensity of jealousy, possessiveness, sacrifice, etc. One neuropsychologist seeks only those brain defects whose consequence consists of total disappearance of named activities. Another seeks those which result in quantitative changes of qualities of activities which as yet have no name.

While scientists collectively recognize both these obligations and their bearing on one another (unreliable knowledge of something important and well-verified knowledge of the trivial being but two ways to make "knowledge" worthless), scientists individually put grossly different emphases on one or the other. And no other decision point in enquiry gives rise to so sharp and unfortunate a division of enquirers into opposed and uncomprehending camps. To many validists, the reliableist is a man without imagination or one of timorous caution, or one who deliberately pursues unexceptionable and frequent exhibition of "research activity" while others take on the difficult tasks. To many reliableists, the validist is unsound or romantic; unappreciative of rigor and precision as the marks of science; too easily moved by the vague claims of common sense; unskilled in the use of Occam's razor.

Some of this blind opposition arises from conditions of work and enquiry, especially on the reliableist side. A subject matter simplified in the interest of reliability is not simplified merely in thought. It is a genuine article, an artifact of the laboratory or field, created by controlling the conditions of enquiry. The facts ignored in conception are suppressed or held constant in fact. Otherwise, the reduction in validity would have no consequent increase in reliability.

Since this relatively invalid subject of enquiry does exist and in those places where the scientist spends most of his time, it is easy for him to become habituated to thinking about his named subject ("learning," "society," "culture") only in the restricted terms of his research. It is almost as easy for him to come to believe in all sincerity that factors omitted in his created version of the subject but claimed by others to exist are products of those others' fancy or gullibility.

Some of the extremism on the validity side also has circumstantial origins. Physicians, teachers, social workers and other engineers are brought, willy-nilly, into contact with unsuppressed and uncontrolled complexities of subject matter which their investigative sciences may have perforce ignored. The contrast is dramatic and, under the circumstances, very likely to be seen invidiously. In general, it will apear as the failure of scientific theory to "work." This failure and its significance for the engineer leads easily to the conviction that what was bought at this price—the reliability—is relatively worthless. When the engineer is also an enquirer or when the enquirer is in intimate contact with the engineer (as in the case of medicine generally and psychotherapy especially) this invidious comparison carries over from practice to enquiry and colors the agent's view of his research.

Yet, many of the extremists in both camps are hard to account for in this way. They appear to be temperamentally as well as circumstantially dedicated to minimizing one or the other of the two criteria rather than to maximizing the one they praise. On the reliability side, for example, one finds many scientists who go well beyond persistent use and defense of their particular, simplified version of the subject. They spend time, words, and energy actively denigrating more complex versions and actively criticizing co-workers who value validity more. Whether or not a temperamental preference is involved, a high level of anxiety certainly appears to be.

The division of enquirers between these camps is so nearly equal, and each of the ideals is so strongly held, that open attack by one or the other is as rare in the printed literature as it is common in the bar and bedroom post-mortems of scientific meetings. Rather, the division is exhibited mainly by flying the flag of one's choice. Thus, B. F. Skinner:

> In English, for example, we say that an organism sees or feels objects, hears sounds, tastes substances, smells odors and likes or dislikes them; it wants, seeks and finds; it has a purpose,

tries and succeeds or fails; it learns and remembers or forgets; it is frightened, angry, happy, or depressed; asleep or awake; and so on. Most of these terms must be avoided in a scientific description of behavior. . . .

. . . Thus the term "try" must be rejected because it implies the relation of a given sample of behavior to past or future events; but the term "walk" may be retained because it does not. The term "see" must be rejected but "look forward" may be retained. . . .[31]

Kurt Lewin answers:

The psychologist . . . finds himself in the midst of a rich and vast land full of strange happenings: there are men killing themselves; a child playing; a child forming his lips trying say his first word; a person who having fallen in love and being caught in an unhappy situation is not willing or not able to find a way out; . . . there is the reaching out for higher, and more difficult goals; loyalty to a group; dreaming; planning. . . . Psychology is out to conquer this continent. . . .[32]

The same near-equal force of the two ideals leads often, in print, to assertion that the other's love, though it be not lovable to me, is yet to be respected. Thus Clark Hull:

Now for certain rough practical purposes the custom of naming action sequences by their goals is completely justified by its convenience. It may even . . . usefully be employed in theory construction, provided the theorist is alert to the naturally attendant hazards. These appear the moment the theorist ventures to draw upon his intuition for statements concerning the behavior (movements) executed by the organism between the onset of a need and its termination through organismic action. . . .

An ideally adequate theory even of so-called purposive behavior ought, therefore, to begin with colorless movement and mere receptor impulses as such, and from these build up step by step both adaptive behavior and maladaptive behavior.[33]

In general, the printed expression of the schism takes the form of avowing both validity and reliability as goods of science but moving thence to assertion that one of them is best attained, like the Blue Bird, by pursuing the other.

What exception there may be to temperate statement in print arises from the slight but undoubted advantage of reliability over validity as

31. Skinner, *Behavior of Organisms.*
32. Lewin, *Field Theory in Social Sciences.*
33. Hull, *Principles of Behavior.*

a status source for contemporary American scientists (excepting physicists and psychiatrists). A validist shares slightly but definitely the askant position of the intellectual, the possessor of moral principles, and the unmarried, adult male.

STABLE VS. FLUID ENQUIRIES (DECISION POINT 4)

Once a set of terms for enquiry in a field has been debated, pretested and settled on, there is usually the opportunity (and the need) to exploit the terms as a program for numerous researches aimed at conclusions about this and that and another instance of the phenomena to which they apply: a thousand primitive societies to be asked the agreed-on set of queries; hundreds of classes, subcultures and regional isolates of a highly structured society; the genetics of any number of characteristics of any number of plant and animal species to be discovered; the structural formulae of an entire encyclopedia of organic compounds.

Research of this kind may be pursued with either of two distinct aims in view. On the one hand, attention may be focused exclusively on the subject matter itself—the cultures, genetic characters, organs, functions, and so on. The terms, as terms, are ignored, especially those which stand for the subject-of-enquiry itself. The fact that the terms are tentative—perhaps incomplete, perhaps inappropriate—and to be tested by determining how and where they fail in the course of detailed enquiries is not permitted to divert the investigator from his interest in the subject-of-enquiry taken as subject-in-fact and from his hope of positive conclusions about it. This is to be called stable enquiry.

On the other hand, after the invention and pretest of terms through debate, there must be extended test of the principle by practice. The extended test involves the pursuit of data and the formulation of conclusions as do researches of the stable sort, but experiments are performed, data educed and interpretations tried in order to test the terms in which the enquiry is pursued. The subject-of-enquiry is taken as a probably imperfect image or model of some supposed subject-in-fact, and research in terms dictated by the subject-of-enquiry is pursued with the aim of discovering and repairing its inadequacies and limitations: whether the subject will speak to the problem as posed; whether the data required can be elicited with the necessary accuracy; whether data will be found for which the terms of the enquiry cannot give an account. This, I call fluid enquiry.

Enquiries pursued as search for "conclusions" may, in many cases, be utilized by others for this second function, but, on the whole, significantly different behavior is required of the scientist in each of the two cases. Stable enquiry lends itself to segmental structuring. Discrete research programs of relatively short duration can be formulated. One may select for investigation those particular members of the set defined by the principle (e.g., organs, traits) which will cause the least trouble; in genetics, for example, hair color, a sixth digit, web feet, which are easily identified either-ors, as against corolla length or intelligence (which exhibit continuous variability) or schizophrenia (which is equivocal and hard to identify). What is required by way of data is unequivocal. The pattern of experiment is laid down. Each program can be envisaged in terms of a definitive termination. Precision, thoroughness, and "technique" are maximized as the criteria of excellence. In the test of principles, on the other hand, the duration of the enquiry is indefinite; what will constitute the significant data is unknown; the outlines of a satisfactory outcome are vague or invisible. In general, the task is not to traverse a marked route but to determine a route and a destination and to do so with uncertainty as a conspicuous factor at each step.

Throughout the biological sciences, in many of the behavioral sciences, in chemistry and geology, there are regiments of journeymen scientists who carry out only stable enquiries while fluid enquiry is carried out by squads or retained as the special privilege and power source of a "Staff." Stable researchers are usually unaware of the existence of fluid enquiry. Where they are aware of it, they are uneasy and offensive. The common epithets are: *just words, speculation, thinking.*

There is reason to think that here, as at the other decision points, psychological factors are operative. Some factor of tolerance of ambiguity appears to characterize the fluid enquirer (as it does the seeker of validity) together with pleasure in the creation of new structures and, perhaps, some sense of exceeding or disposing of fathers. Stable enquirers are often men of fixed habit in other respects and given to worry about nutrition, constipation, and their children's future.

However, there is also operative here, as at no other decision point, a social machinery for encapsulating young scientists into the stable mode and keeping them there. Entire graduate curriculums exist which afford no hint that principles are matters of invention and alteration but, rather, treat current knowledge and practice of a field as its *echt* definition. The practitioner extruded from such a program is later kept in line by his ignorance, by his developed incapacity to understand reports of fluid enquiry and by the system of refreshment programs and special texts by which he is given only as much of new material as his continued usefulness may require.

How far, then, the stable enquirer is a product of his education and how far he selects himself for a limited career is to be determined.

GUIDING, COLLECTING, INTERPRETING (DECISION POINT 5)

I doubt whether this decision point is of much importance and shall treat it accordingly.

Of the numerous possible divisions of the labor of enquiry, three are commonly discriminated as choices by some men of science. There are those who concern themselves primarily with the invention and proposal of principles. There are those who delight in the meticulous and careful accumulation of data for interpretation by others. There are still others who engage primarily in the work of review and monography.

The first of these choices is marked by its variable status among the different sciences. Physics honors the "theoretician"; chemistry, its chemical physicists; psychiatry, its Freuds and Sullivans; sociology, its Parsonses and Durkheims. Geology honors its dead fluid enquirers. Biology tends to reject the role out of hand. Indeed, I recall only two documents in the biological literature which treated a theoretical problem in theoretical terms and found acceptance: the brief letter by Hardy, the actuary, which initiated the development of modern genetical evolution; and a few publications by Sewall Wright in the same field. Usually, biology will tolerate a theoretic contribution only when delivered in a context of experiments done and data collected. Even a field which tolerates theoretical work often demands a price of admission to the activity: an apprenticeship in the sweaty phases of enquiry. Even Einstein served a novitiate. These social restrictions mean that an attempt to study the character and competence of the theoretical man must look closely to its samples. A sample of nontheoreticians is likely to be adulterated by some number of unidentified theoretics.

Of the remaining two choices, a word on the third is in order. The activities of review and monography in the biological sciences (including the clinical) are signs and sources of professional political power. The task of the monographer is to relate diverse researches. The conclusions of such researches are usually less than certain and often contradictory. Their apparatus of terms and techniques will often exhibit wide variability, in respect of generals as well as specifics. The integration of such a diversity requires judgment of the reliability and validity of numerous researches, and in the process of exercising that judgment a monographer has the chance to influence the future course of a field of enquiry and to affect individual careers for better or worse. His power is restricted, in some degree, since his subjects and his audience are largely the same persons, but this restriction is neither greater nor less than that of any elected officer of a polity. Indeed, among monographers, there is a noticeable number of persons who exhibit the social habit of the elected administrator: crony-gregariousness with its collection of loosely held, largely interchangeable, partners in dining, drinking, and story-telling; disinterest in a life of continuity and consequent opportunism.

THE 0-POINT OF DECISION

We began our analysis of enquiry by supposing that all scientists embark upon enquiry with the intention of contributing to our mastered knowledge of the subject matter. This supposition must now be denied. There are two other starting points.

Let it be supposed that in most fields at most times, consensus can be obtained as to the important and outstanding problems yet to be solved. Let the ideal of our original supposition consist of efforts at solving one or more such problems. The enquirer eyes the subject matter as known and as it might be known, and the disparity he sees there constitutes his starting point.

The second choice of starting point is familiar enough: not the subject matter and the hole in the science of it, but techniques and instruments, intellectual or otherwise: path-coefficients, factor analysis, game theory, electron microscopes, computers, tape recorders. The enquirer has his favored instrument and is master of it. Like a child with a hatchet, he looks for something to chop.

The third choice is neither hole in science nor instrument mastered, but virtuosity, *per se*. The enquirer believes he excels others in ingenuity, inventiveness, or what not and looks for means to exhibit it. His starting point is any thing or situation through which he can exhibit his skill. His relation to like-sexed peers is reminiscent of Don Giovanni's and worth investigating.

Persons of the second and third persuasion are probably useful to science in about the degree to which they are tolerated at any given time. The tool master introduces new tools on the one hand and, on the other, tills stony acres. The ingenious, by seeking novelty, occasionally find it.

POSTSCRIPT ON A GRAND STRATEGY

Insofar as this document implies a view of enquiry, a word is in order asserting what is otherwise only suggested—that there are many ways of achieving mastery of a subject of enquiry, no one of them capable of undebatable superiority over the others; each of them capable of illuminating the world of things in a way not precisely duplicated by the others.

Many of these complementarities are obvious. Rational principles confer coherence on what otherwise would be dissevered by holistic principles. Reduction confers coherence in another way. Meanwhile, holistic atacks on problems emphasize the peculiarities of local subject matter while rational and reductive theories tend to subordinate what is local and special to what is common among many subject matters.

Even bull-headed reduction has advantages over its more sophisticated brother in the course of the actual practice of enquiry. For the enquiry which begins by looking to the constituted to tell it the behaviors and qualities to be accounted for is likely to look to the constituents to account for these matters only. The enquiry which looks first to the constituents, on the other hand, is a freer enquiry precisely to the extent that it is unguided. A similar advantage accrues to anti-principled enquiries.

We need not, therefore, *make* a virtue of the necessity of pursuing enquiry through men who are moved by numerous preferences to work in different ways toward differing specifications of their common goal. It *is* a virtue.

Yet, as long as resources for research are limited, there is an itch to believe that one of the several strategies available to science is the best one. It would be very nice to be able to plan the course of a new enquiry and at different stages in the process select enquirers for their appropriate predilections as well as for appropriate abilities.

I have tried to show that this hope must betray us. Consensus on a single pattern of choices will merely enable us to overlook what we have not done in our enquiry. Different principles maximize different dimensions of successful enquiry. One hierarchy of criteria merely legislates definition of the goal. A single ratio of fluid to stable enquiries imposes an arbitrary relation between theory and practice, future and present goods.

This leaves the possibility that some particular *order* of different strategies, constituting a grand strategy may be better than all other orders. This hope may be realizable, though there are two vitiating considerations. In the first place, the possibility of a grand strategy assumes that different subject matters are alike as subjects of enquiry. Yet a good historical case can be made against this premise as well as for it, and a good metaphysical case has, of course, been made on either side. A good scientific case would entail a trial of all such grand strategies on all subjects of enquiry, which amounts to a confusion of types.

In the second place, if we grant that all subjects are alike as subjects of enquiry, we encounter a second and similar trouble. The grand strategy best suited to this homogeneous subject of enquiry may not be the same as the one best suited to the human species *qua* enquirer —a modern instance of the ancient distinction between what is most knowable without qualification and what is most knowable to *us*. And even if these coincided, we must determine whether that common grand strategy coincides with the one best suited to a generation of enquirers caught in a particular web of circumstance—the state of enquiry in other fields; the state of development of instruments of enquiry, such as logic, mathematics, and high-voltage accelerators—at the time that enquiry on some given subject is initiated. In short, the problem of a best grand strategy is a prudential one, contingent on the time, the place, and the subject of enquiry. Within these caveats, I shall now record a speculation on a grand strategy—specifically a grand strategy for subjects far from physics on the Comteian scale, for attack by American scientists, of enquiries instigated in the milieu of current fashions and conditions of enquiry.

Speculation on a Grand Strategy

In the first place, I am convinced that a rational principle should be among the last to be tried. Its early use must be either an illusory and damaging "success" or a wasteful delay of prerequisite enquiries.

These unfortunate possibilities rest on the point that rational enquiries involve the matching of two well-developed bodies of material. On the one hand, there must be the rational scheme itself, whether a geometry, a probabilistic system, some other calculus or a configurative corpus. On the other hand, there must be a body of *relatively* unorganized propositions representing the subject of the enquiry. The rational investigation is completed when one such component is well-matched with the other, when stable relations are established somehow or other, as Einstein put it, between concepts and sense experience.

Now it is pretty obvious that the way to use a rational principle prematurely is to try for the third step when the first two have not been taken an optimum distance. My concern here is with what constitutes the optimum for the second step—development of propositions representing the subject of the enquiry. I shall pretend, knowing little about the matter, that a plethora of rational schemes exist. If I am wrong about that and they too are in need of expansion for the purposes of biology and the behavioral sciences, then I shall be right in my conclusions, a fortiori.

Readiness of a body of propositions for application of a rational scheme involves two criteria. First, the body of propositions must bear a reasonable resemblance (in respect of validity and reliability) to the subject matter. Second, they must exhibit some sort of middle ground between complete variety and complete coherence.

The sense of the second of these conditions calls for some elucidation. The point is this: a highly heterogeneous body of propositions means propositions derived and couched in dozens of different and independently developed sets of terms (as might arise from dozens of workers held together by no achieved consensus about the problems of the field or the character of its subject matter). The independence or "irrelevance" of these terms is what a rational principle is designed to overcome. The number of them is the factor which bears on the question of timing the search for a principle.

Now let us see how these two conditions—the validity of the propositions and their degree of heterogeneity—bear on the success or failure of a rational enquiry. Suppose we have only a few propositions (or many, but couched in a few sets of terms) representing the subject matter. Then the probability is very high that they are low in validity —lacking either adequacy or scope as far as the subject matter is concerned. They will represent either a highly simplified slice through the whole subject matter or a thorough analysis of some small fragment of it. Now suppose that someone successfully fits a rational scheme to these propositions. Who would deny that his success would be a constraining bind on further enquiries? He has a structure whose separate propositions are "true" (reliable). And the structure is a coherent whole. That combination is highly seductive. The vast majority of workers in the field will fall into line and subsequent enquiry will continue in the terms of the "successful" rational principle for a long time— erecting a large, attractive, and illusorily adequate body of knowledge of the subject. For nothing marks off the American scientist more than his readiness to ignore when he can the distinction between the subject as embodied in his terms and the subject as it may be.

If, on the other hand, such a consensus be postponed for awhile— by the absence of a "successful" rational scheme—we leave time for more numerous, relatively independent attacks on the subject matter. Attacks on different facets of it enlarge the scope of the growing body of propositions. Attacks in different terms test out the validity of earlier terms and amend them where they are wanting.

Now if *this* goes on too long, we exceed the second condition for effective rational attack. We get a large collection of heterogeneous propositions, hence a very large number of small sets of terms, and our problem shifts from one of prematurely binding coherence to one of great difficulty in achieving coherence at all. We have too many clues to the kind of rational scheme which would work or, putting it another way, too many conditions which a rational scheme must meet at one fell swoop.

At this point, I appear to contradict myself, for I have claimed that rational attacks should be made late in enquiry while my argument so far suggests a midpoint rather than a late one. The remaining step in the argument consists in showing that we can have our cake and eat it too—extend enquiry and thus increase validity without running into an excessively large number of sets of terms. We can do it by introducing *local* and *interim* coherencies by means of attack with reductive and holistic principles.

Thus, the initial phase of our grand strategy would consist of use of primitive and anti-principles. The second phase would consist of the binding of the results of these enquiries into a small yet varied number of holistic and reductive views, each of which would go its own way for awhile, leading to more comprehensive reductions, then to some very few less-than-comprehensive rationals, and only then to a sweeping rational "synthesis."

Objections to Argument

There are a number of apparent holes in this speculation about a grand strategy. Here are two of them.

It may be argued that the strategy is planned entirely in the interest of validity (both interconnective and adequate). Not at all. Reliability is not sacrificed. Continuity and feasibility are also maximized.

Reliability is maintained in the sense, first, that the strategy is a strategy and not a tactic. In the gathering of the propositions which shall constitute the matter for ultimate integration we assume due regard for precision and consistency of measurement and observation. Second, by asking that early principles stay close to the subject matter, we let the subject and the enquirer's competence rather than the terms of a rational principle lead the enquiry. The individual enquirer in close and relatively undistracted connection with the subject matter determines what will constitute his data. Hence, as long as he affirms reliability as a scientific good, reliability will not be sacrificed for validity. This same argument speaks for feasibility.

This brings us to a second hole—the fact that we propose that reductive and holistic principles, rather than small-scale rationals, do the job of local and intermediate integration. There are two reasons for this, the first of which involves a qualification of that proposal. That first reason is that rationals enjoy entirely too much status at present. (Remember, we said that this strategy was contingent and prudential.) In their own right there is nothing against rationals serving *pro tem* integrations. But the passion of modern scientists for rationals is so abject that, in their eyes, the first rational in the field is likely to assimilate what propositions it can and relegate the remainder to the category of irrelevance rather than leave room for additional local and *interim* integrations.

The second reason for rejecting rationals as intermediate integrators stems from the fact that we are discussing modern enquiries in subject matters high on the Comteian line. This combination is equivalent to remarking that knowledge of subject matters lower on the line are, in fact, reasonably well-developed. If they are—and they are—it would be inefficient and a waste to ignore them. In short, there is much good material available for reductive attacks and that material should be used. This can be done with reasonable safety since the seductiveness of reduction is so much lower than that of rationals just now and because reductives easily invoke holistics as competition (e.g., Durkheim after Mill, Skinner after Pavlov, et al.).

As to continuity, reductives and holistics supervening on primitives and anti-principles have an inbuilt continuity in actual enquiry. Primitives, as practicals, must speak in terms of prediction or control. Since we are discussing a subject matter not yet known in rational terms, controls and predictions of aspects of it must stem in large part from knowledge of the behavior of its constituents (since this is the only large body of knowledge available). Residual items of prediction and control must come from *ad hoc* items of information about the subject matter taken in terms of its own properties. This amounts to saying that primitives will be fragmented bits of reductives and holistics, hence that a movement to systematic use of reductive or holistic principles will stem from the primitives and incorporate them. Similarly, "Laws of Nature" and "Causes" will also speak in the terms of known constituents or recognizable properties of the subject, hence will similarly contribute to and be assimilable to the reductive and holistic principles which may supervene.

Yet, my imaginary critic may have a point here. It may be that interim rationals are more easily assimilable to a large-scale rational synthesis than holistics and reductives would be. If that be the case, we have a choice between validity and continuity. I would choose validity.

APPENDICES

APPENDIX 1. SOME PROBLEMS IN A STUDY OF ENQUIRY

The framework of decision points and choices has been relatively empty of information as to what kinds of persons make what decisions for what utilities. Such information has been suggested as one main line of enquiry for which the framework would be useful.

Eight other lines of enquiry are as follows.

1. To what extent are choices responsive to the exigencies of a subject matter rather than expressive of personal preference? E.g., is there a great difference between the conceptions appropriate to investigation of the organism and those appropriate to investigation of non-living subjects?

2. To what extent are choices responsive to the state of enquiry at a given time rather than expressive of personal preference? For example is the biologists' passionate avoidance of final cause and "anthropomorphism" in the period 1915–1935 a reaction to errors which arose from uncritical use of these notions in preceding decades?

3. To what extent are choices indicative of fashions generated by treatises on method or well-publicized new instruments and models for research? E.g., the radical empiricism of W. K. Clifford and Karl Pearson; "operationalism" more recently; "probabilistic" structures; Game Theory?

4. To what extent do choices reflect a "natural evolution" of enquiry in each field? E.g., from description to causation to quantification, or Euclidian geometry to algebra to partial differential equations? (Without prejudice to the possibility of respectable enquiry along this line it should be remarked, nevertheless, that there is probably no ordering of no set of "methods" or "principles" but has been asserted out of hand to be the evolutionary sequence of science—usually as an argument for a favored principle. Thus: taxonomy, static laws, dynamic laws; or analytic, summative, synholistic; or theological, metaphysical, positive.)

5. To what extent does amount of variance in respect to choices in a given field at a given time reflect the state of communication? E.g., when scientists in a given field read the same noncompetitive journals, belong to the same societies and attend the same meetings, to what extent does variety of strategy disappear? If variety does disappear, does consensus arise via suppression of preferences or via self-selection of those entering the field?

6. To what extent do the choices at the several decision points of given enquirers constitute whole strategies or patterns of choice? I.e., to what extent is choice of *a* at decision point *1* correlated with choice *b* at decision point *2*? I treat each decision point independently of others but the apparent connection between some choices (as choices) is too obtrusive to ignore entirely.

7. What variability exists among scientists with respect to the existence of preference or to efforts at conscious control of personal preference in the interest of such other desiderata as 1 and 2 above? What personality traits mark controllers and indifferentists? This line of enquiry is especially desirable as a countercheck to the psychological relativism of the main enquiry. This countercheck is especially important in view of the fact that though hundreds of scientists exhibit marked preferences in respect to the choices to be described, a few exhibit none and habitually combine what others treat as mutually exclusive.

8. Certain aspects of the personal history of the enquirer are interesting as possible correlates with choices made: (a) stage of career, age, etc.; (b) the preferences of professional father figures, as thesis chairmen, beloved teachers, first boss.

APPENDIX 2. ON "EMERGENT" PRINCIPLES

As far as I can determine, no enquiries are conducted in terms of emergency and no emergent phenomena present themselves for enquiry except by way of an artifact arising from hypostasization of atomic reductive principles. The process appears to run as follows.

When durable reductive principles prevail for a considerable time in a field of investigation, the success of the principle gives rise to an orthodoxy which asserts not merely that reductive principles alone are scientific but that "nature" is reductive. Enquiry then encounters a phenomenon which resists explanation in reductive terms but is successfully investigated holistically. Now, since the phenomenon and the account of it are not discriminated, the combination of the two, misidentified as the phenomenon pure and simple, is seen against the background of phenomena reductively explained as something strange and novel—"extranatural." The novelty in turn becomes something to be explained and this is done by distinguishing two orders of phenomena: ordinary ones and those which arise without due and proper basis in characteristics of the constituent factors. The latter phenomena are dubbed emergent. Of course, their emergency disappears if new properties of the constituent factors are sought and found; or if the earlier body of knowledge in the field is translated from reductive to other terms; or if the phenomena and the mode in which they are investigated are discriminated.

APPENDIX 3. ON OCCAM'S RAZOR

There is a division of scientists with respect to their valuation of economy as a criterion of principles. Among users of rational principles and hunters of historical causations there is much obsessive concern for the minimal while the bulk of scientists, though willing to delete an unnecessary term when it is pointed out by others, are more than willing to let others do the pointing. They seem to be able to take economy or leave it alone.

Whether this indifference is, in fact, true of the bulk of scientists cannot presently be determined. Attitudes about economy tend to be indistinguishable because the degree of economy itself (gross redundancy aside) involved in a structure of terms is hardly capable of measurement. At least, I am not aware of a well-accepted definition and measure of the quality.

For this reason, I omitted economy from the set of choices at this point.

APPENDIX 4. ON RELATIVISM

The charge of relativism can fairly be laid against the viewpoint of this paper but there is a difference between the relativism of Pilate (What is truth?) and that of John Smith (There is more than one way to skin a cat!). Two points are germane here.

First, if scientific knowledge can be sought in many ways, it is not because science is a game, a systematic delusion, or the pursuit of metaphors and mnemonics. Rather, to paraphrase Professor Warner Wick, it is because nature is so rich in matters to be learned and scientists so apt at finding ways to learn them.

Second, there *are* consequences to a choice of principles and it is *not* all one which principle is chosen. Principles not only initiate enquiry; they are tested by it. And if what is tested is not the propriety of the principle to the subject matter alone but to the manifold of matter, enquirer, and circumstances of enquiry, that too redounds to the benefit of the enterprise.

· 8 ·

Education and the Structure
of the Disciplines

STRUCTURE AND EDUCATION
Structure and Knowledge

Before we ask about the structures peculiar to specific disciplines—before, indeed, we ask what "structure" is—there is a prior question: What relevance may the structure of disciplines have for the purposes of education? Why should the curriculum maker or the teacher be concerned with the structure of the discipline with which he or she works?

There are two answers to this question. One answer is relevant when we conceive curriculum and instruction as concerned primarily with the imparting of knowledge. The other is relevant when we conceive curriculum and instruction as concerned primarily with the imparting of arts and skills. Since the reasonable curriculum maker is concerned with both of these, both answers are relevant here.

When curriculum is conceived as the imparting of knowledge, the disciplines seem to be important only as sources from which we draw the truths we intend to impart. We must make decisions as to what knowledges are of most worth, but the sense and significance these pieces of knowledge take on when they are intact as a body called a discipline would appear to be no business of ours.

This position would be defensible were it not for three circumstances which are obscured by the very words "truths" and "knowledge." One of these circumstances centers around the point that not all assertions which appear to be truths are truths. The second centers on the further, even greater complication, that not all truths are equally true or true in the same sense. The third circumstance centers around the point that the meaning of a single proposition or sentence about something-or-other is by no means contained exclusively within that single proposition. It is a commonplace that a single word is given its meaning not only by the "dictionary" but also by the context of the words in which

This chapter is a portion of a paper that was prepared for the Project on the Instructional Program on the Public Schools of the National Education Association, 1961, and has not previously been published.

it is placed in a sentence. What is true of words in a sentence is also true of sentences in paragraphs and paragraphs in whole expositions: that is, isolated statements are not truly isolable. Instead, they, too, are but parts of wholes and their meanings depend on the whole of which they are parts. Clearly, then, the character of the whole of which they are parts determines what they mean, in some degree.

The first point here, that not everything which appears to be a truth is, in fact, a truth, is illustrated by a well-nigh universal mistaking of the structure and, therefore, of the purport, of works of literary art. Consider, for example, the novel *Women in Love*, by a man, D. H. Lawrence. Here is a volume about two sisters in a small English town. Each becomes involved with a man or men. Lawrence describes their visible behavior and their inner feelings at great length.

Now consider a newspaper reviewer who writes a short critical essay on this novel. Amongst other things, let us pretend, he says, "This is a magnificent volume. Never have I seen such thorough and acute insights into the real nature of women and their love-life."

Almost all of us have said something similar about a work of art at one time or another. And, at the time, we thought we meant it. We were so carried away by the artfulness of the artist that we did not stop to realize that what we were reading had nothing whatever in it of the structure which would have justified our taking it as a body of "thorough and acute" truths about women in love. The structures of these novels contained nothing which could be called evidence for the conclusions ("insights") voiced by the author about the love life of females—or whatever. Nor was there a display of a train of inference or interpretation by which the author might have moved from evidence to conclusion.

This point becomes clearer if we ask ourselves what ground we have for thinking that Lawrence knew a great deal about women in love. After all, he was not himself a woman. (And even if he were, we would have not much greater ground for supposing that he knew about women in love, since women, and men too, are notoriously the last people to understand themselves.) Further, the reviewer offers us no information about Lawrence's life which would persuade us that Lawrence knew a great deal about women. In short, the book gives us neither data nor argument to support what it says; and neither reviewer nor author gives us reason to think that the author had lived intimately with his subject.

Now let us go further. Let us ask, not only what ground we have for thinking that Lawrence knew a great deal about women in love, but also ask what basis we have for thinking we can recognize at sight a more subtle truth about women in love when we see such a truth.

Assuming that what we mean by a "deeper insight" is anything like a scientific or commonsense truth, we shall find an embarrassing paradox here. For, to say that we recognize an insight as deeper or a truth as more subtle, is to say that we already know much evidence, already have in hand a large number of other insights and other truths about women in love, and thus are able to make a comparison and recognize the "insight" adduced by D. H. Lawrence as better than previous insights. In effect, every reader who praises a novel for its revelatory insight into some subject is saying that he, the reader, is an expert on that subject.

This, the average reader is not, nor does he think he is. In short, our conviction that we have learned a truth from a novel is an illusion. We were moved by the book—not informed. But the experience of being moved carried with it the illusion of being informed. We mistook the characters for real people, and equated them to other real people. We acted as if a novel were an immaculate and flaw-free window looking out on life.

There is a way to avoid some parts of the argument above. We can entertain the idea that there are two routes to truth, the scientific way and the poetic way. We can suppose, further, that poetic truths are of such a special nature (and man, too, is of such a special nature) that when a truly true poetic truth is presented to a man, something within him resonates, and, by resonating, tells him that indeed he has before him a poetic truth.

There is something to be said for such a view. Indeed, it so impressed Plato that, despite his intense dislike of poets, he was unwilling to dismiss them out of hand. Instead, he proposed that they first be rewarded with a crown of laurel and only then dismissed by being "shown the gates of the city."

But note that this distinction between a scientific truth and a poetic truth arises only if we recognize a fundamental difference between the structure of a novel and the structure of a piece of scientific enquiry: recognize the central role of evidence in one; of something else—perhaps unexplainable "insight"—in the other.

That recognition would not, however, solve all our problems. For the question of the precise character of a poetic structure still remains. Perhaps, as Plato supposed, poets are people who have some sort of a pipeline to the truth and therefore need neither evidence nor argument. Perhaps, on the other hand, poetic works are purely "poetic" in the Greek sense of the word—creations or constructions. In that case, we might conclude that we had been exposed to the effective magic which is wrought by men who deal effectively with the sounds and meanings of words and the power of imagery to persuade. In any case, we would not have supposed that Lawrence's view of women and love was to be juxtaposed, let us say, to the views of Freud or of Harry Stack Sullivan; we would recognize that the latter two were psychiatrists (scientists to some degree) and were using evidence in some sense and in some way, all of which is quite different from the kind of thing done by D. H. Lawrence.

In the above example, we are not certain whether we are dealing with a case of something that looks like truth but is not truth at all or whether we are looking at something which is true in a certain sense (a poetic truth) but a sense not comparable to the sense in which a scientific theory or a scientific conclusion is true. Let us pretend it is an example of the former—a case of something which looks like a truth but is not; something which we mistook for a truth because we had not noted the structure in which it appeared. Let us assume this, not because it is my preferred interpretation of the nature of artistic structures, but because it will leave room for a further example by which to indicate the notion that truths may be true in different degrees or senses.

To illustrate this point, let us take three "things" which are asserted to exist and which, further, are asserted to have such-and-such properties and behavior. Let us take, first, this automobile here-now. Second, let us take the electron. Third, let us take a neutrino. Concerning each of these things, respectively, let us work with three assertions which are alike in form.

A. The automobile in front of the house is black.
B. The electron is a particle with a small mass and a negative charge.
C. The neutrino is a particle with neither charge nor rest-mass.

All three statements, let us suppose, are true in some sense or other. That they are true in different senses becomes pretty apparent when we consider the following points. We have said that the car in front of the house is black because we have looked at it and our assertion is verified by the person to whom we are talking when he looks and nods agreement. By contrast, the statement about the electron most certainly is not made by my looking and by my confrere also looking and nodding. It is not so asserted and verified simply because the electron is not visible. However, the assertion does rest on the fact that a number of specific phenomena have been seen which men have been unable to account for satisfactorily except on the premise that electrons exist. It further rests on certain other, highly specific phenomena which can be understood only on the premise that these particles have a negative charge.

The assertion about the neutrino rests on still a third kind of ground. Not only are they invisible, they have had assigned to them a *lack* of such properties as charge and rest-mass which characterize the electron. Hence, it would be very difficult, indeed, to base our assertion concerning their existence and character on specific phenomena which might be detected in an experiment.

Instead, the ground for positing the existence of the neutrino was roughly as follows. Certain effects occur in a phenomenon called beta decay which raise a doubt about the universality of certain assertions ("laws") which had so far been found to hold for physical phenomena without exception (certain "conservation" laws). These measured aspects of beta decay could, then, have been accounted for by supposing that the conservation laws were not universal but had at least this one exception. But physicists preferred to keep the conservation laws intact and universal. The only conceived way to retain them was to suppose the existence of a well-nigh undetectable particle which carried off the quantities whose disappearance would otherwise have called the conservation laws into question (e.g., the lack of charge and rest-mass, together with certain other lacks leads to the point that a neutrino, if it did exist, could pass through a quantity of matter equal to several times the diameter of the earth before something might happen to betray the existence of said neutrino).

For some time, just this was the only ground for supposing the existence of the neutrino and for assigning to it such a poverty of characteristics.[1]

Clearly, the three different senses in which our three statements are "true" are not revealed by the statements themselves. For the statements are all of the same form. ("The x is —.") Only the context, the structure of problem, evidence, inference, and interpretation, in which each of the statements was originally embedded would have revealed to us the different senses in which each was "true."

(A warning is called for at this point. The example above suggests that the structure of scientific disciplines is entirely a structure arising from different kinds of evidence and different ways of interpreting evidence. As we shall see later, this in only one determinant of the structure of scientific disciplines. There is a second determinant—the kind of question the scientist asks of his subject.)

Now let us examine a case in which structure determines the *meaning* assigned to an assertion. Below, I have written a sentence. Below that

1. This was some years ago. Since then, possible ways of detecting the neutrino—if it existed—were conceived and tried and, indeed, gave positive results. The important point, however, still stands; the conception of the neutrino was devised and used *without waiting* for electron-like verification of it. It was enough for Fermi that it helped him conserve the conservation laws.

I have placed that sentence in a brief part of its context. In the third position, the sentence and its brief context are restated in a still larger context.

Now, play the following game with these quotations, according to the following rules. First, discard, ignore whatever you think you know about current views of physicists concerning light. In this empty frame of mind, read the first short quotation. Assimilate its surface, apparent meaning. Don't *look* for ambiguity. Just take the first meaning it seems to present. Paraphrase it to yourself for emphasis.

Now, go on to the second quotation. Read it through. If your mind works as does that of the ten people with whom I have tested this material, you will find that the original quotation (present in the second quotation in italics) has taken on a new meaning startlingly different from that which it had when presented by itself.

Finally, go on to the third quotation and note what it adds (and subtracts) to the meaning conveyed to you by the second quotation.

Quotation 1: To account for the specular reflection of light from smooth surfaces, therefore, we have to assume that light particles reflect like ideal ball bearings bouncing off resilient surfaces.

Quotation 2: We know that light is reflected when it strikes the surface. Do particles such as steel balls behave in the same way? To answer this question, we merely need to throw some ball bearings on the various surfaces. The balls thrown on to a clean, smooth steel plate bounce off regularly at an angle of reflection approximately the same as their angle of incidence—also the speed after collision with the surface is about as great as before. If, however, either the balls or the smooth surfaces are less resilient than steel, reflection does not take place with equal angles of incidence and reflection. Also, in such cases the speed of the balls after reflection is less than before—unlike light, which does not change its speed on reflection. *To account for the specular reflection of light from smooth surfaces, therefore, we have to assume that light particles reflect like ideal ball bearings bouncing off resilient surfaces.*

Quotation 3: We have seen that light always has its source in some luminous body and that it travels in essentially straight lines. Any model of light must, then, include something that starts with a luminous body and moves along a straight path. The simplest thing that we can imagine traveling in this way is a particle, like a baseball.

We know that light is reflected when it strikes the surface. Do particles such as steel balls behave in the same way? To answer this question, we merely need to throw some ball bearings on the various surfaces. The balls thrown on to a clean, smooth steel plate bounce off regularly at an angle of reflection approximately the same as their angle of incidence—also the speed after collision with the surface is about as great as before. If, however, either the balls or the smooth surfaces are less resilient than steel, reflection does not take place with equal angles of incidence and reflection. Also, in such cases the speed of the balls after reflection is less than before—unlike light, which does not change its speed on reflection. To account for the specular reflection of light from smooth surfaces, therefore, we have to assume that light particles reflect like ideal ball bearings bouncing off resilient surfaces.

We have found that we can make a particle model which accounts for specular and diffuse reflection, which gives Snell's law of refraction, and which leads to the inverse square law for the diminution of the intensity of illumination with distance. The model also suggests that light should exert a pressure and that heat should be associated with light absorption. Both of these effects which we had not previously discussed, are found experimentally to hold true of light. Hence, they exemplify the value of a model in leading us to new investigations.

But now let us ask whether there are any respects in which the particle model is less successful? Are there aspects of the behavior of light which are poorly described by the model or even in conflict with it?

The answer is, "yes." When we come to the phenomenon of refraction, we run into trouble. We can force the particle model to account for refraction but only by making the model much more complicated. And we look with suspicion on a model which requires too many separate complications. Still more trouble arises when we try to account for diffraction. In addition, there is trouble with the speed of light.[2]

Let us now look back at these three quotations. In the first quotation —of the sentence without context—we are forcibly impressed with the phrase, "we have to assume." Had we no knowledge of the wave theory of light as a commonly accepted theory, the utterance would convey to us the notion that scientists explain the reflection of light by positing

2. The above materials are adapted from *Physics*, a high school textbook, prepared by the Physical Science Study Committee (Boston: D. C. Heath, 1960), chap. 15.

the notion that light consists of particles that behave as do ball bearings. I would hazard the guess that no one of the appropriate ignorance except an analytic logician would accept the utterance as having its proper emphasis on the words "ideal" and "resilient surfaces."

Of course, the first context (the second quotation above) supplies precisely the latter new meaning to the original sentence. We now see that it refers not to the necessity for assuming the existence of light particles which behave like ball bearings but, rather, the necessity for assuming, *if* we assume a particle theory, that the particles must be "ideal," etc.

Furthermore, we now find in the second quotation a meaning which will be denied by the third one. The second (especially had we included long passages which described the competence of a particle model to take account of many more of the phenomena of light) conveys the impression that a particle theory *is* a thoroughgoing theory to account for the behavior of light. Only in the third context do we discover that a particle theory has shortcomings and thus realize that we are dealing only with a possibility and that a better possibility exists.

I need not add, I suppose, that the instance above is not as trivial as it may appear. For it is a rare textbook, indeed, which supplies enough of the structure of a discipline to let a student know that he is dealing with a model or a possibility and not with a literal truth or literal falsehood, such as our statement, "This automobile is black."

Let these three examples suffice as illustrations of the relevance of the structures of disciplines for curriculums concerned only with the imparting of knowledge. For this restricted service, structures are desirable or necessary in the service of three functions. First, structures permit us to discover what *kind* of statement we are dealing with— whether it is a verifiably informative statement, a statement designed to move our emotions, a statement of choice, value or decision, and so on. Second, structures permit us to determine to what degree and in what sense an informative statement is "true." Third, structure permits us to discern more completely or more correctly the meanings of informative statements.

Structure and Skills

Let us turn now to the question of the relevance of the structure of disciplines to the imparting of arts and skills.

The skills relative to disciplines which a curriculum might impart are of three kinds. First, and most commonly sought in a curriculum, are the skills by which one applies the truths learned from a discipline. Second, there are the skills of enquiry itself. In their primary use, these are the skills by which the master of a discipline contributes new knowledge to that discipline. But secondarily, they are the skills by which second-ary enquiry (enquiry into enquiries) is conducted. By "enquiry into en-quiries," I mean the kind of study which is involved in an "inductive" approach to the structure of a discipline, learning the structure by study of instances of it. We shall have a little more to say about this below.

The primary role of skills of enquiry may be relevant to but few and highly specialized curriculums (graduate programs, science high schools, courses designed to attract young people to the profession of fields of knowledge). In their secondary role, however, as the skills of enquiry into enquiries, they are relevant to many curriculums, for these are the skills which lead to *critical* understanding of knowledge.

Third, there are the skills of reading and interpretation by which one discovers the meanings of statements which are embedded in a context of structure.

The first and second of these skills are relatively familiar ones in the literature of education. They are most commonly—though too restrict-edly—referred to as "the application of principles," and "the interpre-tation of data." The third of these kinds of skills—those by which the meaning conferred by structure is discovered—is less commonly re-ferred to in the literature. This paucity of reference is due mainly to the fact that the usefulness of these skills becomes apparent only when teachers and students encounter informative statements embedded in a structure. Such encounters have been rare indeed in the past thirty years or more because our textbooks (those for the training of teachers as well as those for students) have conspicuously omitted the structural context of statements.

This neglect of the structures of disciplines is also responsible for the highly restricted sense which is commonly given to the other two skills. Hence, a brief examination of all three kinds of skills is called for in the course of noting the role which structure might play in imparting them and making them more responsibly used.

Let us begin with "application of principles" because this one of the three kinds of skills *seems* to depend least on the structures of the dis-cipline which produced the "principle." Surely, one might suppose, if someone has discovered a principle or method for doing something, all one needs in order to apply the principle is knowledge of it and practice in the technique by which application is made.

For example, if Ohm's law says $E = IR$, all we apparently need to know is how to determine I and R, what units to use when putting them into the equation, and how to multiply the one by the other. The same kind of simplicity seems to hold good for, say, the formula for a sta-tistic. If the formula for Pearson's *Coefficient of Correlation* is known, surely all we need in addition is a convenient method of computation and knowledge of the measurements, etc., to which the terms of the equation apply.

But those of us who have worked with the Pearson *r* and other statistical formulas know that this simple version of application of principles does not hold good. A given formula is properly applicable only to a restricted range of problems or data. The Pearson *r*, for example, becomes more and more undependable as certain properties of the population to which it is applied become less and less linear. In short, intelligent and reliable application of principles requires us to have well in hand an understanding of the types of problems to which the principle is applicable and an understanding of the variations in application which are required for problems of different types.

We can *try* to overcome this difficulty by reducing these restrictions and conditions of applications to a set of rules. Then we impart the rules along with the principles. But we know very well that this method of enhancing the reliable application of principles also has its limitations. For we do *reduce* the restrictions and conditions of application to rules. That is, the rules are incomplete, they do not encompass very much of the relevant conditions of application. They refer only to the cases which we think will be most commonly encountered. And even in terms of this restricted reference the rules are usually only approximate guides, for we try to make them simple, few, and easily remembered. Otherwise, as rules, they become less and less "practical." In short, rules for regulating the application of principles are substitutes for knowledge of the character and limitations of the principles. They tell us something of what to do and not do, but not why we should do it that way. And as one ancient philosopher has remarked, "We do not truly know unless we know the reason."

It is this "reason" which is given to skill in the application of a principle by knowing something of the structure which produced and gives warrant to the principle. For it is the structure of the discipline which lets us know what restricted chunk of the world was studied by the investigation which gave rise to the principle. It is the same structure which tells us of the compromises which are inevitably made when we come to gather data: the data we make-do with because the best data for our purpose are too hard to come by. And it is the structure which tells us of all the doubtful points, the unverified or unverifiable assumptions we have had to make in order to arrive at our principle from our data. Thus, it is structure which ultimately tells us where and how we can apply our principle and how much confidence we can have in what comes of the application.

Now, what about the skills of secondary enquiry, of enquiry into enquiries? First what use is it to anyone other than the professional contributor to a discipline? This has been answered in large part above. For if reasonable and reliable *use* of principles is desirable and if such reasonableness and reliability depend on at least some knowledge of the structure which produced the principle, then, we need the skills which enable us to understand the structure.

But could not this understanding be conveyed by summary statements, descriptions in general terms of the general form which is taken by the structure of the discipline? There are three reasons why this is not the case. First, few, if any, disciplines have a single structure. The problems of any field are usually too diverse to permit their solution by only a single pattern of enquiry. Second, the men who man the field are too diverse in their aptitudes and preferences to admit of unanimity about a one right mode of attack. Finally, even a single structure, did it exist, is not really singular. Rather, as is the case for principles as described above, a structure is a highly flexible pattern which is continually adapted and modified to fit the particular problems and situations to which it is applied.

Hence, a description of structure in general terms has the same limitations as do general rules for the application of principles: by virtue of their generality, they are too sweeping to be informative in a practical way. Hence, here again, some experience with specific instances of the structure of a discipline seems necessary.

There is another and extremely important reason why the structure of a discipline cannot easily be reduced to one general formulation. It coincides with the reason for my remarking earlier that "interpretation of data" is a seriously restricted misnomer for the skills of enquiry into enquiries. Briefly, it is the following.

The name "interpretation of data" suggests that the structure of enquiry is primarily a merely logical structure, a structure arising only from the rules and restrictions by which one makes defensible interpretations of data. Such a restricted view of enquiry is exemplified by the old "five-step" picture of scientific method, when it refers to "relevant" data as a starting point of enquiry but never digs into the question of what makes data relevant or how we tell relevant from irrelevant data. Such a view goes on to suggest that the basic structure of enquiry consists mainly of the formulation of a hypothetical syllogism (If A, then B. A is. Therefore, B is.), followed by experimental determination of the presence or absence of the antecedent, A. Now let us see what this view omits.

The buried four-fifths of enquiry consists of maneuvers which *precede* the collection of data and define what data are relevant. These maneuvers, we can summarize, for the moment, as consisting of certain hidden steps which the old story of stepwise scientific method omitted.

First, data are rarely, if ever, collected at random. Instead, they are collected as means for answering a specific question or for solving a specific problem. For instance, we may take as our question "What is the *cause* of X?" meaning by "cause" an antecedent event which invariably precedes the appearance of "X" and never appears without being *followed* by "X". Then we seek data about this kind of cause by a highly specific experimental pattern which is designed to yield data about cause in this specific sense.

In other researches, we may ask the question "What are the constituent elements or parts whose organization gives rise to the phenomenon which interests us?" In still other cases, we might be asking "What is the special organization of constituents which confers on the thing investigated (e.g., kind of organism, society, or mineral) the properties which set it apart from other kinds?"

Now each such question requires a different sort of datum. Each kind of datum will be elicited only by an appropriate pattern of experiment. Further, once our data are in hand, each kind must be interpreted in its own appropriate way to yield the kind of conclusion for which it was sought in the first place.

Hence, we see that interpretation of data must be preceded by a plan of experiment which will yield the desired data. The plan of experiment, in turn, is preceded by and determined by a commitment to the kind of question we think is appropriate. And the question of what question to ask is preceded and determined by some metaphysical, preferential, or heuristic commitment to a conception of the nature of our subject matter (for instance, whether to treat an organism in biological enquiry as a collection of causes, an organization of interactions, or a set of organs or instruments each serving a special function relative to the whole).

In brief, different items of scientific knowledge are answers to different kinds of questions and the answer can hardly be said to be understood unless one knows the question to which it is an answer. Further, the answers are based on data collected and—as we have remarked earlier—data actually collected in enquiry are rarely the data which would give the best and most unequivocal answer to our question. Hence, again, we must say that an answer can hardly be said to be well understood unless we also understand the degree to which it, rather than another statement, is the right answer. And this depends on knowing the compromises we made by way of deciding what sorts of data short of the ideal sort to settle for.

The overriding point of all this is that the variety of structures in a given discipline arise because several kinds of questions are asked in that discipline, each entailing its own kinds of experiment, data, and manner of interpretation; and for any one kind of question asked, different compromises between ideal and accessible data are made, depending on the particular problem and material under investigation.

Much of this variety can be encompassed in a series of general statements about the structures of a discipline, though not in one such statement. But just because they are numerous, such statements require illustration before they communicate well. The illustrations can hardly be other than instances of the sort of structure being described in the general statement, and if these are really to illustrate, they must be understood. Hence, again, we bump into a need which seems to be best served by recourse to skills of enquiry into enquiries—the skills which make the illustrations actually illustrate as far as the reader is concerned.

It is the circumstances described above, rather than issues about best ways to teach, which lead so many subject-matter specialists to advocate an "inductive" approach to the principles and methods of their field. It is not that these specialists think that "inductive" learning is better or more efficient than "expository" learning but because *what* is learned in the two cases is quite different. "Expository" teaching inevitably tends toward summary and the hiding of variation. "Inductive" learning tends toward summary knowledge *by way of* the variables involved.

The case for mastery of our third kind of skill—that of reading and interpretation—needs little more than we have said above. Critical understanding of structure is, as we have noted, a condition for flexible application of principles, and the skills of reading and interpretation are, in turn, conditions for the acquisition of the skills of critical understanding. For the structures of the disciplines are made accessible through language (both the language of words and the language of mathematics); hence, the importance of skills which penetrate language to arrive at the purport which that language is intended to convey.

Discipline Structure and Pedagogical Structure

We began by asking what relevance the structure of disciplines might have for the curriculum maker. We have so far tried to suggest some of the answers to this question by contrasting the effect on what is learned of the *presence* of the structure compared to its *absence*. Before leaving the question of the relevance of discipline structure to education, we should look briefly at a more extreme and tougher situation: namely, the effect of *replacing* the structure of the discipline with some other structure.

It is hardly necessary to point out in detail the extent to which curricular practice of the past few decades has tended to such a substitutive practice. Because structures were not generally accessible for study, it became easy and habitual to treat the fruits of disciplines as self-evidently whatever we thought they were. Scientific conclusions were treated as collections of separable statements of literal truths. Historical writing was treated as a true report of the indubitably significant matters of the past. Similar but more various dogmas were imposed on the novel, the drama, and the lyric poem.

We thus simplified the fruits of disciplines to the point where it appeared self-evident that they could be correctly understood without reference to the structure which produced them. With that done, there was nothing to give us pause when we felt inclined to incorporate the fruits of disciplines into other structures quite alien to them. Our science textbooks became catalogues of "facts," for example, without regard to the possibility that these "facts" were merely tentative formulations—not facts but *interpretations* of facts. We hardly knew that we were falsifying the ideational and rational character of mathematics by teaching much of it as if it, too, were a physical science—the product of investigations of the shapes of things and of what happens when piles of things are combined into fewer piles or separated into more numerous piles.

Most of this imposition of alien structures was done in the interest of effective teaching and, I repeat, not done willfully, in disdain of the character of what was taught. Rather, it was done because we did not think that what was taught would be affected by our chosen means.

If we are now to reverse the long trend of the past and begin to take cognizance of the structure of disciplines, we should warn ourselves that the task will not only be difficult but painful. We will not only have the task suggested in earlier pages—of finding appropriate ways of including structure as a facet of curriculum *content*. We also have the task of learning to live with a far more complex problem—that of realizing that we will no longer be free to choose teaching methods, textbook organization, and classroom structuring on the basis of psychological and social considerations alone. Rather, we will need to face the fact that methods are rarely if ever neutral. On the contrary, the means we use color and modify the ends we actually achieve through them. *How* we teach will determine *what* our students learn. If a structure of teaching and learning is alien to the structure of what we propose to teach, the outcome will inevitably be a corruption of that content. And we will know that it is.

WHO KNOWS THE STRUCTURE OF THE DISCIPLINES?

This is a double-barreled question. It asks, first, "*Who* knows?" It also asks "Who *knows*?" Let us take the second question first.

Who *Knows*?

Who *knows* the structures of the disciplines? The answer is, *Nobody*. The following will indicate why this answer is correct and why it must be taken seriously. (But please be patient with the exposition. It necessarily runs through several steps before the story is complete.)

First, we must face the fact that, with the possible exception of physics, most disciplines have *several* structures—not one. Some of this multiplicity arises because different canons of "truth," of "verification," are applied to different investigations in a given discipline. Many more variations of structure arise because men have conceived of many different kinds of "telling" questions to ask of their subject matter and each such question gives rise to a different pattern of experiment, different sorts of data, and different ways of interpreting data.

This matter of diversity was discussed briefly in the section on structure and skills above. It would be well to develop it somewhat further here, with emphasis on the way diversity arises. This emphasis will enable us to sketch an important difference in the way scientific disciplines develop and exhibit their diversities.

Science begins, or tries to begin, in ignorance. It will, if it can, turn its back on the folk wisdom and folk need which is the occasion of its existence. In actual deed, however, ignorance cannot originate an enquiry. If data are to be collected and interpreted, there must be some guide to relevance and irrelevance, a determination of what shall constitute the data of that enquiry. To serve this guiding or leading function, the scientist must borrow or invent a conception of the character of his subject matter.

It is at this point that a criterion which dominates much scientific enquiry does its work. That criterion I shall call *reliability*. It requires, first, that the guiding principles of the enquiry be maximally free of vagueness and ambiguity in respect of things, that the referents of its terms have unequivocal location and limit; second, it requires that the manipulations and measurements indicated by the terms be precise and repeatable with uniform results.

These are exigent demands. For a young science faced with a complex subject matter they are impossible to meet except by sacrifice of the subject matter's full complexity. This sacrifice is often made. A conception of the subject matter is adopted which ignores whatever is unamenable to existing methods of reliable investigation.

As investigations proceed under the guidance of these pale images of the subject, new tools and competences of investigation are developed. There will then be revision of the terms of enquiry to make them a better fit to the scope and richness of the subject matter. But this is slow work at best.

Hence most, if not all, conclusions of sciences which emphasize reliability are limited in their fit to a second criterion, that of validity. They may be true, but not of their subject as known to us. They are true of the subject as simplified and devised by the scientist.

There are sciences, on the other hand, which give first allegiance to the criterion of validity. (There are individual preferences, too, in this regard. Some scientists, irrespective of field, prefer validity to reliability, or vice versa.) They prefer guiding conceptions of the subject matter which seem to come closest to fitting its complexity. However, if, again, the science is young, the subject matter is not at all well known. Hence, the validity-determined conceptions which are invented for it depend very much on the personal views of different scientists concerning its character. The result of this is a personalism, a semi-privacy of evidence and emphasis, which contrasts strongly to the *public* character of evidence and emphasis in reliability-determined sciences. The result of this difference is that validity-guided sciences tend to develop and exploit many different principles of enquiry at a given time. By contrast, the reliability-guided sciences tend to show their diverse principles and structures serially instead of concurrently.

A reasonably good picture of the distribution of diversity (especially concurrent diversity) among the various scientific disciplines can be obtained from an adaptation of Auguste Comte's hierarchy of the "positive" sciences. That hierarchy, modernized, runs as follows:

Social Sciences
Psychology
Biology
Chemistry
Physics
Mathematics

Roughly speaking, the variety and number of structures in each discipline on this line is greater as one moves *up* the line. Physics has only a few (two? three?). Biology has five or six which are viable at the present time. (These tend to be reliability-determined sciences.)

Then, the number makes an enormous jump. The situation in psychology is such that Hilgard finds it necessary to describe eleven structures for learning theories alone. And this number arises from a relatively economical differentiation of structures appropriate to an upper-level textbook.[3] If Hilgard were making finer distinctions for the sake, exclusively, of his colleagues, the number might well double. Furthermore, Hilgard omits from his eleven some structures which are cur-

3. E. R. Hilgard, *Theories of Learning* (New York: Appleton-Century-Crofts, 1956).

rently unfashionable. These, be it noted, are not necessarily exhausted or "proved wrong." Some of them might return to fashion in a modified form next year. (Psychology is an arena of conflict between validity and reliability determination.)

When we come to sociology and anthropology the number is even greater—so large in fact, that I have yet to see a treatment of them, such as Hilgard's treatment of learning theory, which reduces them to a reasonable number. Let us take a crystal-ball view and declare that the number of them, distinguished a la Hilgard, would be in the neighborhood of thirty.

Finally, when we come to disciplines, such as history, which fall beyond the Comteian line, the number is still greater.

Now the sheer number of these structures would not, alone, make it impossible to "know" the structures of the disciplines. Large as the total number may be, it poses only a practical difficulty, not a theoretical impossibility, which would bolster my assertion that nobody *knows*. An arduous task of scholarship is posed. But a reasonable number of scholars working on the problem could bring forth fruit in a reasonable length of time, as time goes in the world of scholarship. (Incidentally, there is no such reasonable number at work on it). The problem approaches the point of theoretical impossibility because of *where* and *how* these structures are found and identified.

They are to be found nowhere but in the enormous array of accepted and acceptable research papers which investigators in the disciplines have turned out over the years. Now even this fact poses no theoretically impossible problem—though it shows how very arduous, indeed, the scholarly work would be.

But now, hear this. Every research program worthy of the name has a large number of recognizable properties which distinguish its pattern from the patterns of some other programs. Let us make an *outrageously* conservative estimate of the number of these properties—twenty, let us say. Make the further conservative supposition that the average number of alternatives for each property is five. (E.g., *color* might be one of the twenty properties and, if so, there would be research programs of five different colors.) Suppose further, as we must, that investigators of structure are free to choose any one, any two, any three, (and so on, up to twenty) of these properties as the significant properties for identifying and classifying the structures of the disciplines.

In that case, how many different views of the structures of the disciplines might we get? Even if investigators limited themselves to using but one property as the basis for classification, there would be twenty different schemes of classification, each scheme with a set of five "pigeonholes" quite different from the pigeonholes of the other nineteen schemes. If investigators were free to use two properties at a time as well as one at a time, there would be an additional 210 classifications each with twenty-five pigeonholes. If the investigator is free to take *any* number of properties (one, two, on up to twenty) as basis for his classification, the number of possible schemes, if I remember my algebra correctly, is 2^{20}.

Now the important point about this large number of possible classifications of discipline structures consists merely of this: each of them represents a possible attack on the problem of the structure of disciplines. Each of them is potentially capable of rational defense. And each possible attack is possibly one which might illuminate the question.

All of this is to say for the discipline represented by this paper (the discipline which investigates the structures of disciplines) what we have said for other disciplines: it has a number of structures of its own. Knowledge of the structure of the disciplines is sought in different ways by different men, using different conceptions of the problem.

The different ways in which the problem is conceived are certainly not as numerous as our figure of 2^{20}. But they are numerous enough. And the crucial point is that each of these conceptions usually includes criteria by which other conceptions are made to appear trivial or subordinate. None of them is so much wrong as incomplete, and we have yet to find a widely acceptable new conception which binds them all together. In short, no one *knows*. Instead of knowledge, we have tested models and approximations—like the practitioners of the more familiar sciences.

In this discussion I have tried to meet the problem of diversity by three devices. First, I have made a definite (though not exclusive choice) between two major alternatives. These alternatives can be described very simply. On the one hand, structures of disciplines can be approached *syntactically* in terms of the logical structures they exhibit. In an investigative (scientific) discipline, for example, we would look for different methods of verification and justification of conclusions and describe these as constituting the structures of the discipline. I have illustrated this above, in the example of an automobile, the neutron, and the neutrino.

On the other hand, disciplines can be approached *substantively*, in terms of the conceptual devices which are used for defining, bounding, and analyzing the subject matters they investigate. Thus, we would look for differences of structure which arise when different scientists use different conceptions of their subject matter to guide their enquiries. This is suggested in the quotation from *Physics*, where we are given a hint of the differences which might arise were physics to investigate all phenomena as if they arose from the behavior of particles, as against enquiries which would treat phenomena as wave-motion.

The substantive approach is better seen if we examine some of the different ways in which biologists can conceive the organism for purposes of investigation. In the interests of reliability and simplification, they may conceive the organism as many pairs of fixed and determinate cause-effect connections. This conception permits a very simple pattern of experiment, neat data, and relatively easy interpretation. It yields a body of knowledge which has the structure of a catalogue. We record cause A and its effect, a; cause B and its effect, b; and so on.

Other biologists will seek somewhat greater validity by trying to include in their conception something of the *flexibility* which characterizes the organism. For this purpose, they might replace the idea of a collection of fixed causes and fixed effects with the idea called homeostasis. Under this conception, the organism is treated as a collection of equilibrium points around each of which a limited degree of variation occurs. Researchers guided by this conception try to find what these equilibria are, how far the living body can deviate from each and still return, and what mechanisms there are for permitting deviation and controlling its range and return.

Still other biologists will seek greater validity by trying to include in their conception somewhat more of the *system* or *unity* which characterizes the organism. For example, they may conceive the organism as a vastly complicated "feedback" mechanism in which any damage or change in one part would be followed by "corrective" changes in many others. This would differ from the homeostatic view by refusing to "anatomize" the organism into many distinct corrective mechanisms, each concerned with but a single variable. Instead of trying to identify a *list* of equilibria, it would try to discover the single *general system* of conditions which define "being alive." It would then try to discover what different specific and concrete systems there were which fulfilled these general conditions.

In this last view, be it noted, the very idea of cause-and-effect pairs, of fixed and meaningful anatomical parts, of definite functions of each such part, all disappear. A "normal" organ with its "normal" function becomes merely one of many potentialities of the organism, conspicuous merely because it is frequently visible.

I have gone on at such length about the "feedback" conception because it is relatively easy to see in this case that *substantive* differences of structure have radical effects on what we would call knowledge of the subject being investigated. For example, what was called knowledge of the organism under the cause-effect ("A causes D") now becomes merely one datum among many for the feedback conception. ("Under conditions X, an A is maintained which interacts with temporary D and E to yield B, etc.") Furthermore, this datum is destined to be assimilated into a form of knowledge which would be meaningless in terms of the cause-effect conception.

Because of this potency of the substantive principles of enquiry to determine what knowledge is sought, I shall emphasize the substantive more than the syntactical view of structure in this discussion.

The second way I have tried to solve the problem of the diversity of approaches to the structure of the disciplines is by exercise of "permissive eclecticism." Take, for example, the treatment of "reliability" and "validity" a few pages earlier. They were treated as two different but equally important criteria for the judgment of substantive principles of enquiry. We spoke of some sciences as favoring one, some the other; and of different scientists personally favoring one or the other. We pointed out that both criteria are proper to the scientific enterprise. We tried to indicate that all sciences and all scientists eventually take cognizance of both.

In so holding up both these criteria to clear view, "permissive eclecticism" is illustrated. For, by contrast to this procedure, there are many approaches to the structure of disciplines which take a strong position on what scientists should and should not do. There are approaches, for example, which assert that only reliability is a proper criterion for science. In such an approach, validity is ignored. Other approaches emphasize validity over reliability. And both such approaches tend to explain *away* or condemn what they do not espouse. In short, they are prescriptive, not descriptive.

A prescriptive attitude is not limited to the validity-reliability issue. For example, we would have no trouble at all finding some positivistic students of structure who would raise their hands in horror at Fermi's invention of the neutrino. Such a person might well say, "No scientist has a right to develop a term which is not reducible to 'thing-language.' The neutrino is not. Therefore, the neutrino is not science." Then, in any later discussion of the structure of physics, the case of the neutrino would not appear, would appear as a terrible example—or be relegated to a footnote.

Where we have recognized issues of principle among students of structure, such issues as "validity-reliability," we have treated them not as "validity" *versus* "reliability" but as choices which different scientists make in one direction or another. Thus we have managed, we hope, to be less prescriptive and more inclusive than would otherwise have been the case.

As a third way of facing the problem of diverse interpretations of structure, I include the next section.

In this section, I shall touch on three subjects. First, I shall review one traditional description of the disciplines (with a prelude) together with some variations on it. This review will be in no degree representative. On the contrary, it is designed to serve a special purpose: namely, to introduce some of the terms and distinctions which have proved to be perennially useful in the description of structure. To this end, I have chosen a traditional view which introduces terms and distinctions in a relatively uncomplicated way. My emphasis shall be on these terms and distinctions as such, and not on what the user of them thinks he has discovered about structure from their use.

Second, I shall try to indicate in what general areas of scholarship information about structure can be sought. Third, I shall list a few useful sources of commentary on the structure of the disciplines.

Who Knows?
Prelude: some issues, terms, and distinctions about structure

It is necessary to take full cognizance of the fact that the problem of structure revolves, like a planet, about *two* foci. There is not only the question of what structure each discipline has. There is also the question of what disciplines there are—what specialized practices are sufficiently different from one another to justify separate study. This second question arises because there are no objectively *given* bases which determine, once and for all, what disciplines there are.

It has been widely supposed, for example, that there are indubitable grounds for recognizing basically different *subject matters* for investigation, basically different orders of phenomena, different kinds of *being*, each of which requires a separate discipline because each is amenable to examination by only one method of attack, a method quite different from the one which works on other orders of phenomena, other kinds of being. Many men have espoused such a view. They have asked us, for instance, to recognize a fundamental difference between living matter and non-living matter. In that case, of course, there must be a science of each—biology on the one hand, physics-chemistry on the other. Other men thought they saw a fundamental difference between man and the rest of nature. Nature was bound by immutable, unbreakable laws. Men, on the other hand, were "free." On this basis, then, there would be two fundamentally different disciplines—science, which studied the laws of nature; morals, which studied freedom and right choice.

Still other men have emphasized the difference between the generality of biological and physical phenomena on the one hand, and the *particularities* of human events on the other hand. On this basis, a fundamental distinction between science and history is generated. And the structure of each of these is then studied and formulated with emphasis on the contrast between them.

Similar lines have been drawn to separate mathematics from all other sciences. Mathematics was conceived as the study of ideal forms; the other sciences as study of material things. Since ideal forms and physical things were different kinds of being, they would necessarily be studied in different ways and yield knowledge of different kinds.

Logic has long enjoyed a similar distinction. In company with mathematics, or identified as the master-mathematics, or envisaged as the queen of all sciences including mathematics, it has enjoyed special attention as the science of a subject matter utterly different from the subject matters of all other disciplines.

Some of these splendid isolations and sharp distinctions remain with us to this day. There are few, if any, modern mathematicians, for example, who would take the position that geometry or arithmetic consisted of knowledge abstracted from study of physical shapes and physical things and events. Logic, too, remains isolated in the minds of many of its students. Morals and ethics have resisted assimilation to the other disciplines (" 'Fact' statements and 'value' statements," remains a common distinction.)

On the other hand, it is clear that many such apparently basic differentiations of phenomena are illusions. Do we think that living and non-living are basically different? Then along comes a biophysics and a biochemistry to smudge the difference. Are the movements of the celestial spheres and the behavior of earthly bodies two different orders of phenomena? Then along comes a Newton with a *universal* gravitation and its accompanying laws to make them one. In the same way, psychology and sociology have taken over a part of what was once thought to be the proper subject matter of ethics. And there are even a few attempts to reduce the temporal ebb and flow of human affairs to "scientific" laws of historical change or historical progress.

The reason for the illusion of basic difference of subject matter is of some importance in understanding the structure of the sciences. We can show it most briefly by indicating what it is that makes the illusion disappear. When celestial mechanics and terrestrial mechanics become one, it was because Newton (and those famous giants on whose shoulders he said he stood) had invented a new set of conceptions, a new structure, capable of subsuming the data about both these groups of phenomena—celestial as well as terrestrial. When light and electricity became but portions of one extensive phenomenon, it was because

Maxwell and Faraday had invented a field conception which established connections between the two.

In short, two bodies of phenomena may appear to be different *orders* of phenomena, vastly different *kinds* of things and events, only because we have studied them and discovered knowledge about them using two separate sets of terms, two different bodies of conceptions—one set of conceptions for one collection of phenomena, the other conceptions for the other phenomena. By so doing we create two distinct bodies of knowledge—and no connections between them. Since, perforce, we see the two bodies of phenomena through the knowledge we have of them, and the knowledge of one has no coordinate connection with our knowledge of the other, the phenomena, too, look separate and different. Then, when we develop a new structure which subsumes both bodies of phenomena—or when we perform the lesser miracle of inventing conceptions which connect our formerly unconnected sets of conception—the two bodies lose their apparent difference of kind and become connected parts or aspects of *one* kind of thing.

This business of separate but equal sets of conceptions and their later integration should not blind us, however, to the fact that some boundaries between subjects have never been broken down. Perhaps the boundaries remain only because we have not yet found the embracing new body of conceptions. Perhaps, on the other hand, these are joints in nature, separate bones, separate subjects, so different in kind that unity could be achieved only at the price of ignoring important differences.

There is no demonstration, no *proof* for either of these views. Hence, we should beware of two dogmas, neither of which can be supported —except as dogmas or as hopes. On the one hand, we must beware espousing the notion of a unity of all the sciences (or, more sweepingly, a unity of all knowledge) as the clear end of the evolution of human enquiry. On the other hand, we must avoid being taken in by the present state of things—supposing that the different disciplines which now exist and the differences in structure which distinguish them are differences forever more.

But to return to our original point. There is no fixed catalogue of disciplines, for each of which we must seek the structure. Subject-matter phenomena do not supply a fixed basis for such a catalogue, as we have noted. Nor have other criteria which men have tried to apply been any more successful. There is perennially, for example, the effort to identify fundamental, independent mental abilities (whether called "faculties" or not) and then to try for a catalogue of disciplines based on the abilities which are used in each. Other men have tried to identify fundamentally different human aims (knowing, doing, and making, for example) and then attempted to distinguish kinds of disciplines (science, administration, and art) according to which of these ends they serve. Still other men—notably Kant—have tried to identify the basic ideational content with which the human mind is equipped. Then they have tried to establish a catalogue of disciplines based on the various basic ideas (time, space, and motion yield physics, for example; will and freedom for morals).

Since, then, there is no fixed catalogue of disciplines, we must accord a wide freedom to the investigator. He has the right to distinguish and identify the disciplines as well as tell us about their structure.

The Comtean analysis of structure

Let us review a relatively modern student of discipline structure, Auguste Comte (1798–1857). But before we embark on the details of his view, let us re-emphasize the reason for doing so. We are not interested primarily in his particular catalogue of disciplines, nor in what he says their structures are. He is of value to us because of *the structure with which he attacks the problem of structure.* He uses certain distinctions and conceptions which have proved of continuing value. It is these distinctions and conceptions which are worth our while.

Comte begins by seating himself firmly in the saddle of subject matter. The hierarchy of disciplines which we erected above (mathematics-physics-chemistry-biology-psychology-sociology), is not, as he develops it, so much a hierarchy of disciplines as it is a hierarchy of subject matters. It is more informatively erected as follows (I am here omitting psychology, since it, as we shall see, was a strictly illegitimate affair for Comte):

> Socials
> Biologicals
> Chemicals
> Physicals
> Mathematicals

The above represents a chinese-box system, each entry enclosed in the one listed above it. That is, physicals are the ultimate units of matter. (They might have been represented by the gravitational atoms of Newton in his century. Today, they would be electrons, protons, neutrons, and so on.) Chemicals, as next in line, consist of organizations of these physicals. Today, these would be the atoms of the various chemical elements, each atom being a particular organization of electrons, protons, and neutrons. Biologicals (living organisms) would then be organizations of chemicals. Finally, socials would be organizations of biologicals. (There are no "psychologicals" because Comte's is a hierarchy of the "positive" sciences—which means sciences possessing a *material*, tangible subject matter. Psyches are *not* material.)

Let us listen to Comte himself:

> Chemical phenomena are necessarily more complex then physical and depend upon the physical without influencing them. Everyone knows that all chemical action is influenced by weight, temperature, electricity, etc., and offers in addition something peculiar which modifies the action of the other [physical] agents. This consideration enables us to characterize it [chemistry] as a distinct science.
>
> . . . it is certain that we observe in living bodies all the phenomena, either mechanical or chemical, which we note in gross bodies plus a special order of phenomena, living phenomena properly speaking.
>
> In all social phenomena one notes first the influence of the physiological laws of the individual, then something particular which modifies the effects of the former and which makes the action of individual on individual and generation on generation singularly complex in the human species. Hence it is evident that in order to study social phenomena one must start from a thorough knowledge of the laws pertaining to the individual. On the other hand, this subordination of the one study to the other does not demand, as some eminent physiologists have been led to believe, that sociology be a simple appendix to physiology. Although the phenomena are certainly coherent, they are not identical and the separation of the two sciences is of an importance truly fundamental. It would be impossible to treat the study of the species collectively as a pure deduction from the study of the individual since the social conditions which modify the action of physiological laws are precisely at this point the most essential consideration.[4]

In short, Comte thinks that he can recognize orders or *levels* of organization. Further, since each new level of organization brings forth new behaviors (new phenomena), a new science is required to study it.

But now note carefully what ought to have been the correct referent for the "it" in the sentence above. "It" is not merely the new behaviors, nor the new organization. It is the whole "order" which exhibits the new phenomena, and this new whole has two aspects: its constituent parts and a special organization of those parts.

Thus, the structure of these disciplines emerges. The knowledge sought by each discipline would consist of two subdepartments. Each

4. "Course of Positive Philosophy," chap. 2, from *Organizations of the Sciences* (Chicago: University of Chicago Press, 1946). The phraseology above is a slight modification of the translation which appears in the volume here given as reference.

science (except physics) would first *analyze* its peculiar subject matter, to find out its components—to determine which of the components studied by the science below it make up the subject matter of the science in hand. (Physics would not analyze because its subject consists of the ultimate, unanalyzable units. And what mathematics does, we shall ignore for the moment.) Thus biology would first try to determine what sorts of chemicals enter into the organization of living things. And chemistry would first determine which of the physicals compose each kind of chemical.

This task would not be exceedingly difficult, as Comte saw it. For each science in the hierarchy can begin its truly scientific progress only after the previous science has become reasonably complete. Thus chemistry begins with a reasonably good body of physics behind it. Biology begins when there is a reasonably adequate chemistry already developed. Thus, the analytic phase of enquiry in each discipline begins with prior knowledge of what it is looking for.

After the analytic phase comes the second phase, which completes the science. This must be a study of the *organization*, the pattern of actions and connections among the various components, which makes of each set of constituents something new, something different, a new order of phenomena.

This phase of scientific enquiry would be more difficult than the first phase, as Comte saw it. For note that the organization is unique. What makes a living thing different from a sackful of the chemicals which compose it is the special organization which converts the mere sackful, the mere mixture, into something else. And that special organization cannot be deduced from what the previous science has discovered about the component stuff. In the same way, a society is no mere aggregation of individual live bodies. It too has organization which cannot be inferred from what biology (physiology) discovers about organisms.

Thus we have (so far) an exceedingly simple picture. If this story of Comte's were the whole truth and nothing but the truth, the task of the curriculum maker who takes account of structure would be enormously simplified. In the first place, the *sequence* of the curriculum is already settled for him. There is no understanding sociology without prior study of biology; no understanding of biology without prior study of chemistry; and so on. (In point of fact, this story of Comte's, though not the whole truth, has enough of truth about it to remind us of the problem of "prerequisites" which plagues college programs and high school programs at this moment. Of the sciences on the Comtean line, biology and chemistry, at any rate, currently treat themselves, for curriculum purposes, much as Comte required. Biology wants its students first to have chemistry and physics. Chemistry wants its students to have physics. Only sociology at the present moment is anti-Comtean enough to consider itself independent of biology.)

Not only is the sequence of the curriculum laid down; so also is the manner of teaching. For what each science knows, it *knows*. The components of each subject matter are things—visible things. Hence, the method of investigation is obvious, straightforward, and unequivocal. It consists of *looking*. When one looks, one sees. Hence a science either has it or it doesn't have it. If it can see, it knows. If it can't see, it is in ignorance and must develop ways in which it can see.

Furthermore, the same straightforwardness holds for the organizational phase of investigation. The organization, too, consists, presumably, of visible ties of some sort, various and sundry spatial arrangements, attractions and repulsions, other interactions. Hence, organization, too, is accessible to sensory inspection. There are no questionable hypotheses, no tentative formulations resting on indirect and remote verifications (like our electron or, worse, our brashly unscientific neutrino), no reconstructions and revisions. This being so (since we know, we *know;* and when we know, we *know* that we know) all teaching can be —indeed, should be—dogmatic.

Let us summarize this positive doctrine as it appears so far. From a substantive point of view, we see that each subject matter is conceived as composed of some members from a familiar set of components, members organized in a new and unfamiliar way. The task of enquiry is, therefore, (a) to determine the selection of components and (b) discover the organization.

From a syntactical point of view, the structure of a Comtean discipline is *very* simple. Each discipline presupposes a uniform order of phenomena accessible to observation. Hence, there are no problems of proof or verification, so to speak; only a matter of discovery by inspection.

Now what about the structure with which Comte erected this structure of disciplines? From the syntactical side, there is little to be learned, for, as we have said, Comte is prescriptively simple here. He rejects explorations which do not fit the definition of an "objective," "positive" science—explorations which are not strictly by observation and report. From the substantive side, only two, apparently simple, terms are used —*constituent* and *organization*; or, in a more ancient nomenclature, *matter* and *form*. Since there are but these two terms and because they appear so simple, it might seem that I have sent a man to do a boy's work by using the Comtean structure wherewith to introduce them.

The simplicity, however, is only apparent. Complications lurk unnoticed at two points. They lurk at the bottom of the Comtean line, hidden under the unexplained "mathematics." They lurk, too, in the fact that matter and form are capable of several relations to one another, over and above the relation into which Comte puts them. And for each such different relation, a different structure of the disciplines emerges, with different implications for curriculum.

Let us take the latter first—the matter of relations between matter and form. In the story we have told so far (let us call it the story of Comte-1), the relation is as follows. The material constituents of an object of enquiry have a character of their own. By "a character of their own," I mean a character which belongs to the constituents themselves, which is not imposed on them by the organization and which is not erased or altered by that organization.

The organization, on the other hand, has no "character of its own." It has not because it is *not* an "it," a something. Instead, it is an arrangement of the constituents. We can think of it as an arrangement by which the several constituents are made to interact, restrict, and stimulate one another in certain specific ways. These are ways which the constituents had potentially all along, as a consequence of having a character of their own. But they also had many other possibilities. Hence, we could not have predicted what phenomena would be exhibited by these particular constituents when in this particular organization.

Take the organization called a living system, for example. Its elemental chemical constituents are carbon, hydrogen, nitrogen, sulfur, and a few others. Suppose we had known the properties of these elements from a previous, thoroughgoing chemical investigation which knew everything about them—short of what would be discovered by studying them as constituents of a living system. Could we, from the Comtean point of view, have predicted such things as enzymatic actions, capacity for self-reproduction, for self-regulation, and so on? Not at all. We would have to discover these matters as subjects of enquiry in their own right. However, once we *had* discovered what biologists now know—amino acids, proteins, DNA and RNA—we would find nothing shocking about their character and behavior, could, indeed, trace their behavior (once they were known in their own right) back to properties of the carbon, hydrogen, oxygen, and nitrogen atoms.

Let us present the above relationship of matter, form, and an object of enquiry as follows:

A proper object of enquiry is a level of organization.

The phenomena exhibited by a level of organization are due to:

a) the properties of its constituents (known in general from study by a previous science)

b) as modulated by and in this specific level of organization. (The organization at any level is coherent with but not inferable from the character of what it organizes.)

Now let us look at some of the variations which can be rung upon this theme.

One of the quickest and simplest (and most popular) variations on the Comtean scheme is achieved merely by altering the last item above so that it reads:

(The organization at any level *is* inferable from the character of what it organizes.)

This view let us call reductionism (or Comte-0). It is perennially a refuge of simplicity when research or teaching at a given level of Comtean organization becomes too difficult.

It permits the sociologist, for example, to give up his wearing struggle with the full complexities of society. He can fall back on a previously developed psychology and construct a model of social behavior on the basis of what would be expected from the psychology. Only recently, one school of anthropologists fell back on this procedure. They embraced the Freudian picture of the psyche (id, ego, superego) with its idea of a developmental picture which proceeds through various stages subject to the vicissitudes of its social environment. This picture gave the anthropologists the questions to ask their subject matter.

"How does the Oedipus develop in this society and that one?"

"How many members of this and that society reach the genital stage?"

"—the anal stage?"

"—the oral stage?"

"What happens to the Oedipal crisis in this society where the children have community mothers and fathers instead of own parents and own sibs?"

Now note a curious and important point here. Proceding in this way —asking of a society only the questions suggested by the psychology to which they had reduced the problem—the anthropologists will, for the most part, discover in a society only those aspects of it which *are* relevant to the underlying psychology. Thus, unless the underlying psychology were entirely spurious, every investigation conducted on such a reductive basis would *seem* to bear witness to the propriety of the reductive structure. It works. It poses questions to which the subject matter yields answers. The answers are coherent with one another. Everything is just dandy.

It is this sort of self-guaranteeingness which makes it possible for different structures to operate in a given discipline. Each structure represents some *limited* set of questions to which the subject responds by yielding data. And as long as practitioners of the discipline ask no other kinds of questions, they are unlikely to have doubts about the singular propriety of their favored structure.

We can contrast reductionism to Comte-1 by summarizing it thus:
A proper object of enquiry is a level of organization.
The phenomena exhibited by a level of organization are due to:
a) the properties of its constituents (known in general from a previous science)
b) as modulated by an organization arising from and inferable from the character of what is organized.

Now let us look at a variation on the Comte-1 theme which works at the other extreme—by making *organization* loom large and *constituent* fade away as a source of explanation.

This kind of structure for a discipline has been rarer than reductionism perhaps because it demands, as we shall see, a high level of mathematics or some equivalent source which provides us with knowledge about structure in general. But it has been by no means rare. Histories have been written which selected and explained the events they recorded by reference to a pattern which they thought was in control of human affairs—cycle, expanding sine wave, spiral progress. In the same way, notions of symmetry and parity have long been criteria by which physicists have chosen one explanation as against another.

To take a more concrete example, the Bohr model of the atom, itself reductive in large part, accounted for chemical valence and for the existence of inert chemical elements by a "magic number." That is, chemical combination was supposed to occur only insofar as the combining atoms "filled" the outer electronic orbit of the participating atoms. "Filling" meant that the number of electrons in this orbit, shell, or ring, reached a certain number or numbers. Elements which did not combine (inert elements) were composed of atoms which already had a "magic number" of electrons in the outer shell. This number *was* the explanation, the principle. There was nothing further to explain why it worked as it did.

A substantial part of contemporary sociology, too, has used "reduction upward." Hard on the heels of the Freudian experiment described above, many sociologists suddenly saw that they were selling themselves out by "reduction" and tried to turn the tables. They began a body of investigation embodying the idea that psychology depended on sociology.

They took the position that personality was the outcome of social structure, the product of "socialization," "acculturation," "interpersonal relations," and so on. Of course, this required a conception of personality itself which departed, root and branch, from such conceptions as Freud's. There could be no more semi-biological development of personality, no more "instincts" from which this development could take its start. Instead, the newborn baby had to be conceived as some sort of nearly blank slate, a kind of highly malleable stuff which different societies could mold and shape each in its own way. Similarly, the sociologists had to develop conceptions which would enable society to supply what instinct and developmental pattern had supplied in the Freudian view—a causally forceful pattern (organization) of society which would impose itself on the plastic human infant. Thus "acculturation," "interpersonal relations," etc.

This permutation among the possible relations of constituent-and-organization, form-and-matter, is not one which was given full notice by Comte. Rather, it belongs to the emphases characteristic of other students of the disciplines—Plato and Augustine among the ancients Alfred Whitehead and John Dewey, among modern ones.

These men, though together in their emphasis on organizing principles, differed widely in their view of their origin and nature. For Plato they were Ideas which organized, alike, the world and the human mind. Augustine gave this notion a Christian dye by translating the Platonic Ideas into ordering principles used by Divinity to shape the world. Further, he gave these Ideas a massively mathematical bent, finding in number, proportion, and geometry a large part of these ordering principles. Dewey rings another change by converting the Platonic Ideas into what he calls Logical Forms. These Logical Forms differ from Augustine's by having their origin, not in the Divine, but in human need and human ingenuity: they are constructs, inventions, developed by man to further his enquiries.

In the above fragment of philosophical history, I am not merely wandering in a favorite path. Rather, the history illustrates a point which rises again and again among the structures of modern disciplines: if organization is given hegemony over constituents, form over matter, it becomes almost indispensable to find a source, a science or a discipline, which can approach and study (or invent) organizing forms independently of their embodiment in matter. Thus Augustine distinguishes three major disciplines, the moral, the natural, and the rational. The rational was the study of order itself—mathematics, logic, and so on. The moral studied the orderly life. The natural (corresponding to all of Comte from physics onward) studied the ordering principles of nature.

And it is moving, indeed, to see that we can span the centuries between Augustine and John Dewey, between a Christian Platonism and a modern pragmatism very simply by noting that Dewey, too, envisages corresponding major disciplines:

AUGUSTINE	DEWEY
Moral	Commonsense Enquiry
Natural	Scientific Enquiry
Rational	Enquiry into Enquiry—
	a critical discipline of
	structure
	Mathematics—a creative
	discipline of structure

We can summarize this way of using form-matter, organization-constituent, as follows:

The proper object of enquiry is pattern and patterned things.

The behavior exhibited by a patterned thing is due to:

a) its form or pattern (patterns in general are usually known from a prior science)

b) as imposed upon a matter, the matter affecting the behavior of the thing only a little or not at all.

So far, we have dealt with but two terms in the Comtean treatment of structure: organization and constituents (form and matter). We have watched it run through three combinations. First, we noted their combination in Comte-1. There, they were coordinate and nearly independent factors. The subject matter of an investigation was a combination of the two—almost a simple sum of constituent-conferred behaviors and organization-conferred behaviors.

Then, we examined reductionism (Comte-0). In this view, organization is almost completely subordinated to the constituent factor. Organization arises from potentialities of the constituents and knowledge of organization can be obtained by inference from our knowledge of the constituents.

Third, we examined the case in which organization takes complete power over the constituent factor. Constituents *when un*organized may show properties of their own. (Actually, these are properties conferred by their own inner organization.) When a new organization is imposed upon them to form a new "thing," the erstwhile properties of the constituents become unimportant or disappear. They are repressed by the new organization or radically modified by it. Hence, it is knowledge of organization which gives us knowledge of the organized thing. The constituents do not matter.

We also pointed out that when enquiry is controlled by a structure in which organization dominates constituents, a special feature arises: there is the need for a special discipline which gives us knowledge of organizations in general. Such a discipline is exemplified by mathematics in Comte (and for many others as well). We shall return to this point in the next section.

Meanwhile, it is important to note that there is a third term in Comte with which we have not dealt. It readily passes unnoticed in the Comtean story because it *does* so little. It is important, but it is not operational.

That third term is *end* or *outcome*, the "thing" which arises when form and matter combine. In Comte's own vocabulary, it is the new order of phenomena which arises when the subject materials of a "lower" science becomes constituents in a new organization

In Comte, as we have remarked, this factor is important but not operational. It is important because it is the subject matter to be investigated. A biological, a chemical, or a social is each such an outcome. For each arises when an organization is imposed on the previous subject, and each is the center of attention of a separate discipline.

This factor, this *outcome* is non-operational, though, despite its importance. It is non-operational in the sense that it explains nothing because it "causes" nothing, as far as the science which studies it is concerned. Rather, it is, for the purposes of its sciences, not a cause but an effect, the thing "caused" by the coming together of constituents and organization. In the technical lingo, it is not an agent but a patient, not a doer but a thing done-to.

This factor—outcome or *end*; product of *form* and *matter*—is not always treated as a mere patient, however. It can be treated as an agent and thereby become a major factor in the structure of a discipline. It not only *can* become a major structural factor, it has been so treated in many disciplines at many times.

Mathematics and a revised Comtean story

You will recall that something called mathematics sits at the bottom of the Comtean line. You will recall, too, that it has been sitting there ignored for several pages.

There is ample precedent for this. Most men who have studied the structure of mathematics have been puzzled by mathematics. Their puzzlement has arisen from two major sources: first, because mathematics appears to be so *certain*. Each stage of its development has stood in stark contrast to the other sciences by virtue of the absence of any ground for doubting its content, or, at least, any ground at all comparable to the grounds we appeal to for doubting the complete truth of such sciences as physics and biology.

This first puzzlement about mathematics is made more meaningful by the second source of puzzlement: the fact that it either has no subject matter or, if it has one, that it is not a material subject matter, not things and events accessible to our senses. The equilateral triangle of geometry is a far cry from the triangles we might construct with straight-edge and compass. Indeed, we perform the constructions on the basis of what geometry tells us about such triangles. And even if we did construct them without the aid of geometry, we would not be able to arrive at their properties by some strict induction from the characteristics of our drawings. Similarly, but more obviously, the straight line of classical geometry and the geometrical point are of something other than the world of things, lacking breadth in the one case, length and breadth in the other. It is this absence of a material subject matter to which we refer our conclusions which makes the question of the certainty of mathematics such a perennial puzzle.

There is precedent, too, in Comte, for leaving his conception of mathematics until the last. He says, in the "Positive Philosophy":

> I must now call attention to an immense gap which has been purposely left. . . . The science of mathematics has not been located in our scientific scheme. The reason for this voluntary omission lies in the very importance of this science, so vast and so fundamental. Today, mathematics is more important as an instrument which the human mind can employ in the study of natural phenomena than by virtue of the real and precise knowledge which it offers.
>   . . . the abstract part (of mathematics) is no more than an immense extension of natural logic. . . .[5]

It was not, in fact, until fifteen years later, in another volume, that Comte clarified fully what he meant by a "natural logic." Let us see what it came to, for it survives in one variant or another in many current views of the structure of the sciences.

Comte's idea of natural logic is worth pursuing into some of its modern variations for the sake of three services it can perform for us. First, it resolves certain oppositions between theory and practice. By so doing, it points toward solution of a vexing curriculum problem, the problem of "education for living" versus "education in the disciplines." We shall develop this solution very shortly.

Second, Comte's idea of mathematics as a natural logic provides a springboard for a brief dip into two current conceptions of the structure of mathematics—and a third conception which is popular but hardly current, at least among mathematicians. We can bring these conceptions into view by treating Comte's notion, not in itself, but as one version of a more general idea. This we shall do.

5. Ibid.

Third, the idea of a natural logic will help us bring to a close our introduction to the substantive side of the structure of the scientific disciplines.

Let us begin by talking about the slot which mathematics fills in Comte's hierarchy of the sciences, rather than about his mathematics *per se*. The reason for this shift is highly ironic in view of Comte's passion for constituents. It lies in the fact that the properties of Comte's mathematics arise, not from its constituents, but from the organization in which it has a place. Mathematics is what it is for Comte because of the role it must play for the rest of the positive sciences.

This role will come into view if we ask this basic question: how can the first subject-matter science—physics—get started, *as a science*?

The question arises for physics and not for the other sciences because physics is the *first*, the lowest, of the subject-matter sciences. Thus, it does not have the support of previous sciences while the other sciences do. The other sciences have part of their pattern of enquiry laid out for them by the preceding science. The preceding science enables each following science to ask "Which of the elements of the preceding subject matter are constituents of *my* subject matter?" Since the preceding science has supplied a roster of possible ingredients for the subject matter of the science above it, that following science knows what this part of its problem is.

Physics, however, as the first of the positive, subject-matter sciences, has no such ready guide. Its subject matter consists of *ultimate* elements, elements which have no further investigable inner parts. Hence, physics cannot solve the problem of obtaining knowledge by looking for causally forceful constituents. It must look, rather, in another direction. It must determine what properties and behaviors of its subject-elements are the intrinsically important properties and behaviors—the ones through which these elements exercise causal efficacy when they exist as constituents of more complexly organized subject matters. (Incidentally, Comte would be most unhappy about our phrase "causal efficacy," for he considered the notion of cause as smacking of the prescientific, of the "merely" metaphysical stage of man's thinking. But no matter; we shall use the phrase anyway.)

Now this problem of identifying the important, the efficacious properties of physicals, so as to know what physics should investigate, could be solved handily if the *following* sciences were in some degree developed. For then, chemists and biologists would know some of the peculiar, identifying behaviors which characterize their subject matters —chemicals and biologicals. These known behaviors would, in turn, indicate what sorts of behaviors the properties of the constituent particles

—the physicals—would need to account for. Thus, physics would have its lead, its guideline, to indicate what *its* problems are.

This way of finding for physics what its important problems are involves an apparent paradox. On the one hand, knowledge of physicals is prerequisite to chemical and other investigations. On the other hand, some knowledge of chemicals, biologicals, and socials is prerequisite to the guidance of physical investigation.

Comte resolves this paradox, but to see how he does it requires that we look briefly at another side of the question formulated above: how does physics get started *as a science*?

This second side of the question consists of understanding the reason why Comte specifies physics *as a science* and what he means by the specification. The reason for the specification is contained in the fact that it *is* a specification. That is, to specify physics *as a science* implies that there may be a physics which is *not* science. Or better (and more grammatically) there can be knowledge of physicals which is not scientific knowledge.

This explanation for the specification of physics as a science thus puts the onus on the other half of the matter: what Comte means by *a science*, what difference there is between scientific knowledge and other knowledge, whether of physicals, or biologicals, or any other order of phenomena.

The answer, roughly, is that knowledge is of two sorts, each arising in a different way. On the one hand, it arises as lore, as a collection of know-hows, as *ad hoc* solutions to problems which life with its wants and needs poses to all men. Let us call this kind of knowledge commonsense knowledge or practical knowledge.

Now practical knowledge, in addition to being very important, may also be very complex. But the *acquisition* of practical, commonsense knowledge has a special and peculiar easiness compared with the acquisition of scientific knowledge (which we will define in a moment). That special easiness consists in the fact that the problems of want and need which instigate commonsense enquiries arise from our actions, from our natural endowments (our heredity), and from our situation, our environment. Such problems are *thrust upon us*. We feel them, rather than think them up. More accurately, we feel them first and that leads us to think them, to state them to ourselves in a form which can guide us toward solution.

If we feel cold, it is relatively easy to see that one of our problems is to learn what will give off heat and how to get it alight. If we are hungry, it doesn't take much in the way of thought to start looking for what will satisfy our hunger pangs without substituting some other pangs. Indeed, it may well be that instinctual responses ("instinct," once a naughty word; now once more respectable in the behavioral sciences) will initiate movements toward solving these problems before we have them clearly formulated. For example, hunger pangs make us restless; we move; the movements carry us near things whose odors may make us salivate, reach out, and grab. Thus, we may be directed toward formulation of practical problems not only by the felt want and need but also by what follows—half-intelligent behavior aimed toward meeting the need.

In any case, whether by need alone, or by need plus action, the framing of practical problems is thrust upon us. We do not need a systematic theory of knowledge, or a conception of a subject matter to serve as their root and source.

Thus, numerous, easily generated problems of want and need lead to bits and pieces of commonsense knowledge. We can imagine a primitive man for whom such problems have led to know-how about fires and caves, the ways of wild game and wild plants, some notion of the seasons and of when to plant and when to reap. We do not need to imagine, for we have recorded knowledge of him, a far less primitive man for whom problems of want and need have led to know-how about making soap, cooking food, felling trees, pitching a roof, baking brick and pottery, cheating neighbors, comforting children, and helping friends. Over long periods of time, a culture will develop great catalogues of such know-hows; numerous, separate solutions to many different and separate practical problems.

As time goes on, however, human culture discovers that there are many overlaps among the many entries in its catalogue of know-hows. A way to keep warm, a way to get light, a way to tenderize tough meat, all turn on matters of fire and combustibles, for example. Someone sees, perhaps in a flash of inspiration, that we might better serve our practical needs by being not quite so practical, so immediate, so *ad hoc*. For, surely, if we turned our attention to fire itself, to the question of what will burn and what will not, how burning starts and what it does, we would be achieving knowledge of far greater scope and usefulness than by limiting ourselves only to trying to solve practical problems as they arise.

In short, the idea of a *subject matter*, of a something-to-be-studied, instead of a need-to-be-filled, is born. With it comes the idea of *systematic* knowledge, knowledge which is not a catalogue of separate ways of solving separate problems of want and need but knowledge of the properties and behaviors of a subject matter. The pursuit of this kind of knowledge—of a subject matter and not of ways of doing; knowledge systematic and exhaustive and not *ad hoc*—is what is meant by science.

The Place of Structure in the Curriculum

With science and common sense thus defined, let us take time out to note that we have here a basis, promised above, for solving the vexed problem of practical versus academic curriculum. That problem consists of an apparent competition and conflict for mastery over the curriculum. On the one hand, we are drawn toward a curriculum which is formed by consulting existing wants and needs, social, personal, and economic. We envisage our curriculum as consisting of the know-hows, information, skills, and attitudes most relevant to our existing problems. Numerous groups of men act as spokesmen for these varied needs and press the curriculum maker to include the potentials for solving them in the curriculum.

On the other hand, we are drawn toward a curriculum which is based upon the "disciplines," the sciences, in the most inclusive sense of that word—inclusive of history and language as well as of biology and mathematics. The great age of these disciplines, the very fact of their survival and continued growth through the civilized epochs, speaks for some value they must have. The veneration, the respect, they engender also speaks of something about them worth preserving. Even the vague assertion that "they are our heritage," "our culture," carries weight. And, of course, we do see some use for some parts of some of the sciences: language for talking and writing, mathematics for calculating profit and loss, history for molding loyalties and attitudes, physics for repairing the doorbell, biology for understanding the doctor's instructions.

These two sources of curriculum determination do constitute a problem, however. For the use of the disciplines in the interest of profit and loss, health and conservation, speaking and listening, is not, really, to include the disciplines in the curriculum but only to use them as convenient source books for serving up a practical curriculum. And so we often—though with uneasy conscience—let the many overwhelm the comparatively few and make our curriculum merely practical. Meanwhile the question continues to nag us: why, otherwise, should the disciplines be in the curriculum?

The sketch above, of a relation of theory and practice, gives us an extremely important response to this question. In effect, it points out that the pursuit of science—of systematic knowledge of subject matter—is more practical than the practical. It arises as an improvement on know-how and it does improve upon it.

Its vast superiority lies in the fact that it enables us to *anticipate* practical problems, not merely to wait until they are upon us. It provides for our future as well as our present. For scientific knowledge is knowledge ready and available of the stuff, the things, the doings and undergoings, from which we inevitably must forge all our know-hows. Hence, theoretical or disciplined knowledge is practical knowledge virtual: a massive potential of capacities to do, to make, to alter, and to modify.

Let us restate this point more formally, in terms of the relation of disciplines and practice, for such a restatement will give us a more definite guideline to the problem of curriculum.

The disciplines are knowledges of subject matters. Subject matters are convenient groupings of things and events, groupings designed to facilitate their study in a disciplined way. Hence disciplines, though *virtually* practical, are not *actually* so. For practical problems have the nasty habit of arising in one or another of quite different groupings of things and events. Hence (Comte would say) if we are to harness the advantages of disciplined knowledge over know-how in the solving of practical problems, a correlative semi-discipline is required. This correlative semi-discipline is engineering. Its task is to establish the lines of connection between practical problems as they arise and are recognized with the disciplines whose substance contains the virtual solutions of these problems. Engineering co-relates theoretical and practical, draws on the resources of the disciplines to serve our needs and wants.

But engineering co-relates practical and theoretical in another way, as well. It recognizes disciplined knowledge as its mother-lode, its storehouse and resource. Hence, it sees to it that some of the profits which accrue from the solving of practical problems shall flow back to the sustaining and the nourishment of the disciplines.

Here is a model for the curriculum and the curriculum maker, which suggests the place *and form* of both a disciplined and a practical component in the schools. An old saw revised will give us a view of this place and form: "The layman (non-engineer, non-scientist) is both the *consumer* and the *support* of knowledge."

He is a consumer of knowledge in two senses. First, he is a consumer rather than a producer; that is, he gets what he knows from others; he is not required to discover, to be scholar and investigator. Second, he is a consumer in the sense of the ultimate user; it is he who undertakes the actions and undergoes the consequences which flow from the use of knowledge in the meeting of wants and needs.

The layman is the support of knowledge also in two senses. First, the layman is the support of the disciplines in the sense that only as he gives assent to their activity and pays for them in hard cash can they continue to flourish. Second, the lay public supports the disciplines in the sense that it is from among the members of that public—in smaller numbers, to be sure—that the succession must come, the scholars and investigators of the next generation.

These four roles of the public provide a tetragon in which to place and shape the disciplines in the school curriculum in relation to a practically determined part of that curriculum. There *should*, of course, be a practically determined part. For the disciplines are practical only virtually and it is beyond all bounds of possibility that we can, in the schools alone, teach the disciplines and impart the semi-discipline by which the lay public can extract unaided what it needs from the disciplines for present needs. Hence, there should be not only mathematics as set theory but mathematics as simple arithmetic calculation, as simple factoring of equations, as information about the more useful properties of curves and angles. There should not only be physics as the construction of elegant theories of atomic structure and as the derivation of theorems and equations from fundamental conservation laws and basic constants but also physics as the behavior of levers and dynamos, transistors and atomic energy plants. In biology, there is not only the almost-elegance of genetics and evolution but also some simple consequences of our misbehavior with respect to natural resources; some facts and simple ideas about medicines, digestive tracts, sewage disposal, fluorine in water supplies, diet, and cleanliness.

In relation to this practically determined component of the curriculum, the kind of component the schools have tended toward in the past several decades, the four roles of the lay public show a place for a disciplined component.

Because the layman is a consumer and not a producer of knowledge, he needs enough of each discipline to understand the *kind* of knowledge it produces, the sense in which it is verified knowledge, and the location of its growth points—the places at which it is least complete, or most susceptible of revision.

He needs to know the kind of knowledge produced and the sense in which it is verified knowledge, because good physics, for example, is not good in the sense that good history is good. Good physics is not good in the same sense, even, that sound biology is good. For each of the disciplines has its own syntactical and substantive structure—which is the point of this essay as a whole.

The layman needs to know where the growth points of a discipline are located (and why they are growth points) because ignorance of them will mean that what he learned about a discipline in his schooling will otherwise collapse around his ears. This outcome follows from the fact that the substantive, if not the syntactical, structure of the scientific disciplines now changes so rapidly. In the course of any enquiry, its conceptual frame is tested. Where the conceptual frame—the substantive structure—is found weak or is used up by the continuing enquiry, it is modified or replaced. With that change in conceptual structure, the knowledge of the discipline also changes. And in the physical and biological sciences, if not in other disciplines, this kind of revisionary cycle nowadays is a matter of a few years or a decade, not a matter of centuries.

Because the layman is the ultimate user of knowledge, the man who must act and undergo, he needs a view of the discipline from another vantage point. For actors and undergoers are better as they know what they are doing and why. Blind obedience to a routine, and unquestioning obeisance to authoritative instruction, produce inflexible actors and supine undergoers, neither of which are adequate to the rate of change which our technology and our ways of living now demand.

The layman as giver of assent and cash support must see the disciplines from still a third angle. He must understand something of the sweat, patience, ingenuity, and insight which go into their making. He must understand something of their immediately material value to his pleasure and his comfort. Otherwise, he will not give his assent and his cash. Enquiry will languish, hence the resources of technology will not be replenished. Thus our ability to solve our continuing stream of problems will fade.

Finally, the layman as a possible *member* of a discipline, needs a view of the discipline from still a fourth point of view. He needs to see, first, the kinds of skills and opportunities for individual action which each affords and rewards. Second, at some point, he needs a glimpse of the unsolved problems to which he, as a possible member, might contribute. He also needs, of course, what the giver of assent, and the ultimate user and the servant of knowledge needs—but this goes without saying.

I imagine, then, a school curriculum in which there is, from the start, a representation of the discipline. In the earliest grades—for reasons we need not raise here—this component would be small. The bulk of knowledge learned would appear as simply true; skills would appear as the unquestioned right way to do things. But even here, the discipline would begin to take a stand. It would appear in two forms. First it would appear as small problems—tempered to the age and ability of the child—typical of some or all of the disciplines. There could be a problem of choosing the most convenient mode of classification for some familiar cluster of objects—stamps, toys, picture books. There could be problems in making small inferences from simple data; of thinking of some way of "finding out"; of imagining more than one way in which a visible outcome of hidden processes might have been brought about. There could be problems in detecting the principles of sequences, series, and classes of things. And so on.

However, in instituting such representations of the curriculum I would take care to follow an old rule: when children are given bones to chew on, let there be meat on them and let them chew as if for the meat—not as if for the tempering of their teeth.

The disciplines would appear, second, as fragments of a narrative of enquiry. In a few places each week or month, the child would not be told, merely, "This is right. That is wrong. These are animals. Those are plants." Rather, he would be told, "When we try to grow puppies, kittens, grass and flowers, we find that puppies and kittens need to be fed and warmed. Grass and flowers need water and sunlight. Puppies and kittens are very much alike in still other ways. Grass and flowers are also alike in many other ways. *Therefore.* . . ." In short, *some* knowledge would be imparted, not as truths out of the nowhere but as conclusions from evidence, or decisions from thought about alternatives and their consequences.

As the child moved onward in age and competence, the disciplinary components would increase in length and frequency. Not only would knowledge yet to be imparted appear in these forms but, for the sake of review and introduction, already-known skills, attitudes, and information, earlier taken on faith, would now be related to their origins in investigation, deliberation, or canons of taste and behavior.

At about the high school level or a little sooner, the structures of the discipline would be introduced in still another form. They would be represented by examples of the uncertainties, the differences of interpretation, and the *issues* of principle which characterize the disciplines. Narratives of enquiry would end in doubt or in alternative views of what the evidence shows. Two or more historical works displaying wide differences in the interpretation of important periods, men, and events would replace—in part—the single, indoctrinal history.

Also at the high school level—and perhaps only for some upper fraction of the student population—the disciplines would appear in still a fourth form. Just as narrative of enquiry was earlier used to replace dogmatic instruction, so now original, first-order materials would begin to displace the narrative of enquiry. In history, for example, units of such material would present the student with memorials and documents of a place and time. Some such units would invite the student's own interpretation, a writing of his own history, of this time and place. Other, similar units of historical raw materials would accompany an historian's interpretation of times, places, or events and challenge the student to trace the selections of data and the particular bent of interpretation put on them by the historian.

In the case of the sciences, laboratories might pose problems of obtaining and interpreting data toward conclusions *not* foretold or available from the textbook. In the science classroom, original scientific papers would replace the interpretation of them which had formerly appeared as a narrative of enquiry. The student would learn to interpret, evaluate, and understand such papers on his own; learn, in effect, to construct his own narrative of enquiry.

Through the early years of this increasing contact with the structure of the disciplines, I am assuming that the subject materials taught, the subject materials from which the structure of the discipline emerges, would be subject matter selected primarily on practical grounds. The present needs of the maturing child, later needs appropriately learned at this earlier stage, further needs dictated by the state of our society, our policy, and our economics, would be brought to bear against the content of the disciplines as major determiners of the materials of choice.

Later—beginning at the seventh grade, and surely represented in the high school curriculum—materials dictated by practical criteria would be meshed with additional materials chosen on the basis of the structure of the discipline alone. In physics, for example, the subscience of mechanics would be incorporated, solely because its content is basic to the remainder of the physical sciences, even if mechanics were not of importance on practical grounds. Conceptions from biology such as homeostasis and regulation, whether of immediate use or not, would have their place precisely and solely because they are large and powerful conceptions in that discipline.

It is important to note that structures of importance to the disciplines would not have appeared thus for the first time at the upper levels of the school. Quite the contrary, many of them would have appeared and reappeared as the forms of content or the forms of presentation (narrative of enquiry, problems, etc.) for practically determined materials of the earlier curriculum. The point to be emphasized for the curriculum of the high school is that here, *regardless* of immediately practical value, important aspects of a discipline, as such, would find a larger place than they would at earlier levels of the curriculum.

In one respect, these recommendations appear to violate a common principle of curriculum construction. They do *not* restrict the content of the curriculum at any one state to materials which emerge from and feed back into the daily needs—the common, the extra-academic, experience—of the student. And in the later grades, seven to eight, and nine to twelve, this apparently non-experiential component grows larger and larger.

As we have envisaged the progress of this curriculum, however, the violation of the principle of experience is apparent but not real. The principle appears to be violated only if it is understood in an incomplete and erroneous sense—only if "experience" is assumed to occur only when an individual is caught up in a stream of external, public events. This is not, and never was intended to be, the meaning of "experience" as it operates as a principle of pedagogy.

Common experience, as John Dewey said over and over again, has both an inner (subjective) and an outer (objective) dimension. And without the inner dimension, the outer dimension simply does not exist —as experience. A fool may stand in the midst of the most significant of actions and "experience" nothing more than some human scurrying and talking. A calloused and ignorant individual may witness the most pathetic and damaging humiliation of a child but "experience" nothing more than a parent scolding.

In short, it is our *past* experience as well as present external events which determine our present experience. What we are, what we know, how we have been bent, and what we remember, determine what we experience in the present. It follows, then, that with proper preparation, experience may arise for a child from participation in present events which, on the surface, appear to be without childish significance.

Such a preparation is built into the curriculum plan outlined above. It was suggested that, from the start, a disciplined component would appear as small problems—problems characteristic of the discipline yet problems tempered to the age and ability of the child. One major purpose of this recommended procedure is to introduce the child early to the experience of successfully solving problems, to provide him, through an external, objective element of experience in the school, with the inner experience of his own competence, his own ability to master and control a fragment of the world. It is this experience, which sets the stage, provides the "motivation" for handling larger chunks of disciplined materials whose practical value is not immediately apparent.

Part Three

ON CURRICULUM-BUILDING

· 9 ·

Testing and the Curriculum

A review of the current literature on validity in preparation for this paper disclosed the fact that there is nothing both new and true for me to say. However, the literature also showed that the truth is obscured and fragmented by competitive doctrinaire adhesions, and by an equally patent lack of shared experience among the various specialists who contribute to education. Failure of communication between the test constructor on the one hand and the curriculum-maker-cum-teacher on the other was especially clear.

I have attempted, therefore, to unify the disparate truths seen in the literature by supplying commonplace terms to replace specialists' terms. What emerges can be summarized in two statements. The first recognizes a practically important theoretical limit to the possibility of test evaluation. The second proposes a process and a machinery which would embody a realistic capitulation to the theoretical limits of test evaluation.

First: a test which is highly valid and at the same time highly useful is not possible in the very nature of the case. This opposition between validity and usefulness is inevitable, if by "validity" one means a high degree of conformity to a certifiable standard on the part of a test. This opposition arises because a certifiable standard simply does not exist in most of the areas of the school curriculum.

Second: education at large would benefit much more from a campaign of validation directed conjointly at the teaching process, the curriculum, the principles of curriculum construction, and tests, than it now profits from a campaign which treats only the test as a variable in the system of education factors.

The absence or inaccessibility of a certifiable standard for validation of tests may be illustrated first by the medical curriculum. *Sub specie*

This chapter was previously published in a slightly different form as "Criteria for the Evaluation of Achievement Tests: From the Point of View of the Subject-matter Specialist," in *Proceedings of the Invitational Conference on Testing Problems, 1950* (Princeton, N.J.: Educational Testing Service, 1950), pp. 82–94.

aeternitatis, the medical curriculum is a correct, complete, and effective instrument for the creation of successful medical practitioners; its principles are the powers, habits, and bodies of knowledge possessed by successful practitioners of medicine. To create such a curriculum in fact would require, first, identification of successful practitioners of medicine; second, correct and complete discovery of the powers, habits, and bodies of knowledge which make the practitioner successful; third, determination of the learning "experiences" which would inculcate or evoke these powers, habits, and bodies of knowledge; fourth, determination of ways in which these "experiences" could be instituted; fifth, development of facility in the staff in the application of such "ways." If such steps as these were, in fact, the history of the medical curriculum, a valid test would be a possible and useful goal of a test-making organization. If such steps as these were even possible, there would still be point in the expenditure of funds and energies for the production of valid tests.

But in fact, the medical curriculum neither has been, nor can be, produced by any such valid route. There undoubtedly is such a thing as "successful" medical practice, but it defies clear delineation, and is itself the subject of endless debate. Should it be definitively arrayed by some miracle, the problem of identifying its practitioners remains; and this too would be a matter of doubt and opinion, since success in medical practice is difficult to distinguish from the mere reputation or appearance of success. Should this improbability be achieved, there would remain the problem of identifying the habits, powers, and bodies of knowledge which distinguish the successful from the less successful. And even were this solved, the problems of curriculum construction and execution would remain. Only if all these problems were already solved, would it be prudent and proper to expend funds and energies on the single-minded validation of tests alone.

Meanwhile, what we have is a medical curriculum continually subject to change, as its professors wrestle unsystematically, and as best they can, with the welter of opinion concerning the nature of medicine, the preconditions for its achievement, and the means for evoking and inculcating these means in students. At all these points, "validation" is the need; examiners and test-construction organizations would do much greater service to education than they now perform by their expensive pursuit of the isolated fantasy of the "valid" test were they to consider ways in which tests, and statistical studies of test results, could be made to serve as foci for the systematization of this larger problem of validation.

What is true of the ancient and established profession of medicine is true, *a fortiori*, for general education, where the curriculum is of more recent origin and has an end in view much less concrete than a medical practitioner. This end of general education has something to do with the profession of being a man and a citizen. What a man and a citizen is, or ought to be, however, is subject to far more dispute and elicits far more radically different answers than the question of the nature of a good medical practitioner. Hence, it is obvious enough that a "valid" test of success of general education in general, which would have to proceed by measuring the extent to which each graduate was a good man and a good citizen, is a palpable absurdity.

If the examiner capitulates to this limitation and seeks instead to measure the success of a particular general-education curriculum by measuring the extent to which its products possess the abilities and knowledge in terms of which this particular curriculum has defined man and citizen, the case is little better. The College of the University of Chicago, for instance, at present conceives its contribution to adequate humanity and citizenship to be largely intellectual, and to consist in aiding its students to become able and judicious in their employment of knowledge and their enjoyment of artistic productions. If we were complacently sure that this is the whole and proper aim of a general education, a narrowly valid test of this capacity to use and enjoy would be a useful instrument. But we are not; hence a more valuable kind of test would be one whose items would serve to suggest to the teaching staff alternative or additional aims of education which deserve consideration. And still more valuable would be a test which would disclose the unknown and unanticipated consequences (in addition to those intended) which any effective curriculum inevitably must produce upon its students. Only a test of this kind would be truly "valid" as a measure of the effectiveness of the general curriculum in advancing its students in the professions of humanity and citizenship, and a test of this kind would be explicitly and purposely "non-valid" in the ordinary sense of "validity."

Even if employment of knowledge and enjoyment of art be taken as an adequate statement of the whole aim of general education, a problematic situation still exists which invalidates the notion of a useful and "valid" test. The problematic situation arises out of the indeterminacy of such matters as: the knowledge that is most useful to the student; the nature of *judiciousness* in its use; the habits and abilities which constitute it; the nature of the object of art; the abilities and bodies of knowledge constituent of the capacity to enjoy. These problems are subject to continuous discussion, debate, research, and *revision*. Therefore to embark today upon the task of constructing a valid standardized test based upon today's tentative and merely working definition of the principles of the curriculum is to produce a test instrument at some future time, when, in all likelihood, the matters tested would have been transformed beyond relevance to the "valid" test so produced. And it would be merely petulant for examiners to demand a moratorium on improvement of the curriculum so that they might carry out the ritual dance of "validation."

What is true of the concept of education's aim at Chicago is also true of the concept of education's aim held elsewhere. The concept itself is incomplete and tentative. The terms which constitute it are only partly understood and are continuing subjects of investigation. The terms, in their shadowy and incomplete condition, are in turn represented by curricular intentions and programs whose appropriateness to the terms as ends is a matter of doubt and of continuing enquiry. Finally, the classroom practices which are supposed to realize curricular programs and intentions are valid only to the extent permitted by the competence, the experience, and the state of health possessed by the teacher at the moments when he teaches. A valid test in the ordinary sense is nothing more than an effort to measure the contours of a shifting and altering shadow; the standard for validation does not exist.

The secondary and primary curriculum contains its own version of this guessiness, this flux and uncertainty. The teaching of the arithmetic operation of multiplication is not an end in itself, and the most perfect test of the students' ability to perform this operation is of small value. The operation of multiplication assumes some meaning and significance when it becomes a necessary part of a larger problem, such as is represented by the "story problem" of the arithmetic book. However, a test which measures (however perfectly) the students' ability to translate statements about bananas or working hours still is of limited significance, since, ultimately, the capacity to perform the operation of multiplication takes on its full significance when it is competently performed by a person who detects the proper need for it in a real situation complete with plausible irrelevances, concomitant matters, and affective as well as rational distractors. A test of mere "face validity," which measures the students' capacity to perform arithmetic operations or solve a "story" problem, is the less useful as it is the more valid in the ordinary sense, since the test which impresses, in virtue of its trappings of validity coefficients and standardized achievement levels, is sedative instead of stimulative to the teacher's search for better means of instruction and more adequate conceptions of his aims.

Put backwards, this set of relations is more poignant. The real purpose of arithmetic teaching in the common school is to give its students the ability to perform the appropriate operations of arithmetic upon appropriate matters properly selected by him from the congeries of factors (rational and affective) which are presented to his attention by real situations. This real aim is represented in the school by the thin gray shadow of the "story" problem. And this thin gray shadow is in turn often (and properly) represented by the thinner, grayer shadow of the operations themselves, divested even of the paper trappings of the "story" problem.

A test which speciously boasts of fact validity in virtue of its one-to-one correspondence with only the operations of arithmetic, which are in turn embraced as standards of validity for their plausible-seeming "concreteness" (which is, in fact, merely the simplicity of meaninglessness which comes from being out of context) is really only a shadow of a shadow of a shadow. The delusion that it is real, shared from the examiner to the teacher, a delusion enhanced by the trappings of validation and certification, constitutes the sense in which "valid" tests may be harmful rather than useful to education as whole. Far more desirable would be tests and usages of statistical data which kept the teacher alert to the incomplete and merely representational character of the moment-to-moment content of a curriculum, and which aided and stimulated his effort to put incomplete parts into relation with one another, to make symbols more vividly representative, and to search out and invent means for replacing shadows by the things themselves.

The flux and uncertainty which characterize education arise from two related human limitations, and a realization of what they are and *that* they are can help the examiner in his effort to make his work most useful to education. One of these limitations is the human incapacity to apprehend complex and abstract wholes completely or entirely correctly. As statistical research workers, for example, we are often mistaken in the effective conception of science which guides our choice of problems and methods. As examiners, we are unclear as to the meaning of "validity." As curriculum makers, we are more often wrong or incomplete than right about the nature of our subject matter: for example, we may have inadequate ideas about the nature of artistic works, about what historians can and cannot know, or about the literal character of scientific conclusions and theories.

In the case of general education, the whole which concerns us has something to do with a good and happy life for the men and women our students will become. And whatever other errors we may make when we come to actualizing this abstract notion in a curriculum, the first and commonest error is to be mistaken or incomplete about the abstract idea itself. Our conception of it may arise from conscious thought or be only the product of unexamined experiences; we may even be unaware of the operation of an ethical postulate in our curriculum planning. It functions, however, and it is more often inadequate than correct. And however precise and sound may be our subsequent acts of specifying this abstract notion, choosing materials of study, determining sequence and relation in the curriculum, deciding upon teaching methods and techniques, establishing calendars and time-allotments to parts of our program, the results can be no better than our originating conception of a good and happy life. For "good and happy life," one may read "physician," or "engineer" or "statesman"; the fact that we are always only partly right about these abstract wholes remains.

The question of the nature of these significant wholes, these ends of education, is one perennially settled and perennially re-opened. Hence, a conventionally valid test of the ends of general, professional, or common education, is impossible. Yet an important function of tests, vis-à-vis these wholes, remains. That function is to hold up before the curriculum maker an informing image of his own view of these ends and of the views of them held by others. For abstract conceptions are corrected and made more complete only as men with diverse views of them confront intelligible statements of each other's views and engage in discussion and debate concerning them. The examination has its place in this process because of the difficulty of communicating abstract ideas. Exposition of the meaning we assign them often fails because to hold one view of a given idea is also often to have only one set of terms with which to describe it, and the terms of description may be as strange as the view to be described, to one who holds a different view. We therefore have recourse to examples: if we cannot adequately state the ultimate ends of our curriculum, we hold up the curriculum itself in the hope that through it the observer or colleague can understand the ends it aims at. But a curriculum is only incompletely embodied in any single concrete object. A list of lovingly selected, revised, and polished units of instruction fails to reflect the whole because such a list omits the many alternatives which were rejected in its making, and gives little hint of the debate, study, and discussion out of which meaningful rejection and selection arose. The same can be said of instruction itself: how many of us would wish our purposes in education to be represented in an observer's mind by what he is likely to grasp from a chance visit or two to our classroom?

In the last analysis the adequate communication, which is the only means for improving our conception of ends of education, can arise only from a great variety of embodiments of these ends. With a variety of embodiments or reflections, what is erroneously or incompletely suggested by one is corrected or completed by another, in much the same way that an induction of the characteristics of a class of objects is brought about by correcting the judgment formed from a few members of the class by submitting it to the effect of examining other and varying members of the class. The test or examination for a program of education is a special kind of embodiment of the ends of that program: it is concrete where essays about ends are abstract; its unity can be grasped in a single study; it tends to be precise at just those points where curriculum descriptions are ambiguous; it is the product of leisured thought and correction, where acts of instruction are necessarily the result of the instant's decision. It is because of these virtues of tests as a communicating medium, and because of the need for such communication in the improvement of the curriculum, that it is important that test-construction agencies consider ways in which tests, their statistical study, and other resources uniquely available through such agencies, can be used not as mere "valid," and therefore static, measures of a static curriculum, but as centers of and foci for the discussion and improvement of all parts of the curriculum, including tests.

The second kind of intellectual limitation is not so much mistaking the whole as it is the failure to recognize and correct the consequences of making analyses of that whole which rightly or wrongly we take as the purpose of our educational program. Thus, if we propose to teach students judicious use of the fruits of scientific enquiry, a shattering analysis is required before the purpose can be translated into a curriculum which has real existence from day to day and month to month. We must determine that scientific enquiry consists of this and this and this component act, with this and this effect upon the knowledge which accrues from it. Then we must move to an analysis of "judicious use," deciding that it involves this and this activity. We must further proceed to an analysis which introduces yet another gap between the whole in its original form, and its representation by parts of the curriculum: by hopeful guesses, we must join some notion of the learning organism to our analysis of what is to be learned, in order to say that *this* activity, which constitute the act of judicious use, is to be developed by these and these studies and classroom activities.

There are two ways in which such an analytic process can go astray. In the first place, there is the inherent weakness of analysis per se: that no fracture of a complex and interacting whole but fails to lose the whole. This is as true for the ends of a curriculum as it of a living organism. For instance, a student taught on the one hand to "generalize data," and on the other to correct an incorrect inference, or make a correct one, and so on through a list of alleged components of "scientific method," may become competent at each of these tasks taken alone but remain incompetent to solve a problem in which several of them are required in some particular relationship. The situation is not unlike the relation between arithmetic operations and the "story problem."

In addition to the inevitable shadow of unreality which defaces the curriculum as a consequence of the act of analysis itself, there is the defacement which arises from particular errors and failures of particular analyses. For it is inescapable that a given principle of analysis shall overemphasize differences between the parts it discriminates and obscure differences which would appear were another analytic principle employed. For instance, a program in the humanities concerned with literature may analyze its mass of material in terms of genres with the result that what is unique and important about the lyric poem, the tragedy, the novel, or historical writing, will become clear and significant to the student. But what is unique and important to all genres in virtue of their origin in a given place or epoch will necessarily be obscured. Conversely, a course founded on a historical analysis into periods and places will clarify what is unique and important about the mass of literature of a given time or place but obscure important differences in genres.

Inadequacies which arise from analytic failure are to be corrected by the same means required for correction of mistakes about wholes. In order to perceive that his parts of the curriculum do not reconstitute the whole with which he started, the instructor must confront evidence that students exhibit the partial capacities which constitute his curriculum yet do not possess the whole which he intended to give them. In order to perceive that his particular analysis of his subject matter emphasizes some aspects of it at the expense of others, he must be given the chance to contrast what his students can do with what students trained in differently analyzed curricula can do.

It is the need for these contrasts and comparisons which again illustrates the mutually exclusive character of "validity" and "usefulness." The more valid the test for a particular curriculum, in the sense of more perfect conformity to it, the less its usefulness in pointing toward inadequacies in, and illuminating possibilities of correction and completion of, that curriculum. It is these same needs for contrast and comparison, however, which constitute a task and challenge to the examiner: (1) to produce tests which are not mere slavish replicas of a given established curriculum but which go beyond the instructor's apparent intentions toward his real ones, so that he may become aware of his opportunities for enlarging and correcting his curriculum; (2) to effect, through a variety of tests as foci, communication and discussion among instructors representing varied interpretations of common ends, so that they be reminded and informed of the limitations of their isolated constructions. Nor is the examiner's protest that he is not his brother's keeper a valid reason for eschewing this responsibility.

The invalidity, in the case of the examiner, of Cain's rejoinder to God, can be suggested by indicating the sense in which central-agency examination construction as currently organized pretends that test construction is merely an engineering problem. The essence of the engineering outlook is the notion of separation of ends and means. Someone else tells the engineer what to do. His job is merely to do it. In the case of education, a dean, chairman, or committee states the content and objectives of a curriculum. The examiner receives the statement, and makes a test to fit it, testing its goodness of fit by statistical analyses supplemented by minimal review by the originating dean, chairman, or committee. This is a convenient and pleasant way of life for the examiner, insofar as evasion of responsibility contributes to pleasantness. And it can speciously be defended on the ground of efficient division of labor, a ground whose plausibility is enhanced by appealing to the specialized knowledge demanded by the examiner's task. But efficiency in the accomplishment of a task is not properly measured by the dispatch with which a single component of the job is done; for one component of a complex machine may be produced with dispatch only at the price of reducing the effectiveness of the whole machine of which the component is to be a part. This is happening in the present "efficient" separation of examination construction from the remainder of education; the virtual obsolescence of almost any elaborately standardized and validated test is prevented from being obvious only because the separation of test and curriculum, of examiner and curriculum planner and teacher, hinders the communication which would reveal it.

There is one other way in which an essentially invalid character accrues to "valid" tests in virtue of non-communication among participants in the educational process. It arises from the fact that a conventionally "valid" test may literally test something other than it intends to test, and fail to be caught in this act by the usual statistical methods of validation. This possibility stems from the infinite ingenuity of the student in devising ways to move from a question to an answer. An analogy can be found in biological research where there is need to measure some profoundly buried quantitative factor in the life process. In virtue of its inaccessibility, no attempt is made to measure it directly. Rather, an "indicator" of it is sought, an indicator which can be expected to vary as the wanted factor varies, as, for instance, red blood-cell frequency or hemoglobin concentration, as indicators of the capacity of the body to supply its parts with oxygen. Then some method is devised for estimating the quantity of the "indicator." It is easy to become aware of invalid links between the method of estimating the indicator and the actual fluctuations of the indicator, for these factors are literally on the surface, intrusively in the field of sense experience, as, for instance, the common way to measure blood pressure by measuring the pressure necessary to compress a vessel carrying the blood.

But the possibility that the "indicator" is invalidly taken as a measure of the prime factor is neither obvious nor easy to determine. Yet the possibility is a *prima facie* probability in every case. For it is extremely unlikely that the value at any given moment of any variable quantity in an organism, is a function of one other factor only. The same is clearly true of examinations bearing upon any intellectual skill. The question put, and the alternatives posed for the students' judgment, may be such that the answer can be arrived at by exercise of the skill or ability which the item is intended to measure. What remains problematic is the *actual* skill, ability, or other route, by which the individual student does in fact arrive at the proper response. The obvious instances of this all of us know: the possibility of a student's determining the right response in an information test by using his wit vis-à-vis the way an examiner's mind works; a student's circumventing the intentions of an information test by estimating logical probabilities in the situation; circumvention of a test of the power of inference by using information. But whether routes alternative to the one intended do or do not exist in a wide variety of tests which we currently accept as valid tests of particular skills, can best be determined only by drawing the student, as well as the examiner and instructor, into the conversation which should obtain among educators. Tests need to be tested by "depth" interviews in which the student is taught to think aloud as he answers test items, and thus provide some evidence as to the modes of intellectual operation employed to answer them.

The broader conception of validity outlined thus far suggests that test-construction agencies work toward two relatively neglected aims. First, to assist the individual educator, concerned with his own, indigenous program, to bring his principles of curriculum construction, the curriculum itself, and his tests to a better and more real approximation to his own ultimate ends; second, to bring educators concerned with the same specialty but operating at different institutions into communication with each other so that their conceptions of the ultimate ends themselves, as well as of means, will, by exchange of ideas and of convictions, better approximate the true and useful.

Pursuit of these aims would require four changes in existing organizational structures and procedures of test-construction agencies, relating respectively to their personnel, the tests themselves, the analysis of tests, and the use to which tests and test analyses are put.

1. Concerning personnel, it is proposed first that test analysis become the special responsibility of a small group of specialists designated for the function. Second, the actual construction of tests and items be the responsibility neither of test specialists, recently graduated Ph.D's, nor ad hoc committees superficially supervising the work of one of the aforesaid. Rather, test construction should be the responsibility of individuals who represent in their persons the experience of working with

or toward more than one curriculum in their special fields and levels of education. Such persons would be designated for their examining function by being sought among the staffs of institutions engaged in the development and execution of programs in the field to be tested. Such a person would be released during a stated period for a third or a half of his time to the test-construction agency. His task would be to construct not one but several kinds of tests, each of which would be a formulation *in concreto* of what he thinks his program in science, or humanities, or history, is trying to do.

2. The intention of such a personnel structure is the production of two kinds or *varieties* of tests. One would be a variety of embodiments in several distinctly different tests (not alternative forms of a similar kind) of what is purportedly the same curriculum; this variety, elicited from a representative of one curriculum, is to function in the improved approximation of that curriculum to its ultimate aims. Second, in each field and level, at least three persons would be sought, the three to be representative of as widely differing conceptions of education in that field as seems feasible. The variety of tests which emerge from such varied representation of the field is intended to function to bring educators of widely differing backgrounds and convictions concerning the field into communication with each other for the purpose of sharpening, broadening, and rectifying their ideas and convictions concerning it.

3. This double variety of tests becomes maximally useful for its designed purpose only if submitted to appropriate statistical analysis. Such analysis would include conventional validation procedures, but these procedures would be aimed at the broader goal. Correlations among the test units constituting the set of tests of a single curriculum will be designed to exhibit its unity or lack of it. Lack of it may be interpretable either as an unexpected complexity in the ends of the curriculum, or of ambiguity in the conception of these ends held by the examiner and his staff colleagues. The presence of it may be interpretable as an unexpected simplicity or naiveté in the curriculum as conceived. In either case, what is sought is initiation of thought concerning the tests and the curriculum, of experiment with their methods, materials, and procedures, and, ultimately, considered change in the curriculum and tests.

Correlational and other procedures imposed upon different test-sets representing different curriculums and upon single representatives of several test-sets will be designed to determine the degree of real difference in their effects upon students of apparently different curriculums. It should be noted that in this situation there are two groups of students for each test-set under consideration: students trained in the curriculum represented by a given test-set, and students trained in other curriculums. The possibilities inherent in the series of contrasts thus afforded are too numerous and complex for analysis here. The end of such analysis is, however, simple. It is to bring into the vivid meaningfulness afforded by contrast what it is that each participant curriculum does and does not do for its students. The ultimate aim is the same as before: to initiate thought, experiment, and improvement of the participating curriculums.

In addition to analysis of the relations *inter se* of various images of a single curriculum, and of the images of various curriculums, it is further proposed that ordinary validating procedures be supplemented by "depth interviews" intended to elicit from students in the act of taking tests the content and mode of thought employed for the purpose. Experiments to determine whether such procedures are possible and fruitful have been initiated and appear to speak affirmatively.

4. The potentialities inherent in tests so constructed, designed, and analyzed can become real only if the tests and their results are made genuinely accessible to their consumers, the participant educational institutions. For this purpose, numerous conferences and workshops are means, and responsibility for their initiation and administration becomes a routine function of the test-construction agency.

Parallel to the two ends of the testing program, the two varieties of tests, and the two areas of analysis, the types of conferences would also be dual. One would be concerned with explication of the results of analysis of various tests of a single institution's program, and with speculation as to the significance and cause of the discovered results. It would take place among the teaching staff concerned with the tests and program in question, the staff member responsible for the tests, and the test specialist concerned with their analysis. Out of such conferences should grow a more informed teaching staff, more meaningful instruction, as well as concrete experiments with tests and the curriculum.

The second type of conference or workshop would be concerned with the tests and analyses representative of a variety of curriculums. It would be concerned with the significance to each curriculum of the others it saw reflected in the variety of tests, and of the results exhibited by the measurement of achievement by its own students and those of other institutions, on the variety of matters tested. It would take place among at least two representatives of the several curriculums involved, together with the staff members who constructed the tests and the specialists who supervised their analysis. Out of such workshops should grow a new and larger order of thought, experiment, and revision of curriculum than is remotely possible in the present insular state of most educationists and most educational institutions.

· 10 ·

The Practical:
A Language for Curriculum

THESES AND SYNOPSIS

I shall have three points. The first is this: The field of curriculum is moribund. It is unable, by its present methods and principles, to continue its work and contribute significantly to the advancement of education. It requires new principles which will generate a new view of the character and variety of its problems. It requires new methods appropriate to the new budget of problems.

The second point: The curriculum field has reached this unhappy state by inveterate, unexamined, and mistaken reliance on *theory*. On the one hand, it has adopted theories (from outside the field of education) concerning ethics, knowledge, political and social structure, learning, mind, and personality, and has used these borrowed theories theoretically, i.e., as principles from which to "deduce" right aims and procedures for schools and classrooms. On the other hand, it has attempted construction of educational theories, particularly theories of curriculum and instruction.

These theoretic activities have led to grave difficulties (incoherence of the curriculum, failure and discontinuity in actual schooling) because of the operation of three factors. In the first place, theoretical constructions are, in the main, ill-fitted and inappropriate to problems of actual teaching and learning. Theory, by its very character, does not and cannot take account of all the matters which are crucial to questions of what, who, and how to teach; that is, theories cannot be applied, as principles, to the solution of problems concerning what to do with or for real individuals, small groups, or real institutions located in time and space—the subjects and clients of schooling and schools. Second, many of the borrowed theories, even where appropriate, are inadequate, even as theories, to their chosen subjects: Many are incomplete; some (especially of political structure and personality) are doctrinaire. Third, even where a borrowed theory is adequate to its own subject matter, it

This chapter was previously published by the National Education Association, Center for the Study of Instruction, 1970.

begs or ignores questions about other subject matters. Theories of personality, for example, beg or ignore problems of social structure and ethics or merely dictate solutions to them. Theories of knowledge usually ignore problems of personality. Yet all these matters (values, social and political structure, mind, knowledge) are involved in schools and schooling, and theories concerning them severally cannot be combined into a unified theory adequately covering all of them except by an enormous extension of the genius and assiduity which yielded the separate theories—a task which might or might not be accomplished in a hundred years.

The third point, which constitutes the main body of my thesis: There will be a renascence of the field of curriculum, a renewed capacity to contribute to the quality of American education, only if curriculum energies are in large part diverted from theoretic pursuits (such as the pursuit of global principles and comprehensive patterns, the search for stable sequences and invariant elements, the construction of taxonomies of supposedly fixed or recurrent kinds) to three other modes of operation. These other modes, which differ radically from the theoretic, I shall call, following tradition, the *practical*, the *quasi-practical*, and the *eclectic*.

The Practical

The radical difference of the practical from the theoretic mode is visible in the fact that it differs from the theoretic not in one aspect but in many: It differs from the theoretic in method. Its problems originate from a different source. Its subject matter is of a distinctly different character. Its outcome is of a different kind.

The end or outcome of the theoretic is knowledge, general or universal statements which are supposed to be true, warranted, confidence-inspiring. Their truth, warrant, or trustworthiness is held, moreover, to be durable and extensive. That is, theoretic statements are supposed to hold good for long periods of time and to apply unequivocally to each member of a large class of occurrences or recurrences. The end or outcome of the practical, on the other hand, is a *decision*, a selection and guide to possible action. Decisions are never true or trustworthy. Instead, a decision (before it is put into effect) can be judged only comparatively, as probably better or worse than alternatives. After it has been put into effect, it can be judged by its consequences as good or bad, but this is an afterthought and usually sterile as far as further decisions are concerned. A decision, moreover, has no great durability or extensive application. It applies unequivocally only to the case for which it was sought. Applications to other cases proceed only from analogy and turn out to be good ones mainly by chance.

The subject matter of the theoretic is always something taken to be universal or extensive or pervasive and is investigated as if it were constant from instance to instance and impervious to changing circumstance. The most obvious examples are among the subject matters of scientific and mathematical investigation: mass, equivalence, time, class (among the universals); the mammalian thyroid gland, Homo sapiens, igneous rock (among the extensive); electrons and protons (among the pervasive). The subject matter of the practical, on the other hand, is always something taken as concrete and particular and treated as indefinitely susceptible to circumstance, and therefore highly liable to unexpected change: this student, in that school, on the South Side of Columbus, with Principal Jones during the present mayoralty of Ed Tweed and in view of the probability of his reelection.

The problems of the theoretic arise from areas of the subject matter marked out by what we already know as areas which we do not yet know. This is to say that theoretic problems are states of mind. Practical problems, on the other hand, arise from states of affairs in relation to ourselves. Specifically, they arise from states of affairs which are marked out by fulfilled needs and satisfied desires as being states which do not satisfy, which hurt us, or which deprive us of more than they confer. They are constituted of conditions which we *wish* were otherwise and we think they *can be made* to be otherwise. (The duality of this origin of practical problems has an important corollary: Practical problems can be settled by changing either the state of affairs or our desires. The latter kind of solution is as legitimate as the former. It follows, then, that practical problems intrinsically involve states of character and the possibility of character change.)

The differences in outcome, subject matter, and origin of problem which distinguish the practical from the theoretic are paralleled by an equally radical difference in method. Theoretic methods proper (those used directly in the pursuit of knowledge) are numerous, but each of them is characterized by the same defining feature: control by a principle. The principle of a theoretic enquiry determines the general shape of its problem, the kind of data to seek, and how to interpret these data to a conclusion.[1] In the theoretic, then, the formulation of a good specific problem and the devising of the right experiment may challenge wit and reward genius, but the direction in which the experiment is to

1. For a more complete treatment of the principles of theoretic enquiry, see my "What Do Scientists Do?" chap. 7 in this volume, and "The Structure of the Natural Sciences," in *The Structure of Knowledge and the Curriculum*, ed. G. W. Ford and Lawrence Pugno (Chicago: Rand McNally, 1964), pp. 31–49.

go and what is to be done with the data, once collected, are dictated by the guiding principle of the enquiry.

The practical has no such guide or rule. We may be conscious that a practical problem exists, but we do not know what the problem is. We cannot be sure even of its subjective side—what it is we want or need. There is still less clarity on the objective side—what portion of the state of affairs is awry. These matters begin to emerge only as we examine the situation which seems to be wrong and begin to look, necessarily at random, for what is the matter. The problem slowly emerges, then, as we search for data, and conversely, the search for data is only gradually given direction by the slow formation of the problem.

At some indeterminate point along the way, as the problem assumes shape and the data search becomes more clearly directed, the character of the process alters. It becomes more of a search for solutions and less of a search for the problem. In this second phase, we envisage alternative actions, consider their possible consequences, and estimate their cost and feasibility. Even here, however, the problem cannot be taken as fixed nor, in consequence, can we rest on our definition of what data are relevant. For the consideration of means determines ends as much as ends determine the search for means. We may have thought, for example, that our problem was one of increasing our income or reallocating resources. However, it may prove so difficult to adjust our budget or make more money that we shift our problem to learning how to want less of what money can buy. Then, the relevant data no longer concern only credit, cash, extra pay, and the price of things; relevance suddenly embraces what personal resources of satisfying arts we have yet to discover in ourselves, how they might be discovered and developed; how, that is, we can alter our behavioral and emotional habits.

One case of the interplay of ends and means, of problem, data, and solution, deserves special attention: the selected fruits of practical enquiry which go by the name of *policy*. Policy seems to be an exception to the assertion that practical enquiries have no guiding principles, for, in the course of some deliberations, alternative ends or means may be rejected as "contrary to policy." Now, "policy" deserves some degree of special stature, for it is, if properly constructed, a summary of the past effective deliberations of the institution whose policy it is. It is both a memorial to the coherence and continuity of the institution and, to some extent, a guide toward maintenance of that continuity. But policy as a quintessence of past decisions is no better than its origins. It arises in and from *past* deliberations. Deliberations are the better to the extent that they take account of circumstances, but circumstances notoriously change. Hence, policies grow obsolete. A policy may be conceived, indeed, as one part of an institution's circumstance. As such, it is a factor which deliberation must take into account. But, by the same token, it is one of the factors which deliberation must entertain as possibly subject to deliberate change. To some extent, then, policy is a guide to deliberation, but it is, in more than a punning sense, only a practical guide. It can be used only to the extent that present problems and circumstances permit, and sometimes they do not permit at all. Furthermore, it is by deliberation that we determine the relevance of policy to a present situation. Thus policy determines the course of a deliberation no more than deliberation permits.

The method of the practical (called "deliberation" in the loose way we call theoretic methods "induction") is, then, not at all a linear affair proceeding step-by-step, but rather a complex, fluid, transactional discipline aimed at identification of the desirable and at either attainment of the desired or at alteration of desires.

The Quasi-Practical

So much, then, for the practical per se. The distinction of the quasi-practical from the practical per se is partly one of convenience and partly one of substance. It is an extension of practical methods and purposes to subject matters of increasing internal variety. This increasing variety makes it more and more difficult to *be* effectively practical. It is one thing to make wise choices for the instruction of a homogeneous group of children. It is more difficult and less feasible to make an equally definite and equally wise choice for many groups, each containing children of different ages and different social origins. Firm decisions may be made about rates and ways of integrating one school. Equally firm decisions on the same matter for a whole school system or all the schools of an entire state are likely to be less wise and more difficult to make. The increasingly doubtful character of quasi-practical decisions does not, however, permit us to avoid making them. At least two factors involved in the practical per se (at least, as applied in the field of education) require that we extend its application to more varied, less amenable subject matters.

In the first place, if the practical decisions made by each member-group of a heterogeneous grouping are not to go astray, something approximately practical must be done for the larger collection as a whole. This necessity arises from the fact that actions taken by the member-groups affect one another. Actions have consequences, and the consequences spread beyond the unit for which the decision was made. Consider as obvious examples the consequences on neighboring schools of a unilateral action by one school involving an increase of its salary scale, or the effect on sister disciplines of a cancellation of examinations by the social studies. Indeed, decisions alone, apart from actions and consequences of action, may have effects. Consider the effect on a neighboring community's schools of the mere news that a nearby school community has adopted (or rejected) the "new" science curriculums en masse.

The solution to such problems (of practical guidance for increasingly heterogeneous groupings) is one business of the quasi-practical. The methods appropriate to such problems are the methods of the practical per se plus two special emphases, one concerning the process of decision itself, the other concerning formulation of decisions made. In making choices and decisions for heterogeneous groupings, the special obligation of the quasi-practical is to those areas of pertinent circumstance which vary or are likely to vary from member-group to member-group. It must identify these areas of variation. It must estimate the different directions and degrees of variation likely to occur among the member-groups. It must determine (as far as it is possible to determine anything in the practical) the different ways in which different variations will affect the wisdom of its decision. It must discern some of the ways in which its decision ought to be modified or qualified in each specific application in order to take best account of each varying circumstance.

In formulating its decisions, the special obligation of this aspect of the quasi-practical is to certain human weaknesses. The process of deliberation is not only difficult and time-consuming, it is also unsatisfying—because there is no point at which it is clear that the course has been completed and completed well. As a result, there is always the temptation in deliberation to look for principles where none exist, to seek "rules" which can be interpreted as requiring that choices of a certain restricted kind be made or as forbidding choices of some kinds. The special obligation of formulation is, then, to communicate the merely *quasi*-practical character of the decision: pointing to some of the considerations which ought to be taken into account in translating it into the practical, suggesting some of the ways in which the decision can be modified in the light of these considerations. The special obligation, in short, is to see to it that quasi-practical decisions are not mistaken for "directives"—either by those who make them or by those who are to translate them into action.

The channels of effect and reaction among similars (six schools, ten groups of learners, four producers of nickel-steel) which render each such similar vulnerable to the decisions and actions of others constitute one of the factors which require exercise of the quasi-practical. There are also connections among dissimilars, organic connections channeling effect and reaction to an even greater degree. Consider, for example, the relations which exist among divisions of a corporation: research and development, promotion and sales, finance, production. Each can pretend to have merely its own practical problems. These "own" problems are, in one sense, real enough. The practical problems of research and development concern the wise disposition of human talents, the feasibility of one project as opposed to another, the most effective utilization of space and equipment. The problems of sales and promotion are problems of the audiences to be reached and the "messages" delivered to them, problems of pricing, profits, and dealer relations, problems of delivery. The practical problems of finance are problems of interest rates and dividends, of foreseeing markets for equities, debentures, bonds, of the repute of the corporation in the financial community and among receivers of dividends.

We have here, however, a patent instance of the extent to which each practical case confronts us, not with a problem clear in its boundaries and nicely subsumed in one set of terms, but with a cloudy problem-situation. It is part of our practical problem to discern the problem, and we do it well or badly to the extent that we keep our boundaries flexible and our terms fluid. It is *not* wisely practical to conceive the problems of research and development, for instance, as merely problems of disposition of investigative talent and laboratory resources and of the relative feasibilities of projects. A project which uses resources to the full and yields an interesting new device will be a wholly successful project only if the device can be produced and the product marketed. Conversely, the problem of sales and promotion may be less a problem of how best to sell what the corporation makes than a problem of discerning what improvements or revolutions in the product may make it saleable. (If the market for two-channel stereo sound is nearly saturated, let us ask R & D about the possibilities of four-track reproduction.) Each department of the corporation, in short, is not solely responsible for its own problems. Each other department also has a proprietary interest. The terms proper to each department apply also to problems of other departments. The corporation's parts have organic connection.

The same organic connections exist in education. Effective teaching of reading and writing cannot be left only to teachers of reading and writing. The success or failure of such teaching affects and is affected by the reading and writing demanded in science and the social studies. The way in which scientific knowledge is presented to students (as contingent on enquiry, indubitable truth, or *only* indubitable truth) affects the credibility of the content of the humanities and the social studies. The timing of long papers and examinations in one department affects students' performance in other areas. Treatment of literary works as fair reports of the milieu they describe has immediate impact on the teaching of history (and vice versa). Such organic connections ramify into still further reaches. The attitudes praised or otherwise instilled in the social studies become factors in the maintenance of order in the school. The moralities and mores conveyed by the attitudes of all teachers affect the relations of children to the school, of children to their parents, and of parents to the school. The proprieties of language usage imposed by an English teacher, the accents and idioms derided by a science teacher (or merely not understood), the standards of dress and deportment, the demands for docility, the encouragement of prejudices and xenophobias by any teacher, affect the problems of all and become parts of their problems.

The same kind of organic connections relates (or should relate) the parts of the larger educational establishment. Research into learning and teaching, educational sociology, tests and measurements, and statistical analysis have their practical problems: establishment of priorities among their research projects and allocation of their human and financial resources. Establishment of such priorities takes place, in part, in terms of the progress of the field, the blank spaces in its body of knowledge, the availability of techniques and methods appropriate to its researches. In part, however, problems of priorities in research extend beyond the bounds of the sciences involved. They involve human needs. The presence of a new class of students in the schools posing a new problem in the mastery of the written word is a matter which should concern psychologists and sociologists when they choose what work to do. In general, the needs of a people and the difficulties faced by the institutions which serve these needs are considerations in the guidance of research—in even the "purest" sciences.

The solution to such problems (of organic connections among the diverse organs of the school, the school community, and the educational establishment) constitutes a second business of the quasi-practical. The methods appropriate are, again, the methods of the practical per se but with a heavy special emphasis on the *cherishing of diversity* and the *honoring of delegated powers*.

What is required is that the deliberations narrowly proper to each organ of the system (department of a high school, field of educational research, administrative office, publisher of textbooks) be carried on in part with the help and advice of able representatives of the other organs involved. Deliberation about the physics course requires the comment of the English teacher as well as the teacher of biology, the learning theorist as well as the science educator. Deliberation about allocation of funds among researchers on "creativity," perception of meaning, and enquiry readiness is the business of teachers and school administrators as well as of educational psychologists. In seeking and obtaining such advice, however, each seeker will face a specially heavy intellectual and moral obligation. He will be confronted by unfamiliar vocabularies. He will hear terms which he does not use brought to bear on "his" problems. Considerations which, in his framework, are alien and irrelevant will be raised and debated. His problem will be to listen, to master the new vocabularies, to appreciate the effect of new terms, and to begin to discern and honor the relevance of "alien" considerations to his problems and his interests. Eventually, his problem will be to discover that the diversity which poses these problems and obligations does, in fact, operate in his interest—since every additional factor taken into account in making a practical decision is one less factor which might otherwise frustrate the success of the ensuing action.

Each representative who gives advice and shares the deliberations on another's problems has a complementary moral and intellectual obligation. In the course of the corporate deliberations he discovers, perhaps for the first time, the existence of numerous remote agencies whose decisions affect his professional life (the teacher, for example, discovers the extent to which textbook publishers, national and private foundations, and other distant executives predetermine the curriculum he will teach). He recognizes corporate deliberations as one of the few means by which he can influence the course of these remote agencies. Meanwhile, from the very act of participation in the deliberations, he acquires an additional sense of proprietorship in the others' problems. Such recognitions by a participant constitute a great temptation to influence the deliberations, not in the direction of the decision best for the organism as a whole, but in the direction which best serves his own part-interest. The same recognitions urge the giver of advice to insist in any way he can that his advice be taken. Yet, in the interest of the whole, the ultimate practical decision, subsequent to the reception of quasi-practical advice, must be taken by the organ which the problem most concerns. From this constellation of factors the special obligation of the giver of advice arises: the honoring of delegated powers.

The Eclectic

The third mode of operation commended to curriculum—the eclectic—recognizes the usefulness of theory to curriculum decision, takes account of certain weaknesses of theory as ground for decision, and provides some degree of repair of these weaknesses.

Whether applied eclectically or not, theory has two major uses in decision making. First and most commonly, theories are used as bodies of knowledge. Skinnerian theory is used, for example, as knowledge of the learning process or Freudian theory is used as knowledge of personality. In this way, theory provides a kind of shorthand for some phases of deliberation and—rightly or wrongly—frees the deliberator from the necessity of obtaining firsthand information on the subject under discussion. Second, the terms and distinctions which a theory uses for theoretical purposes can be brought to bear practically. For purposes of curricular deliberation, for example, we may bring the Baconian distinction of memory, reason, and imagination to bear to divide subject matters (and curriculum problems) into three corresponding classes: historical, scientific, and literary. Or the ancient differentiation of disciplines into logic, ethics, and science may be applied to separate three classes of educational problems: development of cognitive competencies, development of values and attitudes, and acquisition of knowledge.

The weaknesses of theory arise from two sources: the inevitable incompleteness of the subject matters of theories and the partiality of the view each takes of its already incomplete subject. Incompleteness of subject is easily seen in the entirely cognitive learning theory which takes no account of emotional needs and satisfactions. It is equally visible in economic theories which begin with supply and demand but which are unable to take account of emotional-cultural factors which affect the direction and intensity of demand. (The force of such theoretical delimiting of a subject matter is often so great that the reader of such a sentence as the preceding often recoils with the remark, "But that isn't economics! That's psychology," i.e., the curtailments imposed by theory are treated as real and irreparable.) Incompleteness of subject is also visible in personality theories which reduce the whole of society to an appendage of personality and in sociological theories which reduce personality to an artifact of society. Partiality of view is exemplified by the Freudian treatment of personality after the analogue of a developing, differentiating organism (a treatment which makes it extremely difficult to deal directly with problems of interpersonal relations). It is equally visible in interpersonal theories which make it difficult to deal with autogenous behaviors and feelings. (We shall examine instances of these weaknesses of theory and their wide diffusion again.)

These weaknesses vitiate the value of either of the two uses of theory in the making of decisions. Incompleteness of subject and partiality of view together render the use of theory as a replacement for firsthand information a dangerous procedure. Partiality of view is incorporated in the structure of terms and distinctions of the theory; hence adaptation of the distinctions to other uses is highly likely to bring with it something of the same partiality. For example, the distinction of development of cognitive competence from development of values and attitudes makes it very difficult to consider ways of education which might put it within the power of some individuals to choose and effect deliberate, rational changes in their felt values and attitudes.

Eclectic operations repair these weaknesses (to some extent) in two ways. First, eclectic operations bring into clear view the particular truncation of subject characteristic of a given theory and bring to light the partiality of its view. Second, eclectic operations permit the serial utilization or even the conjoint utilization of two or more theories on practical problems. The first consequence of the eclectic, even without the second, at least enables us to know what we are doing (and omitting) when we use a theory in practical situations. The first and the second together enable us to make sophisticated use of theories without paying the full price of their incompleteness and partiality.

The eclectic begins by identifying the terms and distinctions which constitute the skeleton (the structure) of a theory—not merely what the terms are but how they are related. In Freudian theory, for example, the initial analysis would disclose not only the centrality of ego-id-superego but also the genetic relations they bear: ego and superego developing out of id and forever bearing with them the stigma of their origin. It would note the primary attachment of pleasure and energy to the id as further consequences of its assumed dominance. It would note the limited potency assigned to the ego and the near-imperviousness assigned to the id as limiting psychotherapy mainly to alteration of the superego and casting society as the villain of the piece. By such means (there are, of course, other terms and relations in Freudian theory omitted from this analysis) the initial analysis reveals the extent to which the Freudian theory is primarily a theory of the vicissitudes of the instincts, that its treatment of sociality is curt and subordinate to its treatment of the "inner" life, that it has little to say about the development of cognitive components of the personality, including those cognitive competences by which the infant begins to differentiate itself from other persons and other things and which only some adults carry far (clearly an important practical matter both for psychotherapy and for education). In addition to noting these curtailments of subject matter, the initial analysis discloses, too, the special bias (partiality of view) imposed on the selection and interpretation of facts by the use in Freudian theory of the embryological notion of development of psychic organs by differentiation from a primary organ, the id. (It is clear, I hope, that curtailments of subject and partiality of view in Freudian theory are merely illustrative of curtailments and biases in theory generally, and not of peculiar weaknesses of Freud.)

After such a primary analysis, the eclectic may go in either of two directions. It may concern itself with competing theories of one or similar subject matters (for example, some of the considerable variety of personality theories). Or it may concern itself with theories constructed in other sciences to deal with subject matters omitted from the theory initially treated (for example, theories of learning, theories of culture, and theories of society, supposing these matters to have been dealt with curtly or not at all by the theory initially treated).

In the former case (treating differing theories of similar subject matters), comparison of the different sets of terms with one another and with their approximately common subject matters makes it possible to identify a set of elements shared among all the theories examined, and embodied (though differently) in each theory's set of terms. This set of common elements then makes it possible to discriminate and relate the biases of each theory: what its terms illuminate, what light cast by others' terms it fails to shed, what aspects of the subject it brings to the foreground, and what it thrusts into the background. In brief, this branch of eclectic method makes it possible to see what each member of the collection of theories does and does not do with and to their approximately common subject matter.

This knowledge makes it possible to apply different competing theories *appropriately* to different practical problems. It also makes it possible to discriminate what can be treated in deliberation by the shorthand of extant theory and what must be left to the harder labor of deliberation. It even makes it possible to bring two or three different theories of the same subject matter (which, as theories, are mutually exclusive) to bear on the same practical problem. Thus, materials which could otherwise be treated only as source for a merely "preferred," doctrinaire choice, or as a mere conspectus of incomplete "opinions," are converted by this powerful branch of the eclectic into a battery of varied and useful tools. (The eclectic does *not* make it possible to combine the alternative theories into one coherent theory. An inventive genius may profit from an eclectic analysis, but for the invention of a single coherent theory, genius is still required.)

The second branch of eclectic method (which treats theories of different but related subject matters) proceeds by analogous methods to somewhat different ends. Comparison of sets of terms and subject matters found in these theories makes it possible to determine, for a given theory, what violence it has done its chosen subject in order to disconnect it from related subjects and give it the appearance of an independent whole. The complementary violence done to the remaining, "other" subject mass is similarly identified. Third, the points of possible contact between the selected subject and "adjacent" subjects which have *not* been polished into invisibility are identified. One theory of personality, for example, is found to have separated "personality" from "society" and given independent wholeness to "personality" by (a) positing the incorporation of one feature of sociality *into* personality at an early age; (b) treating most of the remainder of "society" as only an unpleasant but necessary arrangement for procurement of food, shelter, and protection; and (c) converting conjoint work and play into mere preludes or substitutes for sexual gratification. One group of social theories gives society the appearance of completeness by rendering personality almost entirely as a reflection of social action and social need, and by treating instinctual needs as trivial or as important only in infancy.

The second branch of the eclectic thus makes possible the practical conjunction of some theories of one part-subject with some theories of other part-subjects without having to wait on a unified theory of the united whole.

ARGUMENT AND COROLLARIES

We turn now to the evidence and argument in support of the views here summarized and to examination of some of the ways in which the proposed modes of operation—especially the practical—might operate in curriculum and for the education of teachers and curriculum workers.

Crises of Principle in General

The frustrated state of the field of curriculum is not a sickness peculiar to that field nor is it a condition which warrants guilt or shame on the part of curriculum practitioners. All fields of systematic intellectual activity are marked by rhythms which involve such crises. The crises arise because any intellectual discipline must begin its endeavors with *untested* principles. In its beginnings, its subject matter is relatively unknown, its problems unsolved, indeed, unidentified. It does not know what questions to ask, what other knowledge to rest upon, what data to seek, or what to make of them once they are elicited. Any new field requires a preliminary and necessarily untested guide to its enquiries. It finds this guide by borrowing, by invention, or by analogy, in the shape of a hazardous commitment to the character of its problems or its subject matter and an additional commitment to untried canons of evidence and rules of enquiry. An early version of sociology, for example, chose "the city" as its subject and conceived of the city in terms borrowed from physics and physiology. From physiology it took the notion of organism, thus conceiving the city as an outcome of the operation of laws of growth, maturation, and aging inherent in it. From physics it borrowed the notions of point-sources of force and of fields of influence surrounding such points. Consequently, it sought the laws of growth and deterioration of cities, and tried to locate the focal points of their growth and deterioration and further laws expressing the rates at which the fields of growth and deterioration spread outward from these points.

What follows such commitments to principles of enquiry are years of their application, pursuit of the mode of enquiry demanded by the principles to which the field has committed itself. For example, the sociologists who committed themselves to an organic view of cities spent years gathering and studying statistics on the changes which ensued on the establishment of industrial developments, business districts, and successive waves of immigration and changes in the economic status of the inhabitants of streets and neighborhoods.

To the majority of practitioners of any field, these years of enquiry appear only as pursuit of knowledge of its subject matter or solution of its problems. They take the guiding principles of the enquiry as givens. These years of enquiry are, however, something more than pursuit of knowledge or solution of problems. They also serve as tests, reflexive and pragmatic, of the principles which guide the enquiries. The years of enquiry determine whether the data demanded by the principles can, in fact, be elicited and whether, if elicited, they can be made to constitute knowledge adequate to the complexity of the subject matter or solutions which, in fact, do solve the problems with which the enquiry began. Organismic sociology spent more than a decade collecting its data, making growth maps of city after city, and searching for regularities among these maps.

In the nature of the case, these reflexive tests of the principles of enquiry more often than not are partially or wholly negative. After all, the commitment to these principles was made before there were well-tested fruits of enquiry by which to guide the commitment. Inadequacies of principle begin to show, in the case of theoretical enquiries, by failures: failure of the subject matter to respond to the questions put to it; incoherencies and "contradictions" in data and in conclusions which cannot be resolved; or by clear disparities between the knowledge yielded by the enquiries and the behaviors of the subject matter which the knowledge purports to represent. Organismic sociology, for example, had no trouble in finding its data, but it found, too, that these data were shot through and through with incoherences, that few regularities were disclosed, and that these few were wholly inadequate as representations of the complex changes which cities underwent. In the case of practical enquiries, inadequacies (bad habits of deliberation) begin to show by incapacity to arrive at solutions to the problems, by inability to realize the solutions proposed, by frustrations and cancelings out as solutions are put into effect.

Although these exhaustions and failures of principle and method may go unnoted by practitioners in the field, at least at the conscious level, what may not be represented in consciousness is nevertheless evidenced by practitioners' behavior and appears in the literature and the activities of the field as signs of the onset of a crisis. These signs consist of a large increase in the frequency of published papers and colloquiums marked by *a flight from the subject of the field*. There are usually six signs of this flight or directions in which the flight occurs.

The first and most important, though often least conspicuous, is a flight of the field itself, a translocation of its problems and the solving of them from the nominal practitioners of the field to other men. Thus, one crucial frustration of the science of genetics was resolved by a single contribution from an insurance actuary. The recent infertility of academic physiology has been marked by a conspicuous increase in the frequency of published solutions to physiological problems by medical researchers. In similar fashion, the increasing depletion of psychoanalytic principles and methods in recent years was marked by the onset of contributions to its lore by internists, biochemists, and anthropologists.

A second flight is a flight upward, from discourse about the subject of the field to discourse about the discourse of the field, from *use* of principles and methods to *talk* about them, from grounded conclusions to the construction of models, from theory to metatheory, and from metatheory to meta-metatheory. In physics, for example, Einstein, Max Planck, and Niels Bohr had demonstrated to the satisfaction of many physicists, in the years 1900–13, that the "laws" of classical electrodynamics and mechanics did not hold for the behavior of electrons within the atom or even for events following collision between free electrons and electrons in the atom. In the years following, the journals were overwhelmed by proposed alternative models of the atom, papers attacking these models as metaphysically impossible, papers attacking and defending the possibility that entirely different laws might govern large particles and small ones, and still other papers attempting to reconcile the two states of affairs.

A third flight is downward, an attempt by practitioners to return to the subject matter in a state of innocence, shorn, not only of current principles, but of all principles, in an effort to take a new, pristine, and unmediated look at the subject matter. For example, one conspicuous reaction to the warfare of numerous inadequate principles in experimental psychology has been the resurgence of ethology, which begins as an attempt to return to a pure natural history of behavior, to intensive observation and recording of the behavior of animals undisturbed in their natural habitat by observers equally undisturbed by mediating conceptions, who attempt to record anything and everything they see before them.

A fourth flight is to the sidelines, to the role of observer, commentator, historian, and critic of the contributions of others to the field.

A fifth sign consists of marked perseveration, a repetition of old and familiar knowledge in new languages which add little or nothing to the old meanings embodied in the older and more familiar language, or repetition of old and familiar formulations by way of criticism or minor additions and modifications.

The sixth is a marked increase in eristic, contentious, and *ad hominem* debate. Consider, for example, the warfare of words among contending exponents of different theories of personality. Freudians, existentialists, Gestaltists, and defenders of ego theories are not only meticulous in pointing out the errors and omissions of their colleagues, they are also assiduous in suggesting their shortcomings of character, morals, and intelligence.

I hasten to remark that these signs of crisis are not all or equally reprehensible. There is little excuse for the increase in contentiousness nor much value in the flight to the sidelines or to perseveration, but the others, in one way or another, can contribute to resolution of the crisis. The flight of the field itself is one of the more fruitful ways by which analogical principles are disclosed, modified, and adapted to the field in crisis. The flight upward, to models and metatheory, if done responsibly, becomes, in fact, the proposal and test of possible new principles for the field. (Responsible proposal has certain defining marks. In the first place, models are constructed and proposed for the solution of clearly defined and formulated unsolved problems in the field. They are not constructed merely at random or proposed merely because they are new. Second, responsible proposals are accompanied by clear indications of how and where the research they require might be instituted. Ideally, they are accompanied by an instance of their use: the actual solution of a previously difficult problem by means of the new conception.) The flight backward, to a state of innocence, is at least an effort to break the grip of old habits of thought and thus leave space for needed new ones, though it is clear that in the matter of enquiry, as elsewhere, lost virginity cannot be regained.

In the present context, however, the virtue or vice of these various flights is beside the point. We are concerned with them as signs of collapse of principles in a field, and it is my contention, based on a study not yet complete, that most of these signs can now be seen in the field of curriculum. I shall only suggest, not cite, my evidence.

Crises of Principle in Curriculum

With respect to flight of the field itself, there can be little doubt. Of the five substantial high school science curriculums, four of them—PSSC, BSCS, CHEMS, and CBA—were instituted and managed by subject matter specialists; the contribution of educators was small and that of curriculum specialists near the vanishing point. Only Harvard Project Physics, at this writing not yet available, appears to be an exception. To one of two elementary science projects, a psychologist appears to have made a substantial contribution but curriculum specialists very little. The other—the Elementary Science Study—appears to have been substantially affected (to its advantage) by educators with one or both feet in curriculum. The efforts of the Commission on Undergraduate Education in the Biological Sciences have been carried on almost entirely by subject matter specialists. The English Curriculum Study Centers appear to be in much the same state as the high school science curriculums: overwhelmingly centered on the work of subject specialists. Educators contribute expertise only in the area of test construction and evaluation, with a contribution here and there by a psychologist. Educators, including curriculum specialists, were massively unprepared to cope with the problem of integrated education, and only by little, and late, and by trial and error, put together the halting solutions currently known as Head Start. The problem posed by the current drives toward ethnicity in education finds curriculum specialists even more massively oblivious and unprepared. And until recently I found myself alone with respect to the curriculum problems immanent in the phenomena of student protest and student revolt. (Of the social studies curriculum efforts, I shall say nothing at this time.)

On the second flight—upward—I need hardly comment. The models, the metatheory, and the meta-metatheory are all over the place. Many of them, moreover, are irresponsible in that they are concerned less with the barriers to continued productivity in the field of curriculum than with exploitation of the exotic and the fashionable among forms and models of theory and metatheory: for example, systems theory, symbolic logic, language analysis. Many other models, including responsible ones, are irreversible flights upward or sideways. That is, they are not models or metatheories concerned with the judgment, the reasoned construction, or the reconstruction of curriculums, but with other matters—e.g., how curriculum changes occur or how changes can be managed. In this respect, they are almost patent confessions of impotence in the face of curricular problems. They come close to suggesting that what ought to be done about curriculums is the business of some other expert, that the actual institution of curricular changes is the business of still another group of workers, and that the business of the curriculum specialist is only to observe these others working in the hope of finding rules or laws of their operations.

The flight downward, the attempt at return to a pristine, unmediated look at the subject matter, is, for some reason, missing in the case of curriculum. There are returns—to the classroom, if not to other levels or aspects of curriculum—with a measure of effort to avoid preconceptions (e.g., the work of Smith and Bellack, and the studies of communication nets and lines), but the frequency of such studies has not markedly increased. The absence of this symptom may be significant. In general, however, it is characteristic of diseases that the whole syndrome may not appear in all cases. Hence, pending further study and thought, I do not count this negative instance as weakening the diagnosis of a crisis of principle.

The fourth flight—to the sidelines—is again a marked symptom of the field of curriculum. Histories, anthologies, commentaries, and criticisms of curriculums and proposed curriculums multiply.

Perseveration is also marked. I recoil from counting the persons and books whose lives are made possible by continuing restatement of the Tyler rationale or of the character and case for behavioral objectives or of the virtues and vices of John Dewey.

The rise in frequency and intensity of the eristic and *ad hominem* is also marked. Thus, one author climaxes a series of petulances by remarking that what he takes to be his own forte "has always been rare—and shows up in proper perspective the happy breed of educational reformer who can concoct a brand-new, rabble-rousing theory of educational reform while waiting for the water to fill the bathtub."

There is little doubt, in short, that the field of curriculum is in a crisis of principle.

A crisis of principle arises, as I have suggested, when principles are exhausted—when the questions they permit have all been asked and answered, or when the efforts at enquiry instigated by the principles have at last exhibited their inadequacy to the subject matter and to the problems they were designed to attack. My second point is that the latter holds in the case of curriculum: The curriculum movement has been inveterately theoretic and its theoretic bent has let it down. A brief conspectus of instances will suggest the extent of this theoretic bent.

Incompetences of Theory: Failure of Scope

Consider first the early, allegedly Herbartian efforts (recently revived by Bruner). These efforts took the view that ideas were formed by children out of received notions and experiences of things, and that these ideas functioned thereafter as discriminators and organizers of what was later learned. Given this view, the aim of curriculum was to discriminate the right ideas (by way of analysis of extant bodies of knowledge), determine the order in which they could be learned by children as they developed, and thereafter present them at the right times with clarity, associations, organization, and application. A theory of mind and of knowledge thus solves by one mighty coup the problem of what to teach, when, and how; what is fatally theoretic here is not merely the presence of a theory of mind and a theory of knowledge, though that presence is part of the story, but the dispatch, the sweeping appearance of success, the vast simplicity which grounds this purported solution to the problem of curriculum. And lest we think that this faith in the possibility of successful neatness, dispatch, and sweeping generality is a mark of the past, consider the concern of the National Science Teachers Association only four years ago with (italics mine) "identifying the broad principles that can apply to *any and all* curriculum development efforts in science," a concern crystallized in just seven "conceptual schemes" held to underlie all science. With less naiveté but with the same steadfast concern for a single factor—in this case, a supposed fixed structure of knowledge—one finds similar efforts arising from the National Society of College Teachers of Education, from historians, even from teachers of literature.

Consider, now, some of the numerous efforts to base curriculum on derived objectives. One effort seeks to ground its objectives in social need and finds its social needs in just those facts about its culture which are sought and found under the aegis of a single conception of culture. Another grounds its objectives in the social needs identified by a single theory of history or politics. Consider, for example, the following two:

> First, there is the goal of a world-wide democracy or a series of democracies. . . . Second, . . . the goal of a world government with authority to enforce its mandates . . . the crucial problems of political, economic, religious, esthetic and educational life should be brought into the center of the curriculum. . . .[2]

> In every changing culture of the world today, two insistent problems should engage the attention of educators: (1) What are the concepts and problems of our changing civilization which should constitute both the needed social program of action and the outline of the educational program? (2) What are the elements of a creative philosophy which shall be appropriate for the new social order? . . . Thus through the schools of the world, we shall disseminate a new conception of government—one that will embrace all of the collective activities of men. . . .[3]

(Currently, we are more likely to find "participative democracy," anarchy, or minority rule instead of Marxism or Wilson-Roosevelt liberalism as the one true doctrine—but the point is the same.)

2. Theodore Brameld, "A Reconstructionist View of Education," in *Philosophies of Education*, ed. Philip H. Phenix (New York: John Wiley & Sons, 1961), p. 106.

3. Harold Rugg, "Social Construction Through Education," in *Readings in the Philosophy of Education*, ed. John M. Rich (Belmont, Calif.: Wadsworth Publishing Co., 1966), p. 112.

A third group of searches for objectives is grounded in theories of personality. The seductive coherence and plausibility of Freudianism persuade its followers to aim to supply children with adequate channels of sublimation of surplus libido, appropriate objects and occasions for aggressions, a properly undemanding ego ideal, and an intelligent minimum of taboos. Interpersonal theories, on the other hand, direct their adherents to aim for development of abilities to relate to peers, inferiors, and superiors in relations nurturant and receiving, adaptive, vying, approving, and disapproving. Theories of actualization instruct their adherents to determine the salient potentialities of each child and to see individually to the development of each.

Still other searches for objectives seek their aims in the knowledge needed to "live in the modern world," in the attitudes and habits which minimize dissonance with the prevailing mores of one's community or social class, in the skills required for success in a trade or vocation, or in the ability to participate effectively as members of a group. Still others are grounded in some quasi-ethics, some view of the array of goods which are good for man.

Three features of these typical efforts at curriculum making are significant here, each of which has its own lesson to teach us. First, each is grounded in a theory as such. We shall return to this point in a moment. Second, each is grounded in a theory from the social or behavioral sciences: psychology, psychiatry, politics, sociology, or history. Even the ethical bases and theories of "mind" are behavioral. To this point, too, we shall return in a moment. Third, each theory concerns a *different* subject matter. One curriculum effort is grounded in concern only for the individual, another in concern only for groups, others in concern only for cultures, *or* communities, *or* societies, *or* minds, *or* the extant bodies of knowledge.[4]

The significance of this third feature is patent to the point of embarrassment: No curriculum, grounded in but one of these subjects, can possibly be adequate or defensible. A curriculum based on a theory about individual personality which thrusts society, its demands, and its structure far into the background or which ignores them entirely can

---

4. It should be clear by now that "theory" as used in this paper does not refer only to grand schemes such as the general theory of relativity, kinetic-molecular theory, the Bohr atom, the Freudian construction of a tripartite psyche. The attempt to give an account of human maturation by the discrimination of definite states (e.g., oral, anal, genital) and the effort to aggregate human competences into a small number of primary mental abilities—these too are theoretic. So also are efforts to discriminate a few large classes of persons and to attribute to them defining behaviors: e.g., the socially mobile, the culturally deprived, the creative.

be nothing but incomplete and doctrinaire, for the individuals in question are in fact members of a society and must meet its demands to some minimum degree since their existence and prosperity as individuals depend on the functioning of their society. In the same way, a curriculum grounded only in a view of social need or social change must be equally doctrinaire and incomplete, for societies do not exist only for their own sakes but for the prosperity of their members as individuals as well. In the same way, learners are not only minds or knowers but also bundles of affects, individuals, personalities, and earners of livings. They are not only group interactors but also possessors of private lives.

It is clear, I submit, that a defensible curriculum or plan of curriculum must be one which somehow takes account of all these sub-subjects which pertain to man. It cannot take only one and ignore the others; it cannot even take account of many of them and ignore one. Each of them is not only one of the constituents and one of the conditions of decent human existence but each also interpenetrates some or all of the others. That is, the character of human personality is one of the determiners of human association and the behavior of human groups. Conversely, the conditions of group behavior and the character of a culture or society determine in some large part the personalities which their members develop, the way their minds work, and what they can learn and use by way of knowledge and competence. Even the patterns of scientific enquiry are determined to some extent by social conditions (especially economic ones) and by the personalities attracted to science in a given culture. These various "things" (individuals, societies, cultures, patterns of enquiry, structures of knowledge or of enquiries, apperceptive masses, problem solving), though discriminable as separate subjects of differing modes of enquiry, are nevertheless parts or affectors of one another or coactors. (Their very separation for purposes of enquiry is what marks the outcomes of such enquiries as "theoretic" and consequently incomplete.) In practice, they constitute one complex, organic agency. Hence, a focus on only one not only ignores the others but vitiates the quality and completeness with which the selected one is viewed.

It is equally clear, however, that there is not, and will not be in the foreseeable future, one theory of this complex whole which is other than a collection of unusable generalities. Nor is it true that the lack of a theory of the whole is due to the narrowness, the stubbornness, or the merely habitual specialism of social and behavioral scientists. Rather, their specialism and the restricted purview of their theories are functions of their subject, its enormous complexity, its vast capacity for difference and change. Even the relatively simple and highly uniform subject matter of mechanics had to wait centuries for development of principles of enquiry adequate to the behavior of physical bodies in motion. Physiology has only recently developed shifts of principle which take account of an order of complexity of the animal body beyond that represented by the simple and ancient notions of structure and function. Human behavior, whether one-to-one or in groups, is of a still higher order of complexity, vastly more difficult to encompass in a usefully viable set of ideas. There have been efforts to conceive principles of enquiry which would encompass the whole variety and complexity of humanity, but they have fallen far short of adequacy to the subject matter or have demanded the acquisition of data and modes of interpretation of data beyond our capabilities. There are successful efforts to find bridging terms which would relate the principles of enquiry of one subfield of the social sciences to another and thus begin to effect connections among our knowledges of each, but the successful bridges are few and narrow to date and permit but little connection. As far, then, as theoretical knowledge is concerned, we must wrestle as best we can with numerous, largely unconnected, separate theories of these many, artificially discriminated sub-subjects of man.

I remarked in the beginning that renewal of the field of curriculum would require diversion of the bulk of its energies from theory to the practical, the quasi-practical, and the eclectic. The state of affairs just described, the existence and the necessarily continuing existence of separate theories of separate sub-subjects distributed among the social sciences, constitutes the case for one of these, the necessity of an eclectic, of arts by which a usable focus on a common body of problems is effected among theories which lack theoretical connection. The argument can be simply summarized. A curriculum grounded in but one or a few sub-subjects of the social sciences is indefensible; contributions from all are required. There is no foreseeable hope of a unified theory in the immediate or middle future, nor of a metatheory which will tell us how to put them together or order them in a fixed hierarchy of importance to the problems of curriculum. What remains as a viable alternative is the unsystematic, uneasy, pragmatic, and uncertain unions and connections which can be effected in an eclectic. And I must add, anticipating our discussion of the practical, that *changing* connections and *differing* orderings at different times of these separate theories will characterize a sound eclectic.

The whole character of eclectic arts and procedures must be left for discussion on another occasion. Let it suffice for the moment that witness of the high effectiveness of eclectic methods and of their accessibility is borne by at least one field familiar to us all—Western medicine.

It has been enormously effective and the growth of its competence dates from its disavowal of a single doctrine and its turn to eclecticism.

Incompetences of Theory: The Vice of Abstraction

I turn now from the fact that the theories which ground curriculum plans pertain to different sub-subjects of a common field to the second of the three features which characterize our typical instances of curriculum planning—the fact that the ground of each plan is a theory as such.

The significance of the existence of theory as such at the base of curricular planning lies in what that theory does not and cannot encompass. All theories, even the best of them in the simplest sciences, necessarily neglect some aspects and facets of the facts of the case. A theory covers and formulates the *regularities* among the things and events it subsumes. It abstracts a general or ideal case. It leaves behind the nonuniformities, the particularities, which characterize each concrete instance of the facts subsumed. Moreover, in the process of idealization, theoretical enquiries may often leave out of consideration conspicuous facets of *all* cases because its substantive principles of enquiry or its methods cannot handle them. Thus, the constantly accelerating body of classical mechanics was the acceleration of a body in "free" fall, fall in a perfect vacuum, and the general or theoretical rule formulated in classical mechanics is far from describing the fall of actual bodies in actual mediums—the only kinds of fall then known. The force equation of classical dynamics applied to bodies of visible magnitude ignores friction. The rule that light energy received varies inversely as the square of the distance holds exactly only for an imaginary point-source of light. For real light sources of increasing expanse, the so-called law holds more and more approximately, and for very large sources it affords little or no usable information. And what is true of the best of theories in the simplest sciences is true *a fortiori* in the social sciences. Their subject matters are apparently so much more variable, and clearly so much more complex, that their theories encompass much less of their subjects than do the theories of the physical and biological sciences.

Yet curriculum is brought to bear, not on ideal or abstract representations, but on the real thing, on the concrete case, in all its completeness and with all its differences from all other concrete cases, on a large body of fact concerning which the theoretic abstraction is silent. The materials of a concrete curriculum will not consist merely of portions of "science," of "literature," of "process." On the contrary, their constituents will be particular assertions about selected matters couched in a particular vocabulary, syntax, and rhetoric. They will be particular novels, short stories, or lyric poems, each, for better or for worse, with its own flavor. They will be particular acts upon particular matters in a given sequence. They will be perceptions conditioned by particular past conditionings of particular things and events. The curriculum constructed of these particulars will be brought to bear, not in some archetypical classroom, but in a particular locus in time and space with smells, shadows, seats, and conditions outside its walls which may have much to do with what is achieved inside. Above all, the supposed beneficiary is not the generic child, not even a class or kind of child out of the psychological or sociological literature pertaining to the child. The beneficiary will consist of very local kinds of children and, within the local kinds, individual children. The same diversity holds with respect to teachers and what they do.

The generalities about science, about literature, about children in general, about children or teachers of some specified class or kind, may be true, but they attain this status in virtue of what they leave out. The matters omitted vitiate the practical value of theory in two ways. They are not only in themselves often matters of importance; they also modify, by their presence, the general characteristics encompassed in the theories. A species of some genus is characterized, not only by specific traits added on to the generic, but also by modifications and qualifications of the generic traits by the specific ones. A Guernsey cow is not only something *more* than a cow-in-general; some of its generally cow-y traits are modified by its Guernseyness.

These ineluctable characteristics of theory and the consequent disparities between real things and their representation in theory constitute one argument for my thesis that a large bulk of curriculum energies must be diverted from the theoretic, not only to the eclectic but to the practical and the quasi-practical. The argument, again, can be briefly summarized. The stuff of theory is abstract or idealized representations of real things. But curriculum in action treats real things: real acts, real teachers, real children, things richer than and different from their theoretical representations. Curriculum will deal badly with its real things if it treats them merely as replicas of their theoretic representations. If, then, theory is to be used well in the determination of curricular practice, it requires a supplement. It requires arts which bring a theory to its application: first, arts which identify the disparities between real thing and theoretic representation; second, arts which modify the theory in the course of its application in the light of the discrepancies; and third, arts which devise ways of taking account of the many aspects of the real thing which the theory does not take into account. These are some of the arts of the practical.

Incompetences of Theory: Radical Plurality

The significance of the third feature of our typical instances of curriculum work—that their theories are mainly theories from the social and behavioral sciences—will carry us to the remainder of the argument toward the practical. Nearly all theories in all the behavioral sciences are marked by the coexistence of competing theories. There is not one theory of personality but many, representing at least six radically different choices of what is relevant and important in human behavior. There is not one theory of groups but several. There is not one theory of learning but half a dozen. All the social and behavioral sciences are marked by "schools," each distinguished by a different choice of principle of enquiry, each of which selects from the intimidating complexities of the subject matter the small fraction of the whole with which it can deal.

The theories which arise from enquiries so directed are, then, radically incomplete, each of them incomplete to the extent that competing theories take hold of different aspects of the subject of enquiry and treat it in a different way. Further, there is perennial invention of new principles which bring to light new facets of the subject matter, new relations among the facets, and new ways of treating them. In short, there is every reason to suppose that any one of the extant theories of behavior is a pale and incomplete representation of actual behavior.

There is similar reason to suppose that if all the diversities of fact, the different aspects of behavior treated in such theory, were somehow to be brought within the bounds of a single theory, that theory would still fall short of comprehending the whole of human behavior—and in two respects. In the first place, it would not comprehend what there may be of human behavior which we do not see in virtue of the restricted light by which we examine behavior. In the second place, such a single theory will not only seek its data in the restricted light of its principles, it will also necessarily *interpret* its data in the light of its *one* set of principles, assigning to these data only one set of significances and establishing among them only one set of relations. It will remain the case, then, that a diversity of theories may tell us more than a single one, even though the "factual" scope of the many and the one is the same.

It follows that such theories are not, and will not be, adequate by themselves to tell us what to do with actual human beings or how to do it. What they variously suggest and the contrary guidances they afford to choice and action must be mediated and combined by eclectic arts and must be massively supplemented, as well as mediated, by knowledge of some other kind derived from another source.

Some areas of choice and action with respect to human behavior have long since learned this lesson. Government is made possible by a lore of politics derived from immediate experience of the vicissitudes and tangles of legislating and administering. The institution of economic guidances and controls owes as much to unmediated experience of the marketplace as it does to formulas and theories. Even psychotherapy has long since deserted its theories of personality as sole guides to therapy and relies as much or more on the accumulated, explicitly non-theoretic lore accumulated by practitioners as it does on theory or eclectic combinations of theory. The law has systematized the accumulation of direct experience of actual cases in its machinery for the recording of cases and opinions as precedents which continuously monitor, supplement, and modify the meaning and application of its formal knowledge, its statutes. It is this recourse to accumulated lore, to experience of actions and their consequences, to action and reaction at the level of the concrete case, which constitutes the heart of the practical. It is high time that curriculum do likewise.

Practical Curriculum: Assessment and Change of Curriculum

Because the arts of the practical are onerous and complex, only a sampling can be added here to what we have already indicated of its character. I shall deal briefly with only four aspects of it, together with some of the changes in educational investigation which would ensue on adoption of its discipline.

The practical arts begin with the requirement that existing institutions and existing practices be preserved and altered piecemeal, not dismantled and replaced. Changes must be so planned and so articulated with what remains unchanged that the functioning of the whole remains coherent and unimpaired. These necessities stem from the very nature of the practical—its concern with the maintenance and improvement of patterns of purposed action, and especially its concern that the effects of the pattern through time shall retain coherence and relevance with one another.

This is well seen in the case of the law. Statutes are properly repealed or largely rewritten only as a last resort, since to do so creates diremption between old judgments under the law and judgments to come, and the resulting confusion must lead either to weakening of law through disrepute or a painful and costly process of repairing the effects of past judgments so as to bring them into coherence with the new. It is vastly more desirable that changes be instituted in small degrees and in immediate adjustment to the peculiarities of particular new cases which call forth the change. Consider, as a particularly clumsy case in point, the release of known and convicted murderers, some of them threats to society, in consequence of a Supreme Court ruling on the conditions for admission of confession as evidence.

The consequence, in the case of the law, of these demands of the practical is that the servants of the law must know the law through and through. They must know the statutes themselves and the progression of precedents and interpretations which have effected changes in the statutes, and they must especially know the present state of affairs: the most recent decisions under the law and the calendar of cases which will be most immediately affected by contemplated additions to precedent and interpretation.

The same requirements would hold for a practical program of improvement of education. It, too, would effect its changes in small progressions, in coherence with what remains unchanged, and this would require that we know *what is and has been going on in American schools*.

At present, we do not know. My own incomplete investigations convince me that we have not the faintest reliable knowledge of how literature is taught in the high schools or what actually goes on in science classrooms. There are a dozen different ways in which the novel can be read. Which ones are used by whom, with whom, and to what effect? What selections from the large accumulation of biological knowledge are made and taught in this school system and that, to what classes and kinds of children, and to what effect? To what extent is science taught as verbal formulas, or as congeries of unrelated facts, or as so-called principles and conceptual structures, or as outcomes of enquiry? With what degree and kind of simplification and falsification is scientific enquiry conveyed, if it is conveyed at all?

A count of textbook adoptions will not tell us, for teachers select from textbooks and alter their treatment (often, quite properly), and can frustrate and negate the textbook's effort to control the pattern of instruction. We cannot tell from lists of objectives, since they are usually so ambiguous that almost anything can go on under their aegis and, if not ambiguous, reflect pious hopes as much as actual practice. We cannot tell from lists of "principles" and "conceptual structures," since these, in their telegraphic brevity, are also ambiguous and say nothing of the way they are taught or the extent.

What is wanted is a totally new and extensive pattern of *empirical* study of classroom action and reaction; a study, not as basis for theoretical concerns about the nature of the teaching or learning process, but as a basis for beginning to know what we are doing, what we are not doing, and to what effect; what changes are needed, which needed changes can be instituted with what costs or economies, and how they can be effected with minimum tearing of the remaining fabric of educational effort.

This is an effort which will require new mechanisms of empirical investigation, new methods of reportage, a new class of educational researchers, and much money. It is an effort without which we will continue largely incapable of making defensible decisions about curricular changes, largely unable to put them into effect, and ignorant of what real consequences, if any, our efforts have had.

A very large part of such a study would, I repeat, be direct and empirical study of action and reaction in the classroom itself, not merely the testing of student change. But one of the most interesting and visible alterations of present practice which might be involved is a radical change in our pattern of testing students. The common pattern tries to determine the extent to which *intended* changes have been brought about. This would be altered to an effort to find out what changes have occurred, to determine side effects as well as main consequences, since the distinction between these two is always in the eye of the intender and side effects may be as great in magnitude and as baneful or healthful for students as the intended effects.

A second facet of the practical: Its actions are undertaken with respect to identified frictions and failures in the machine and to inadequacies evidenced in felt shortcomings of its products. This origin of its actions leads to two marked differences in operation from that of theory. Under the control of theory, curricular changes have their origin in new notions of person, group or society, mind or knowledge, which give rise to suggestions of new things curriculum might be or do. By its nature, this origin takes little or no account of the existing effectiveness of the machine or the consequences to this effectiveness of the institution of novelty. If there is concern for what may be displaced by innovation or for the incoherences which may ensue on the insertion of novelty, the concern is gratuitous. It does not arise from the theoretical considerations which commend the novelty. This characteristic of theory-instigated change is one of the factors leading centrally to the bandwagon phenomenon in American public education: the wholesale but short-term adoption (or pseudo-adoption) of enquiry teaching, creative training, programing, and what not. The practical, on the other hand, because it institutes changes to repair frictions and deficiencies, is *commanded* to determine the whole array of possible effects of proposed change, to determine what new frictions and deficiencies the proposed change may unintentionally produce.

The other effective difference between theoretical and practical origins of change is patent. Theory, by being concerned with *new* things to do, is unconcerned with the successes and failures of present doings. Hence present failures, unless they coincide with what is altered by the proposed innovations, go unnoticed—as do present successes. The practical, on the other hand, is directly and deliberately concerned with the diagnosis of ills of the curriculum.

These concerns of the practical for frictions and failures of the curricular machine would, again, call for a new and extensive pattern of enquiry. They require curriculum study to seek its problems where its problems lie—in the behaviors, misbehaviors, and nonbehaviors of its students as they begin to show the effects of the training they did and did not get. This means continuing assessment of students as they leave primary grades for the secondary school, secondary school for jobs and colleges. It means sensitive and sophisticated assessment by way of impressions, insights, and reactions of the community which sends its children to the school; of employers of students; of new echelons of teachers of students; the wives, husbands, and cronies of ex-students; the people with whom ex-students work; the people who work under them. It will look into the questions of what games ex-students play; what they read, if they do; what they watch on TV and what they make of what they watch, again, if anything. Such studies would be undertaken, furthermore, not as mass study of products of the American school taken *in toto* but of significantly separable schools and school systems, suburban and inner-city, Chicago and Los Angeles, South Bend and Michigan City.

I emphasize sensitive and sophisticated assessment because we are concerned here, as in the laying of background knowledge of what goes on in schools, not merely with the degree to which avowed objectives are achieved but also with detecting the failures and frictions of the machine: what it has not done or thought of doing, and what side effects its doings have had. Nor are we concerned only with successes and failures as measured in test situations but also as evidenced in life and work. It is this sort of diagnosis which I have tried to exemplify in a recent treatment of curriculum and student protest.[5]

Practical Curriculum: Anticipatory Generation of Alternatives

A third facet of the practical, I shall call the anticipatory generation of alternatives. Intimate knowledge of the existing state of affairs, early identification of problem situations, and effective formulation of problems are necessary to effective practical decision, but they are not sufficient. Effective decision also requires that there be available to practical deliberation the greatest possible number and fresh diversity of alterna-

5. Joseph J. Schwab, *College Curriculum and Student Protest* (Chicago: University of Chicago Press, 1969).

tive solutions to problems. One reason for this requirement is obvious enough: The best choice among poor and shopworn alternatives will still be a poor solution to the problem. A second aspect is less obvious. Many of the problems which arise in an institutional structure which has enjoyed good practical management will be novel problems, arising from changes in the times and circumstances and from the consequences of previous solutions to previous problems. Such problems, with their strong tincture of novelty, cannot be solved by familiar solutions. They cannot be well solved by apparently new solutions arising from old habits of mind and old ways of doing things.

A third aspect of the requirement for anticipatory generation of alternatives is still less obvious. It consists of the fact that practical problems do not present themselves wearing their labels around their necks. Problem situations, to use Dewey's old term for it, present themselves to consciousness, but the character of the problem, its formulation, does not. The character of the problem depends on the discerning eye of the beholder. And this eye, unilluminated by possible fresh solutions to the problems, new modes of attack, new recognitions of degrees of freedom for change among matters formerly taken to be unalterable, is very likely to miss the novel features of new problems or dismiss them as "impractical." Hence the requirement that the generation of problems be anticipatory and not await the emergence of the problem itself.

To some extent, the *theoretical* bases of curricular change—such items as more sophisticated conceptions of scientific enquiry, discovery learning, structure of the disciplines, and creativity—contribute to the need for anticipatory solution to problems but not sufficiently or with the breadth which permits effective deliberation. That is, these theoretic proposals tend to arise in single file, each of them out of connection with other proposals which constitute alternatives to them, or, more important, out of connection with other matters which constitute circumstances which ought to affect the choice or rejection of proposals. Consider, in regard to the problem of the "single file," only one of many relations which exist between the two recent proposals subsumed under "creativity" and "structure of knowledge." If creativity implies some measure of invention and if "structure of knowledge" implies (as it does in one version) the systematic induction of conceptions as soon as children are ready to grasp them, an issue is joined. To the extent that a child is effectively conditioned to bring an induced, imposed, body of conceptions to bear on each of a number of subject matters automatically perceived as requiring conceptions a——d and not conceptions p——t, to that same extent the scope for creativity is curtailed. On the other side, to the extent that children are identified as capable of profit from creativity "training" and are encouraged to treat subject matters in unusual or whimsical ways, to that extent the putative benefits accruing from inculcated and clearly directed "organizers" are foreclosed. Only if the two were carefully considered *together*, with particularized practical concern for how much is done of each, to whom, and with what timing relative both to the child's development and to each other, is a durably effective improvement in education at all likely.

A single case, taken from possible academic resources of education, will suggest the new kind of enquiry entailed in the need for anticipatory generation of alternatives. Over the years, critical scholarship has generated, as remarked earlier, a dozen different conceptions of the novel, a dozen or more ways in which the novel can be read, each involving its own emphases and its own arts of recovery of meaning in the act of reading. Novels can be read, for example, as bearers of wisdom and insights into vicissitudes of human life and ways of bearing them. Novels can also be read as moral instructors, as sources of vicarious experience, as occasions for aesthetic experience. They can be read as models of human creativity, as displays of social problems, as political propaganda, as revelations of diversities of manners and morals among different cultures and classes of people, or as symptoms of their age.

Now what, in fact, is the full parade of such possible uses of the novel? What is required by each in the way of competences of reading, of discussion, and of thought? What are the rewards, the desirable outcomes, likely to ensue for students from each kind of reading or combinations of them? For what kinds or classes of students is each desirable? There are further problems demanding anticipatory consideration. If novels are chosen and read as displays of social problems and depictions of social classes, what effect will such instruction in *literature* have on instruction in the *social studies*? What will teachers need to know and be able to do in order to enable students to discriminate and appropriately connect the insights of artists, the accounts of historians, and the conclusions of social scientists on such matters? How will the mode of instruction in science (e.g., as verified truths) and in literature (as "deep insights" or artistic constructions or matters of opinion) affect the effects of each? (Here, obviously, is also an instance of the need cited earlier—for control of organic connections within the school structure.)

The same kinds of questions could be addressed to history and to the social studies generally. Yet, nowhere, in the case of literature, have we been able to find cogent and energetic work addressed to them. The journals in the field of English teaching are nearly devoid of treatment of them. College and university courses, in English or education, which address such problems with a modicum of intellectual content are as scarce as hen's teeth. We cannot even find an unbiased conspectus of critical theory more complete than *The Pooh Perplex*, and treatments of problems of the second kind (pertaining to interaction of literature instruction with instruction in other fields) are also invisible.

Under a soundly practical dispensation in curriculum, the address of such questions would be a high priority and would require recruitment to education of philosophers and subject matter specialists of a quality and critical sophistication which have been rarely, if ever, sought.

Practical Curriculum: Deliberation

As the last sampling of the practical, consider its method. It falls under neither of the popular platitudes: It is neither deductive nor inductive. It is deliberative.

It cannot be inductive because the target of the method is not a generalization or explanation, but a decision about action in a concrete situation.

It cannot be deductive because it deals with the concrete case and not abstractions from cases, and the concrete case cannot be settled by mere application of a principle, for almost every concrete case falls under two or more principles, and is not, therefore, a complete instance of either principle.

Moreover, every concrete case will possess some cogent characteristics which are encompassed in no principle. The problem of selecting an appropriate man for an important post is a case in point. It is not a problem of selecting a representative of the appropriate personality type who exhibits the competences officially required for the job. The man hired is more than a type and a bundle of competences. He is a multitude of probable behaviors which escape the net of personality theories and cognitive scales. He is endowed with prejudices, mannerisms, habits, tics, and relatives. And all of these manifold particulars will affect his work and the work of those who are to work for him. It is deliberation which operates in such cases to select the most appropriate man.

Deliberation is complex and arduous. It treats both ends and means and must treat them as mutually determining one another. It must try to identify, with respect to both, what facts may be relevant. It must try to ascertain the relevant facts in the concrete case. It must try to identify the desiderata in the case. It must generate alternative solutions. It must make every effort to trace the branching pathways of consequences which may flow from each alternative and affect desiderata. It must then weigh alternatives and their costs and consequences against one another, and choose, not the *right* alternative, for there is no such thing, but the *best* one.

I shall mention only one of the new kinds of activity to ensue upon commitment to deliberation. It will require the formation of a new public and new means of communication among its constituent members. Deliberation requires consideration of the widest possible variety of alternatives if it is to be most effective. Each alternative must be viewed in the widest variety of lights. Ramifying consequences must be traced to all parts of the curriculum. The desirability of each alternative must be felt out, "rehearsed," by a representative variety of all those who must live with the consequences of a chosen action. And a similar variety must deal with the identification of problems as well as with their solution.

This will require penetration of the curtains which now separate educational psychologist from philosopher, sociologist from test constructor, historian from administrator; it will require new channels connecting the series from teacher, supervisor, and school administrator at one end to research specialists at the other. Above all, it will require renunciation of the specious privileges and hegemonies by which we maintain the fiction that problems of science curriculum, for example, have no bearing on problems of English literature or the social studies. The aim here is *not* a dissolving of specialization and special responsibilities. Quite the contrary: If the variety of lights needed is to be obtained, the variety of specialized interests, competences, and habits of mind which characterize education must be cherished and nurtured. The aim, rather, is to bring the members of this variety to bear on curriculum problems by communication about them with one another.

Concretely, this means the establishment of new journals, and the education of educators so that they can write for them and read them. The journals will be forums where possible problems of curriculum will be broached from many sources and their possible importance debated from many points of view. They will be the stage for display of anticipatory solutions to problems, for a similar variety of sources. They will constitute deliberative assemblies in which problems and alternative solutions will be argued by representatives of all, for the consideration of all, and for the shaping of intelligent consensus.

Needless to say, such journals are not sufficient alone. They stand as only one, concrete model of the kind of forum which is required. Similar forums, operating *viva voce* and in the midst of curriculum operation and curriculum change, are required—of the teachers, supervisors and administrators of a school; of the supervisors and administrators of a school system; of representatives of teachers, supervisors, and curriculum makers in subject areas and across subject areas; of the same representatives and specialists in curriculum, psychology, sociology, administration, and subject matter fields.[6]

A downright pathetic sign of the great need for such face-to-face confrontation and journal forums and for an education in their uses appears in the educational literature. The sign consists of the frequency with which reviews and critical papers say of the materials under review: "This is a *scientific* treatment of the enquiry problem." "This is an interesting *hortatory* book." "This is a plea for creativity training but the author provides no data to *prove* his point." "The author *feels* that arithmetic ought to be taught so as to provide insight into arithmetic processes. . . ." "Not a *research* article."

Again and again, the prevailing distinction is the limited one of "scientific" or "hortatory," theoretic or homiletic. Of course, "review" papers and "methodological" papers are recognized, but these, too, are usually seen as dealing with just the other two: scientific or hortatory. There is little visible discrimination of the mere special or interested pleading for "a cause" (the hortatory) from papers which propose alternatives to present or envisaged practices, discriminate possible consequences (good or bad) of alternatives, trace these consequences to their further probable effects, and in other ways contribute to the responsible deliberation necessary for defensible choices of new or altered practices. Either the educationist community has no common apparatus for recognizing such papers or few of them are written—or both.

The education of educators to participate in this deliberative process will be neither easy nor quickly achieved. The education of the present generation of specialist researchers to speak to the schools and to one another will doubtless be hardest of all, and I have no suggestion to make on this hardest problem. But we could begin within two years to initiate the preparation of teachers, supervisors, curriculum makers, and graduate students of education in the uses and arts of deliberation, and we should.

For graduate students in education, this should mean that their future enquiries in educational psychology, philosophy of education, educational sociology, and so on will find more effective focus on enduring

6. It will be clear from these remarks that the conception of curricular method proposed here is immanent in the Tyler rationale. This rationale calls for a diversity of talents and insists on the practical and eclectic treatment of a variety of factors. Its effectiveness in practice is vitiated by two factors. First, its focus on "objectives," with their great ambiguity and equivocation, provides far too little of the concrete matter required for deliberation and leads only to delusive consensus. Second, those who use it are not trained for the deliberative procedures it requires.

problems of education, as against the attractions of the current foci of the parent disciplines. It will begin to exhibit to graduate students what their duties are to the future schoolmen whom they will teach. For teachers, curriculum makers, and others close to the classroom, such training is of special importance. It will not only bring immediate experience of the classroom effectively to bear on problems of curriculum but will also enhance the quality of that experience, for almost every classroom episode is a stream of situations requiring discrimination of deliberative problems and decisions thereon.

By means of such journals and such an education, the educational research establishment might at last find a means for channeling its discoveries into sustained improvement of the schools instead of into a procession of ephemeral bandwagons.

· 11 ·

The Practical:

Arts of Eclectic

PREFACE AND RECAPITULATION
Introduction

Though titled "The Practical" and concerned with practice, the series of papers of which this is one is grounded in a consideration of theory as well as practice. The series is concerned with theory because a study of educational literature reveals that education in general and the field of curriculum in particular have been inveterately theoretic and that this theoretic bent has let education down. Educators have sought theory (theory of curriculum, theories of teaching and learning) as if such theories would be sufficient to tell us what and how to teach. Educators have applied theories from the behavioral sciences toward solution of practical problems as if these borrowed theories could be applied simply and directly. Meanwhile, educators themselves, as well as others, bear witness to the fact that problems so attacked have been poorly solved. Extant curriculums with the stamp of theoretic legitimation often fail in practice. Teaching which is coherent with theory often misses its practical mark.

Some of this failure is inherent in the character of practical problems. They are never solved completely or once and for all. Much of the failure, however, can be traced to marked disparities between theory and practice and to peculiarities of theory from the behavioral sciences.

Theories of curriculum and of teaching and learning cannot, alone, tell us what and how to teach, because questions of what and how to teach arise in concrete situations loaded with concrete particulars of time, place, person, and circumstance. Theory, on the other hand, contains little of such concrete particulars. Theory achieves its theoretical character, its order, system, economy, and, above all, its very generality only by abstraction from such particulars, by omitting much of them.

This chapter was previously published in slightly different form in the *School Review* 79 (1971): 493–42.

Theories borrowed from the behavioral sciences are marked by two other forbidding traits. Each of these sciences treats only a portion of the complex field from which educational problems arise, and, in the course of enquiry, the science isolates its treated portion from the portions treated in other behavioral sciences. Second, each behavioral science brings to bear on its treated portion not one but many principles of enquiry, each of which affords a different perspective and leads to a different treatment of its subject. Thus, pluralities of theory arise, no one member of a plurality complete, each member throwing its own useful light on the subject treated.

The incongruity of theory and practice cannot be corrected by a fundamental change in either one or the other. The practical is ineluctably concrete and particular. The strength and value of theory lie in its generality, system, and economy. Nor can the peculiarities of the behavioral sciences be removed easily or swiftly. They arise, as indicated in the first paper of this series,[1] from the complexity of their subject matters and the limitations of human ingenuity.

The problems posed by these complications can, however, be solved by other means. First, the particularities of each practical problem can be sought in the practical situation itself, the search guided by resources much richer than any one theory can afford. Second, in each instance of application of a borrowed theory to a practical situation, incongruities can be adjusted by mutual accommodation. Third, restricted subject and limited treatment so characteristic of behavioral theories can be transcended by using more than one such theory.

The methods by which these ends might be achieved, have, however, a complication of their own. Although they can be described and exemplified, they cannot be reduced to generally applicable rules. Rather, in each instance of their application, they must be modified and adjusted to the case in hand. Because of this complication, I call them *arts*. These arts can be divided, though only for purposes of discussion, into two sorts: arts of the practical and arts of eclectic. The former are arts which supplement theory, which do for practice and the charting of practice what theory cannot do. The eclectic arts are arts by which we ready theory for practical use. They are arts by which we discover and take practical account of the distortions and limited perspective which a theory imposes on its subject.

In this paper, I shall deal mainly with the eclectic arts and, indeed, with only one subgroup of them. Nevertheless, let us look more closely at all these matters.

---

1. See "The Practical: A Language for Curriculum," chap. 10 in this volume.

Arts of the Practical

The radical difference between practice and theory is visible wherever they occur together: in medicine, politics, law, and engineering, as well as in education. The practical is always marked by particularity, the theoretical by generality. The generality of theory ranges widely. At one extreme, it consists of such elegant, encompassing constructions as the postulates of Euclidean geometry, the system of terms which describes the wavelike condition and statistical location of small particles in the atom, and the Freudian blueprint of the soul. It consists, at the other extreme, of such neat, restricted summations as empirical generalizations, delimitations of species and genera, types and subtypes, and simple measures of populations so delineated, such as means and modes.

Always and everywhere, whether at one extreme or the other, generalities are achieved only by processes of abstraction or idealization. Species are differentiated and defined on the basis of only *some* differences and similarities. Many others are ignored. Euclidean treatment of plane figures is concerned only with their conformation: the particular size of one figure or another is not included. The geometrical triangle, with its perfect sum of angles, takes no account of the variations in sum of angles which will mark any collection of any visible triangular surfaces. The height of any one Scotsman will only infrequently correspond with the mean height of Scotsmen. Very few women correspond precisely with Botticelli's Venus, and the intensity of very few lights varies with the square of the distance from their sources.

The very fabric of the practical, on the other hand, consists of the richly endowed and variable particulars from which theory abstracts or idealizes its uniformities. The road we drive on has bends and potholes not included on the map. We teach not literature, but this novel and that. The child with whom we work is both more and less than the percentile ranks, social class, and personality type into which she falls. Yet, we will drive our car smoothly, convey *Billy Budd* effectively, and teach 'Tilda well only as we take account of conditions of each which are not included in the theories which describe them as roads, literature, and learning child. We must take notice of these conditions, make some estimate of the relevance of each to the task in hand, and devise some means by which to cope with them.

The particularities of the practical, merely by existing, constitute one difficult problem for the practical arts. The problem is to *see* them—to take note that each is there and to honor it as possibly relevant to our concerns. This is difficult because we normally see only what we are instructed to look for and we are instructed by theory. Hence, if we take

'Tilda only as a learning child, we see only what a theory of learning, of childhood cognitive development, or of personality tells us to see. We will be blind to other particulars.

The practical arts operate in at least one semisystematic way to meet this problem. The way consists of deliberately "irrelevant" scanning of 'Tilda: looking at her through a succession of lenses which have nothing to do with her studentship. One looks at her as small brother's sister, as Mommy's first, as occupant of the third floor apartment, as slightly overweight with a hint of southern accent. One wonders whom she will marry and what her married life will be like.

There are additional ways in which arts of perception may operate. First, it is quite possible that, if we perceive enough of 'Tilda's rich detail by "irrelevant" scanning, what remains will become conspicuous by virtue of not being included in any of the categories ("theories") we have brought to bear. That is, when only a few categories are used and, therefore, few details seen, the rich remainder constitutes a large undifferentiated background. If, however, the bulk of that background is subjected to differentiation, is nibbled away by successive "irrelevant" scannings, the situation is reversed. The now large mass of differentiated detail becomes background for the small remainder made noticeable by its very isolation—the conspicuously dark and lonely figure wandering at the back of the lighted crowd sitting around the bonfire.

Second, and despite prevailing psychological dogma, I think it probable that immediate perception, perception without the aid of learned organizers, categories, "theory," may occasionally occur—though such perceptions are doubtless fleeting and fragmentary. There are a few good arguments and much anecdote to support such a view. There is notably the argument that not all our learned categories are demonstrably taught us by telling and pointing. Some may have been taught us by experiences to which we were not directed. At any rate, the first teller and pointer could not have been told.

There is also reason to think that there are ways in which accessibility to immediate perception can be enhanced. The electronics troubleshooter, faced with an intermittent crackling of a hand-wired amplifier, first seeks the trouble systematically. He checks each tie point for loose connections, tests each one for a cold solder joint. This procedure fails to expose the trouble. He then, figuratively, throws his eyes out of focus, though still staring at the maze of wiring. Not quite so figuratively, he throws his mind out of focus, stops or disconnects the guiding mental machinery, loosens his muscles. Very often, this relaxation of guided attention works. The source of the electronic difficulty "leaps to the eye."

There are, of course, additional practical arts. There are arts of problemation. These are arts by which we assign various possible meanings to perceived detail of the situation and group them in different ways in order to perceive and shape different formulations of "the" problem posed by the displeasing situation. There are arts for weighing the alternative formulations of a problem thus achieved and for choosing one to follow further. There are arts for generating alternative possible solutions to the problem, arts for tracing each alternative solution to its probable consequences, arts for weighing and choosing among them. There are also reflexive arts for determining when the deliberation should be terminated and action undertaken. These must be left for discussion on another occasion.

Arts of Eclectic: Legitimation of Curriculums

Besides the radical difference between theory and practice which is visible wherever they occur together, there are special peculiarities of the theories which education borrows from the behavioral sciences. These peculiarities pose their own barriers to the easy application of theory to the solution of educational problems, and there are arts which surmount these barriers. These additional barriers and a first sketch of the eclectic arts are best seen in the context of ways in which we currently try to legitimate curriculums.

Exhortation and special pleading

One group of exhortations in the literature is represented by the following paraphrases:

1. The schools of the world should disseminate a new conception of government, one that will embrace all of the activities of man, wherever he is throughout the world.
2. The organization of the school, of every classroom in it, and of every activity in every class should aim to disclose to the young the desirability of rules of the game: the possibility of devising and emending rules and the benefits which accrue from playing according to the rules. Only by this means, intensively and consistently carried out, can we hope to reduce government and imposition of order by force and sanction to their proper place as courts of last resort.
3. The population of every school and classroom should be highly heterogeneous in its clientele. These heterogeneous students should be encouraged and enabled to form subgroups which recognize and give social force to the differences in interest and preference which bind and separate them. These subgroups should be encouraged to choose agents. These agents

should function to adjudicate and compromise the different demands of different subgroups on limited resources and to resolve other conflicts which arise between group and group. Only in this way will representative government be rediscovered and returned to its proper function.

Another set of exhortations:

a) We must embody in an *un*structure of the schools our realization that the attention span of children is brief, their interests fleeting and numerous, their capacity to profit from an experience limited to the duration of their interest in that experience. Schools must become informal, unstructured, affording a wide variety of activities for every child and permitting him to move from one to another at will.

b) The child requires a structuring of space and time against which he can test his growing ego strength and into which he can retreat when the anxieties raised by uncertainty exceed his moment's capacity for enlarging his external reality. Hence, the early school should supply a firm divisioning of time and effort and a clear demarcation of "home" and "other." These divisions are not to be imposed willy-nilly, but their rhythms should be sufficiently enforced to be ever present in the immediate background of the child's awareness.

c) In sum, the schools must first supply each child with occasions and objects of aggression which are at once satisfyingly destroyable but not so irreplaceable that the ensuing guilt is too great. It must supply appropriate objects of libidinal cathexes. It must supply activities and occasions for increasing the child's capacity for suspense of impulse, including, of course, adequately supportive, guiding, and punishing adult figures. Finally, it must supply the child with resources for adult sublimation of instinctual energies.

One characteristic of these exhortations is immediately noticeable. Each draws on one science while ignoring others. Each item of the numbered set speaks from a view of the nature of government, drawn from annals of political theory. Each item of the lettered set speaks from a view of the child's inner life, drawn from annals of psychology. Other exhortations can be found which draw on sociology while ignoring politics and psychology. Others draw singly on economics or some other single field.

It is noteworthy that each of these singularly based exhortations is plausible, appealing. They are so because each speaks to one or another human need or desire to which education might contribute. Their very coexistence, then, points to an inadequacy of each and to the problem posed by this inadequacy. Each omits what another includes. They need, then, somehow to be joined and reconciled. This is one task of the eclectic arts.

A second characteristic is equally obvious. Each numbered item draws on a view of government which differs from the views of government drawn upon by the other numbered items. Each lettered item draws on a view of the child's inner needs and conditions which differs from the views employed by the other lettered items. It is also clear that these differing views are not merely contradictory views, one of which may be right and the others wrong. Most of them are literally different *views*: each stands in such a relation to the subject matter it shares with others that it sees a different facade or sees it in a different perspective. Thus, *a* sees large a present state of the child's existence; *b* sees large a condition of its continuing growth; and *c* sees large the instinctual impulses with which the child must cope. Again, the coexistence of the three points to an incompleteness of each. This mode of being incomplete constitutes the second problem with which the eclectic arts are designed to cope.

A third characteristic of these exhortations flows from the first and second: they constitute frighteningly one-sided educational commendations. If they be taken as curricular prescriptions, the result could be only chaos as far as the child in school is concerned. Any one of the proposals would lead to a curriculum so inadequate, so incomplete, that displacement would quickly ensue. The replacement, if it stemmed from another such one-sided commendation, would do something the first failed to do but would fail to do what the first accomplished. It, too, would be displaced in favor of another, and so on indefinitely. The child's education, in consequence, would be a series of abortive jerks and startings with no course charted and followed to a defensible destination.

Special pleadings reveal the same fault. The defense of one science curriculum points with pride to one set of strengths. The defense of another praises it for quite different strengths. One best fits the structure of scientific enquiry. Another is most up to date in content. A third is accessible to a wider range of student competences. A fourth is designed to meet certain social needs. These different pleas cannot speak to one another because they are speaking from different grounds: different subjects of different behavioral sciences or widely different views of one of these subjects. Again, the effect on curriculum, if effect there were, would be a splintering of children's education.[2]

2. It can be argued that exhortations and special pleadings are not to be taken as curricular prescriptions, that their one-sidedness does not represent the character of curriculum legitimation generally. The first of these claims

This third characteristic of curriculum legitimations—that they are frighteningly one-sided commendations—constitutes the moral and pragmatic reason why educators ought to attend to the first and second characteristics. If education is to be good for students and if the institution of education is to avoid the punishment with which societies threaten institutions which fail their function, educators must attend to the problems posed by the inadequacy of borrowed theory: the incompleteness of their subjects and the incomplete view which each takes of its incomplete subject.

Eclectic arts and incomplete subjects

The problems of education arise from exceedingly complex actions, reactions, and transactions of men. These doings constitute a skein of myriad threads which know no boundaries separating, say, economics from politics, or sociology from psychology. For example, the way I allocate my scarce resources is tied to my infantile experiences. My infantile experiences, in turn, were determined in part by my parents' economic resources, in part by their political allegiances, in part by their small-town milieu. It is just such a complex web which must somehow be taken into account if we are to effect durable solutions to educational problems.

Yet our fullest and most reliable knowledge of these matters is not knowledge of the web as a whole. It is knowledge of various shreds and sections of the whole, each shred and section out of connection with other shreds and sections. It is the knowledge conferred upon us by the various behavioral sciences. Some six sciences are involved: a kind of behavioral epistemology, concerned with what men know or can find out; a kind of behavioral ethics, concerned with what men need and

is often true. Many exhortations and special pleas are designed to bring into the light considerations long neglected. They are, in effect, invitations to more extended use of eclectic arts. It is not true, however, that one-sidedness is limited to this mode of legitimation. The other three modes I can identify exhibit the same or analogous faults. Measurement of the relative success of one curriculum against another can treat only the efficiency of each in achieving one aim or another. It has no apparatus for weighing alternative aims. The legitimation which occurs in the course of planning and developing curriculums (aims sought, considerations taken into account) again basically shows concern for only one or a few determinative factors, rarely a full or even wide complement. A third mode consists of theories which purport to show that one determinative factor always takes precedence over others or assimilates others. Most arguments to such views covertly take their premises from the factor which is nominated king. Hence, there are as many such arguments and resulting theories as there are determinative factors to consider.

want and what among these wants and needs conduce to a satisfying life; sociology-anthropology; economics; political science; and psychology.

This separation of the whole of human affairs into subjects of various sciences is not a fault of these sciences but a condition of all scientific enquiry. All communities of enquiry are controlled by principles of enquiry which distinguish in the awful complexity of the world lesser complexities with which enquiries can deal. These same principles supply terms for the questions to be asked of each subject matter and point to the various kinds of data which each enquiry will seek.

In the course of thus readying a subject of scientific, of theoretic, enquiry, the principles which distinguish it from the whole tend to confer on the partial subject an appearance of wholeness and unity. The connecting and entwining threads which originally made it one aspect of a larger whole are smoothed down and covered over. The notion of a social fact, for example, gives to the subject of some sociological enquiry an appearance of independence from psychological fact. The notion of an epigenetic development of individual personality from factors inherent in each organism confers on psychological fact a pseudoindependence from social facts and confers on social facts, indeed, the appearance of being mere expressions of individual personality.

These separations and smoothings of subjects of enquiry are reflected in the knowledge we inherit from the sciences which treat these subjects. The bodies of knowledge are themselves separated, each couched in its own set of terms. Only a few terms of each set have connections with terms of another set. Hence, the bodies of knowledge we inherit from the behavioral sciences are, taken separately, only imperfectly applicable to practical problems, problems which arise in the whole web of the original complexity.

We cannot hope for an early theoretical healing of these ruptures of subjects and of knowledges about them. New principles of enquiry which knit together what earlier principles cut asunder come only occasionally and in the long course of enquiry. What is required is a practical healing, a recourse to temporary and tentative bridges built between useful parts of bodies of knowledge in the course of their application to practical problems. This is the function of one group of eclectic arts.

These arts are addressed to the underlying structure of theories. They are arts which identify the devices which confer the appearance of completeness on the subject of the enquiry. They are arts which trace their devices to their effects—to the distortions and smoothings they impose on the subject of enquiry and the complementary subordinations and alterations they confer on adjacent subjects. They are further arts which determine what portions of other sciences, other theories, can be made to run in harness with the theory in hand and which cannot. They are, finally, arts by which to effect the temporary harness and apply the team to our practical problem.

Eclectic arts and incomplete views

Each separated and simplified subject of a behavioral science is still so complex that it affords scope for application of numerous principles of enquiry. Each such principle makes its own selection of the data relevant to its enquiry. Each one effects its own subordinations and superordinations among the facets of the subject. Each asks different questions of the subject and gives rise to different answers. In consequence, a plurality of theories arises in each behavioral science, each one incomplete, each throwing its own light on the subject.

Some members of a plurality are more useful than others on a given practical problem. No one throws all available light on the subject. One member may complement another more effectively or more immediately than would some other. Hence, another set of eclectic arts is required—arts which will disclose what a given principle of enquiry does to its subject, what emphases it induces, what perspective it takes, what it leaves clouded, obscure, or ignored. These are the arts which will occupy us for the remainder of this paper.

Interim Summary

We can distinguish, for purposes of discussion, three sets of arts for reconciling the incongruities of theory to practice in attacking problems of education. There are practical arts concerned with particulars of the practical omitted by theory. There are eclectic arts concerned with the incompleteness of each subject of the behavioral sciences. There are other eclectic arts which select among, adjust, and sometimes combine the incomplete views which constitute the plurality of the theories generated in each behavioral science.

These sets of arts are not, however, wholly separable from one another. Much usage of the practical arts is, indeed, focused wholly upon the unpleasing concrete situations which rouse our concern for practices and urge us toward their modification. Much usage of the eclectic arts is focused wholly on the theories which seem to bear on our practical concerns. Collectively, however, these arts are concerned with *bringing a principle to its case*. This is achieved not by bringing one to the other, but by mutual accommodation. The principle (theory) must be selected and adapted to the case. But the case becomes a case of (an instance of) this theory or another only as it is made to be so. We carve it from the situation in a fashion which makes it so: we select from facts of the situation what we shall treat as relevant facts of the forming case; then we divide the relevant facts into those we shall entertain as alterable and those we shall treat as fixed. The steps in this mutual accommodation are taken first from one side, then from the other. Hence, arts of eclectic and arts of the practical commingle.

Transition

In what follows, we are concerned with the arts which treat pluralities of theory about a single subject. We are concerned with how their function and use can be conveyed to prospective educators. But how they can be taught depends on the character of the arts themselves. The character of the arts, in turn, depends on the peculiarities which distinguish one member of a plurality of theories from others. Hence, we must be dealing with all these three simultaneously. We shall use one example throughout the treatment: theories of personality. We shall therefore consider some of the peculiarities of these several theories, the means by which these peculiarities are detected, and how these means can be conveyed to students of education.

THE TEACHING OF ECLECTIC
The Problem

Nearly all theories in all the behavioral sciences are marked by the coexistence of competing theories. There is not one theory of personality but many, representing radically different choices of what is relevant and important in human action and passion. There is not one theory of groups but several. There is not one theory of learning but half a dozen. All the social and behavioral sciences are marked by "schools" distinguished from one another by different choices among principles of enquiry, each choice of principle determining a selection and arrangement of different aspects, and different relations among aspects, of the subject under treatment.

Even the best theories which arise from enquiries so directed (and there is no other way of directing theoretical enquiries) are, then, radically incomplete in their views. Vague and ambiguous theories, trivial theories, and unsupported speculations can be identified and eliminated by various familiar methods of analysis and criticism and are, in the course of the history of most fields of enquiry, in fact, eliminated. The theories which survive this winnowing—good theories—are nevertheless incomplete, each taking its own view of the subject matter and throwing its own peculiar light upon it.

If this incompleteness were patent, we would have no problem. If there could easily be an immediate (by theory unmediated) apprehension of an instance of the actual, existing subject matter of these theories, then an instant's comparison of the real thing with its representation in theory would betray the incompleteness of the theory. This happy possibility unhappily does not exist. Good theories are persuasive theories, plausible theories. Each of them formulates in its own way some truths about some men under some circumstances; each is "true," *in its own terms*, of some, perhaps many or all, instances of its subject matter. If these truths, once well presented to us by a theory, find their referents in our own experience of men, this resonance of experience with assertion persuades us not only of the "truth" of the theory but of its whole truth. We not only seek what it tells us to seek, we do not seek and only rarely note what it does *not* instruct us to search out. This constitutes our problem as educators.

"Problem" has here its usual two senses. It stands for something we complain about or ought to complain about: a handicap, an undesirable, a vice. It also stands for the query by means of which we begin to seek correction of the vice complained of. Both senses deserve formulation.

Tunnel vision

The problem in the first sense is obvious enough. The vice is tunnel vision. The possessor of only one of a collection of competing theories sees its subject matter in only the peculiar light cast by that theory and conceives as alternatives of education (ends or means) only the ones suggested by the one view and judges among them only in the light of the one. The teacher of art or literature possessed by only one critical theory sees only a limited array of the polyvalences of literature or art for education. The curriculum planner possessed by only one theory of personality conceives of a healthful and satisfying life for his students in unnecessarily narrow terms. The architect of school systems possessed by only one view of the relations of school and society sees only one or a few modes of school organization and polity.

The problem in the second sense is equally obvious—at least in initial and general form: by what alternatives to doctrinaire instruction can some of the riches of the radical pluralism of theory be made accessible to educators in training? I shall suggest four such alternatives, three of them useful and two of these three almost immediately available for use by intelligent and well-informed faculties.

A note on "objectives"

It should be noted in advance that the suggested alternatives to doctrinaire instruction may each contribute to somewhat different outcomes. "The riches of radical pluralism" takes on different meanings. An alternative may contribute to informed use of a *single* theory. That is, it will contribute mainly or solely to the potential educator's understanding of the idiosyncrasies of his chosen tool: what it foregrounds and suppresses, where its accuracy or reliability is worst and best. On the other hand, it may contribute to informed choice among a battery of alternative theories, choice appropriate to the specific problem to be solved or to the concrete case in hand. Third, it may contribute to the ability to bring a multiplicity of theoretic stands to bear on a concrete case, thus ensuring a wider view of what might be done by way of education, a wider view of the considerations relevant to choice among alternatives, and a wider view of the hardships and facilitations to be expected in the course of instruction.

It is not at all clear which of these possible outcomes, if any, is the most desirable for prospective educators. Theoretically, I suppose, the best case could be made for the last. In practice, however, all will depend on the concrete case. In some cases, time may be of the essence. Then, it may be far more desirable that an intelligent choice be made among limited alternatives than a hurried and anxious choice among many. In other cases, the person or group of persons involved may be unable to tolerate much uncertainty or uncertainty long sustained. It may be far better for such persons that they possess limited tools, knowing them well, than a larger armament which, like all armament, presses for its use but brings much anxiety in its train.

Mere Conspectus

The most obvious and least useful alternative to doctrinaire instruction is a trio of doctrinaire instructions. Says a junior faculty member at a meeting considering Professor June's course syllabi: "He proposes one-quarter courses in each of such broad conceptions as friendship, family, and aggression. It would be much better, much more just, to make them year courses with several different professors teaching each concept. After all, there are many points of view on such matters. All of them ought to get a hearing—or at least more than one."

There are good intentions behind such proposals, and they constitute good beginnings. There is recognition of a kind of pluralism. There is distaste for arbitrary choice among the plurality. There is also the firm promise, however, that arbitrary choice is merely postponed and transferred to another elector. The realization of this unfortunate promise can be seen in actual student responses to merely conspective courses, and the inevitability of the promise can be seen in the nature of the suggestion itself.

A very common and most pathetic student response is the query, sometimes brazen, sometimes simple and unembarrassed, sometimes shy and troubled: "So there are three theories. Which one is right?"

The pathos of this kind of response lies in the fact that it is not the fault of students. The whole burden of their education (not only at the primary level, where it is probably desirable, but at the secondary level, where it may not be, and at the collegiate level, where it almost certainly is not) has been a collection of unique solutions to sharply separated problems and of single bodies of "fact" about each of many isolated subject matters. With such a background, students are quite unprepared to recognize the character of theoretic pluralism, much less cope with it. This circumstance, in turn, points to the notable practical weakness of mere conspectuses: they are neither understood nor believed. And they will not be until and unless two distinct factors are added to instruction in general or to conspectuses in particular. We shall name them in a moment.

A second, very common, student response, though rarely voiced unless solicited, consists, in effect, of assigning to each member of a conspectus a curious, equal validity. Each member of a conspectus has evidence and argument to support it. Each is espoused by one substantial voice of authority. Each, therefore, must be, in some sense, right. Each, then, deserves respect and mastery.

At first glance, this student response appears a grade more sophisticated than the first. It seems to recognize plurality as a fact of life instead of treating it as an illusion the professor can dispel. In fact, it is this apparently greater sophistication which is the illusion. With nothing more to go on than the conspectus itself and the apparently equal distribution of evidence and praise among the members of the plurality, most students reason that the problem posed by the plurality is a problem of congenial choice. Respect for and mastery of each member of the conspectus are taken as preludes and requisites to discovery of that one of the plurality which is most congenial and therefore to be chosen. In effect, the student treats the plurality as an odd outcome of enquiry (to which he is not privy) but not as a fact of his life.

The suggestion itself—that doctrinaire espousal be replaced by conspectus—promises little more than can be seen in these student responses. It provides a sort of *pro forma* justice or impartiality with respect to alternative views but no apparatus by which to understand, judge, or exploit the array of views. That the suggestion is often coupled with the proviso that each view be presented by an advocate of it— "several different professors teaching each concept"—suggests that the professoriat is in much the same condition as some students: pretty much at a loss for means to deal with the plurality other than by impartial presentation (i.e., partial advocacies but *equal* partial advocacies).

The phrase "understand, judge, or exploit" suggests the two factors which are wanting in mere conspectus. We need, on the one hand, a mode of communication which will explain how it can be that different men of intelligence, knowledge, and goodwill can arrive at such different views of a common subject. We need, on the other hand, means by which students can discover the various powers of perception which a variety of theories can confer.

Inappropriate accounts of enquiry

A beginning toward the first of these needs would be achieved by no more than a general and introductory disquisition on enquiry and its difficulties couched in terms which speak pointedly to the existence of pluralities of theories and account for the origin of such pluralities.

The terms of the most familiar accounts of enquiry (e.g., hypothesis and verification, induction and generalization) will not, however, serve this purpose, since they ignore or understate precisely the factors requiring emphasis.

The typical hypothesis-verification narrative, so popular among natural scientists and now becoming popular even among psychiatrists, puts its emphasis on verification and ignores or underplays the alternatives available as the content of hypotheses. Such narratives, differing somewhat among themselves, give different views of the method of *proof* employed in science but have little or nothing to say about methods of *discovery* and *invention*—that is invention of new terms in which to frame new kinds of hypotheses which embody the possibility of obtaining new forms of knowledge of things, as against obtaining knowledge of hitherto unknown things.

Yet such inventions, and the discoveries consequent on their use lie at the heart of enquiry and constitute one origin of pluralities of knowledge. It is one thing to have conceived knowledge as knowledge of invariant sequences of classifiable events and to shape hypotheses concerning which class of events is the invariant antecedent of the class of events under scrutiny (e.g., whether wars follow economic deprivations of a nation or threats to the power of a ruling class; whether the sensation of thirst is the consequence of reduced salivary flow or of neural impulses triggered by increased concentration of blood salts). It is quite another thing to have conceived knowledge as knowledge of formal relations among invented quantities or processes which "account for" a selected body of phenomena (e.g., $F = Ma$ to account for the motion and rest of bodies), to have invented a few alternative formal structures of this kind and subjected them to successful test. In the same way, our verification tests may be aimed at choice among hypotheses concerning the efficacy of determining factors (e.g., analysis of variance and covariance) or among hypotheses concerning which irreducible elements of a set of such elements constitute the matter under investigation (e.g., classical inorganic chemical analysis and synthesis). The existence of such invented alternatives as these (accounts in terms of antecedent-consequent relations, in terms of formal relations, or of multifactorial determiners, or of constitutive elements) is one of the matters which require emphasis in any account of enquiry which will begin to display the whys and wherefores of pluralities of knowledge.

The typical induction-generalization account will not serve our purposes either. Such accounts put their emphasis on the process brought to bear on a subject matter and the character of the emergent knowledge but treat the subject matter as a *singular* given. They pay little or no attention to the degrees of freedom, made available by the multitudes of similarities and differences among things, for varieties of groupings (taxonomies) on which to bring to bear the inductive process. Yet, varieties of ways in which a segment of the world can be bounded and sectioned (sliced, divided) are another principal source of pluralities of enquiry.

The logical positivist account which speaks in terms of observed facts, observed relations among facts, and a *choice* of mathematical languages into which to incorporate the observed obviously speaks to one of the sources of plurality (alternative accounts) but equally obviously ignores the other (alternative matters accounted for). Quasi-platonic accounts assert the merely contingent character of any and all joints, seams, or separations in nature and emphasize the potential diversity of subject matters, but denigrate pluralities of theory based on such diversities and obscure their usefulness by treating all contingent joints and separations as merely imperfect starting points of intermediate enquiries to be used only as stepping-stones to an ideal, wholly unified theory of everything, of all the world, seen as an englobed unity.

An appropriate account of enquiry

The account which would begin to quicken conspectuses into useful life requires a set of terms which would describe the complexity of the subjects of the behavioral sciences, show how this complexity affords scope for (indeed forces on enquirers) a multiplicity of questions to be addressed to the subject under enquiry, and gives further scope for a variety of selections and emphases among the numerous facets of the complex subject as resources for answering each question addressed.

The notion of principles of enquiry, together with the notion of issues of principle, embodies such a set of terms.[3] The notion of a principle of enquiry supposes that a given body of enquiry has its origin in commitment to a conception of the subject matter which is prior to the in-

3. The notion of a principle of enquiry and description of the forms of principle conspicuous in biology and the behavioral sciences are described in "What Do Scientists Do?" chap. 7 in this volume.

vestigation. Such a conception sets the boundaries of the subject and names the crucial relations, parts, elements, range of properties, array of actions, or related participants which give it its character. Thereby, the principle locates the data to be sought in investigation, indicates the way in which these data are to be interpreted, and determines the form which the resulting knowledge will take on. The notion of issues of principle merely adds that, for any reasonably complex subject matter, there is scope for a conflict of principles and scope for a variety of selections of determining parts, properties, and relations within the bounds of one principle of enquiry.

It is probable, indeed, that an economical and educationally effective account of this kind could be limited to a single form of principle. The part-whole principle is a likely candidate, since it is ubiquitous in the behavioral sciences. Organs and organism in biology constitute one case in point. Ego and id as organ-like parts of the personality represent the principle in psychology. Individuals or institutions as constituting society, and ideas, ideals, and values as parts of "culture," are two other instances.

With any one of these as concrete examples, the disquisition could exhibit some of the issues of principle involved in this form: the whole determinative of the parts (e.g., cultural determination of personality): the parts determinative of the whole (e.g., psychoanalytically oriented sociology): mutual determination (e.g., social conditioning and purposed reform). It could then exhibit the scope for various selections of constitutive parts: not only ego-id-superego but cognitive-conative-appetitive, or ego—external nonego—internal nonego—core, for example.

Accounts of actual enquiries

Even if no more than this were added to the conspectus, students would at least be saved from the expectation, forced on them by earlier doctrinaire education, of a unique solution to every problem. This and no more, however, would provide only some understanding of plural enquiry in general and not understanding of the practical and concrete enquiries which constituted the theories which compose the plurality under treatment in a given conspectus. To serve this end, it is necessary that each theory be seen as it arises from the concrete enquiry which gave birth to it. The principles and premises which governed the enquiry should be identified. What data were selected by these principles as the data relevant for the enquiry must be seen. The mode of interpretation by which the data are transformed, encompassed, or traversed to the finished formulation of the theory should be disclosed. (A sketch of such an account is contained in the section below on polyfocal conspectus.)

From such an exposition, students might begin to discern the fact that the members of a plurality of theories are not so much *equally* right and *equally* deserving of respect, as right in different ways about different kinds of answers to different questions about the subject and as deserving different respects for different insights they are able to afford us. A teacher of literature, for example, might begin to discover that a critical view of literature as the repository and expression of archetypical problems of human existence and a critical view of literature as formal orderings of plot and character, music, imagery, and language are not contradictories, one or both of which must be wrong, but contrarieties, different facets differently viewed, each of which is *some* part of the whole.

I remarked that what is wanting in a mere conspectus is an apparatus by which students can understand, judge, and exploit a plurality. Addition to the conspectus of an account of the enquiry which generated each member of the plurality provides ground for understanding. It also rectifies a common mistaking of the notion of "judgment" in this context, the mistaken notion that what is to be judged is only the strength, the soundness, the reliability, of each theory. It begins to show that, on the contrary, the good theories constituting a plurality (the educational usefulness of poor theories or bad theories is not at issue here) are to be judged also and primarily in reference to the contribution of each to validity: what and how much of the subject matter each reveals, what incomplete light it casts on the subject matter, and what consequent omissions and distortions characterize its view. (In order to make this judgment, one ignores, of course, the claim appended to many doctrines that it is the only possible doctrine or the only defensible one.)

The possibility of commonplaces

The additions so far suggested do not, however, provide an apparatus sufficient for taking full advantage of this correction. The additions permit recognition of what needs to be done but not a tool for doing it. This tool, too, can be supplied. It is constructed by a certain mode of systematic comparison of the principles, premises, methods, and selections used by and in each enquiry. This mode of comparison generates a set of factors to be called "commonplaces" or "topica" (the names pilfered from Aristotle and Bacon). These commonplaces represent, in effect, the *whole* subject matter of the whole plurality of enquiries of which each member-theory reveals only one facade at best, and usually only one facade seen in one aspect.

An adequate set of commonplaces, then, provides a map on which each member of a plurality can be located relative to its fellow members. It not only permits the student to know that through each theory he will see *some* part of the whole, it also enables him to know—to some degree, at any rate—*what* part of the whole he will see.

I hasten to emphasize that comparison of enquiries aimed at disclosure of commonplaces is a task of enquiry, not of instruction. The recommended pattern of instruction would consist in the introduction of the appropriate set of commonplaces as means for dealing with the members of the plurality under scrutiny. Unfortunately, I must add also that little scholarship of this kind has been done in the behavioral sciences. Few sets of well-established commonplaces are to be found in the literature. Hence, this addition to conspective programs of instruction must await the requisite research.

The foregoing taken in its entirety—the notion of an appropriately constructed account of enquiry in terms of principles and issues of principle, the notion of narratives of the concrete enquiries composing a plurality, and the notion of the commonplaces of a family of enquiries —constitutes a forbidding, indeed an intimidating, prescription for instruction. It is not, however, intended to be taken in its entirety for any instruction of any and all students. For some purposes and for some clienteles, it may be sufficient to provide no more than an appropriate general account of enquiry. Certainly, if a general account be well given once in a context of pointed instances, it need not be repeated in subsequent courses. Rather, subsequent courses would move immediately into the concrete enquiries which constitute their interests.

Furthermore, such a later course need not necessarily treat all the constituents of its conspectus in terms of their origin in enquiry. If four or five doctrines constitute the program, it may be positively desirable as well as prudent to treat only two or three as outcomes of enquiry. Those presented only in their rootless, doctrinal form may then serve as provocations to students to search out for themselves the enquiries which produced them, or to engage in speculative reconstruction of the enquiries. Meanwhile, the two or three which are treated via their producing enquiries may be used (especially with students aiming toward careers of research and scholarship) as backgrounds against which to construct models and plans of alternative enquiries.

The third component of these suggestions—commonplaces—would, where available, be means by which to systematize accounts of concrete enquiries and render them susceptible of treatment with greater dispatch, instead of constituting an additional time-consuming pattern of instruction.

Arts and disciplines of critical analysis

A program of initiation into pluralities can, on the other hand, be rendered even more complete (and complex). It can provide an induction into the arts and disciplines of sophisticated enquiry into enquiries, as well as give accounts of the character and content of enquiries. For potential investigators, as against potential consumers and users of doctrine, it probably should do so.

The means are fairly obvious. Conjoint critical analysis (by instructor and students) of concrete enquiries replaces narrative about them —wholly or in part. Students examine the records of an inquiry. They press past the "answers" propounded in the papers to the suppressed questions (problems) to which the answers speak. They press through the recitals of data sought and found, and interpretations made, to the terms in which the recitals are couched and to the distinctions imposed by the enquirer upon the subject matter. The order and relation of the terms and distinctions, to one another and to the questions they generate, are schematized as a record of the supporting skeleton of the enquiry. The procedure is repeated for a second and third line of enquiry in the same family and the several structures of terms and distinctions are compared with one another.

From such analyses, reconstructions, and comparisons then arise, first, vivid awareness of some of the alternative attacks available to the family of enquiries under scrutiny and perception of the differing consequences of different patterns of attack on the character and content of the knowledge which accrues. There comes, second, increasing mastery of the critical competences which disclose these structures of enquiry.

At some point in the developing mastery of critical competence student interest turns, or can be turned, away from the enquiries of others to possible enquiries of his own. One or more of the batteries of attack now known are directed toward other but homologous subject matters of enquiry. Later, subject matters may be selected which differ—as subjects of enquiry—in a few marked ways from the subject matter on which the learned pattern of enquiry was seen to bear, thus posing to students the problem of modification of the pattern of enquiry, its adaptation to different subject matters.

Still later, attention can be directed to the generation of "new" patterns of enquiry, patterns not so far seen in operation by the student but rendered discernible to him because they are, by contrariety or another relationship, implicated in the patterns known by the student. Finally, with very good students and a representative set of enquiries, the skeletal structures developed may in turn be scrutinized for discovery of the commonplaces which relate them to one another. We shall turn to instances of some of these devices later.

So much, then, for understanding and judgment—theoretical mastery —of pluralities. Such theoretical mastery has value as ground for expectation and comprehension of pluralities of enquiries and as leading toward facility and flexibility in enquiry. It also provides (in its simpler forms) an almost ideal ground for practical mastery—exploitation—of pluralities. It is probably not, however, always a necessary ground for practice (i.e., the *use* of pluralities of view as means for fuller grasp of the facts, circumstances, and possibilities which constitute actual educational problems). Almost certainly, it is not a sufficient ground—at least for many students. Students will not, by virtue of intelligent possession of a plurality of views, necessarily use them when examining instances of the persons, groupings, or events treated by the views. It is notorious, for example, that theoretic mastery of pluralities of critical doctrine by students of literature leads "upward," more often than not, to preoccupation with systems and schemas of critical doctrine and *not* "downward" to more flexible and comprehensive views of literary works. Exploitation of alternative views, their practical utilization, ought, then, to be pursued (at least on the part of educators in training) in its own right, as a capstone to theoretic mastery. A pattern of such a pursuit follows immediately.

Polyfocal Conspectus
First cycle

Polyfocal conspectus is a pretentious name for what may appear at first glance to be a simple procedure. Its unit consists of alternation of mastery of a view-affording doctrine with thoroughgoing involvement in bringing the doctrine to bear as a revealing lens on real, simulated, or reported instances of its subject matter.

The student first masters, let us say, Freud's tripartite construction of human personality. He reads, discusses, and debates (with fellow students and instructor) appropriate chapters from the *New Introductory Lectures, The Ego and the Id*, and *Beyond the Pleasure Principle*.[4] The characters, the roles, and the relations of ego, id, and superego are clarified and made vivid. Freud's view of the normal progress of the person's maturation is followed. Some of the numerous vicissitudes which beset the progress of this development are duly noted and the behaviors heeded which arise from vicissitudes undergone (and overcome or not overcome) in the course of development. This adventure constitutes the first phase of a cycle.

The second phase begins, for example, with a viewing of a composite motion picture or video tape. The viewing reveals, let us say, five episodes drawn from the ongoing activities of a teacher and a group of

---

4. Sigmund Freud, *New Introductory Lectures on Psychoanalysis* (New York: W. W. Norton & Co., 1933), *The Ego and the Id* (London: Hogarth Press, 1957), and *Beyond the Pleasure Principle* (New York: Liveright Publishing Co., 1950). For a thorough documentation of some of the analyses used in the body of this paper, see Seymour Fox, *Freud and Education* (Springfield, Il.: Charles C. Thomas, 1975).

children, a "class." The episodes, singly and together, reveal something of the behaviors of all the students involved and of the teacher, but they focus, by means of conventional directorial and camera techniques, on one student, on his behavior and his transactions with fellow students and the teacher.

At the end of the first viewing, the instructor invites response from his trainees, unstructured invitation inviting first reactions. They come sparsely at first, then more richly: characterizations of the child's behavior, of the teacher's behavior; attempts at formulation of the educational problem involved; tentative diagnoses of the child's condition, speculations about causes. From these resources, the instructor selects (covertly) the two or three starting points he considers most promising for his purposes and most appropriate to the training group in hand.

These purposes cannot be nicely specified, since they depend in part on the responses to the unstructured invitation and what these responses reveal to be the strengths and weaknesses of the group. The overriding purpose is to begin to imbue students with ability to bring the principle to the case. The instructor will be concerned, then, with drawing students' attention to the problem of selecting among exhibited behaviors those to which the Freudian theory demands attention. However, since he is looking ahead to *poly*focal conspectus, he will also be concerned that students see in the situation behaviors to which the Freudian view does not command attention and recognize these behaviors as outside the purview of the theory. He will be concerned to evoke continuing self-criticism by students of the appropriateness and precision of their Freudian interpretation of the selected behaviors—though again with an eye to their recognizing scope for other interpretations. He will also be concerned with relations between observers and the observed apart from considerations of theory: whether students see well and wide-rangingly: whether they see what, indeed, was there, or some altered version of it. (For these purposes, the video tape should be available for playback.) In all of this, he will play the part of a *prejudiced* monitor: he will honor selections of Freudianly nonrelevant behaviors and instances of non-Freudian interpretation but insist on the priority of the Freudian view.

Overtly, he responds to some one of the trainee comments with an answering challenge or question: what evidence (in the exhibited behavior) the trainee bases his diagnosis upon; the trainee's ground (in the Freudian theory) for characterizing as he has the behavior noted; whether the putative cause asserted is plausible; whether the educational problem noted is indeed a problem, and, if it is, whether it is likely to be solved by educational means or require therapeutic intervention. By such challenges, response to challenge, and the discussion which ensues on challenge and response, the original (selected) comment is clarified, corrected, and expanded.

The discussion then moves a second step toward bringing the principle to its case. The instructor asks of trainees what additional information they wish or require to test the clarified diagnosis, to check the characterization, to verify the speculation concerning causes, to serve, in sum, whatever purposes the selected starting point, as clarified and seen by the trainees, requires. The requests for information will suffer one of two fates. They may be granted forthwith (from a second viewing of the film, from documents readied for the purpose, from additional film held in reserve). They may be challenged: with respect to their relevance to the case in question, with respect to their possible discoverability, with respect to the mode of interpretation which the trainee will use upon the data, or with a question concerning the ground in Freudian theory which legitimizes the request as an appropriate request in the circumstances. (Whether requests are granted or challenged depends on particulars of the moment.)

If the request is granted forthwith, the discussion moves on to incorporation of the new data into the ongoing treatment of the case, to expression of doubts and challenges concerning the way they are used, to defenses or revisions made in the light of the challenges or doubts. If the request is challenged, discussion moves to clarification and revision of what is challenged, to successful rebuttal of the challenge, or to reasoned withdrawal of the originating request. If the latter is the outcome, the instructor and trainees turn to another or revised request. If the outcome is one of the former, the data are provided and discussion moves on to their interpretation and use by the group, the interpretation and use being subject, again, to challenges from the instructor and, by now increasingly, to challenges from trainees. Eventually, the discussion is brought to a reasonably satisfying and reasonably defensible close in the shape of a diagnosis agreed upon, a program for amelioration of the originating condition, or a recommendation concerning curriculum and instruction which will take account of such needs as the child's behavior suggests.

The purpose of this program of question, challenge, response, and counterresponse is twofold. The general and obvious purpose is to transform the Freudian (or other) material from a doctrine to a *view*, from a body of "knowledge" to a *habit* of observation, selection, and interpretation of the appropriate facts of concrete cases. This purpose is, or should be, characteristic of any program devoted to training toward a profession, whether pluralities are involved or not. The second purpose lies within the first and is crucial to the *poly*focal aim of the endeavor. It consists in ensuring that each selection of facts from the multitude visible in the original portrayal are the facts dubbed relevant by the Freudian view, that characterizations made are Freudian characterizations, that diagnoses are from the Freudian nosology, that the causes sought are the kinds of causes that the Freudian doctrine conceives as the efficacious causes. The second purpose, in short, is to avoid *bad* eclectic: the *unaware* mixing of elements of two views, even though the mix be coherent, or the mixing of the immiscible without knowing that the mixture is incoherent.

The latter subpurpose is patently desirable. It is avoidance of a confusion. The former is less obviously but equally desirable for two reasons. First, a merger of ideas, for example, the collapse of a distinction into a larger whole, is not inherently more desirable than the distinction. To view a cat and a dog as two instances of animal reveals one sort of thing; to view a cat as one thing and a dog as another reveals other facets of the two. Each such act of viewing is desirable, and without awareness of which device one is using (making the distinction; collapsing it), one is unlikely to use the other. This is to say that a small measure of polyfocality is lost and one contribution toward the habit of polyfocal scrutiny is not only lost but obscured. The second reason concerns the two whole views from which the merged elements are drawn. If the two views are indeed two (as they should be in a well-chosen plurality), the unaware merging of miscible elements from the two obscures the differences which render them two. One view is unconsciously assimilated to the other, is lost as a separate view as far as the unaware user is concerned. This is to say that a large measure of polyfocality is lost and a large contribution to the discipline of polyfocal scrutiny obscured. These reasons for maintenance of the "purity" of the Freudian view are also the reasons why the instructor plays the part of the *prejudiced* monitor. He is retaining conceptual space for the other whole views which later cycles of the program will introduce. When each of these is treated, he will be prejudiced in its favor.

This ends the first cycle: a phase of mastery of a doctrine, a phase of involvement in bringing it to bear as one revealing lens. The second and successive cycles, which treat other doctrines and bring them to bear as additional revealing lenses, are *not* mere repetitions of the first. A new factor is introduced, a factor of cumulation.

Cumulative cycles, phase 1

The second cycle begins as did the first, with mastery of a view-affording doctrine. The second doctrine may be one which appears to be immediately comparable with the first, using the same form of principle, parts, and relations among parts, and having parts which *seem* to be much the same as the Freudian parts. The Aristotelian construction (*Ethics*, bks. 1–6)[5] is a useful case in point, with its appetitive and actively rational parts and a quasi part connecting the rational and appetitive.

Alternatively, the second doctrine may use the same form of principle but conceive and assign parts which appear to be radically different from the parts of the first construction. The construction by Carl Frankenstein (*The Roots of the Ego*)[6] is an interesting case in point, with an ego in transaction with internal and external nonegos plus a central "core." (It is pleasant to have a construction with four parts instead of three.)

The second doctrine may, on the other hand, use a radically different form of principle. In the more extreme interpersonal theories, for example, not only are parts dispensed with but the whole envisaged is an altogether different whole, no longer "the personality" encased in one skin and possessing a character which determines relations with other personalities. Instead, the whole envisaged is a system of relations which determine the relata. The "personality" loses its entitative status and becomes, instead, the intersect of its friends and enemies.

In the beginning, the new doctrine is mastered in much the same way as was the first. The new view is taken in its own terms, the text studied, interpreted, discussed, and debated. Comparison with the first doctrine is avoided. This pattern of restricted attention is followed until responses to text and query which unreflectively identify features of the new doctrine with features of the old diminish to a trickle.

The point of this restriction is probably clear. The overwhelming tendency of students faced with a new member of a family of doctrines is to assimilate the new one to the first-learned. He treats the new one as being the same as the first, or as deviating in only a few identifiable and unremarkable ways, or as being flatly contradictory of discrete passages of the first. (Whether this tendency is a result of schooled expectation of a one right answer, is due to some general tendency to favor the first-learned, or is due to some other or combination of factors need not concern us now.) If this kind of operation is allowed to go unchecked, no plurality can arise, only a one view with variations and some "errors"—hence, the initial habituation toward treatment of the new in its own terms.

5. Aristotle, *Nicomachean Ethics* (numerous editions in English). In addition to books 1–6, see sections on pleasure in book 9.
6. Carl Frankenstein, *The Roots of the Ego* (Baltimore: Williams & Wilkins, 1960).

Once assimilation efforts have diminished, however, attention can be fully turned to the cumulative factor, a comparison of the two doctrines aimed at clarifying the distinctness of their views. This clarification does not require an exhaustive treatment of the differences of principle, premises, terms, and distinctions which distinguish the theories, or even a very thorough treatment, since we are not concerned in polyfocal conspectus with establishing the disciplines of critical analysis or sophisticated enquiry, or even with imparting a thoroughly informed conspectus of doctrines as doctrines. What is required, rather, is just that degree and kind of treatment which will impart to students a readiness to try the doctrines as distinctly different ways of looking on personality, each with its own defensible point of view and perspective.

If the second doctrine is the Aristotelian construction, one might well begin with the posited parts in each doctrine which appear to students to be much the same—the Freudian "id" and the Aristotelian "appetitive." By focused reexamination of the new text via question and answer, one begins to disentangle what students have tacitly merged. The two parts *are* generically similar: each is the repository of the impulsions we share with other mammals. But Freud assumes an ineluctable hegemony of the id over the other parts: its demands cannot be ignored except at the price of sickness; it is the origin and sole proprietor of the "psychic energy" on which all the parts depend; it is the sole source of pleasure. The other parts "borrow" their energy and their capacity for pleasure. Since Freud assumes this hegemony, he forecloses the possibility of enquiries into possible modification of the id by the other two parts. (Freudian "sublimation" is not a modification of the id but a rechanneling of its energies.) On the other hand, the same assumption thrusts into the foreground the question of the dynamics by which illness arises from frustration and the further problem of discriminating the ways, other than modification of the id, by which the requirements of the various psychic organs are reconciled.

In Aristotle, on the other hand, the appetitive is assigned a considerable plasticity. There are not only the possibilities of sublimation and repression of its impulsions but also the possibility of symptom-free renunciation: not only the possibility of renunciation, indeed, but of cultivation, the nurturing of potential impulsions and pleasures which others may hardly feel at all.

The difference between the appetitive in Aristotle and the id in Freud leads to a differing construction of other psychic parts as well, since each part in each view is in organic connection with its fellow parts. Aristotle assigns to his rational part (the rough equivalent of the Freudian ego) an original (built-in) potential for modification of the appetites. He then assigns to it a possible course of development through which it becomes eventually capable of determining what aspects of the appetitive are most profitably to be changed and in what direction— a kind of self-diagnosis and self-therapy.[7]

Thus, Aristotle investigates precisely what Freud can ignore—the question of the instruments available in the psyche for modification of impulsion and the processes by which modification occurs. But by the same token, Aristotle's assumption forecloses for him the matters in Freud: the origin of neurosis and the character of the shunts (sublimations) by which neuroses are avoided.

The instructor then indicates to students the plausibility of each assumption. No man, at least no young one, can deny the imperiousness of sexual demands. On the other hand, no one, at least no older one, can deny that many men pursue vastly different objects and activities with much the same energy, zest, and single-mindedness which Freud reserves for pursuit of objects of the "instincts." One goes on to indicate the heuristic defensibility of the assumptions as well. Each of them indicates and instigates enquiries which the other relegates to the background or to oblivion.

There is another kind of question of great potency for our purpose. One can ask how Aristotle (or Maslow or Hartmann) takes account subordinately of the matters in the forefront of the Freudian (or Allportian) investigation and, conversely, how Freud takes account of the Aristotelian emphases. The "answers" are then exhibited. Aristotle introduced a scale of continence and incontinence constituting a wide range of genetic individual differences in the accessibility of the appetitive to modification and control; Freud posited especially effective and desirable channels of "sublimation"—art and science.

This form of question yields two profits which potentiate each other. In the first place, it casts a bright light on the degrees of freedom available for explanation as a component of enquiry. Theories do not differ only in the facts they subsume; different explanations are not necessarily one right, one wrong. Rather, under the control of different premises and principles of enquiry, different theories may organize and explicate their common stock of facts in different ways, each of the ways as defensible as the other. In the second place, students find the question of different accountings for similar facts highly attractive. They see its

7. With students especially interested in personality theory, it may be useful to point out that some recent efforts to assign greater powers to the rational—some of the "ego psychologies"—are frustrated in their efforts by failure to take account of the organic connection among the various parts: they do not reduce the "size" of another part in order to make room for a larger ego.

import, enjoy addressing it on their own to works examined, and are often able, with little or no new training, to elicit the data it requires. In brief, the question and its answers achieve a large measure of the outcome which cumulative first phases are designed to serve. They convey a sense of the useful and defensible otherness of the doctrines treated and convey a measure of the discipline which will expedite later treatments of the same sort.

In any case, with a clear indication that the two doctrines' similar organic parts (id and appetitive) differ in pointed ways, one can go on to exhibit some of the larger differences in doctrine which stem from these first differences. If these parts differ in their respective schemes, so must the relations of each to its accompanying parts. If the relations differ, then it is highly likely, if not necessary, that the other parts differ, too, that Aristotle's rational may have powers or properties assigned to it which differ from the powers and properties of Freud's rational ego. There is no need, of course, to pursue all these possibilities into the actual fact, since we are not concerned in polyfocal conspectus with exhausting the systems of difference between doctrines. With some students, it may be enough merely to indicate the possibilities. In most cases, it is essential to locate one or two of the actuals for the sake of reinforcing the student's appreciation of the possibilities.

One may then step back and try for a characterization of the difference of the two doctrines as a whole: that the Freudian is a physicianly work concerned mainly with the etiology, diagnosis, and treatment of disease; that Aristotle's is a political work concerned mainly with a program for rearing the young. One is primarily therapeutic, the other orthogenic. (This omnibus characterization will become important for us when we come to speculate on the probable and desirable outcomes of a polyfocal pattern of instruction.)

Other doctrines, other questions

Of course, if the second doctrine is not Aristotle's but some other, such as the suggested Frankenstein or interpersonal, the useful questions will differ too, since they depend on the actual relations and most generative differences of the doctrines under treatment. To be sure, examination of the Frankenstein might easily lead students to recognition of much similarity in the origins of Freud's superego and Frankenstein's external nonego. (Both are environmental, with heavy weighting on the social environment.) Pursuit of this similarity would again lead to detection of differences which eventuate in radically different treatment and use of the environmental factor in the two theories.

However, pursuit of the critical differences between these two similars, as in the comparison of Freud and Aristotle, would prove to be

a long way around to the telling differences between Freud and Frankenstein. One might better begin by pointing out that if the approximately same whole can be discriminated by different men into substantially different sets of parts, it could be because they had anatomized
the whole in different planes, taken different cuts through the subject
matter.

With this possibility clarified by simple examples, one or another of
its corollaries can be pursued. If the two sets of cuts intersect, then each
coherent organ or part disclosed by one cut will be found distributed as
subordinate constituents among some or all of the coherent organs disclosed by the other cut. One can then search for the substantive equivalents of this imagery: what fate has overtaken the materials of Freud's
superego, say? Into what new parts in Frankenstein have they been assimilated and in what new way organized with what newly accompanying materials? What emphases of Freud have consequently dropped into
obscurity? What new emphases emerge in consequence of the new combinations of materials and their new organization? What are the possible uses and disuses of these different emphases for problems and
situations in education?

Another line of attack emerges from the probability that men of intelligence taking different cuts through a subject matter may well have
done so with different intent. They may have intended different dis-
closures as personae in different dramas. One asks therefore, to what
use the parts are put, what accounts they make possible.

This question proves to be highly revealing in the case of Frankenstein and Freud. Freud wishes to give us an embryogenic account of
the development of the psyche. This account must have two characteristics. It must be an account with beginning, turning point, and definitive close. It must be an account in which parts arise by differentiation
from the matter of a primal part which must forever tinge the character
of what arises from it. Freud's ego, id, and superego serve these purposes admirably. The id, the instincts, constitutes a primal part from
which ego and superego arise but from which they can never become
wholly independent. The Oedipal crisis and the superego it generates
constitute the turning point. If and when the ego develops strength and
experience enough for good scanning and employment of the world (in
the service of the id) and for effective mediation between superego, id,
and world, development is complete. There will be continuing and satisfying life, but it will be the life of a matured community (the psyche)
with a stable constitution.

Freud wishes personae which will also make vivid an account of the
inner conflicts which his clinical experience revealed. Again, the Freudian parts serve admirably. The demands of the id, the strictures and

ideals of the superego, and the opportunities afforded by the world have built into them a great unlikelihood that they will often coincide.

Frankenstein, on the other hand, is only subordinately interested in a definitive embryogenic account. His first concern is for an account which will legitimize the possibility of ego growth indefinitely prolonged, of a lifetime not marked by a definitive plateau but, rather, continuing its increase in content, in flexibility, coherence, and versatility as long as physical health permits. His account, too, must have certain additional characteristics. It must account for a growth of individual egos which preserves, despite generic similarity, the possibility of unique egos. Second, in order to make possible indefinite growth, it must find a way in which the ego, far from exhausting what it feeds on, replenishes its sources in the very act of growing.

The parts discriminated by Frankenstein serve these difficult purposes admirably. The only practicable limit to the ego's continuing growth is misdirection by chance or bad nurture, misdirection which limits the permeability of the ego's membranes to the kinds of matters it earlier fed upon. The possibility of a unique ego is preserved by the diversity of the worlds to which a permeable ego can turn for nurture. The plenitude of its resources for continued growth is insured by assignment to the ego of capacity for increasingly *catalytic* autonomy. That is, the more autonomous the ego grows, the greater its competence to recognize, confront, and profit from a correspondingly increasing autonomy of the inner and outer nonegos which are its resources.

Again, as in the earlier examples, one moves from notice of differences in organizing (explaining) principles to indication of their plausibility. (By "plausibility" here and earlier, I mean merely that the conception can be matched with corresponding facts.) Some men do bloom throughout their lives. Many men conform for the most part to a prevailing model, but some do not. It is indeed the experience of some of us (and conveyed to others by drama and the novel) that the more we are, and know that we are, the more recognizable, interesting, and profitable become the differentnesses of others.

And still again, as earlier, one may move from here to indication of some ways in which facts made foreground in one view are taken into subordinate account in the other. In the case of Frankenstein, for example, what for Freud is seen as central conflicts among the parts of the psyche become, for Frankenstein, the defenses and maneuvers by which the deprived or misdirected ego avoids the growths which threaten its inadequate autonomy. Similarly, the relations of parent and child which, for Freud, precipitate the Oedipal crisis are transformed by Frankenstein into means by which the child is inducted into the world of growth.

Radical difference of principle

To round out this budget of examples, let us take the possibility of comparing Freud with a theory which is completely interpersonal, yet takes account of all the facts treated by Freud. If there were such a pure and "complete" interpersonal theory, it would stand to the Freudian theory as a beautifully simple and therefore extraordinarily vivid example of polyfocal plurality.

On the theoretical side, each would include the same materials. Each would also involve both relata and relations. That is, each must talk of John and James, of Paul and Paula. Each must talk too, of enmity and alliance, of wanting and being wanted, fearing and feared, aggressing and being aggressed upon, nurturing and nurtured. The difference between the two theories would consist in the simple, wholesale, and symmetrical exchange of roles between these two—between relata and relations—in the dramas of the two theories. In each theory, there are the roles of explanation and that which is explained, explicans and explicandum. But in one of the theories (Freud's), it is the relata which, predominantly, constitute the explicans while relations are explained. The personality is thus and so, or these two persons are thus and so. *Therefore*, he fears or wants her; she rouses his anxiety; he identifies; she projects.

In a thoroughgoing interpersonal theory, on the other hand, it is (predominantly) relations which constitute the explicans while relata are explained. There were such relations as nurturance neglect, or failure of conscientious neglect; there are such relations as exploitation, ruling and being ruled, alliance, love, competition, cronyism. *Therefore*, he is impulsive; she is withdrawn; the man is gregarious, she will fear authority figures; he will recoil from tall ones, be drawn to the short. (In fact, the exchange of roles here is even more vivid than I have suggested. The factor which plays the role of explicans not only explains but generates. The explicandum is not only explained but sired by the explanation.)

On the practicable side, the difference in emphasis, the view afforded by the two doctrines, is equally wholesale, simple, and vivid. From the one view (Freud's), behaviors are primarily symptoms. Causes must be sought in the normal pattern of personality development as such and in deviations from that pattern imposed by the particular vicissitudes suffered by this particular personality during its ontogeny. Radical modifications of behavior must be instigated by some knd of renewal of ontogeny which will reconstitute the personality as a whole. Amelioration of behavioral symptoms must be sought in accessible parts and characteristic processes of the personality which can be put in the service of other parts (e.g., supplying new channels of sublimation; supplying less destructible objects of aggression).

From the interpersonal point of view, on the other hand, behaviors are *not* only symptoms but are causally efficacious. They consist of provocations which evoke responses which provoke still other responses, all of this repeating and reinforcing old patterns of provocation and response. Consequently, modification of behavior can be sought in relations deliberately established between client and therapist, between student and teacher, which suggest to the client, encourage and abet, new ways of address which evoke new responses which function as new stimuli to still further new responses which break the ancient patterns and establish new and more rewarding ones. (The distinctions between radical and ameliorative treatment disappear.)

Given theories of such neat contrariety, the instructional operations which will make clear their polyfocal potential can be very brief and simple. They may consist of no more than an exposition of the radical difference between the two (much as in the paragraphs above) together with indications of differences in perception and interpretation of noted behaviors which would arise from their use as perspectives. It is almost certainly desirable, however, that some measure of student initiative and participation be enlisted. This can be added to the lectorial explication by questions put and answers sought from the texts under study or from experience.

One such pattern of questioning is suggested by the fact that most students recoil in disbelief from interpersonal doctrines. Each of us is usually well wedded to belief in our own existence as enduring and determining persons and are inclined to extend the same courtesy to others. This prevalence of selfhood suggests mischievous questions to students designed to elicit examples of the contrary from their own existences. One asks if anyone present recalls a moment in a group when his behavior altered on the entrance of an addition to the group. To one of those courageous enough to identify himself, further questions are addressed, designed to probe the alteration of behavior: the new feelings which accompanied the change of behavior, the new intentions or impulses which seemed to engender it, the enhancements or diminutions in pleasures and pains which followed on the new entrance, even changes consequent on the new entrance in perception and valuation of persons present throughout the period of the group's assembly. With the ice thus broken, one is usually well able to go on to instances from the lives of other students and from there even to the tentative characterization of classes of occasions in which one student or another "becomes a different person."

One point to this line of questioning and response is obvious enough: it helps to raise interpersonal doctrine toward the threshold of possible belief by conferring on it a measure of plausibility drawn from students' own experience. This outcome is, of course, necessary if the view is to function as a lens coequal with the Freudian (or other) lenses. There is a second, less obvious, point to the line of enquiry. Precisely because it is addressed to experience instead of the text, it is a foretaste of phase 2 (the viewing phase) of this second cycle of polyfocal conspectus. It is the preparatory, fumbling *use* of a doctrine as a lens looking out on the world.

Before we can pass on to a brief description of a cumulative phase 2, a postscript to this treatment of interpersonal theory must, in conscience, be given. There not only is no pure interpersonal theory extant, there is not likely to be one. Relations, however efficacious they may be, are usually conceived to require some ground, some matter originating from another source, on which to act. (In one recent translation of the Old Testament, not even God is seen creating *ex nihilo*. The opening line of Genesis reads, "When God began to create the heaven and the earth, the earth was void and without form." The earth may have been formless and void, but it was there.)

The converse, of course, holds for Freud's theory. It is not purely entitative. A primal part, if it is truly *one* part as usually conceived (homogeneous), cannot, of itself, differentiate into other parts. Some secondness is required as trigger and probably as guide. This triggering and guiding may be chance or it may be a relation to some factor outside the primal part or to some factor embedded in the primal part in earlier (phylogenetic) times. Both of the latter possibilities are used by Freud. The rise of the superego is triggered by the child's relations to its parents. The potential for emergence of the ego is instituted phylogenetically by irritations of life matter by influx of energy from the environment.

Fiction though it be, this notion of a *pure* entitative theory and a *pure* relational one is useful—useful, indeed, in three ways. First, if this or a similar account is conveyed to students without prior signaling of its fictional character, it permits communication with dispatch of the important difference between two kinds of theory, each of great value in the planning of curriculum and the execution of instruction. (I assume that I need not defend the desirability of noting and interpreting the behavior of students in the course of teaching and learning, or the desirability of considering the character of human personality in deliberating about ends and means of curriculum. I assume, further, that neither entitative theories nor relational ones need defense against the other.)

Once the first function is served, the fiction can be corrected in either of two ways: as I have done here, by simple confession; or by the careful examination of real instances of the two kinds of theory (Harry Stack Sullivan's *The Interpersonal Theory of Psychiatry*[8] would be a useful representative of the interpersonal). The second means is the more desirable, since it conveys much more vividly to students the refusal of the facts of life—even the facts of such a refined life as the life of enquiry—to be wholly encompassed in clear and simple ideas. This is the second usefulness of the fiction.

Third, the notion of pure alternatives has enabled me to convey here with considerable dispatch what otherwise might have been a difficult and extended exposition: that explanation in scientific enquiry is not a kind of *thing* (as in the vulgarism "fact versus explanation") but a kind of role. "Explanation" is what organizes and conveys. The explicandum is what is organized and conveyed. "Facts" may be used *to* explain as well as to *be* explained. And different accounts can arise merely from different choices of which facts or which kind of facts to elect for which roles.

A second reflexive comment is in order. I have used as example throughout this discussion materials drawn from only one field—personality theory. I have drawn on a single field in order to establish between us—you and me—a common body of exemplary material and to establish between theses, between one point and another, a body of common examples. The body of common examples between one point and another constitutes a first and concrete order of connection between points made, connections which supplement and undergird the connections expounded in general terms. The example used at a given point should, then, throw light upon earlier points (and later ones) as well as on the point exemplified in the moment. These instances of different accounts of personality, for example, are intended to illuminate one of the earliest points made—the need for an account of enquiry appropriate to the existence of pluralities of theory—as well as to exemplify phase 1 of a cumulative cycle of polyfocal conspectus. The same instances lay much of the ground, too, for what we shall treat later in the sequel on commonplaces.

I have deliberately drawn on the single field, personality theory, because it is one of the softest of the soft behavioral sciences on which decisions and conclusions in education rest. This softness constitutes a positive advantage, for it arises in large part from the complexity of the subject, a complexity which, in turn, gives rise to very wide freedom for

8. Harry Stack Sullivan, *The Interpersonal Theory of Psychiatry* (New York: W. W. Norton & Co., 1953).

choice of principle of enquiry, of terms of explanation, of emphases among accumulated facts. This latitude in turn makes easier the task of indicating the character and origins of plurality.

It must not be supposed, however, that plurality necessarily disappears as sciences get "harder." Sociology, even biological ecology, have their own diversities. A community can be investigated, for example, as an oversized organism depending for existence on execution of definite vital functions. Enquiry will then proceed by attempting to specify these vital functions or roles and proceed by determining for each of a set of discriminated kinds of communities what organisms or species of organisms serve each function, occupy each "niche." (A similar pattern characterizes "Parsonian" investigations of human communities and the investigations of classical comparative physiology.) On the other hand, a community can be conceived in terms of the exchanges between members of materials involved in their metabolism. In that case, enquiry aims to establish the network of exchanges which define a community: what is exchanged, at what rate, with what equilibria maintained or upset. (A similar pattern characterizes "economic" studies of human communities and international relations, except that the goods and services exchanged are not limited to material ones.)

In brief, the pluralism with which we are concerned is conspicuous in the softest sciences but not limited to them.

Interim summary

Let us consolidate position after this excursion into personality theory. We are concerned with a definite pattern of instruction called "polyfocal conspectus." It is concerned with imparting to students a measure of inclination toward and competence for examining educational situations and problems in more than one set of terms. (It does not aim to impart thorough knowledge of the structures of pluralities, or disciplines of sophisticated analysis and enquiry—only as much as is necessary for effective use of tools, not their construction and criticism.)

The pattern of instruction proceeds in cycles, the number of cycles depending on the number of alternative perspectives one wishes to impart, but preferably not less than three. Each cycle has two phases.

The first phase of a first cycle is concerned with imparting a doctrine.

The second phase of a first cycle is concerned with transforming the doctrine into a view, moving it from the status of "knowledge" toward being one mode of discriminating certain kinds of problems and materials appropriate to their solution in educational situations. The second phase proceeds by confronting students with real and simulated situations sufficiently "busy," unstructured, and various to admit discrimination of many problems and materials and, indeed, of many different kinds. The discipline imparted consists of ensuring that each selection of facts from the multitude presented in the situation, each formulation of problem, and each search for materials of solution are the facts, the problems, and the materials appropriate to the doctrine under study. This discipline is made necessary by the need to reserve perceptual space for second and additional doctrines, and views of the world by means of these other doctrines.

Second and subsequent cycles are not duplicates of the first. A cumulative factor is added to each phase. The cumulative factor is appended to ensure that perceptual space, discrimination of one view and doctrine from another, is maintained or, if not maintained, is knowingly violated and to good purpose.

The cumulative factor in first phases consists of a *few* questions addressed and followed which clarify the distinctness of the doctrine under study from the doctrines which occupied earlier first cycles. The selected questions can be addressed, on the one hand, to differences in the apparatus of enquiry: differences in formal principle (Freud and the interpersonal); differences in purpose (Freud and Aristotle); differences in the materials selected for embodiment of the formal principle (Freud and Frankenstein); differences in other sorts of premises, terms, and distinctions. The selected questions can be addressed, on the other hand, to the fates of materials (data) acted on by the apparatus: what retreats and advances, what foreground-background reversals occur as one moves from doctrine to doctrine; translocations of explicans and explicandum. Better and best questions cannot be specified, since their value depends on the actual differences between the doctrines under study. It is nevertheless the case that a *few* questions well treated will suffice. The numerous questions suggested in our excursion into personality theories constitute *alternatives*.

Cumulative cycles, phase 2

We can turn now to description of a cumulative second phase. It begins, as did phase 2 of the first cycle, with presentation of a real, recorded, or simulated problem situation.[9] The trainees, again, are asked to discriminate a problem in the situation, a problem of the kind signified by the doctrine under study. By now, however, with the experience of phase 2 of the first cycle assimilated, this initial maneuver can be enriched. The trainees are asked to identify and formulate silently the problem they "see." They watch, request a rerun if the material is

9. For discussion of the character and criteria of material for such a simulation, see my *College Curriculum and Student Protest* (Chicago: University of Chicago Press, 1969).

recorded, make written note of their formulation. (It is important to request that they make written note, since *oral*-cerebral commitments have a way of being erased or overridden by a first-voiced view, and we are concerned in this enrichment with evoking some diversity of problem perceived.) When notes are finished, the instructor asks for first one and then another description of "the" problem. From the several problems voiced, he asks students to select a pair (and their advocates) which joins an issue. The issue may be one of accuracy or reality of perception. (It is astonishing to discover with what frequency trainees "see" what did not occur or embroider what did.) It may be an issue of fitness of the problem formulated to the doctrine in hand. In any case, he requests criticisms from fellow students of the problem as voiced; invites the voicer to rebut or to adapt his or her description to the cogent criticism; uses the materials thus evoked to emphasize aspects of the guiding doctrine overlooked, or to clarify aspects of the doctrine which this foray into practice reveals to have been obscure, or more firmly to establish connections between the generalities of the doctrine and the particularities of actual cases.

When one such debate has run its course and served its purpose, another is joined, and the same procedure is continued until the urgencies, doubts, and uncertainties signaled by students have had their day. (I urge you to compare this procedure with the procedure earlier suggested for phase 2 of a *first* cycle. The differences are telling and mark one aspect of cumulation: the much larger measure of student participation, the extent to which the initiative passes to them, the frequency with which they *ask* the important questions as well as answer them.)

When several problems have been clarified and agreed upon, the group selects one for further pursuit. (Note again the contrast with the first experience of this kind. Then, the instructor made the choice; now it is made by the group.) Requests for additional information are honored, discussed, or challenged for their relevance. The new data are assimilated to the problem or the course of its solution, and the discussion is brought to a satisfying and defensible close: a sound diagnosis, a program for amelioration, an outline of curriculum or instruction.

All of this is much as in the first cycle except for the enhanced amount of student participation and control. Only one factor not so far named marks off this episode from its counterpart in the first cycle: *its work must be done on an entirely different case.* If, for example, the chosen cases are classroom situations, the room and the children must be different: older or younger, brighter or dingier, of a different size and shape. The occasion for the children's behavior should be different; so also the tone and temper of their behavior. The reason for this condition is dramatic but simple. It concerns the heart of our problem: polyfocal conspectus and the maintenance of perceptual space.

In the cumulative phase 2 as so far described, the problem of maintenance of perceptual space has been minimized. The first doctrine examined and the first essay toward its application (the first cycle) are days in the past. Mastery, discussion, and debate of the second doctrine have intervened and occupied the recent time and attention of students. Even though the difference of second doctrine from the first formed a part of that discussion, the discussion centered on the second doctrine and will have closed with it as solo occupant of the stage. The choice of an entirely different case maintains and enhances this distance of the two doctrines and views and affords a highly dramatic (affectively powerful) contrast to what follows.

What follows is sudden and unsignaled re-presentation of the *original* case. At once, the trainees are faced with what "they had finished with." It is in fact finished as far as the trainees are concerned: organized, structured, given shape by the doctrine earlier treated, neat and disposed. Now the problem of the trainees is to escape the tyranny of the first doctrine, a tyranny made doubly tyrannical over them, since they had served as its agents in shaping the present case. Their new task is to de-compose the finished picture they had earlier shaped, resolve it into its original busy and polyvalent potentialities, then reshape it into a new picture, a new kind of problem, and a new kind of solution, and do all this without destroying beyond possibility of recovery the first picture composed. Only then will trainees have experienced a polyfocal conspectus.

Applications

With respect to the behavioral sciences, little more need be said about the poignancy of eclectic treatment. Sociology, social psychology, cultural anthropology, psychology, and political science are loaded with studies arising from competing principles leading to solutions which invite eclectic treatment, and these solutions are, in turn, loaded with purport for educational problems. The following come to mind as especially demanding polyfocal conspective treatment on the part of educators:

Child development, especially studies involving notions of "concepts" and their formation.
Learning theories.[10]
Studies of styles of enquiry, creativity, and other envisaged varieties of pattern for perception of, response to, and manipulation of the environing world.

10. For a report on an interesting eclectic treatment of learning theory, see Paul F. Kleine, "From Learning a Theory to Theorizing about Learning," *Education at Chicago* (Winter 1971), pp. 15–21.

Studies of intelligence and scholastic aptitude, under whatever other name and with whatever distinctions may be further imposed.

Studies of groups, group behavior, and the behavior of persons in groups.

Studies of family, social class, and subcultural determination of life style, character, and personality.

Treatments, whether from jurisprudence, sociology, politics, or psychology, which assert the "real" or "proper" relations between society and the individual.

Conceptions of motivation, especially those which raise issues involving oppositions of autogenous rewards as against external attractions, and competition as against collaboration.

There is another and wholly different sphere in which conspective treatment would reward education: the commonly recognized fields of knowledge which education draws upon for content, materials, and aims of curriculum. History, literature, even the sciences, are richly polyvalent resources for curriculum. Yet little is done in the education of teachers and curriculum planners to afford them a vivid and systematic view of these numerous options. Educators-in-training are usually left merely to stumble upon one or a few of the available alternatives, and the circumstances of their accidental discovery are usually such as to lead trainees to choose one as "the" nature of the field. Other valences, if encountered later, are then usually perceived as mistaken, effete, or enemy aliens.

What is radically impoverishing here is not merely that only a few of many resources are seen but that they are seen and judged only by reference to a narrow conception of a field of knowledge. What is wanted is a furniture and frame of mind in which a field of knowledge would appear as affording such numerous, viable alternatives for education as virtually to demand that they be scrutinized and judged not merely as sound or unsound conceptions of the field, but also as more or less appropriate in the education of young people of differing competences, needs, and circumstances. Polyfocal conspectus would afford such a furniture and frame of mind.

The field of literature is an accessible case in point. As indicated in the first paper of this series, critical scholarship has generated a dozen conceptions of the novel, short story, and drama, each constituting a different way in which a literary work can be read and a different significance of it to the reader. A work can become a vicarious experience, a display of a social problem, a light thrown on the reader's own circumstance or problem, an evidence concerning the author's epoch, an occasion for aesthetic pleasure, a disclosure of devices by which to organize thought and move the hearts of men, or an accessible and moving ideal of existence and action.

The problem posed by this diversity to the educator of educators is, first, to bring these alternatives to light for his trainees, second, to provide them with grounds for judging the efficacy of literature in each of these possible roles, and third, to provide occasions for deliberation by the educators-in-training concerning which of these options, if any, literature should be for various kinds of students' schools and other circumstances.

History affords an even wider range of options and therefore poses the same educational challenge and educational opportunity. Different historians seek different facts as the pertinent facts of history. Some seek to know all aspects of what they call a culture. Others focus on the economy and the conditions of life of the producing members of that economy. Others examine what they take to be the products of ordering intellects—religions, languages, legal codes, literatures, and technological inventions. Still others focus on national, class, and cultural combats, others on modes of political order. Historians differ, too, in the means they use to order, organize, or "explain" their chosen facts. Some find their explanations in supposed laws of history: cycles of growth and decay, spiral or linear progress toward freedom, order, or some other fulfillment. Others look for psychological laws: notions of challenge and response, of habituation and revolt, of a warfare of reason and passion, of an evolution of human potentiality or a growth in human character. Some look backward for the origins and causes of what they take to be important states and conditions of the present. Others look forward to find causes, treating history as a tendency toward these causes. Still others try to avoid causes and to exhibit merely the temporal order of events. Some even seek the causes of events in history itself: a people's idea of their past and how that idea influenced their decisions about their present.

As in the case of literature, each kind of historical work may have its peculiarly appropriate contribution to make to one group of students in one place and time, while other modes of selection of the pertinent past and other modes of their interpretation may have most value for other students. Hence, again, resources for education and opportunities to match resources with educational needs are overlooked if educators-to-be are not apprised of this richness of history and helped toward competence in making defensible choices for different students amid the available riches.

The sciences exhibit their own polyvalency. A science is at once a body of highly sophisticated knowledge about some segment of the world, a body of conceptual habits which tends to isolate that segment of the world from other segments, and a body of rules for coping with its segment of the world. It is also a source of technological means for alteration of that world. A science is, in addition, a discipline (or several) consisting of a rational order of problems posed and of principles and methods brought to bear upon the problems. It is also a community of a certain kind and a subculture with an ethos which distinguishes it from other subcultures. It is a human activity which affects the rest of human action (economic, political, social, personal) and in turn is affected by the rest of human action. For some group of students in some set of circumstances, any one or any combination of these may constitute the appropriate guise which science should wear in their schooling.

Polyfocal conspectus can be readily adapted to the opportunities afforded by history, literature, and the plastic arts as curricular resources. The basic pattern of a series of two-phase cycles remains appropriate, although the desirable number of cycles will be larger, and, fortunately, first phases briefer, than in the treatment of theories from the behavioral sciences. The character of first phases will also remain much the same. Each will examine a "theory" of the field of knowledge under consideration: a critical theory of literature or the arts;[11] an essay in historiography or philosophy of history.[12]

Second phases retain the role they play in the case of behavioral scientific materials—transformation of a doctrine to a view—but materials and procedures will require adaptation to the object viewed. In the case of literature, the simplest but least effective procedure would consist of following each doctrine with a literary work selected for its appropriateness to the doctrine brought to bear upon it. The weakness of such a procedure lies in its failure to provide experience of actively different viewings, since the object itself constrains the view. The ideal procedure would operate on a single work so rich as to permit reading and rereading in as many different ways as there are doctrines under consideration. The most practical procedure will probably prove to be one of progressive overlap in which, for example, of six critical doctrines the first and second are brought to bear on one work, the second and third on a second work, and so on, with variations.

11. For planning and construction of first phases on literature, the following are suggested: R. S. Crane, ed., *Critics and Criticism*, abr. ed. (Chicago: University of Chicago Press, 1970); and Lionel Trilling, ed., *Literary Criticism, an Introductory Reader* (New York: Holt, Rinehart & Winston, 1970).

12. For first phases on history, see Ronald H. Nash, ed., *Ideas of History* (New York: E. P. Dutton & Co., 1969); Thomas N. Guinsberg, ed., *The Dimensions of History* (Chicago: Rand McNally, 1971); and Fritz Stern, ed., *The Varieties of History* (New York: Meridian Books, 1956).

In the case of history, analogous procedures apply. The simplest procedure would present for each historiographic theory a historical work which closely follows the doctrine enunciated by the theory. The ideal procedure would present a large, heterogeneous body of raw materials (a simulation of the chaos in fact posed by the past to the historian) from which the trainees would select, in the light of each doctrine, the appropriate facts and submit them to the organization or interpretation demanded by the doctrine. The most practicable procedure will doubtless prove to be some compromise between these two.

It should be kept in mind, however, that second phases as applied to curricular resources serve a second function. They are not intended merely to make educators-in-training flexible readers or cognizant of the varieties of history. They are also intended to present alternative readings of literature and alternative forms of history as alternatives for curriculum. Consequently, a second phase should provide extended occasions for deliberations concerning the matching of kinds of readings and kinds of histories to the differing needs and circumstances of different students.

Most regrettably, the procedure of polyfocal conspectus is not adaptable at present to the sciences as curricular resources. Materials which would constitute an appropriate range of "theories" for first phases are both too few and too widely scattered throughout a range of journals to serve the purpose, and materials appropriate for second phases are scarcer still.

Outcomes

Educators have long been accustomed to ask at this point in a curricular discussion, "What is the intended outcome?" The question arises from the dogma that curriculums should be devised, controlled, and evaluated in the light of "objectives" taken as the leading principles. Consideration of the practical character of curriculum and instruction convinces me that this dogma is unsound. There are principles, alternative to objectives, which generate defensible curriculums. There are coprinciples, for use with objectives, which guard against some of the errors and excesses which arise from dependence on objectives as sole leading principles. I shall discuss these matters at large in the next paper of this series. One detail of the matter, however, concerns the question of intended outcome as addressed here to polyfocal conspectus.

The detail is merely this: I do not intend or expect one outcome or one cluster of outcomes but *any one* of several, a plurality. Recognizance of the several stems from consideration not of possible outcomes, but of the materials under treatment: pluralities of theory, their relations to the matter they try in their various ways to subsume, their relations to one another.

Sartre describes one conceivable outcome thus:

> Consider the example of the cube: I know it is a cube provided I have seen its six sides; but of these, I can see only three at a time, never more. I must therefore apprehend them successively. . . . When I see three sides of the cube at the same time, these three sides never present themselves to me as squares: their lines become flat, their angles become obtuse, and I must reconstruct their squareness. . . . We must *learn* objects, that is to say, [conjugate] upon them the possible points of view. The object itself is the synthesis of all these appearances.[13]

I doubt very much that such an outcome of polyfocal conspectus is likely. I base this doubt on consideration of the complexity of the objects represented by a plurality of theories, on the complexity of the theories, and on the competence of the men who constructed the theories. The objects are more complicated than a cube. The partialities and distortions of them by theory are more complicated than the perspectives of a cube. The theorists are highly competent.

This outcome is, nevertheless, possible. I base this faith on consideration of one of the states of mind and character that afflict constructors of theory; they are often bent more on constructing a new one than on enlarging the purview of one constructed by others.

Other outcomes are likely. The adventure with the conspectus may drive some students away from the field of education. It may convey to some a merely *general* appreciation of the complexity of theory and its incongruity with the practical. It may convey to others an informed awareness of the strengths and weaknesses of their preferred instruments. It may convey to some an ability (and its accompanying habit) to choose different instruments on different occasions, instruments appropriate to the practical situation they confront. It may convey to some an ability to use several instruments serially. To still others, it may convey a wider perspective on the range of educational problems and the range of possible solutions to them, but little or no increment in their ability to manage practical situations. (I base these anticipations on experience of students who undertake training in education.)

Any of these outcomes is desirable, at least for education. Some of them are too expensive.[14]

13. Jean-Paul Sartre, *The Psychology of Imagination* (New York: Washington Square Press, 1966).

14. For a highly sophisticated treatment of the relations of theory and practice generally, see Richard McKeon, "Philosophy and Action," *Ethics* 62, no. 2 (January 1952): 79–100.

· 12 ·

The Practical:
Translation into Curriculum

Scholars, as such, are incompetent to translate scholarly material into curriculum. They possess one body of disciplines indispensable to the task. They lack four others, equally indispensable. As scholars, they not only lack these other four, but also, as individuals, they are prone at best to ignore and at worst to sneer at them. Possessors of the other four necessary disciplines have an equal handicap; they do not possess the discipline of the scholar; they do not know the bodies of knowledge which his discipline has produced; they are often overawed by him. Yet, all five disciplines are necessary, and the curriculum work their possessors do must be done in collaboration. They must learn something of the concerns, values, and operations which arise from each other's experience. They must learn to honor these various groupings of concerns, values, and operations, and to adapt and diminish their own values enough to make room in their thinking for the others. They must bring these partially coalesced bodies of judgmental factors to bear on the body of scholarly materials.

These three operations—*discovery* of one another by collaborators, *coalescence* of what is discovered, *utilization* of the coalesced body of concerns as tools for generating new educational materials and purposes —take place, not serially, but simultaneously. The first two take place as the third is undertaken. The process is carried forward in a spiral movement toward a body of generated educational alternatives and choices among them—choices which satisfy entirely no one party to the collaboration but which do satisfy the collective more than does any other constellation of educational means and purposes among those considered.

AGENTS OF TRANSLATION

What are the five bodies of experience which must be represented in the group which undertakes the task of curriculum revision?

This chapter was previously published in the *School Review* 81 (1973): 501–22.

Subject Matter

There must be someone familiar with the scholarly materials under treatment and with the discipline from which they come. Suppose the materials under consideration are historical: then a member of the group must be familiar not only with this body of historical material but must also know what it is to be a historian.

Learners

There must be someone familiar with the children who are to be the beneficiaries of the curricular operation. This experience, too, must be manifold. It must include general knowledge of the age group under consideration: what it already knows, what it is ready to learn, what will come easy, what will be difficult, what aspirations and anxieties which may affect learning must be taken into account, what will appear to the child as contributing to an immediate desire or need. It should include intimate knowledge of the children under consideration—knowledge achieved by direct involvement with them. This is required in order to know the ways in which this unique group of children depart from generalities about similar children of the same age. These special attributes will include not only an impression of the direction and degree by which these children depart from the average on the scales used by the gatherers of general knowledge but will also include knowledge of attitudes, competences, and propensities not taken into account by the gatherers of general knowledge about children.

Knowledge of the children should include a range of information about their present state of mind and heart treated as a stage in development toward their probable destiny as adults. This should include some probabilities about their future economic status and function; what leisure they will enjoy; what adult aspirations and attitudes they, their friends, and neighbors are likely to have; what roles they will play in the family, their political community, their ethnic or religious community.

The Milieus

References to community suggest a third body of experience which should be represented in the curriculum-making group: experience of the milieus in which the child's learning will take place and in which its fruits will be brought to bear. The relevant milieus are manifold.

These milieus include the school and classroom in which the learning and teaching are supposed to occur. What are likely to be children's relations to one another? Will the classroom group overlap the play or neighborhood group or any other group in which the children function? Will the children begin as friends and acquaintances or as strangers? Will their relationships be dominated by cliques or other subgroups?

What structure of authority (or status) will characterize the relations of teachers to one another and to the educational leaders of the school? In what ways are these relations of adults in the school likely to affect the relations of teachers to students or to what and how the teachers are likely to teach?

Relevant milieus will also include the family, the community, the particular groupings of religious, class, or ethnic genus. What aspirations, styles of life, attitudes toward education, and ethical standards characterize these parents and, through their roles as parents, affect the children (as well as the character of what can and cannot be attempted in a curriculum)?

These milieus suggest others. What are the relations of this community to other communities of the same religious, ethnic, or class genus? What similarities or differences of rite or habit characterize them? What are the relations of the entire religious, ethnic, or class genus to the other genera which constitute the town or city and are represented in miniature by the children of each genus as they interact with children of other genera in the playground and public school? What are the conditions, dominant preoccupations, and cultural climate of the whole polity and its social classes, insofar as these may affect the careers, the probable fate, and ego identity of the children whom we want to teach? A dominant anti-intellectualism, a focus on material acquisition, a high value on conformity to a nationwide pattern and on the cloaking of cultural-religious differences are possible influences.

Teachers

So far, three bodies of experience are to be represented in the curriculum group: experience of the scholarly subject matter and its discipline, of the child, and of the child's milieus. Another required body of experience is knowledge of the teachers. This should include knowledge of what these teachers are likely to know and how flexible and ready they are likely to be to learn new materials and new ways of teaching. We need good guesses, too, about their personalities, characters, and prevailing moods: how they are likely to relate to the children, to one another, to the directors of the school, to visiting master teachers or scholars; how they tend to feel about themselves. It may be desirable to know something of their backgrounds: what biases they bring with them, what political affiliations they champion.

Curriculum-Making

The final required body of experience has to do with the curriculum-making process itself. Each representative of a body of experience must discover the experience of the others and the relevance of these radically different experiences to curriculum making for a partial coalescence of these bodies of experience to occur. These are necessary, "concurrent preliminaries" to the actual process of making a defensible curriculum which has some likelihood of functioning effectively. They are necessary preliminaries which are highly unlikely to occur of themselves. The usual developing behavior of such curriculum groups operating without a representative of this fifth body of experience is one of resentful or resigned submission of three of the group to a fourth.

It is easy for the scholar-specialist to overawe the group and to impose the character and structure of his discipline as the correct model for the character and structure of the curriculum. Only if the representative with knowledge of and sympathy with the children intervenes as an equal in the deliberation is the discipline represented by the scholar likely to be treated as a *resource* of education rather than as a model for it.

It is easy for the representative of the children to overwhelm the scholar with his warnings of what children will and will not, can and cannot do, thus opposing his expertise—what children *have* habitually done in other curricula taught by methods appropriate to them—to the efforts of the scholar to urge trial of new purposes by new means.

It is also possible for the representative of the milieus to urge successfully the conventional caution that a member of a complex structure cannot hope to change the whole of which he is a mere part, or even effect a partial change contrary to prevailing habits and attitudes. Similarly, it is possible for the representative who knows the teaching group to urge conformity of the curriculum to what teachers currently can and are willing to do.

THREE FUNCTIONS OF THE CURRICULUM SPECIALIST

One vital task of the representative of the curriculum-making process is to function as a countervailing force of these common tendencies. It is he who reminds all others of the importance of the experience of each representative to the (curriculum-making) enterprise as a whole. It is he, as chairman, who monitors the proceedings, pointing out to the group what has happened in the course of their deliberations, what is currently taking place, what has not yet been considered, what subordinations and superordinations may have occurred which affect the process in which all are engaged.

The first function of the curriculum specialist concerns these preliminaries to the curriculum-making process, the second concerns curriculum making itself.

Embodiments

It is the curriculum specialist who knows the concrete embodiments, the material objects, which are the indispensable constituents of a curriculum. It is a mistake to suppose that a curriculum-planning group can safely and appropriately terminate its activities merely with statements of purposes and explanation of the reasons for choice of these rather than other purposes.

Curricular purposes, and reasons for them, must be communicated by language, by formulation. Such formulations will inevitably fall short of encompassing the full meanings and real intentions of the parties to the curricular deliberation. The meanings which matter are those which determine whether a given text, a given pattern of teaching, a given treatment of a topic, when examined and momentarily submitted to, is both felt and seen to be appropriate to the curriculum which has been envisaged. These meanings lie in the whole course of the deliberations which created them. The meanings lie as much in what was decided against as in what was decided for. They lie in the reasons for rejection of alternatives as much as in the reasons for preferring those which are preferred. They lie in nuances of expression in the course of the deliberation.

These are meanings which are impossible to encompass in a formulation to be read and acted upon by individuals who were not privy to all the deliberation and become related to it only later through a terminal formulation of its chosen purposes and reasons. Others, not privy to the deliberation, cannot, like bronze molders, take a terminal statement of purposes as a pattern and, from it, realize a curriculum, constructing materials for students, guides for teachers, and patterns of teaching and learning which are appropriate.

Equally, however, a curriculum-planning group can rarely afford either the time or the expertise necessary for the construction of embodiments of the curriculum. Others must be enlisted in that effort in collaboration with the planning group, a collaboration which proceeds by formulation followed by discussion of what the reader of the formulation has garnered from it, followed by trial construction of a bit of concrete curriculum, followed by scrutiny of this trial by the planning group, followed by discussion of it among both makers of the bit and planners, followed by a corrected bit or an additional bit, and so on.

The second function of the curriculum specialist is to instigate, administer, and chair this process of realization of the curriculum.

Values

There is another way in which terminal formulation fails to encompass and communicate the real intentions of a planning group. This second inadequacy stems from the deep psychology of intentions. Educational intentions are specified and projected *values* of the planning group, values possessed and understood in terms broader than education and much broader than any one concrete bit of educational curriculum.

The breadth and generality of these values are so great that only in a rare instance can a merely rationally guided concrete specification of a stated educational intention be confidently identified (by merely rational means) as embodying or satisfying one or more of the broad values held by the planning group. Only if there is added to rational scrutiny of a proposed segment of a curriculum the felt experience of it, an undergoing of it in imagination and empathy, only then can it be identified with some confidence as probably appropriate.

What we usually distinguish as ends and means—stated curricular intentions and curricular materials—are more realistically seen as elements in a maturation process by which values are realized reflexively. A value is embodied in a stated educational intention but only equivocally and imperfectly. The stated intention then serves as an imperfect guide or pattern for construction of a curriculum bit. Experience of the curriculum bit reduces by a little the equivocation of the stated intention and illuminates a little more the value which lies at its roots. Substitution of another curriculum bit, or modification of the first may follow from the illuminating experience but there will also be reflexive modification of the formulated intention itself or modification of the way it is understood. It may even be discarded or replaced. The underlying value which gave rise to the stated intention has itself come closer to the surface and may be better understood. The value may even be so well illuminated that it becomes accessible to scrutiny, criticism, and change. At least, we may hope that, though the value may not be examined with an eye to changing it as a living value of the curriculum planner, it will be scrutinized with an eye to whether it should be imposed upon the student by way of the curriculum.

Instigation, encouragement, and monitoring of this process is a third function of the curriculum specialist.[1]

Size of a Planning Group

Although five bodies of experience must be brought together to effect translation of scholarly materials into defensible curriculum, it does not follow that five persons are required. The group may be smaller or larger than five. It may be smaller to the extent that two or more of the required bodies of experience may be found in one person. The member who knows the child may also know the milieus of the teachers. The scholar may have adequate, living experience of the child or teachers.

---

1. For an illuminating statement of the role of the curriculum specialist, see Seymour Fox, "A Practical Image of the Practical," *Curriculum Theory Network*, no. 10 (Fall 1972).

There are also reasons why the group should be larger than five. Our knowledge of social milieus and of the development of children is knowledge produced out of the variform disciplines of the behavioral sciences. Different investigators in these sciences go about their enquiries in different ways, guided by differing conceptions of problem, method, and principle of investigation. More than one useful body of knowledge arises about an approximately common subject matter. Too often, the purveying possessor of such knowledge possesses only one of the several useful bodies of knowledge about the subject matter in question and needs to be complemented and corrected by another purveying specialist who knows another of the relevant bodies of knowledge.

The same pluralism holds for scholarly disciplines. There are, as has been noted, dozens of critical conceptions of the novel and the short story. There are manifold conceptions of the character of historical investigation and knowledge of moral-political behavior, of the ways in which appropriate religious behavior should be determined. Some measure of these pluralisms should be represented in the curriculum-making group if the embodiment of doctrine is not to be so narrow as to invite rejection when it sees the light of day.

Even experience of the curriculum might well be supplied in more than one person. For one such person will be possessor of values of his own as well as of curricular expertise. Consequently, only one such person in the role of chairman might well suppress some aspects of the deliberation rather than evoke them. If the notion of two chairmen is bizarre, then let us say, at least, that some additional person should be present to monitor the behavior of the chairman, someone alert to the movement of discussion, alert to its purport and removed from both the discipline under translation and from the educational purposes it is intended to serve.

MATERIAL TO BE TRANSLATED

Defensible educational thought must take account of four commonplaces of *equal* rank: the learner, the teacher, the milieu, and the subject matter. None of these can be omitted without omitting a vital factor in educational thought and practice. No one of them may be allowed to dominate the deliberation unless that domination is conscious and capable of defense in terms of the circumstances. Despite the educational bandwagons which bear witness to the contrary, neither child nor society nor subject matters nor teachers is the proper center of curriculum. Indeed, the short merry life of many bandwagon curriculums often has arisen from just such overemphases: the child-centered curriculums of Progressivism; the social-change-centered curriculums of the 1930s; the subject-matter-centered curriculums of recent reforms; the teacher-centered curriculums which may arise from unionism.

Coordinating Four Commonplaces

Coordination, not superordination-subordination is the proper relation of these four commonplaces. We can demonstrate this by considering the possible domination of one in the light of another. Imagine a child-centered planning which emphasizes above all else the present inclinations of students, the interests they bring with them or those which can be aroused by the shrewd placement of provocative objects and events in the educational space. In a curriculum so initiated and thoughtfully planned, the other three commonplaces will not be ignored. Indeed, they may be honored but in a subordinate role. The milieus will be honored as limiting conditions. They will be examined with an eye to predicting interests and facilitating planning of curricular activities. The milieus will also be honored as targets of education by emphases in which collaboration of children, establishment of "rules of the game," and the role of umpire made necessary by rules, constitute socializing aspects of the curriculum. Subject matters will be honored by being the source from which and by which selection is made of the provocative objects and events which serve as catalysts of curricular activity. The teacher will be honored as the person who will most often serve in the role of umpire and serve more extensively as the more mature member of the learning community.

Despite these honorings of the other commonplaces of education, the dominance of the fourth, the children, creates clear and present ground for worry with respect to the subject-matter factor. What of the many things the children may *not* learn which they need to know? We hear this core concern reverberate in the question: Can any planner, any teacher, know enough, know variety enough, and choose wisely enough among so many bodies of knowledge to plant in the learning area the appropriate provocatives of interest and learning? We hear the concern echo again in the question: But what if the "provocative" objects do not provoke? These worries are not allayed by assurances that a knowledge which is needed in the days when the child is no longer a child will be sought and learned. We know of nothing and are given nothing in the way of evidence to support this assurance.

In such worries we are tacitly affirming that subject matter—bodies of knowledge, of competences, of attitudes, propensities, and values—constitute the most inclusive and most telling checklist of possible desirables and possible human interests which mankind possesses. It is this characteristic of subject matter which makes it one of the commonplaces of education.

This characteristic of subject matter appears to argue for subject matter as the ruling commonplace of curricular deliberation. But recall what occurs when subject-matter concerns initiate the planning of curriculum. Subject matters are bodies of knowledge. As knowledge, they tend to shut out other educables: competences, attitudes, propensities, values. As *bodies* of knowledge, they are organized. There is a thread which leads us from one bit of subject matter to the next. Each bit appears to be contingent on what went before and to make necessary what comes after. It becomes difficult to *select* from a subject matter those parts which are defensible in the curriculum because they serve the child, the teaching function, or the polity. In a curriculum enterprise which begins in an effort to adapt a given subject matter to curricular purposes, it is virtually impossible to question whether that subject matter as a whole is desirable in the curriculum and whether it should be given much or little time and energy—inevitably taken from other subject matters or other curricular activities.

There is also ground for worry with respect to the child. Is this subject matter worthy now or in the future of the time and energy demanded of the child? Has there been generous and just concern for the amount of time apportioned to it, relative to time apportioned to other subject matters, on the basis of what is better and worse for children? Or has the decision been made by the weightiness, the dignity, the current esteem, in which the subject matter is held or because the curriculum planners are dominated by lovers of that subject matter? We hear this concern reverberate in the question whether every subject matter is equally accessible or equally useful to all children, or whether individual differences, regional differences, and many other grouping differences among children ought not to determine how much of a given subject matter should be taught, what different selections ought to be made for different children, and what different versions and emphases, even in a single selection of content, should be made in the interest of the needs and abilities of different children. The reverberation is heard again as we wonder whether the heavy hand of self-interested adulthood may not be bearing too heavily on childhood and whether the past and what the past found useful may be weighing too heavily on the present and the future.

Through such worries we affirm that, in a consideration of a subject matter as affording materials for curriculum, one vital criterion must be what is best or good or satisfying to the learner as a child, as a human being, and as a citizen.

Our worries in these two cases taken together affirm that the commonplaces must be coordinate in the planning of curriculum. Amid the concerns of child-centered planning, we note the vital role of organized subject matter. Amid concerns for subject matter, we note the vital role of the child's present and future.

Maintaining Coordinacy

All this fails to speak directly to the practical problem of how to maintain coordination. The practical problem arises from the fact that a group of men is rarely commissioned or financed to think about *education*. (If they were, half of the practical problem would disappear, since that very commission raises all the commonplaces to equal visibility.) Instead, men are usually commissioned and financed to think about satisfying manpower requirements or about how to "modernize" the curriculum in biology, in social studies, in physics, in English. Such questions immediately raise the flag of one commonplace above others.

Four factors, no one sufficient in itself, no one indispensable, are concerned in maintaining coordination. First, there is the makeup of the planning group. Ordinarily the nucleus of a group commissioned to translate a body of scholarly material into curriculum is drawn from the disciplines to be dealt with. The members of this nucleus make the curricular decisions. Men who represent the child, the teacher, and the milieu are usually drawn in only as subordinate temporary "consultants" who speak their pieces and depart. Their pieces are inadequate. They can speak only in generalities. They cannot speak to problems of the subject matter because they have not been peers in the discussion of it. They cannot speak to concrete curricular alternatives because they have not been parties to the generation of these alternatives from the scholarly body of material. The design of the deliberating body guarantees that commonplaces other than that of the subject matter will be effectively silent.

Part of the solution is obvious: representatives of all four commonplaces must be included in the deliberating group from the start. Almost as obvious is the need that these representatives be men who are not overawed by the scholar. But let us go further. Let us require that the first order of business be an explanation of the scholarly material by the representative of that material to the skeptical minds of the remainder of the group. Let these unawed skeptics question the specialist closely, pointedly, indeed, personally, on all matters that are unclear, on all unsupported assertions about the importance or the character of his field and of the particular body of materials to be treated. Let there be questions about adequacy of problem and of evidence in the scholarship which produced the material. Let there be questions about the existence of competing questions and competing solutions. In brief, let us establish from the beginning the place of the scholarly member as only one among many and not the "first among peers."

A second desirable factor leading to coordination of commonplaces is a process of evaluation of tentatively accepted bits of curriculum, a formative evaluation which operates *concurrently* with the deliberations. This formative evaluation is to be done in course; it is to be done in order to improve curricular materials before they are widely distributed. This "improvement" must go considerably beyond the usual. The usual concern is for the efficiency with which the curricular bit serves the stated intention which generated it. We are concerned, in addition, with clarification of the intention itself and of the values from which it arises. Consequently, the character of the evaluation, its timing, and its use require specification.

It should be an evaluation which goes beyond tests of efficiency and aims at methods which will break the limits imposed by the stated intention. I have in mind an evaluation procedure in which the evaluator joins the experimental teacher in the classroom situation in which the materials are tested. Teacher and evaluator engage in an alert, sensitive watch to identify reactions and responses of children as they deal with the materials being evaluated, with a special eye for reactions and responses *un*anticipated in the stated intention. From these reactions and responses, evaluator and teacher, with the collaboration of the curriculum-specialist member of the planning group, select those which they deem most representative of unanticipated characteristics of the curriculum bit and most significant in the education and development of the child. The frequency and intensity of these selected untoward reactions are then evaluated. Most important of all, the selected reactions are disclosed to the planning group in *two* embodiments—not only in the usual statistical report, but also in a direct confrontation of members of the planning group with the student behaviors themselves. Teacher and evaluator stage demonstration classes (and class aftermaths) for the deliberating body. This is the confrontation through which the planners will be able to go beyond rational scrutiny of what they are doing toward a felt experience of what they are proposing to do to and with the children. This is one way in which the child, as one important commonplace of curriculum consideration, can speak for himself.

SCHOLARSHIP AS CURRICULUM POTENTIAL

Let us consider two important attitudes which should be taken toward scholarly materials when they are translated into curriculum. First, they must be treated as *resources*. The import of this can be conveyed by an instance of its negation and an instance of its affirmation drawn from the field of literature.

The statement which introduces "Discussions of the Short Story" reads: "A short story is neither plot nor character nor statement nor style; it is simultaneously plot and character and statement and style. In language a short story records moving character reflecting an attitude toward existence. The elements of the experience are separable only for the pleasures of discussion. For authoritative communication with any story, we return to the complicated experience of the story itself."[2] The author is asserting (*a*) a definition of the character of the "scholarly" material under treatment, a definition which asserts precisely and completely the character of the material, and (*b*) that translation of short stories into curriculum must, by whatever means will work, treat the short story as what it is. The curriculum must realize the short story as what it is; the curriculum must realize the short story in the minds and hearts of the student in its full character or try to do so as far as the condition of the student permits.

The passage is thus a sterling instance of refusal to use scholarly material as a curriculum resource. It insists on conformity of the curriculum to the nature of its source materials. The domination of subject matter is made complete; the other commonplaces are ignored; the "malleable" student is to be given the shape indicated by the material.

Compare that with a passage taken from "Literature in the Revitalized Curriculum."

> In more recent time . . . the new English [has been] rather much under the supervision of the academic. . . . We are now, in my view, on the threshold of the fourth stage, which I shall call the Humanitarian. If there is a "new English" . . . it has taken the development of the imagination, conceived in the most liberating sense, as its ultimate aim. . . . The imagination is no narrow faculty, but filters through and colors every part, every corner of our lives. Let us take for example the matter of morality. . . . The curriculum should be open to a great variety of values and visions, including those that rub against the grain of society. . . . As the teacher is concerned with developing and expanding the student's total imaginative capacity, so he must be concerned with all aspects of the imagination. . . .[3]

This author, too, starts from a characteristic of the scholarly material. But, unlike the first, he moves immediately to concern himself with

2. Hollis Summers, ed. *Discussions of the Short Story* (Lexington, Mass.: D. C. Heath, 1963).

3. James E. Miller, Jr., "Literature in the Revitalized Curriculum," *Bulletin of the National Association of Secondary School Principals*, no. 318 (April 1967), pp. 25–38.

what service this characteristic can perform which is good and satisfying for students. By this move, he illustrates what is meant by the treatment of scholarly material as curricular resource. The curriculum is not to conform to the material; the material is to be used in the service of the student.

The use of scholarly material as a resource for curriculum can be perverted, and its perversion is as pernicious educationally as deprival of it is. Perversion consists of warping the scholarly materials out of their character in order to force them to serve a curricular purpose which fascinates the planners. Such perversions are exemplified by terminal formulations which begin, "How can we use science (or literature, or history, or moral dilemmas) to achieve x, y, or z?" where the x, y, or z originate the deliberation and the scholarly materials are dragged in by the heels. The perversion consists in degrading subject matter to the role of servant.

The second attitude to be taken toward scholarly material when it is translated into curriculum is that scholarly material possesses three faces, *is* three different things. It is, first, that which it conveys, its purport. A piece of historical material is an account of what happened to someone somewhere. That event as it happened to those people at that time is one of its faces. A short story conveys a moral dilemma or a vision of a social class or the operation of a facet of human character. Any one of these constitutes one of its faces. A body of scientific material tells us something about a grouping of phenomena. That is one of the faces of a piece of scientific material.

A piece of scholarly material is also that which produced it. It is the outcome of an originating discipline, a coherent way of bringing a body of principles, methods, and problems to bear upon some inchoate mass in order to give it order and meaning. A short story is the outcome of a discipline which selects material, clothes it in a certain language, gives it a certain form, and selects and uses certain devices in order to evoke a certain effect. A piece of scientific material is the outcome of a discipline which predetermines the character of some selected grouping of phenomena in order to formulate questions which it can answer by means of the techniques presently available to it.

Third, a piece of scholarly material is a compound object, a complex organization requiring certain access disciplines. There are numerous questions which must be addressed to a short story before that story will reveal itself fully. There are different questions which must be addressed to a piece of history or science before one of them will reveal its full purport.

Constant awareness of the existence of these three faces in every piece of scholarly material is crucial to the translator into curriculum because each face possesses and suggests its own richness of curricular possibility. The purport may have many curricular uses—and this is the face to which most curricular efforts are addressed. But the other two faces have curricular potential as great or greater. Where the purport speaks to those curricular possibilities, which can be summarized under "knowing that," the two disciplinary faces speak to the curricular possibilities summarized under "knowing how."

The potential curricular values of access disciplines to a complex work are clear. Access to the intricate content and structure of a short story, a lyric poem, a psalm, a work of plastic art, or music is access to a highly durable and virtually inexhaustible source of satisfaction.

Access to a scientific work is access to ground for critical judgment which avoids the misinformation, the extremes of belief, and the confusion which are often the outcomes of popular renderings of such materials. Access to the structure of argument, whether toward political or moral action, is access to a judgment about better and worse commitment of our time, our energy, and our developing character. Access to historical works is access to one of the factors which determine who we think we are, what problems we think we have, and how we ought to act. In general, possession of such disciplines is possession of avenues toward freedom of thought, feeling, and action. The potential curricular values for the young of the originating disciplines, such as rhetoric toward production of argument, science toward production of warranted conclusions about natural things, history toward interpretations of the past, are less obvious. Their potential for the young becomes clearer when we note what it might mean to convey such disciplines to them.

We do not mean that all the young are to be made into expert historians, investigators, artists. This is fatuous. We do not mean merely that the young are to be given thin versions of some scholarly discipline to pursue as a hobby. We mean that we ought to consider as curricular possibilities the conveyance of such knowledge about and exemplary experience with originating disciplines that the student (1) is better prepared to master those disciplines which give access to the finished outcomes of the scholarly disciplines; (2) is equipped with insight into the methods and principles of an originating discipline sufficient to add a critical component to his access disciplines. The attempt to *write* a lyric poem and to have one's effort submitted to analysis conveys aspects of the character of lyric poetry, aspects to be sought in the reading of lyric poems, which no mere instruction in the reading and analysis of lyric poems can convey. The attempt to formulate a scientific problem, however simple, and to carry out the investigation required by the problem, is to learn about questions to be addressed to scientific material which no mere lectorial presentation can convey. To grasp some of the many ways in which different historians conceive the character of historical knowledge, to identify the facts pertinent to each history, and to seek out these facts is to understand the kind of history one is reading at a given moment. It is a means of realizing the limitations of a particular kind of history as one among a number of ways of throwing light upon the past and interpreting the present, and it enhances competence to judge the dependability of the history under scrutiny. At the same time, the student's ability to read such a history is enhanced. He knows more of the questions to be addressed to the text and is better prepared to extract answers to these questions from the text.

In some cases, our stricture against conveying a thin version of a scholarly discipline and encouraging its actual use can be an overstatement. Simple versions of some scholarly disciplines may be of serious use to some laymen. Rhetoric is one. Since the good of every man is bound up in the communities of which he is a member, the decisions made by such communities affect him. Thus, his ability to affect consensus is clearly an ability which redounds to his benefit. Casuistry, the discipline by which principles (especially moral and religious principles) are scrutinized for their relevance to a situation demanding choice and action and adapted to the case, is another discipline which can redound to the benefit of both individual student and the moral, religious, and political communities of which he is part. Some firsthand experience of scientific disciplines vastly sharpens one's understanding of what constitutes reliable and sufficient evidence for conclusions.

The possible benefit of mastery of simple versions of some originating disciplines extends into the emotive realm. The ability to compose a lyric poem, or a moving statement of praise, of thanks, of awe, or of fear is a contribution to our ability to clarify and so to understand our emotions, to control them where control is desirable, to discharge them where discharge is desirable. By such means, melancholy can often be transformed into realistic grief rather than being allowed to deteriorate into pathological melancholia. A debt to the character or action of another person can be shaped into worthy gratitude rather than being permitted to degenerate into debthood or thoughtless worship. Some mastery of historical disciplines may enable us to organize and understand our own pasts, our personal histories, and thus to gain additional ability to think about our future and plan it.

METHODS OF TRANSLATION

The methods by which scholarly materials are translated into a defensible curriculum are not mere transformations of one kind or style of material into another. They are methods for assessing privations, perversities, errors, and misdevelopments in those who are to be recipients of the putative benefits of curriculum; then, methods for discovering in scholarly materials curricular potentials which serve the purposes which have been envisaged in the light of detected student needs; then, assessment of the probable advantages of one potential against others as a means toward educational benefits.

First Phase: Curriculum Effects

The method begins in two sources: (1) in knowledge of the young students and knowledge of their predecessors, now grown and exhibiting the good and bad effects of previous curriculums; (2) in a vision of the best student-grown (or several different "bests"), a vision deriving from the scrutinized values of the planning group. The method begins with an intertwining of two radically different strands: information and soul-searching.

Each item of one strand must serve as an occasion for locating an item of the other. Each piece of information on the present condition of students or former students ought to be followed by voiced discoveries of how the planners feel about the condition in question: whether it is approved, and why; if disapproved, what alternate condition or conditions ought to replace it. The planners should then invite statements of differences or concurrences of view on the desirability of replacing the condition and what might be done about it. Similarly, each statement of value or desired intention ought to evoke consideration of students or milieus as they are known or thought to be, with speculations on how they arrived at that desirable or undesirable condition.

This initial stage of the deliberation serves two purposes. First, precisely because the group is commissioned to concern itself with scholarly materials, it begins by emphasis on other commonplaces, especially the student and his milieus. Second, it is the prime means by which each planner begins to discover himself—his values and their projections into educational intentions—begins to discover his colleagues, and begins to discover the loci at which each must begin to modify or contract himself to accommodate his colleagues' views and arrive at a collegiality which can function effectively in pursuing the task at hand.

These purposes justify expenditure of considerable time, ten or fifteen two-hour meetings apportioned over as many weeks. The time should not be allotted, neither should one attempt to determine its end point by some estimate of achieved consensus. It should not be a move toward consensus, but an airing and accommodation which will continue in other guises in all stages of the deliberation. The terminus of this first phase should be signaled by a growing distaste for its continuance, a demand, generally agreed upon, that something more concrete take its place.

There is no warrant that men gathered together for the purposes outlined will discover anything of themselves or their colleagues or modulate their views to accommodate the views of their colleagues. Collegiality will arise only to the extent that a minimal capacity for shame and a degree of humility characterize each member of the group. It is "normal" for men to treat their own values as if they were well examined, to ignore contrary or different values utilized by others, and, most of all, to elevate automatically the area of their own expertise to the role of ultimate arbiter of matters under consideration. These "normalities," especially the arrogance of specialism, will wreck any attempt at responsible translation of scholarly materials into defensible curriculum. I know of no device of chairmanship or tactic of administration which can avert this danger without the assistance of a measure of humility and shame among the participants.

The Second Phase: Discovery of Curriculum Potential

The second phase of the deliberation is occasioned by introduction of a piece of scholarly material whose potential for the curriculum is to be determined. This phase has two subphases. There must be, first, the generation of alternatives. The piece of scholarly material is scrutinized in its three existences (its purport, its originating discipline, and its access disciplines) for its curriculum potentials. The basis for inventiveness in this regard consists of the other commonplaces, as these have come to be envisaged in the phase of self-discovery. One figuratively turns the piece of scholarly material from side to side, viewing it in different lights. What use might it serve in the development of more critical loyalty to a community? What might it contribute to the child's resources of satisfying activity? What might it contribute to the moral or intellectual virtue held to be desirable by the planning group? To what convictions might it lead concerning conservation or reform of a community setting? To what maturation might it contribute?

The second subphase is entered when several pieces of scholarly material have been successfully treated in the first subphase. Now there are several potential curriculum bits competing for the time and energies of the students, for place in the curriculum. The second subphase is a process of choosing and deciding among the competing curricular bits, the intentions they seem to realize, the values they try to embody.

In this subphase, the central problem consists of discovering the considerations which ought to be brought to bear on the alternatives. The resources from which to derive the appropriate considerations are the four commonplaces. From the subject matter: Is the purport of the material an important historical event or condition, for example? Is it good history, arising from well-validated facts, interpreted in a defensible way toward insights useful to our time and circumstance? From the milieu: Does it contribute toward improvement of a community? Is it likely to be acceptable to that community? If it is novel or disturbing, are there steps we can take to facilitate its acceptance? From the children: Is the good it is supposed to do more urgent or more important than the goods served by competing curricular bits? Is it appropriate to the age and experience of the children under consideration? What consequences may it have for the relations of children to parents and to other significant adults? What effect may it have on the relations of children to one another? What effect may it have on the relation of each child to himself? From the teacher: Is he or she prepared to teach it as it should be taught? Can this training be successfully entered upon? Will the teacher be in sympathy with the values embodied in the curricular bit? If not, are there prevailing values among teachers which can be used to help enlist them in the service of the embodied values?

It is impossible to forecast the precise questions which ought to be asked of the alternatives under consideration. The appropriate questions are made appropriate by the character of each particular curricular bit, by the attitudes, values, and cognitive skills of the planners, by the community for which the planning is done, by the peculiarities of the children to whom the curriculum is to be submitted. Discovery of the "right" questions to ask depends in the last analysis on the deliberative skill of the planners and the alertness of the chairing curriculum specialist.

The role of the curriculum specialist here is one which derives from a most marked and peculiar characteristic of the deliberative process: it must compare incommensurables. The task is not merely a technical one of forecasting consequences and costs. It is not adequately stated as merely determining *the* value or good of the forecast consequences. For "the" value is in fact a number of different values: a valued contribution to the maturity of the child; a valued effect on the present state of mind of the child; a valued effect on the community. These different values are the incommensurables, which must be weighed against one another. There are no weighting factors which can be supplied to the deliberating group by which to simplify this process.

The special obligation of the curriculum-specialist chairman is to ensure that the group hunt out, recognize, and juxtapose the different considerations which are pertinent. Even when the arrogances of specialists have been mastered and collegiality established, there will still be a tendency to perseverate, to maintain attention on the one cluster of values which, for whatever reason, has initially interested the group at the start of one of its meetings. It is this perseveration which the chairman must interrupt. His task is to see that the deliberations of the group are appropriately saltatory—that the group turn from concentrating on the affective values to the child, for example, and consider the value of putative effects on the curriculum bit on parents, on the finances of the operation, on the personality of the school principal. Clusters of values left behind are revisited—again and again. The aim is not to make the deliberations less thorough but to ensure juxtaposition of incommensurables so that they will be weighed against one another.

The generation and consideration of alternatives do not follow one another in strict seriality. There must be alternatives to consider, hence some must be generated before the second subphase can be entered. But the deliberations involved in the consideration of alternatives are themselves rich sources of new alternatives. The moments when such flashes of invention occur to a member of the group must be honored, however important the considerations under discussion may appear to be.

Neither generation nor consideration of alternatives conclude when the planning group has agreed on the curriculum bits it proposes to sponsor. The processes of invention and choice run on through the operations of evaluation earlier described and especially in that aspect of the evaluation which involves confrontation of the planning group with the untoward responses of the children to the sponsored curriculum bit. The confrontation is one way in which the child can enter the curricular discussion, and speak for himself. Other devices directed toward the same end—with reference to teacher and community as well as the child—should be sought.

Publications by
Joseph J. Schwab

"A Further Study of the Effect of Temperature on Crossing-over." *American Naturalist* 69 (1935): 187–92.

With Edna Bailey and Anita D. E. Laton, *Suggestions for Teaching Selected Material from the Field of Genetics*. Bureau of Educational Research in Science, Monograph I. New York: Columbia University, Teachers College, 1939.

"A Study of the Effects of a Random Group of Genes on Shape of Spermatheca in Drosophila melanogaster." *Genetics* 25 (1940): 157–77.

"Deriving the Objectives and Content of the College Curriculum." In *New Frontiers in Collegiate Education, Proceedings of the Institute for Administrative Officers of Higher Education*. Vol. 13, ed. John Dale Russell. Chicago: University of Chicago Press, 1941, pp. 35–52.

"The Role of Biology in General Education: The Problem of Value." *Bios* 12 (1941): 87–97.

"The Fight for Education." *Atlantic Monthly* 169 (1942): 727–31.

"The Science Programs in the College of the University of Chicago." In *Science and General Education*, ed. Earl McGrath. Dubuque, Iowa: William C. Brown Co., 1947, pp. 38–58.

"The Nature of Scientific Knowledge as Related to Liberal Education." *Journal of General Education* 3 (1949): 245–66.

"Criteria for the Evaluation of Achievement Tests: From the Point of View of the Subject-Matter Specialist." In *Proceedings of the Educational Testing Service Invitational Conference on Testing Problems, 1950*. Princeton, N.J.: Educational Testing Service, 1950, pp. 82–94.

"The Natural Sciences: The Three Year Program." In *The Idea and Practice of General Education: An Account of the College of the University of Chicago*, by Present and Former Members of the Faculty. Chicago: University of Chicago Press, 1950, pp. 149–86.

"Dialectical Means vs. Dogmatic Extremes in Relation to Liberal Education." *Harvard Educational Review* 21 (1951): 37–64.

"Population Equilibrium." *Bios* 23 (1951): 191–97.

"John Dewey: The Creature as Creative." *Journal of General Education* 7 (1953): 109–21.

"Eros and Education." *Journal of General Education* 8 (1954): 54–71.

"Relating Sciences: An Introduction." *Pedagogia* 2 (1954): 129–36.

"Is Consensus Enough?" *Educational Leadership* 14 (1956): 408–13.

"Science and Civil Discourse: The Uses of Diversity." *Journal of General Education*, 9 (1956): 132–43.

"Norms for Promotion: A Symposium *De Magistris*." *Journal of General Education* 10 (1957): 125–26.

"On the Corruption of Education by Psychology." *Ethics* 68 (1957): 39–44.

Eros and Education—The Problem of Discussion. Rio Piedras, Puerto Rico: University of Puerto Rico, Faculty of General Studies, 1958.

"Inquiry and the Reading Process." *Journal of General Education* 11 (1958): 72–82.

"On the Corruption of Education by Psychology," *School Review* 66 (1958): 169–84.

"The Teaching of Science as Inquiry." *Bulletin of the Atomic Scientists* 14 (1958): 374–79.

"The 'Impossible' Role of the Teacher in Progressive Education." *School Review* 67 (1959): 139–59.

"Inquiry, the Science Teacher, and the Educator." *School Review* 68 (1960): 176–95.

"The Teaching of Science as Enquiry." In Joseph J. Schwab and Paul F. Brandwein, *The Teaching of Science*. Cambridge, Mass.: Harvard University Press, 1960.

"What Do Scientists Do?" *Behavioral Science* 5 (1960): 1–27.

"The Concept of the Structure of a Discipline." *Educational Record* 43 (1962): 197–205.

Supervisor and co-author. *The Biology Teacher's Handbook*. American Institute of Biological Sciences. Biological Sciences Curriculum Study. New York: John Wiley and Sons, 1963.

"A Radical Departure for a Program in the Liberal Arts." *Journal of General Education* 15 (1963): v–viii.

With William Brownson. "American Science Textbooks and Their Authors." *School Review* 71 (1963): 170–80.

"Enkele Beschouwingen in Verband met de Wetenschappelijke Opleiding." *Tijdschrift Belgische Nationale Vereninging der Leraren in de Biologie.* 10 (1964): 155–58.

"Problems, Topics, and Issues." In *Education and the Structure of Knowledge*, ed. Stanley Elam. Chicago: Rand, McNally, 1964, pp. 4–47.

"The Professorship of Administration: Theory, Art, and Practice." In *The Professorship in Educational Administration*. Columbus, Ohio: University Council for Educational Administration, 1964, pp. 47–70.

"The Religiously Oriented School in the United States: A Memorandum on Policy." *Conservative Judaism* 18 (1964): 1–14.

"The Structure of the Disciplines: Meanings and Significances." In *The Structure of Knowledge and the Curriculum*, ed. G. W. Ford and L. Pugno. Chicago: Rand McNally, 1964, pp. 1–30.

"The Structure of the Natural Sciences." In *The Structure of Knowledge and the Curriculum*, ed. G. W. Ford and L. Pugno. Chicago: Rand McNally, 1964, pp. 31–49.

With Burton Cohen. "Practical Logic: Problems of Ethical Decision." *The American Behavioral Scientist* 8 (1965): 23–7.

"On Scientific Inquiry." In *Talks with Scientists*, ed. C. F. Madden. Carbondale, Ill.: Southern Illinois University Press, 1968, pp. 3–24.

College Curriculum and Student Protest. Chicago: University of Chicago Press, 1969.

"Integration and Disintegration of Education." In *Education and the Urban Renaissance*, ed. R. Campbell, L. Marx, and R. Nystrand. New York: John Wiley and Sons, 1969, pp. 37–43.

"The Practical: A Language for Curriculum." *School Review* 78 (1969): 1–23.

The Practical: A Language for Curriculum. Washington, D.C.: National Education Association, 1970.

"Planned Programs." In *Higher Education for Everybody*, ed. Todd Furniss. Washington, D.C., American Council on Education, 1971, pp. 18–25.

"The Practical: Arts of Eclectic." *School Review* 79 (1971): 493–542.

"Praktische Legitimierung von Curricula." *Bildung und Erziehung* 24 (1971): 334–41.

"The Practical 3: Translation into Curriculum." *School Review* 81 (1973): 501–22.

"A Quiver of Queries." In *Beyond the Punitive Society*, ed. H. Wheeler. San Francisco: W. H. Freeman and Co., 1973, pp. 247–55.

"Decision and Choice: The Coming Duty of Science Teaching." *Journal of Research in Science Teaching* 11 (1974): 309–17.

"Private Lives." *The Center Magazine* 7, no. 5 (September-October 1974): 2–7.

"Learning Community." *The Center Magazine* 8, no. 3 (May-June 1975), pp. 30–44.

"On Reviving Liberal Education." In *The Philosophy of the Curriculum*, ed. Sidney Hook et al. Buffalo, N.Y.: Prometheus Books, 1975, pp. 37–48.

"Education and the State: Learning Community." *The Great Ideas Today, 1976*. Chicago: Encyclopaedia Britannica, 1976, pp. 234–71.

"Freedom and the Scope of Liberal Education." In *The President as Educational Leader*. Washington, D.C.: Association of American Colleges, 1976, pp. 610–88.

"Teaching and Learning." *The Center Magazine* 9, no. 6 (November-December 1976): 36–45.

Name Index

Subject Index

Affect, 20, 172, 345–49, 350–55; in education, 108–32; in teaching, 110–24. *See also* Discussion

Biological Sciences Curriculum Study, 24–25, 302, 303

Causation, in science, 73–74, 76, 85, 87–93, 200–202, 225
Causes, Aristotelian, 19, 28, 34, 73–74, 194–95, 200–202, 226, 255–65, 288–91
Character, as an educational goal, 30, 37, 372
Chicago, University of, College, 1, 4, 7–8, 9, 10–11, 14–18; goals of, 4–5, 12–14, 43–44, 55–56, 66–67, 277–78. *See also* Natural Sciences
Citizenship and liberal education, 21–22, 137–48
Classroom organization, 122–23
College curriculum, history of, 4–5, 137–40
College Curriculum and Student Protest (Schwab), 1, 2, 30, 32, 36–37, 303, 357n
Columbia College, 5–6, 14
Commonplaces, 19, 20, 29, 339–40; of curriculum, 366–68, 371–75
Community, 12, 22, 30, 37, 138–48, 379, 382
Community colleges, 147
Culture, in liberal education, 11–12
Curricula: and the disciplines, 24–26, 28, 66–72, 98–104, 281, 316–18, 360–63; goals of, 266, 268–69, 372–73, 375–83; organization of, 120–21; sources of, 266–67. *See also* History; Humanities; Literature; Natural Sciences; Science
Curriculum development, 35, 43–67, 266–72, 275–383; behavioral sciences in, 226–29, 329, 333, 337–38, 359–60, 366–67; commonplaces in, 366–68, 371–75; community in, 366–67, 382; crisis in, 287, 302–4; deliberation in, 363, 379–83; disciplines in, 266–72, 281, 316–18, 360–63, 372–73, 374, 375–83; evaluation in, 375; high school projects as examples of, 302–3; methods of, 380–83; objectives in, 105, 275, 279–81, 326–27, 333–34, 363–64, 368–69; plurality of theories in, 338–39; practical arts in, 323–64; structures of disciplines in, 255, 316–18, 366, 371–73, 375–79, 381–82; testing in, 314, 315; theory in, 287–88, 296–99, 304–12, 322–23; values in, 396–70. *See also* Curriculum evaluation; Curriculum specialist; Practical; Tests
Curriculum evaluation, testing in, 275–86
Curriculum specialist, roles of, 361–71, 382–83

Deliberation, 30, 143–44, 318–21
Discussion: and affect, 124–32; qualities of, 105, 124–32; in teaching, 158–63, 343–59; uses of, 105–6, 158–60

Education, goals of, 180–82, 229, 236–41, 305–7, 371, 326–29, 376–79. *See also* Affect; Character; Habits; Liberal education; Public education; Science; Teaching
Educational research, 31, 32, 34, 275–86; crisis in, 302–4; problems for, 282–83, 303–14, 305; tasks of, 283–87, 315–19
Enquiry. *See* Fluid enquiry; Principles of enquiry; Stable enquiry
Eros. *See* Affect

391